THE LITERARY CRITICISM OF F. R. LEAVIS

TO MY MOTHER

THE LITERARY CRITICISM OF
F. R. LEAVIS

R. P. BILAN

Assistant Professor, University College, University of Toronto

CAMBRIDGE UNIVERSITY PRESS

CAMBRIDGE

LONDON · NEW YORK · MELBOURNE

Published by the Syndics of the Cambridge University Press
The Pitt Building, Trumpington Street, Cambridge CB2 1RP
Bentley House, 200 Euston Road, London NW1 2DB
32 East 57th Street, New York, NY 10022, USA
296 Beaconsfield Parade, Middle Park, Melbourne 3206, Australia

First published 1979

Printed in Great Britain at the
University Press, Cambridge

Library of Congress Cataloguing in Publication Data

Bilan, R. P.
The literary criticism of F. R. Leavis.

Bibliography: p. 320
Includes index.
1. Leavis, Frank Raymond, 1895–1978. 2. English
literature – History and criticism. 3. Criticism –
England – History. 4. Lawrence, David Herbert,
1885–1930 – Criticism and interpretation – History.
1. Title.
PR29.L4B5   801'.95'0924   78-18089
ISBN 0 521 22324 5

CONTENTS

Contents

ACKNOWLEDGMENTS

I am deeply indebted to a number of friends for their help, and I would like to take this opportunity to record my thanks. W. J. Keith and Sam Solecki read this work from its beginnings and then, as I re-wrote, faithfully read it again and again; their unflagging help was of decisive importance. T. H. Adamowski also gave freely of this time; he provided an extensive critique of my work and, in our endless debates, forced me to re-think and clarify my ideas. Michael Kirkham and Deborah Jurdjevic read specific chapters and they both offered extremely useful suggestions not only on particular points but on the handling of the chapters as a whole. I would also like to thank Michael Black of Cambridge University Press for his detailed comments on my manuscript. Finally, I am grateful to Mrs Q. D. Leavis and Chatto and Windus Limited for permission to quote from *Culture And Environment, Education And The University, Anna Karenina And Other Essays, English Literature In Our Time And The University, Lectures In America, Nor Shall My Sword, Letters In Criticism, The Living Principle, Thought, Words And Creativity, Determinations: Critical Essays, The Common Pursuit, New Bearings In English Poetry, Revaluation, The Great Tradition, D. H. Lawrence: Novelist, Dickens The Novelist.*

Parts of this book were first published in *College English, D. H. Lawrence Review, The Dalhousie Review, Novel* and *University of Toronto Quarterly*; the *Novel* essay was reprinted in *Towards a Poetics of Fiction* (Indiana University Press).

PART ONE: SOCIETY, CULTURE AND CRITICISM

INTRODUCTION

> Literary criticism, then, is concerned with more than
> literature...A serious interest in literature cannot be
> merely literary; indeed, not only must the seriousness
> involve, it is likely to derive from, a perception of – which
> must be a preoccupation with – the problems of social
> equity and order and of cultural health.[1]

The nature of the literary criticism of F. R. Leavis cannot be
properly understood apart from his social and cultural concerns;
as he indicates above, behind all his work lies the preoccupation
with the cultural health of society. His basic assumption is that
modern civilization is diseased, and his primary concern is to foster
the growth of the activities that will alleviate and remedy this
condition.

Perhaps more cogently than any other critic in the twentieth
century, Leavis has continually argued the case for the importance
of literature and of literary criticism in modern society, but the
importance he attributes to them must be seen in the context of
his other concerns. The various answers that Leavis gives to the
contemporary plight are clearly indicated by the titles of some of
his early works: *Mass Civilization And Minority Culture* (1930), *Culture
And Environment* (1933), *For Continuity* (1933), *How to Teach Reading*
(1932), *Towards Standards of Criticism* (1933), and *Education And The
University* (1943). In the face of the modern disintegration Leavis
argues for the necessity of maintaining the continuity of the English
cultural tradition, now largely represented by English literature,
and the finer values that it embodies. But this continuity can only
be maintained by the existence of a strong minority or educated

3

public, which in turn makes possible the function of criticism and the maintenance of standards. Leavis looks to education, in particular to the university, to help create the necessary educated public and to sustain the effective life of the cultural tradition. Only by these means, he thinks, can we begin to strive towards cultural health.

The cultural diagnosis and the cure Leavis offers remained consistent over a period of more than forty years. There is not only consistency but also a certain symmetry in his writing career: he began by presenting his cultural diagnosis in *Mass Civilization And Minority Culture* in 1930 and in two of his last books, *English Literature In Our Time And The University* (1969), and particularly in *Nor Shall My Sword* (1972), he explicitly returned to the concerns of the earlier work. These later books show no great divergences from his earliest position; while there are changes, modifications, a sense that things have become worse, the continuity of Leavis's concerns is more striking. In *Anna Karenina And Other Essays* (1969), for instance, he reprinted, as apparently still representing his views, one of the earliest statements of his general position, 'Towards Standards of Criticism' (1933). Also, Leavis occasionally quotes from his earlier works. For example, in *Nor Shall My Sword*, in order to present his analysis of the effects of technological change, he refers to a crucial passage from *Education And The University*. Since the early and later works are this closely connected, rather than discuss the separate books, I intend to examine Leavis's key social/cultural ideas: his ideas on past and present society, on cultural tradition, and on the educated public.

There is, however, a problem here that needs to be cleared up at the outset. Although I am beginning with a discussion of Leavis's views on society – his analysis of modern society and his various remedies or therapies – he is, of course, primarily a literary, rather than a social critic. The insight and authority he repeatedly demonstrated in speaking on literary texts does not necessarily carry over into his general comments on society. And, in a sense, Leavis himself recognizes this clearly enough. In his essay, 'The Function of Criticism at Any Time; or the Responsible Critic', he makes a very definite distinction between literary and social criticism:

> The business of the literary critic as such is with literary criticism. It is pleasant to hope that, when he writes or

talks about political or 'social' matters, insight and
understanding acquired in literary studies will be engaged
– even if not demonstrably (and even if we think it a
misleading stress to speak of his special understanding of
'contemporary social processes'). But his special
responsibility as a critic (and, say, as the editor of a
critical review) is to serve the function of criticism to the
best of his powers. He will serve it ill unless he has a clear
conception of what a proper working of the function in
contemporary England would be like, and unless he can
tell himself why the function matters. If he tells himself
(and others) that it matters 'because a skilled reader of
literature will tend, by the nature of his skill, to
understand and appreciate contemporary social processes
better than his neighbours', he misrepresents it and
promotes confusion and bad performance.[2]

Leavis does, nonetheless, offer a critique of industrial society. But
in his comments on, say, working conditions in industrial society
he is not saying anything new, and certainly a far more precise
analysis of this aspect of society, and this aspect of technological
change, is offered by Weber, Durkheim and Marx, with their
respective diagnoses of progressive rationalization, anomie and
alienation. When Leavis approaches this kind of topic – and in *Nor
Shall My Sword*, for instance, he often does – his analysis is frequently
vague.

But, in commenting on society, Leavis does have his own
distinctive area of concern, and within this area his analysis is often
trenchant. He is, in his concern with continuity, the educated
public and standards, the main twentieth-century representative
of a central line of English social thought that reaches back through
Arnold to Coleridge. Much of his importance lies in keeping this
tradition – a tradition of social-cultural thought – alive. Much of
his commentary on society is focused on the *cultural* effects of
technology; in particular, the ways in which technological change
influences language and literature. And as he points out in 'The
Responsible Critic': 'There *is*, however, a special understanding
of 'contemporary social processes' and a special preoccupation
with them, that a critic as such, and above all, the editor of a critical
review, ought to show. I am thinking of. . . the social processes that
have virtually brought the function of criticism in this country into

abeyance.'[3] Hence his concern with the literary world. Further, much of his 'social' analysis focuses on education – particularly on the role of the university. In his diagnosis of the state of the university and of the state of culture, Leavis is often illuminating; he is, in fact, one of our leading cultural critics.

There is, moreover, a way in which Leavis *is* qualified to speak more generally about industrial society. Much of his life's work is devoted to trying to get recognized how important the study of literature is to any proper understanding of society. In *English Literature In Our Time And The University* he argues for the importance of criticism in, indirectly, providing a distinctive approach to the study of civilization and society. And he further insists on 'the immense importance of the novel in a literary education that should vindicate the idea of the university... In English the novelists from Dickens to Lawrence form an organic continuity, and the intelligent study of them entails a study of the changing civilization (ours) of which their work is the criticism, the interpretation and the history; nothing rivals it as such.'[4] More than anyone else in our time Leavis shows how literature is relevant to the study of history and society.

1

Leavis's View Of Society: The Past And The Present

*i. Literature and Seventeenth-Century
English Society*

Like many other modern critics and writers – I. A. Richards, T. S. Eliot, D. H. Lawrence, and W. B. Yeats, to name a few – Leavis believes that we live in a time of marked cultural decline, and, like most of these writers, he looks back to a period in the past which he sets against the present. Much of Leavis's work, in fact, involves an argument about the nature of the past: this was a central issue in his quarrel with C. P. Snow, and he found T. S. Eliot's literary criticism so stimulating in part because he agrees with Eliot's theory of 'the dissociation in sensibility', that a great change in civilization in the seventeenth century is manifested in the language of poetry. The period before this change became decisive, the era of the seventeenth century that includes both Shakespeare and Bunyan, is, for Leavis, the time of the fullest cultural vitality of English life.

In one of Leavis's earliest statements of his view of the positive nature of seventeenth-century society he discusses the conditions that made Shakespeare's language and writing possible:

> The dependence of the theatre on both court and populace ensured that Shakespeare should use his 'linguistic genius' – he incarnated the genius of the language – to the utmost. And what this position of advantage represents in particular form is the general advantage he enjoyed in belonging to a genuine national culture, to a community in which it was possible for the theatre to appeal to the cultivated and the populace at the same time.
>
> A national culture rooted in the soil – the commonplace

metaphor is too apt to be rejected: the popular basis of
culture was agricultural. '
   . . . the strength and subtlety of English idiom derives
from an agricultural way of life.[1]

Shakespeare's achievement, that is, was made possible by the
existence of a rich social order, an organic society, out of which
arose the richness of the English language.

It is important to understand the features of this culture that
Leavis admires, for, whatever the truth of his view – a point to
which I will return – it implicitly serves him as a social model. One
aspect of this society Leavis considers absolutely essential for
cultural health: its religious quality. Writing on Bunyan in 1938
Leavis insisted that *The Pilgrim's Progress* has a cultural content that
the Marxists, for example, were blind to: he is referring to the
religious sanction in the book and the nature of the affirmation
made at the end of part two. He writes: ' *The Pilgrim's Progress* must
leave us asking whether without something corresponding to what
is supremely affirmed in that exaltation. . . there can be such a thing
as cultural health.'[2] In his later essay on Bunyan in 1964 Leavis
is much more explicit about the religious quality which pervades
Bunyan's work, a religious quality that overrides any doctrinal
intention. Leavis argues that in considering the novel 'we have to
recognize that we do very much need the two words "theological"
and "religious". Bunyan's religion, like his art, comes from the
whole man. And the man, we can't help telling ourselves as we
reflect on the power of his masterpieces, belonged to a community
and a culture, a culture that certainly could not be divined from
the theology.'[3] As Bunyan the man cannot be seen apart from his
culture, no more can his works: the religious quality of *The Pilgrim's
Progress*, the suggestion is, reflects something essential in the culture.

The feature of this society that Leavis especially directs our
attention towards is the organic relation between popular and
sophisticated culture. The theatre, Shakespeare, appealed to the
cultivated and the populace at the same time. Moreover, 'Bunyan
himself shows how the popular culture to which he bears witness
could merge with literary culture at the level of great literature.
The converse, regarding the advantages enjoyed by the literary
writer, the "intellectual", need not be stated: they are apparent
in English literature from Shakespeare to Marvell.'[4] This organic
relation not only made the literature of the period possible, but all

levels of society benefited; it was the necessary condition of a general cultural vitality.

Further clarification of Leavis's grounds of praise of rural, early seventeenth-century society is provided by his disagreement, in *Nor Shall My Sword*, with the negative view of that society that T. S. Eliot expresses in 'East Coker'. After quoting Eliot's poem Leavis objects:

> Yet the country-folk whom Eliot reduces to this created the English language that made Shakespeare possible... Their speech developed as the articulate utterance of a total organic culture, one that comprehended craft-skills of many kinds, arts of living formed in response to practical exigencies, and material necessity through generations of settled habitation, knowledge of life that transcended the experience of any one life-span, subtly responsive awareness of the natural environment.[5]

Unquestionably, this is an extremely generalized description, and, in the end, Leavis does not give us a totally clear understanding of his social model. But the vitality of language, exemplified pre-eminently by Shakespeare, the religious quality, and the close connection of popular and sophisticated culture are obviously central to the society he deeply admires.

It is of vital importance to understand how Leavis *arrives* at this view of the seventeenth century, for, while ultimately I think he presents a simplified, idealized picture of seventeenth-century life, he does, *qua* literary critic, call attention to certain key facts about the age. Although as a university student Leavis was a scholar in History who took English as a Second Part of the Tripos, his view of history is derived mainly from literature, and it is the use he makes of literature that gives his historical argument, whatever its shortcomings, a valid claim on our attention. Essentially he bases his case on his belief in the intimate connection between literature and society. While Shakespeare is the primary 'proof' of the cultural vitality of the period, Leavis proposes his view of the seventeenth century mainly in his writings on John Bunyan.* He

---

* He deals with Bunyan in two essays in *The Common Pursuit*, 'Bunyan Through Modern Eyes' (1938), and 'Literature and Society' (1943), and more fully in the introduction he wrote to *Pilgrim's Progress* in 1964.

writes: 'Saying that there was in the seventeenth century, a real
culture of the people, one thinks first...of Bunyan...A humane
masterpiece resulted because he belonged to the civilization of his
time, and that meant...participating in a rich traditional culture.'[6]
And Leavis concludes: 'We must beware of idealizing, but the fact
is plain. There would have been no Shakespeare and no Bunyan
if in their time, with all its disadvantages by present day standards,
there had not been, living in the daily life of the people, a positive
culture which has disappeared.'[7] In Leavis's view, then, the
existence of the positive culture makes possible Shakespeare and
Bunyan. This question of the relation of literature and society is
obviously a complex, and controversial one, and certainly there are
critics like Northrop Frye, for example, who deny that particular
social conditions nourish great literature.[8] But Frye's view cuts
literature radically, in fact, entirely, off from life, and surely
Leavis's insistence that literature, like the language it is a manifestation of, does arise out of the whole culture is the more
acceptable, as well as the more traditional, view. Thus, for Leavis,
literary achievement is a direct index of quality of life in a society.
Bunyan's *Pilgrim's Progress* then he takes as 'evidence' of the
richness of *popular* English cultural life.*

In a further way Leavis's approach to the seventeenth century,
the kind of argument he presents, is distinctly that of a literary
critic: he derives his evidence of the nature of this culture from the
literary text by examining Bunyan's use of language. Leavis's
comments reveal his basic assumptions about the nature of
language:

> Bunyan the creative writer wrote out of a 'moral sense'
> that represented what was finest in that traditional
> culture. He used with a free idiomatic range and vividness

---

* It is perhaps necessary to explain what might appear to be a
contradiction in Leavis's thinking on the relation of literature and society.
Both Dickens in, say, *Little Dorrit* and Lawrence in *Women In Love* have
written what Leavis considers great novels, but he does not regard them
as indicating a correspondingly rich society. But in both cases he points to
still remaining positive aspects of society that made possible the respective
achievements: he claims that much of Dickens's strength comes from
being in touch with the last traces of popular culture, and that
Lawrence's work was nourished by the influence of the Nonconformist
tradition. Bunyan was more fortunate in that he was part of, and his
work reflects, a wider flourishing cultural life.

in preaching...the language he spoke...A language is much more than such phrases as 'means of expression' or 'instrument of communication' suggest; it is a vehicle of collective wisdom and basic assumptions, a currency of criteria and valuations collaboratively determined; itself it entails on the user a large measure of accepting participation in the culture of which it is the active living presence.

The vigour of Bunyan's prose is more than a matter of earthy raciness.[9]

Leavis's argument for the existence of a rich, living traditional culture is based primarily on the quality of language in *The Pilgrim's Progress*, for, as he remarks, 'it is upon the reader approaching as a literary critic that this truth compels itself (others seem to miss it)'.[10] An historian approaching Bunyan's work and not responding to the language might well find in it only a doctrinal and sectarian Puritanism; Leavis, concentrating on the language, finds evidence of a rich way of life. Quoting an example of the typical use of dialogue in the novel, he comments:

That is plainly traditional art and, equally plainly the life in it is of the people...The names and racy turns are organic with the general styles and the style, concentrating the life of popular idiom, is the expression of popular habit – the expression of a vigorous humane culture. For what is involved is not merely an idiomatic raciness of speech, expressing a strong vitality, but an art of social living, with its mature habits of valuation.[11]

Again, it is by commenting on style – the approach of the literary critic – that Leavis tries to establish his point.

If the strength of Leavis's approach is that he stays within his field, showing, as a literary critic, what literature can reveal about society – and what might be missed by the historian – the weakness in his argument seems obvious. While Leavis himself occasionally comments on the benefits that historians could get from literary criticism, asking them to accept an historical argument, the *entire* burden of proof of which is laid on literature is surely excessive. The nature of Leavis's evidence about the seventeenth century is simply too limited and selective. He in effect judges the society *only* by its literature and thus fails to provide a full perspective on seventeenth-century life. Leavis ignores the fact that while literature may provide special insights into history, these insights need to be supported by the usual data of historians – documents, journals, church records, and so on. And his argument particularly avoids facing the complications that arise when the historical insights of literature conflict with the 'facts' of historians.

The question of the actual nature of life in seventeenth-century England is obviously too large a question for me to go into here, but even a cursory glance at the work of historians indicates that, in certain respects, Leavis's picture of that society needs to be seriously qualified. He does acknowledge that this positive society has 'disadvantages by present day standards', but the fact that he tends to ignore the disadvantages leads to a distortion in his view. His picture of the day-to-day life of the working people seems, if not simply idealized, certainly open to debate. In *The Century of Revolution 1603–1714* Christopher Hill emphasizes the extreme harshness of the life of the poor in the early seventeenth century – the famine, pestilence and sudden death they were subject to. And he contends 'the [urban] poor were treated as utterly rightless'.[12] And Raymond Williams, who, in *The Country And The City*, like Leavis, draws primarily on literary evidence, argues that the condition of the rural workers was not much better: 'This economy, even at peace, was an order of exploitation of a most thoroughgoing kind; a property in men as well as in land; a reduction of most men to working animals.'[13] The positions of Hill and Williams, it is true, given their bias can hardly be accepted uncritically but they do provide evidence that the harsher realities of life are left out of Leavis's historical picture.

On the other hand, Leavis's view of the positive aspects of seventeenth-century society does receive support from historians. Speaking of Bunyan and the traditional popular culture reaching back to the Middle Ages Leavis insists that 'the place of religion in the culture is obvious enough'. In *Contrasting Communities: English Villagers in the Sixteenth and Seventeenth Centuries* (1974), Margaret Spufford argues convincingly, and in great detail, that the parish church and the meeting house were important in the villages; that religious life was central to the peasantry. For all that he might ignore, in pointing to the religious quality, the richness of language, and the organic relation of popular and sophisticated culture, Leavis is emphasizing those features of seventeenth-century society that are admirable, and that are lacking in the present.

Leavis wants us to understand not just the nature of the past, and what he thinks has been lost, but the nature of the changes that have produced our modern civilization. He argues that it is of crucial importance to understand the decisive start of science in the seventeenth century

> because a proper aliveness to the fundamental nature of the world's present sickness depends upon some knowledge and perception in relation to that field, and these entail an understanding of what happened there in the seventeenth century when the great change became irreversible. I am thinking of course of the confident start of science upon its accelerating advance. What the student needs to acquire a minimum knowledge of is the way in which the 'common-sense notion of the universe' (Whitehead's phrase) took possession of the ordinary man's mind, and with what consequences for the climate of the West and the ethos of our civilization. This involves being able to state intelligently what the Cartesian-Newtonian presuppositions were and to what kind of philosophical *impasse* they led – that still exemplified in the philosophies of science and the positivist and empiricist fashions that prevail.[14]

The scientific attitude, with its concomitant technology, which led to the Industrial Revolution, is at the centre of those changes in civilization Leavis is concerned with. He argues that by 1700 'all the forces of change that had been at work through the century had come together to inaugurate the triumphant advance towards the civilization, technological and Benthamite, that we live in'.[15]

Leavis praises Eliot's criticism, particularly the essays on Marvell and the Metaphysicals, mainly because of Eliot's theory of the 'dissociation of sensibility'. Leavis explains: 'About the causes of the process of "dissociation" Eliot says very little. He is aware (as who is not?) that civilization underwent something like a total change in the seventeenth century.'[16] This interpretation of the seventeenth century, it is true, has been challenged – Frank Kermode, for example, in his essay on 'Dissociation of Sensibility' in *Romantic Image* explicitly attacks Eliot's theory of history, and his objections, if they apply to Eliot's view, would apply to Leavis's as well. Kermode claims that 'the notion of a pregnant historical crisis, of great importance in every sphere of human activity, was attractive because it gave design and simplicity to history'.[17] There is an implicit parallel with the original fall in the notion of a decisive change in the middle of the seventeenth century, but Kermode finds this view unsupportable: 'It is not merely a matter of wrong dates; however far back one goes one seems to find the symptoms of dissociation. This suggests that there is little historical propriety in treating it as a seventeenth-century event.'[18] But Leavis himself points to signs of a decisive change: the contrast between Shakespeare's use of language and Dryden's reveals the loss of distinctly poetic-creative language – and this indicates a loss of creativity in the culture. Moreover, the striking contrast between the religious quality of Bunyan's Nonconformism and the secular Nonconformism of Defoe reveals a further impoverishment of sensibility. And certainly science, technology and mechanization – and 'the Cartesian–Newtonian presuppositions' – began to take command by the end of the seventeenth century. As Whitehead argues in *Science And The Modern World*, the mechanist theory of nature became dominant in the seventeenth century, and 'has reigned supreme ever since'.[19]

ii. The Organic Community

Leavis argues that despite the growing impact of science and the Industrial Revolution, local variations of the positive culture which made Shakespeare and Bunyan possible did survive, that up to the late nineteenth century the organic community still existed in rural England. Although Leavis only infrequently referred to the organic community after the 1930s, his dispute with C. P. Snow was partly about the nature of rural life in the nineteenth century, and in a fairly recent essay on George Eliot's *Adam Bede* he argues that her novel provides a record of this way of life at the end of the eighteenth century. He describes the world that she preserves in her novel as locally rooted and locally self-sufficient and claims that 'there is a sense in which, paradoxically, the inhabitants of that provincial England live in a larger world than their successors'.[20] In particular, the advantage of life in that rooted community, Leavis maintains, is that

> not only is the typical workman master of a craft,
> practising a skill and serving a function that bring a man a
> sense of his meaning something in life; George Eliot shows

us a world in which people possess and practise arts of
living, the creative products of generations. For us, the one
there is perhaps most point in insisting on is the art of
speech.[21]

And, Leavis adds, intellectual and artistic culture owe an essential
debt to this creative use of speech.

The central text, however, for Leavis's view of the organic
community is *Culture And Environment*, where he makes use of the
works of George Sturt. On the first page of *Culture And Environment*
Leavis states:

> What we have lost is the organic community with the
> living culture it embodied. Folk songs, folk dances,
> Cotswold cottages and handicraft products are signs and
> expressions of something more: an art of life, a way of
> living, ordered and patterned, involving social arts, codes
> of intercourse and a responsive adjustment, growing out of
> immemorial experience, to the natural environment and
> the rhythm of the year.[22]

This, with its emphasis on the natural environment and the cycle
of the year, sounds strikingly like D. H. Lawrence in *A Propos of
Lady Chatterly's Lover*, and Lawrence's influence is apparent in the
book. Leavis sympathizes with a rural way of life, but it is the
general loss of the sense of community that he laments: 'It is not
merely that life, from having been predominantly rural and
agricultural has become urban and industrial. When life was rooted
in the soil town life was not what it is now. Instead of the
community, urban or rural, we have, almost universally,
suburbanism.'[23]

From Sturt's books Leavis derives a picture of a truly satisfying
way of life. *Change In The Village* indicates that the folk were able
to live primarily in their work, thus their use of leisure was
according; *The Wheelwright's Shop* shows, Leavis argues, that 'their
work was such that they were able to feel themselves fulfilled in it
as self-respecting individuals'.[24] This picture includes not just the
skilled craftsman depicted in *The Wheelwright's Shop*, but also the
unskilled majority – those represented by Old Turner in *Change In
The Village*. There was no separation of life and work, work gave
meaning and dignity to life, and in general life in the old order was
richer, fuller than in modern experience. Is Leavis, with this
positive view, simply offering us a nostalgic pastoral dream?

While the use to which Leavis puts Sturt is in the main justifiable,
in the sense that Sturt does bring out a distinct contrast between
the old order and the new, between Turner and the coal carter,
Sturt also makes some criticisms of the old village life that Leavis
does not mention. The main defect that Sturt saw in the peasant
system as he knew it was that the mental activity of the people
was cramped, for while they were perceptive of details their power
of abstraction was extremely limited, their imaginations stifled,
and, notably, the range of their language was narrow. In fact, we
can see clearly how the qualifications that Sturt makes are dropped
in Leavis's account. Sturt writes: 'The work they did, though it left
their reasoning and imaginative powers undeveloped, called into
play enough subtle knowledge and skill to make their whole day's
industry gratifying.'[25] This is positive, but qualified; Leavis
translates it into: 'Besides their hands their brains, imagination,
conscience, sense of beauty and fitness – their personalities – were
engaged and satisfied.'[26] Sturt's portrayal is generally positive, but,
unlike Leavis, he was aware of definite shortcomings.*

Sturt, of course, is writing about a time of change, so much of
the old order has already gone; life in the present village is not as
full as he thinks it had been in the past: 'It is true that there are
never any signs in the valley of that almost festive temper, that glad
relish of life, which, if we may believe the poets, used to characterize
the English village of old times.'[27] Even for Sturt, who, like Leavis,
gets some of his history from literature, the true village was a thing
of the past. The fact that Sturt glances backwards to a better time
might lend some credence to Raymond William's objection that
Leavis's 'version of history is myth in the sense of conjecture' and
reveals 'a surrender to a characteristically industrialist, or urban,
nostalgia. . . If there is one thing that is certain about the 'organic
community', it is that it has always gone.'[28] This is similar to
Kermode's argument about the 'myth' of the dissociation of
sensibility in the seventeenth century. Williams's view, which has
a certain personal authority because of his own experience of a part

---

* In considering Leavis's idyllic picture of work in the organic community
  we should perhaps think back to the opening chapter of *Adam Bede* where
  all the men but Adam cease work immediately at six, much as they
  would in a modern factory. When Adam objects, 'I hate to see a man's
  arms drop down as if he was shot, before the clock's fairly struck, just as
  if he'd never a bit o'pride and delight in's work', Wiry Ben replies, 'Ye
  may like work better nor play, but I like play better nor work; that'll
  'commodate ye – it laves ye th'more to do.'

of rural England, seems to represent a large body of opinion, of those outside the *Scrutiny* group, about the reality of the organic community. Yet there are those who support Leavis; John Fraser, for example, insists: 'The organic community was not, and is not, a myth.'[29]

Some clarification, perhaps, can be thrown on this debate by considering one other 'text' Leavis refers to: Thomas Hardy's essay 'The Dorsetshire Labourer'. In *Nor Shall My Sword* Leavis turns to Hardy's essay in order to answer the claim made by C. P. Snow and J. H..Plumb that the poor readily walked off the land into the factories. He quotes Hardy: 'This process, which is described by the statistician as the tendency of the rural population to the large towns is really the tendency of water to flow uphill when forced.' Leavis then comments: 'What Hardy describes is a positive civilization that made the poverty and hardship he also describes (his point depends on that) acceptable to the "rural population" who had, under economic compulsion, to suffer, with the utmost reluctance, its loss.'[30] Here Leavis presents a more balanced response – he insists on the fact of the 'positive civilization' but also makes explicit his awareness of the 'poverty and the hardship'. Hardy unquestionably is extremely knowledgeable in this matter and his own response to the rural community is particularly instructive. In the essay, Hardy is less concerned with the contrast of the town and the country than with the change that has been introduced *within* the rural community by the necessity of migratory labour. He presents a complex assessment of the gains and losses that have accrued. On the one hand, the change has positive results as the people move out of the 'organic community'. He observes that the habitually-moving man is 'much more wide awake' than one of the old-fashioned stationary sort, and that the labourers are now 'more independent since their awakening to the sense of an outer world'.[31] He concludes: 'They are losing their individuality, but they are widening the range of their ideas, and gaining in freedom.'[32] Against these gains, however, Hardy sets certain losses. Before migration, the labourer had a long personal association with his farm; consequently his employer assumed the character of natural guardian. Now the labourers have lost touch with their environment, and they are moving towards uniformity. Hardy, like Sturt, then, portrays a life that was less fulfilling than what Leavis would have us believe, but he makes it clear that there have been substantial losses.

Whatever we think about the question of the organic community, we should be careful not to misunderstand Leavis's attitude towards the past. C. B. Cox and A. E. Dyson, in 'Word in the Desert', give a false impression of Leavis's response; they claim that 'the nostalgia for rural life, repeatedly expressed in *Scrutiny*, has been mocked by historians...Advocates of the myth of decline have wanted to retain old habits and values and have therefore reacted blindly and emotionally to modern developments.'[33] Cox and Dyson imply, by their references to 'nostalgia' and 'retain', that Leavis wants the old ways restored unchanged. In contrast, let us recall what Leavis writes towards the end of *Culture And Environment*:

> We must beware of simple solutions. We must, for instance, realize that there can be no mere going back: it is useless to think of emulating the Erewhonians and scrapping the machine in the hope of restoring the old order. Even if agriculture were revived, that would not bring back the organic community. It is important to insist on what has been lost lest it should be forgotten; for the memory of the old order must be the chief incitement towards a new, if ever we are to have one.[34]

Leavis frequently reiterated this point – it is central to his argument in both *Education And The University* and in *Nor Shall My Sword*. Leavis's focus is on the present, there is no desire on his part (as there is at times in Ruskin, say) to escape from the present into the past, nor to make the present simply accord with the past. But he does insist that awareness of the past is the essential condition under which there can be any hope for the present and the future; if we forget the past there can be no hope. The past provides us with a model, not as something to be imitated, but as offering a sense of human possibilities, a creative stimulus to further living in the present.

iii. Technologico-Benthamite Civilization

The twentieth century is for Leavis – as for many other intellectuals – a time of dissolution and disintegration; it is, as the title of his first pamphlet indicates, a period of mass civilization. The primary cause of this new and menacing civilization is clear to Leavis: 'In support of the belief that the modern phase of history is unprecedented it is enough to point to the machine.'[35] As he argues in 1930: 'The traditional ways of life have been destroyed by the machine, more and more does human life depart from the natural rhythms.'[36] This kind of social analysis obviously belongs in the line of thought Raymond Williams has discussed in *Culture And Society*, but whereas Carlyle, for example, was concerned that the machine would produce a mechanization of mind and feeling, Leavis's primary early concern is that the change consequent on the machine 'can hardly replace the delicate traditional adjustments, the mature, inherited codes of habit and valuation, without severe loss, and loss that may be more than temporary. It is a breach in continuity that threatens.'[37]

Leavis's main early statement on the society being shaped by the machine comes in *Culture And Environment* (1934). He sets out at greater length his analysis and critique of the effects of the machine:

> The great agent of change, and, from our point of view, destruction, has of course been the machine – applied power. The machine has brought us many advantages, but it has destroyed the old ways of life, the old forms, and by reason of the continual rapid change it involves, prevented the growth of the new. Moreover, the advantage it brings us in mass production has turned out to involve standardization and levelling-down outside the realm of mere material goods.[38]

Leavis's concern is with the *cultural* effects of the machine – the way in which it tends to affect those aspects of society which shape taste, sensibility, emotional response and value. We need to keep this focus in mind to understand properly the opening words of *Culture And Environment*: 'Many teachers of English who have become interested in the possibilities of training taste and sensibility must have been troubled by accompanying doubts. What effect can such training have against the multitudinous counter-influences – films, newspapers, advertising – indeed, the whole world outside the classroom.'[39] Leavis's phrasing here, it is true – seeing the 'whole world' outside the classroom as harmful – represents his characteristically embattled stance, causing him to set things in sharp opposition; but by 'whole world' he means primarily those aspects of the environment affecting taste and sensibility, which are his special concern.

In the face of this hostile environment, *Culture And Environment* is offered as a textbook for schools to train in discrimination and resistance, for, whereas in the past, in a healthy state of culture a citizen could be formed unconsciously by the environment, in the modern world a satisfactory idea of living must be worked for consciously. A large part of *Culture And Environment* is devoted to an analysis of one particular cultural effect of the machine – the impact of advertising on current fiction and on the national life generally. This aspect of the book now seems somewhat elementary, and while Leavis considerably expands on suggestions I. A. Richards made in *Principles of Literary Criticism*, the substance of this part of his argument clearly derives from Q. D. Leavis's *Fiction and the Reading Public*. Nonetheless, Leavis's overall proposals for training schoolchildren in the critical analysis of popular culture – newspaper, films, fiction – were in many ways original and pioneering and have earned him deserved praise. Raymond Williams, for instance, observes that 'the kind of training indicated in *Culture And Environment...* has been widely imitated and followed, so that if Leavis and his colleagues had done only this it would be enough to entitle them to major recognition'.[40]

Moreover, Leavis presents a very distinctive kind of social analysis, one directly related to his concerns as a literary critic – he concentrates on the use of language in society. Examining some typical examples of the influence of advertising on journalism and popular fiction he states: 'It should be brought home to learners that this debasement of language is not merely a matter of words; it is a debasement of emotional life, and of the quality of living.'[41] The impoverishment of language that Leavis finds in modern society he takes as indication of an impoverishment of emotional life. As a way of bringing home the difference between the present and the past Leavis suggests that 'classes moderately advanced in training might be asked to consider the probable concomitants of a change from the Bible, the Prayer-Book, Bunyan, Shakespeare and Milton as the main influences upon our emotional vocabulary, to newspaper, advertisements, best-sellers and cinema'.[42] While this obviously is an overly-sharp contrast – not everyone in our society reads best-sellers, nor, on the other hand, did everyone in the seventeenth century read Milton – the Bible was a pervasive influence in the past, and advertising, with what Leavis calls its 'crude emotional falsity', is a new feature of the environment.

Leavis goes on in *Culture And Environment* to present a further critique of the modern world; he contrasts modern work and leisure with what he sees as more enriching kinds of work in the past. There are, however, obvious simplifications in this aspect of Leavis's social diagnosis and he has been properly criticized for them by Raymond Williams in *Culture And Society*. Moreover, Leavis's analysis of work and leisure is in no way distinctive; the Marxist critique, say, of work – alienation – is far more comprehensive and trenchant. But one aspect of Leavis's critique is worth noting, for it shows the way in which certain of his literary-critical interests derive directly from his wider social concerns. In discussing the relation of work and leisure in the modern world, he argues that work which allows no fulfilment 'unfits one for making the *positive* effort without which there can be no true recreation'.[43] Such work leads people to seek not true leisure, which is re-creation, and demands an active, involved response, but passive distraction. Distractions or compensations tend to take the form of day-dreaming or fantasizing which habituate one 'to weak evasions, to the refusal to face reality at all.'[44] If we think of Leavis's negative assessment of the weakness – the day-dream quality – of Victorian poetry, of the poems of Walter de la Mare, and even of parts of George Eliot's *The Mill on the Floss* or D. H. Lawrence's *The Ladybird* – we can see the close relation between his social analysis and his literary criticism. The most important works of literature are these that offset the harmful effects of the modern environment.

Leavis's later response to the modern world is best set out in *Nor Shall My Sword*. With the passage of over thirty years he clearly feels that the situation of industrial society has grown worse. He expresses a stronger sense of the menacing quality of modern civilization and there is a deeper urgency in his diagnosis of cultural sickness. Leavis's essay on Snow, the first of his social writings of the 1960s, and certainly his most famous and controversial, provides a forceful statement of his view of contemporary life:

> Today's America: the energy, the triumphant technology, the productivity, the high standard of living and the life – impoverishment – the human emptiness; emptiness and boredom craving alcohol – of one kind or another. Who will assert that the average member of a modern society is more fully human, or more alive, than a Bushman, an

Indian peasant, or a member of one of those poignantly primitive peoples, with their marvellous art and skills and vital intelligence?[45]

This could have been written by D. H. Lawrence, and considering Leavis's earlier negative response to both *Mornings in Mexico* and *Etruscan Places*, it indicates a certain shift in his thinking, a sense of how desperate he finds the contemporary situation.*

What, in the 1930s, Leavis had called mass civilization, he calls, in his later years, technologico-Benthamite society, a more specific description of the prevailing ethos that he rejects. Leavis regards both technology and Benthamite attitudes as leading to a simplified, reductive conception of human values. He tries repeatedly to call attention to what he sees as the effects of technology: 'A general impoverishment of life – that is the threat that, ironically, accompanies the technological advance and the rising standard of living, and we are all involved.'[46] He goes on to explain how this impoverishment of life occurs:

> Technological change has marked cultural consequences. There is an implicit logic that will impose, if not met by creative intelligence and corrective purpose, simplifying and reductive criteria of human need and human good, and generate, to form the mind and spirit of civilization, disastrously false and inadequate conceptions of the *ends* to which science should be a means. This logic or drive is immensely and insidiously powerful. Its tendency appears very plainly in the cultural effects of mass production – in the levelling-down that goes with standardization.[47]

Leavis does not develop in any detail this diagnosis of the effects of technology; he is not, that is, a social critic in the same sense as, say, Jacques Ellul who in *The Technological Society* analyses very specifically how technology – technique, efficiency – come to domi-

---

* The negative description that Leavis gives here of America needs some explanation; it is characteristic and George Steiner has criticized him for this. However, the disease that Leavis is calling attention to is, he argues, not just American; rather, it is inherent in industrial civilization. He explains that the blindness, the inability to perceive that characterizes our civilization 'isn't peculiarly American, it is a vacuity that technologico-Benthamite civilization is creating and establishing in this country'.

nate, and supplant, human values. Leavis characteristically concentrates on the *cultural* effects of technology and is mainly calling attention to, rather than fully analysing, what he sees as the primary problem of our time. He does, nonetheless, provide a fuller statement of his view of the destructive impact of technology. The statement was originally made in *Education And The University* but he quoted the passage in *Nor Shall My Sword*, indicating that his diagnosis remained constant:

> American conditions are the conditions of modern civilization...On the one hand there is the enormous technical complexity of civilization, a complexity that could be dealt with only by an answering efficiency of co-ordination – a co-operative concentration of knowledge, understanding and will (and 'understanding' means...a perceptive wisdom about ends). On the other hand, the social and cultural disintegration that has accompanied the development of the inhumanly complex machinery is destroying what should have controlled the working. It is as if society, in so complicating and extending the machinery of organization, had incurred a progressive debility of consciousness and of the powers of co-ordination and control – had lost intelligible memory and moral purpose...The complexities being what they are, the general drift has been technocratic, and the effective conception of the human ends to be served that accompanies a preoccupation with the smooth running of the machinery tends to be a drastically simplified one.[48]

'Benthamite', the other half of Leavis's coinage, is a short-hand way of referring to an entire set of attitudes that he sharply opposes: excessive rationality; the Benthamite calculus, that is the attempt to measure, average and quantify, and thus reduce human values; an atomistic conception of the individual and society; an emphasis on equality at all costs, ignoring essential differences; and, perhaps most importantly, a view of the mind as passive and mechanical and a completely secular response to life. Leavis sees as the end result of 'technologico-Benthamite' civilization the mechanization of man. In his recent book, *Thought, Words And Creativity* (1976), he praises D. H. Lawrence's critique of this process:

> What he inveighs against is the misuse of the mind that makes it an enemy of life. He exposes and inveighs a great

> deal, because that misuse is the distinctive mark of our
> scientific-industrial civilization...the mind, mental
> consciousness, [offers] to work life according to its ideas,
> which, with the mental consciousness they belong to, have
> been cut off from the well-head and from the centres of
> living power. It is with thought...Lawrence sets about
> rescuing life from this inner mechanization.[49]

What is so sinister about this process to Leavis is that 'industrial civilization, with the power to mechanize what lives in it or by it' threatens the distinctively human quality of 'the creativity...that can draw on the source that lies deep down'.[50]

Creativity derives from the 'source'; that is, it, and human life, have a religious basis. I will later take up the matter of Leavis's religious language; here it is necessary simply to note that his critique of modern society is written, ultimately, from a religious point of view. Both Benthamism and technology take no account of, and in fact cut us off from, the religious source of life. Writing of Blake, to whom he does attribute a religious spirit, Leavis remarks: 'The contrast of Blake to Bentham may serve to enforce the main point I have been trying to make. You could hardly attribute a religious spirit to the Benthamite inspiration.'[51] Technologico-Benthamite civilization impoverishes by having no awareness of the need for a religious sense of life. In *Thought, Words And Creativity* Leavis forcefully states his case for the necessity of recognizing the religious basis of life, and the danger that will ensue if we do not:

> Lawrence in his discursive treatises, *Psychoanalysis and the
> Unconscious*, makes plain why he treats the hidden source as
> the access to the real and profound authority that may
> properly be called religious, and why, in his diagnosis of a
> sick world, he makes indifference to the source the lethal
> malady – a blankness inherent in technologico-Bentham-
> ism – that will destroy our civilization.[52]

2

Language, Literature, And Continuity

At the centre of Leavis's thought is the question of how to retain and develop a full sense of human ends, values and significance in a society increasingly dominated by science and technology. The answer that he gave was the same for over forty years: by maintaining cultural continuity. The title of his first collection of essays, published in 1933, was simply *For Continuity*. In his recent book *Nor Shall My Sword* most of the essays end in the same way – in a plea for continuity. One of the essays is entitled '"English", Unrest And Continuity' and the essay '"Literarism" Versus "Scientism"', originally a lecture Leavis gave in the modern section of the ancient university of York, concludes: 'Looking round at this beautiful university city, I have said to myself: "Surely here the creative battle to maintain our living cultural heritage – a continuity of profoundly human creative life – must seem worth fighting; must be seen as a battle that *shall* not be lost."'[1]

In this concern with continuity Leavis is the heir of Matthew Arnold. Leavis's 1930 minority culture pamphlet shows the clear influence of Arnold and in his recent *English Literature In Our Time And The University* he elaborates on the nature of the influence. Arnold saw, he claims, that the growth of material civilization and the changes brought about by technological advance entail a lapse of the creatively human response which *is* a cultural tradition; further, 'Arnold saw, and said, that to preserve continuity – continuity of cultural consciousness – a more conscious and deliberate use of intelligence was needed than in the past.'[2] The emphasis on the importance of the poetic tradition, on standards, the educated public, the central place given to the function of

25

literary criticism – these are Arnold's major concerns as well as Leavis's, and they are all aspects of the 'conscious and deliberate' effort to maintain continuity.

Mass Civilization And Minority Culture is Leavis's first attempt to explain the answer he thought was necessary in the present condition; to explain, that is, what he means by 'culture'. Leavis begins with a quotation from *Culture and Anarchy*, then remarks that he must face problems of definition which Arnold could pass by (a comment which is rather ironical considering Leavis's deliberate and perpetual refusal to define important words, insisting that they must live and gain meaning in use). Leavis then states: 'When, for example, having started by saying that culture is in minority keeping, I am asked what I mean by "culture", I might (and do) refer the reader to *Culture And Anarchy*; but I know that something more is required.'[3] In a well-known passage Arnold states his definition of culture:

> The whole scope of the essay is to recommend culture as
> the great help out of our present difficulties; culture being
> a pursuit of our total perfection by means of getting to
> know, on all the matters which most concern us, the best
> which has been thought and said in the world; and
> through this knowledge, turning a stream of fresh and free
> thought upon our stock notions and habits.[4]

Leavis's own position has obvious affinities with this. His statement that '"civilization" and "culture" are coming to be antithetical terms'[5] clearly relates him to Arnold and to the tradition of cultural thought that Raymond Williams has discussed as the culture and society debate; culture is now thought of as a body of values superior to those prevalent in society. Further, in asserting the difference between his interpretation of culture and that of the Marxists, with their emphasis on social and economic determinants, Leavis sounds very much like Arnold: 'There *is*, then, a point of view above classes; there *can* be intellectual, aesthetic and moral activity that is not merely an expression of class origin and economic circumstances; there *is* a "human culture" to be aimed at that must be achieved by cultivating a certain autonomy of the spirit.'[6]

The difference, however, in Leavis's conception of culture is brought out when he claims that 'a culture expressing itself in a tradition of literature and art – such a tradition as represents the finer consciousness of the race and provides the currency of finer living – can be in a healthy state only if this tradition is in living relation with a real culture, shared by the people at large.'[7] Leavis's concern is always with defining and bringing to a focus the English culture represented by English literature; Arnold's concern is with the culture of the 'world'. Their remedies for the troubles of an external and material civilization take different forms: we only have to think of *Essays In Criticism* (first series) where Arnold presents Heine, the De Guérins, Joubert, Spinoza and Marcus Aurelius to the English nation to see the contrast. Whereas Arnold looks to the intellectual culture of the continent as a remedy to British provinciality, Leavis concentrates on the strength of the native English culture.

This characteristic difference between Arnold and Leavis is also seen in their attitude to Nonconformist religion. Arnold's view of the Nonconformists is highly critical: 'But we have got fixed in our minds that a more full and harmonious development of their humanity is what the Nonconformists most want, that narrowness, one-sidedness, and incompleteness is what they most suffer from; in a word, that in what we call *provinciality* they abound, but in what we may call *totality* they fall short.'[8] In contrast to Arnold, Leavis defended the centrality and importance of Nonconformist religion in English life. It is one aspect of his commitment to the culture intimately related to British civilization.

Arnold's comment, however, raises the matter of provinciality; Leavis has often been charged with being narrow and provincial in being concerned only with English literature and English culture. In contrast, Arnold and T. S. Eliot are often seen as having a greater range of awareness in their concern with European culture. In this sense Leavis obviously is 'provincial', but this is not necessarily the fault that it is usually taken to be. This narrowing of interest is very deliberate on Leavis's part, and he himself replies to the charge of provincialism: 'Better, then, be provincial than cosmopolitan, for to be cosmopolitan in these matters is to be at home nowhere.'[9] I think it must be seen that if the narrowness is, in one sense, a weakness, it also involves a corresponding strength; Leavis's knowledge of English culture is deeply rooted, and this rootedness is the source of that insight and authority with which he speaks on English literature and English culture.

Ultimately the reason for Leavis's difference from Arnold and Eliot, the reason for his concentration only on English culture, is

that he thinks of culture as being inseparable from language: to be
responsive to cultural values is to be responsive to a language. In
the 1930 pamphlet on minority culture he directed us to Arnold's
use of 'culture', then remarked: 'something more is required'. The
'something more' is an explanation of the relation of language and
culture. Referring to the educated minority, Leavis writes:

> In their keeping...is the language, the changing idiom,
> upon which fine living depends, and without which
> distinction of spirit is thwarted and incoherent. By
> 'culture' I mean the use of such a language. I do not
> suppose myself to have produced a tight definition, but the
> account, I think, will be recognized as adequate by
> anyone who is likely to read this pamphlet.[10]

For Leavis, then, unlike Arnold, culture is intimately related to
language; as he adds, 'when we used the metaphor of "language"
in defining culture we were using more than a metaphor...Without
the living subtlety of the finest idiom (which is dependent upon use)
the heritage dies.'[11] There are, however, certain difficulties with
this view. First, the definition is *not* very tight. Leavis in fact has
always been somewhat vague in his efforts to 'define' culture. In
the much later essay 'Luddites? or There Is Only One Culture'
he writes:

> It may be commented at this point that I am not absolved
> from explaining what positively I mean by 'culture' in the
> sense I invoke when I criticize misleading uses of the term.
> I won't proceed by attempting to offer a direct formal
> definition; that wouldn't conduce to economy, or to the
> kind of clarity that for the present purpose we need.[12]

Instead, he again refers us to language. To say that 'culture' is the
'use of such a language' seems to be a simplified, because *single*,
explanation of culture. Also, once one begins to define culture in
relation to language, it becomes difficult to keep distinct Arnold's
sense of culture as 'the best' and the anthropologist's use of culture
referring to a whole way of life. Leavis's use of the word is often
loose. While in the minority culture pamphlet he means by
'culture' the finest 'use of language', more typically he writes: 'The
more one ponders it the more difficult a concept does "language"
become to delimit. To be sensitive to a language is to be sensitive
to a culture. You can only hope to be sensitive to a language of

the past, or to a foreign language, out of your sensitiveness to your own language.'[13] Here he is using 'culture' in its wider sense, and this perhaps justifies Raymond Williams' remark that 'the difficulty about the idea of culture is that we are continually forced to extend it, until it becomes almost identical with our whole common life'.[14] While Leavis's references to language incline him to extend his idea of culture in this way, his final concern is with the 'best' culture that is an expression of the wider English civilization.

Culture is closely allied with tradition in Leavis's thinking. In explaining that he is concerned with more than the 'culture' of individuals he writes: 'It is to the culture that transcends the individual as the language he inherits transcends him that we come back; to the culture that has decayed with tradition.'[15] Whether Leavis refers to the continuance of culture or tradition, however, in both cases the transmitting agent is language. In *Culture And Environment*, in a section entitled 'Tradition', he comments on the relation of culture, tradition, and language:

> At the centre of our culture is language, and while we have our language tradition is, in some essential sense, still alive. And language is not merely a matter of words – or words are more than they seem to be:
> 'From the beginning civilization has been dependent upon speech, for words are our chief link with the past and with one another and the channel of our spiritual inheritance. As the other vehicles of tradition, the family and community, for example, are dissolved, we are forced more and more to rely upon language.' I. A. Richards, *Practical Criticism*, pp. 320–1.
> Largely conveyed in language, there is our spiritual, moral and emotional tradition, which preserves the 'picked experience of ages' regarding the finer issues of life.[16]

The survival of English culture depends upon sustaining tradition, and it is to English literature, to the English literary tradition, that Leavis looks to accomplish this – to maintain continuity: 'The fact that the other traditional continuities have...so completely disintegrated make the literary tradition correspondingly more important, since the continuity of consciousness, the conservation of collective experience, is the more dependent on it: if the literary tradition is allowed to lapse, the gap is complete.'[17] Literature fulfils this function by keeping the language fully alive. Whereas in the past the moral, emotional tradition embodied in language was kept alive both by the creative art of speech, and by the crafts represented by the wheelwrights that Sturt describes, in the present, conscious preservation is necessary. Since the decisive use of words in the modern world, Leavis claims, is in association with advertising, journalism and best-sellers, it 'becomes plain why it is of so great importance to keep the literary tradition alive. For if language tends to be debased...instead of invigorated by contemporary use, then it is to literature alone, where its subtlest and finest use is preserved, that we can look with any hope of keeping in touch with our spiritual tradition.'[18] Leavis, it is true, by concentrating *only* on language, and the literary tradition, slights the other ways – the other arts, history, philosophy – of conserving the collective experience. But that literature is pre-eminent in enriching the language and has a central place in maintaining the spiritual tradition is surely undeniable.

Leavis's most concise early statement on the nature of literature, and on its relation to language and tradition, comes in his 1933 pamphlet *How To Teach Reading*. He begins by criticizing Ezra Pound's idea of literature. While Leavis approves of Pound's attempt to define literature in terms of language – 'language charged with meaning to the utmost degree' – he observes that Pound fails to realize the relation of literature to cultural tradition. For Pound literature remains merely a matter of individual works, but for Leavis it involves a literary tradition and must be seen as the expression of a particular cultural tradition:

> A given literary tradition is not merely, as it were by geographical accidents of birth, associated with a given language: the relation may be suggested by saying that the two are *of* each other. Not only is language an apt analogy for literary tradition; one might say that such a tradition is largely a development of the language it belongs to if one did not want to say at the same time that the language is largely a product of the tradition. Perhaps the best analogy is that used by Mr. Eliot in *Tradition and the Individual Talent* when he speaks of the 'mind of Europe'. 'Mind' implies both 'consciousness' and 'memory', and a literary tradition is both: it is the consciousness and memory of the people or the cultural tradition in which it has developed.[19]

By being 'consciousness' as well as 'memory', a literary tradition maintains and carries on the cultural tradition.

Leavis's conception of literature is here explicitly indebted to T. S. Eliot, and in the essay 'Literature and Society' he gives a fuller acknowledgement of the importance of Eliot's idea of tradition on his own thinking about the nature of literature; it was Eliot who helped him to come to think of literature as an organic order rather than as an accumulation of separate works. But when Eliot thinks of the order of literature he is concerned with realizing a European order; Leavis is concerned to define the order and reality of 'English literature', to insist that the two combined words do in fact, necessarily, go together. In the *Scrutiny* retrospect essay Leavis states that those founding *Scrutiny* recognized,

> for all our diversities of creed and 'philosophy', that we belonged to a common civilization and a positive culture. That culture was for us pre-eminently represented by English literature. We believed there *was* an English literature – that one had, if intelligently interested in it, to conceive English literature as something more than an aggregate of individual works. We recognized, then, that like the culture it represented it must, in so far as living and real, have its life in the present – and that life is growth.[20]

As Leavis indicates, he believes that we still have a positive culture, that we do share a common cultural tradition. In *Education And The University* he explains that if education were only directed at resisting modern civilization the effort would be hopeless; however, those who make an effort in education 'must feel it to be the insistence of essential human needs; needs manifested in a certain force of tradition that they, in promoting the effort, represent and are endeavouring, by bringing it to greater consciousness of ends and means and urgencies, to strengthen and direct'.[21] Education, that is, has a positive basis in the existing cultural tradition. Despite Leavis's great pessimism about modern civilization, and despite his strong sense of the unprecedented menace of living in our time (what Kermode calls 'the sense of an ending' is apparent in Leavis's thought as well as Lawrence's, although with Lawrence it is more extreme), one of Leavis's fundamental assumptions is that the gap in continuity has not been absolute, the disintegration has not been complete. As he explained in 1943:

> I assume that the attempt to establish a real liberal
> education in this country...is worth making because, in
> spite of all our talk about disintegration and decay...we
> still have a positive cultural tradition. Its persistence is
> such that we can...count on a sufficient measure of
> agreement, overt and implicit, about essential values to
> make it unnecessary to discuss ultimate sanctions, or
> provide a philosophy, before starting to work. This I
> assume;...the kind of effort I have in mind would be the
> effort of an actual living tradition to bring itself to a focus,
> and would see itself...in terms of the carrying-on of a
> going concern.[22]

This is a very large assumption Leavis is making, but the belief in
the effective presence of a positive tradition is basic to all of his work;
this assumption makes it possible to conceive of a university and
to engage in literary criticism. In the years after this passage was
written Leavis thought the threat of technological society had
grown, yet he did not waver in his belief in the existence of a positive
culture of shared values. In 1967 he affirmed that the business of
the university entails

> carrying on a vital continuity in which the promoters and
> executants are already involved in such a way that, but for
> their being so involved, there would have been no
> conception, no planning, no point in founding a
> university. They have, that is, a common culture in which
> (say), for all their differences, agnostics, Catholics and
> diverse kinds of Protestants can work together for common
> human ends. Such a cultural tradition, like the language
> that is at the heart of it, has been formed and kept
> living...by continuous collaborative renewal. The
> participants tend to be hardly conscious of the basic values
> and assumptions they share, but it is the sense of
> something basic shared that makes possible the assumption
> (for instance) that there is point in founding new
> universities.[23]

Some of Leavis's critics have attacked his pessimism about modern
civilization, but it could be possible to regard his assumption that
there is a common tradition, a shared sense of values, as overly
optimistic.

There are obvious difficulties in trying to argue that there still is a homogeneous cultural tradition. First, until the twentieth century, English culture has predominantly been a Christian culture. Whatever the disagreements between Anglicans, Baptists, Nonconformists, Methodists, etc., it was the general commitment to Christian values that unified society. But the cultural tradition that Leavis is trying to preserve is not, primarily, Christian. In outlining his approach in *Education And The University* he touches on the problem involved here:

> Of course, it is the preoccupation with cultural values as human and separable from any particular religious frame or basis, the offer at a cultural regeneration that is not to proceed by way of a religious revival, that prompts the description 'humanist'. Literary criticism must, in this sense, always be humanist...It seems to me obvious that the approach needed in education must be in the same way humanist...The point is that, whatever else may be necessary, there must in any case be, to meet the present crisis of civilization, a liberal education that doesn't start with a doctrinal frame, and is not directed at inculcating one...When [the Christian] says that the cultural tradition we belong to and must aim to preserve is in very important senses Christian he commands assent. But this is the age not of Dante or of Herbert, but of T. S. Eliot.[24]

Leavis acknowledges, in fact insists, that there has been a change in the nature of religious belief: whereas Dante and Herbert could give total allegiance to their faith, for a modern such as Eliot, belief is much more tentative, a searching exploration, rather than a committed affirmation. But Eliot's way does not seem representative; modern society has become increasingly secular and the influence of Christianity has continually waned – it is no longer a dominant unifying force. Where a religious belief does continue, rather than being Christian, it is just as likely to be in the form of the 'religious sense' represented by Lawrence, and Leavis himself. This 'religious sense', however, increasingly becomes an individual matter and does not provide the common ground of Christian faith.

With the decline of Christianity, many critics and writers would argue that what characterizes the modern era is the very point that we no longer share a common world of values, that value has

become much more personal and subjective. Certainly there has
been a shift in this direction since the nineteenth century and any
claim that we share basic values is more tenuous now than it was
in the Victorian age. For Leavis, however, there is a sense in which
we inevitably live in a world of shared values; he would never think
of purely individual values, or of the individual, in the manner, for
instance, of John Stuart Mill. One can only conceive of purely
personal experience or of purely personal values by thinking of
society in an atomistic way, by making a sharp separation between
the individual on the one hand and society on the other. Leavis
never does this; and, for instance, in his Introduction to *Mill on
Bentham and Coleridge* he criticizes Mill's atomistic conception of
society:

> As we go on in the *Autobiography*, we see the original
> Benthamite individualism modifying itself radically. . . [but]
> his thinking is still that of a mind for which the individual
> is the prior fact; he works out from that to the idea of
> society, and doesn't seem to arrive at any very full inward
> recognition of the complexities covered by the
> 'individual-society' antithesis.[25]

Leavis in fact argues that the primary importance of literature for
students of society is to help them learn a much more subtle and
complex view of the relation of the individual and society, and he
rejects not only the Benthamite, and the romantic, view of the
unaided individual forming his world and values alone, but also
the Marxist or positivist view of society shaping the individual; the
real relation is much more inward than either of these views. One
of the many features of Snow's 'Two-Cultures' lecture that Leavis
objected to was the opposition Snow made between the individual
condition and social hope. Leavis retorted that Snow emptied the
word 'society' of everything not congenial to the technologico-
Benthamite ethos and he claimed that 'to challenge the crude
antithesis, individual-social, is to demand genuine recognition for
the fact, nature and significance of human creativity'.[26] An
atomistic view of man and society would regard creativity simply
as an individual act, and the values created could be conceived as
solely individual, but for Leavis the relation of the individual,
society and values is organic. Blake would seem to be an example
of an almost individual form of creativity, yet Leavis refers to Blake
to illustrate the point that,

except in the individual there is no creativity...But the potently individual such as an artist is discovers, as he explores his most intimate experience, how inescapably social he is in his very individuality. The poet...is...a focal conduit of the life that is one, though it manifests itself only in the myriad individual beings, and his unique identity is not the less a unique identity because the discovery of what it is and means entails a profoundly inward participation in cultural continuity – a continuous creative collaboration, something that must surely be called 'social'.[27]

According to Leavis's understanding of the relation of the individual and society our experience is necessarily social and our values inevitably shared cultural values.*

Further, Leavis insists, our experience is not only inherently social, but any adequate conception of society must take into account the presence of the past. In *Nor Shall My Sword* he argues that 'the Snow-Todd mode of thought, or non-thought, eliminates cultural continuity, excluding thus any more adequate idea of "society" than that which belongs to Social Studies'.[28] In order to defend his own conception of society, and to support his argument that the past is an inherent part of modern society, be quotes Michael Polanyi: 'Each of us interiorizes our cultural heritage, he grows into a person seeing the world and experiencing life in terms of this outlook.'[29] And in *The Living Principle* he argues more cogently that the cultural tradition is inescapably present in modern society. Referring to Marjorie Grene's discussion of the way in which a child is born into, and develops within, 'the human world', he writes:

> Of the child she says, virtually, that it is able to grow into full humanity because it lives in a fully human world, a world shaped by all kinds of human value-judgments and

---

* In Leavis's view, then, the notion of personal and subjective values is a very carelessly held, and mistaken, idea. Everyone is shaped by some common body of assumptions; to have entirely personal, subjective values is to be almost superhumanly heroic – even Blake cannot be so described. But the common centre of value is disintegrating into value-cliques – what Leavis calls the "social-personal valuations" of a coterie. And the values of the coterie are much less serious, coherent, and adequate than those that derive from the cultural tradition.

informed by distinctly human 'values'. The 'total
community' to which she refers is, properly considered,
both the actual enumerable community which, as the
bearer of cultural tradition, is its effective presence, and
the wider human community, transcending statistical fact,
to which, by participating in a living culture, one belongs,
having access to the profit of many centuries of human
experience.[30]

The values of the cultural tradition, however, must be consciously
maintained in the modern world and to accomplish this Leavis
looks to the university. In *Education And The University* he argues that
'the universities are recognized symbols of cultural tradition – of
cultural tradition still conceived as a directing force, representing
a wisdom older than modern civilization'.[31] Leavis's emphasis, we
should note, falls on a 'sense of value' which should direct society,
not on any moral doctrine. In both of his later books dealing with
the university he again emphasizes their function in maintaining
the cultural tradition. In *English Literature In Our Time And The
University* arguing for the importance of the university he contends:
'the living heritage on which meaning and humane intelligence
depend can't, in our time, be maintained without a concentrated
creativity somewhere'.[32] In the introduction to *Nor Shall My Sword*
Leavis explains that his focal preoccupation is with the creation of
the university, but he then adds that

> the university as I contend for it is not an ultimate human
> goal; it is the answer to a present extremely urgent need of
> civilization. The need is to find a way to save cultural
> continuity, that continuous collaborative renewal which
> keeps the 'heritage' of perception, judgment, responsibility
> and spiritual awareness alive, responsive to change and
> authoritative for guidance.[33]

In the above passage Leavis puts 'heritage' in quotation marks
to indicate the qualified sense in which it is authoritative. Leavis
never was a traditionalist like T. S. Eliot or Allen Tate, for
example. The difference can be seen by considering Solomon
Fishman's summary of the position of the Southern new critics:
'The agrarian is conservative. Perceiving continuity to be the
condition of culture, he is more dedicated to permanence than to
change.'[34] Leavis does not have this conservative dedication to

permanence. It is true that the way he spoke of tradition as the locus of values in the 1930s could possibly be taken as representing a very conservative stance, but even then his insistence was on the need to understand the idea of a living, changing tradition. And Leavis's recent explanations of his position should make it clear that he in no sense simply adheres to the past, and that conservative traditionalism is not the only alternative to progressive enlightenment. In his reply to C. P. Snow, he explains: 'I have used the phrase "cultural tradition" rather than Snow's "the traditional culture", because this last suggests something quite different from what I mean. It suggests something belonging to the past, a reservoir of alleged wisdom, an established habit, an unadventurousness in the face of life and change.'[35] That is clearly not what Leavis advocates, rather he insists that in order to control science and technology, mankind

> will need to be in full intelligent possession of its full humanity (and 'possession' here means...a basic living deference towards that to which, opening as it does into the unknown and itself immeasurable, we know we belong). I haven't chosen to say that mankind will need all its traditional wisdom; that might suggest a kind of conservatism that, so far as I am concerned, is the enemy. What we need...[is] creative response to the new challenges of time.[36]

Leavis's language here unquestionably includes rhetoric and cliché – 'creative response to the new challenge of time'; nonetheless, he successfully makes his point that in his view of cultural tradition, change and growth are central. If we fully grasp this conception of cultural tradition and continuity, then the difficulty which René Wellek thinks he finds in Leavis's thought largely disappears. Wellek, in discussing Leavis's standards or criteria, suggests that the two central ones are tradition and life. He argues that Leavis thinks of tradition as primarily literary and social, but Wellek thinks that this standard of tradition is often modified or even contradicted in Leavis by a concern for life or vitality. Wellek concludes therefore that 'there is a contradiction, or at least a tension between Leavis's emphasis on civilized tradition, or humanism, and on his advocacy of life for life's sake'.[37] Whatever 'life for life's sake' is supposed to mean, one can see why Wellek would think there was a problem here, but he misunderstands Leavis's

view of tradition and continuity – they are not opposed to his
advocacy of 'life'. Leavis explains that '"handing things on" is
rather to be called "maintaining a continuity", and perhaps I can
make clear the difference I have in mind by adding immediately
that for "continuity" you can substitute a "life" – maintaining a
life'.[38]

Leavis's recent position involves only a shift of emphasis from his
stance of the 1930s, but he increasingly came to emphasize that
continuity depends on collaborative creativity. In '"English",
Unrest And Continuity', which is perhaps the most important
though not the most famous of the essays in *Nor Shall My Sword*,
he clearly explains how literature illustrates this view of continuity:

> The truism that English literature has its life in the
> present, or not at all, has to be effectively asserted: it is
> basic. If we have the means of bringing home
> strongly...the force of the associated truth, that life is
> growth (not economic growth) and creative responsiveness
> to change, we should *use* them. The progressivist's
> acceptance of the fact of change has for a corollary a
> contempt for tradition, conceived as a timid clinging to old
> habits, and implicitly posited as the only alternative. That
> is why I avoid the word 'tradition', and, in speaking of
> the need to maintain cultural continuity, insist that the
> maintaining, being either a strongly positive drive of life or
> pitifully nothing, is creative. Only in terms of literature
> can this truth be asserted with effect in our world...And
> here I state the unique nature, and the central
> importance, of English as a university study.[39]

Part of the attraction Eliot's essays on the seventeenth century had
for Leavis lay in their illuminating, in the matter of the relation
between the present and the past, 'the way in which an organic
(and therefore changing) English Literature exists, transcending
the "past" and "present" of empiricist commonsense'.[40] The
phrase 'English literature in our time', from the title of Leavis's
book, partly indicates this aspect of his concern with continuity.
He maintains that only in terms of the present can the literature
of the past exist, that the reality of English literature for each age
changes and not just by accretion, but that the chart of the organic
structure changes; that is, the use of the past, the reality and life

of the past in the present must be creative – there is no mere handing down or taking over.

Leavis's fullest explanation of the essentially creative nature of continuity comes in the introductory essay in *Nor Shall My Sword*, entitled, '"Life" Is A Necessary Word', and the explanation given there further clarifies the problem posed by Wellek. In the essay Leavis explains what he means by 'life' and the nature of the continuity that sustains it. He uses that centrally Laurentian word 'wonder' to express his sense of 'life': 'Wonder is the welcoming apprehension of the new, the anti-Urizenic recognition of the divined possibility. It is the living response to life, the creative – the life of which the artist in his creativity is conscious of being a servant. To be spontaneous, and in its spontaneity creative, is of the essence of life.'[41] This is an expression of a sense of life that certainly would be amenable to Lawrence, and although as a definition it is, inevitably, somewhat vague, Leavis's comments on Blake bring it into sharper focus. Leavis uses Blake in order to 'define' what he means by 'creativity': 'Blake was incapable of supposing that in his creativity he "belonged to himself".'[42] There is clearly a religious resonance in Leavis's use of the term. Leavis's discussion of Blake further reveals just how fundamentally his idea of continuity involves an openness to the new. Leavis praises Blake in general but does not endorse his Jerusalem, for in Jerusalem Blake attempts to present the final goal of humanity, a state that would deny the need for any further development or growth. The attempt to present a final goal entails life being 'known', but Leavis claims: 'Life in its continued livingness is what, of its very nature, can't be convincingly imagined in terms of a final cause vindicated in an achieved ultimate goal, for livingness is creativity, and creativity manifests itself in emerging newness.'[43] Leavis's emphasis in this essay, in fact, is so heavily on the apprehension of the new that he no longer seems to be speaking about the continuity 'which keeps the "heritage" of perception, judgment, responsibility and spiritual awareness alive'. But his point, of course, is that the "heritage" has always been a creative achievement, and that the human world of values and significances must be continually created.

3

The Educated Public

The values and the sense of the complexity of life derived from the cultural tradition can be effectively asserted in modern society, Leavis insists, only through the existence of an educated public. In urging the necessity of an educated public Leavis obviously is following the argument of Matthew Arnold. His conception of the educated public descends from Arnold's concept of the aliens, and, as well, from Coleridge's notion of the clerisy. Leavis, however, adapts this key line of English thought to the present situation, and his statements on the nature and function of the educated public are an important, although neglected, part of his work.

Throughout his career Leavis tried to get recognized the importance of this educated public. In his very early publication 'Mass Civilization and Minority Culture' (1930) he first explained the nature and function of the minority:

> Upon this minority depends our power of profiting by the finest human experience of the past; they keep alive the subtlest and most perishable parts of tradition. Upon them depend the implicit standards that order the finer living of an age, the sense that this is worth more than that, this rather than that is the direction in which to go, that the centre is here rather than there. In their keeping...is the language, the changing idiom, upon which fine living depends and without which distinction of spirit is thwarted and incoherent.[1]

From the very beginning Leavis places a tremendous burden on the minority; they alone, in effect, are responsible for, and can change, the health of modern society. In his later work – *English Literature In Our Time And The University* (1969), *Nor Shall My Sword* (1972), especially the concluding essay, 'Elites, Oligarchies, And An Educated Public', and *The Living Principle* (1975) – his insistence on the importance of the minority has become, if anything, more emphatic. In the preface to *The Living Principle* he gives a clear statement of his later position:

> I myself see as my business in this book to present with all
> the cogency I can achieve the full necessity of a living
> creative literature, of the cultural continuity without
> which there can be no valid criteria of the humanly most
> important kind, and of the cultural habit... that once
> meant that there was some vital touch and communication
> between the experience and sensibility represented by a
> living literary tradition on the one hand, and on the other,
> the intellectual and political life of the age. Such
> communication must depend on the existence of an
> influential and truly cultivated public – a public in which
> the continuity has a potent life.[2]

The role of the educated public, then, is to make influential the 'best that is known and thought' and to maintain and impart the standards or sense of value essential to the health of all society; it is to be, in effect, the centre necessary to direct technological society. With these very large claims the question of the nature of the minority is obviously a crucial one for the very possibility of there being a real centre for society depends largely on the range of concerns of those who constitute the minority. Raymond Williams, in *Culture And Society*, claims that in the early 1930 pamphlet Leavis is thinking primarily of a literary minority and criticizes him for this. Williams compares Leavis's conception of the minority with that of Coleridge and Arnold and contends that 'for Leavis, the minority is, essentially, a literary minority, which keeps alive the literary tradition and the finest capacities of the language. This development is instructive, for the tenuity of the claim to be a "centre" is, unfortunately, increasingly obvious'.[3] Leavis's formulation does appear to narrow the nature of the minority; yet Williams, drawing on the 1930 pamphlet, misrepresents his position – as can be seen by looking no further than Leavis's introduction to *Determinations*, a collection of essays he edited in 1933. The title *Determinations* was chosen rather than 'Determinations In Literary Criticism' to make the very point that the minority must take account of and represent the general intellectual climate. In his introduction Leavis emphasizes that in an age where so many specialisms are insisting on their authority it is of great consequence that a minority educated public exist to assert another authority. He then adds: 'I hope I have left no one any excuse for supposing that I assign the business of forming this public to literary criticism alone.'[4] Whatever doubts may arise from Leavis's early formulations, in his later writings – especially in *The Living Principle* – he became very explicitly concerned with the influence of the general intellectual climate. As he explains:

> I am of course not assuming that, where expression in words is concerned, the 'significant' is confined to the creative work we call 'literature'. The educated public we need...will represent, for the creative writer and the critic (both of whom require collaboration), a general lively awareness...of the significance of (say) Whitehead, Collingwood and Polanyi: I exemplify with a line of creative thought that is clearly of major significance for non-specialist intelligence and sensibility.[5]

While Leavis's interest undoubtedly centres in literary criticism he always maintained that one of the factors giving literary criticism its special importance is that it continually leads outside itself. *Scrutiny*, we should recall, was never strictly a literary review; it consistently published articles on contemporary civilization, history, education, music, art and philosophy. And Leavis's educational proposals, as we shall see, especially as formulated in 'Sketch for an English School' in *Education And The University* make it quite evident that the minority he is concerned with cannot be dismissed as a narrow, literary minority. His conception may fall short of Coleridge's idea of an allegiance to all the sciences, but he does not argue simply for a literary minority. Rather he contends: 'What in fact we want is the kind of public implied, at any rate as an ideal, by the reviews of the last century, where literary criticism had its place among the diverse intellectual interests of a cultivated mind in its non-specialist activity.'[6] It is only by representing these 'diverse intellectual interests' that the educated public can possibly be conceived of as being a true centre in society.

Granting that Leavis is concerned with more than a literary minority, his insistence on the crucial importance of the educated

minority is, in modern democratic society, frequently challenged
or resisted. While the importance of the educated public may have
been recognized in the nineteenth century of Coleridge and Arnold,
in modern society the dominance of egalitarian ideas often leads
to a straightforward rejection of the role of minorities. Leavis
himself regards the prevalent hostility towards minorities, towards
the educated public and thus to standards, as one of the sicknesses
of contemporary society. William Walsh, in his essay on 'The
Literary Critic And The Education Of An Elite', makes two
observations that seem relevant to any egalitarian critique of
minorities. First, Walsh notes that 'Civilization, or "culture" in
Coleridge's and Arnold's sense, has always been the direct concern
and the immediate product of minorities.'[7] The importance of
minorities in the past seems a fact, and there seems little reason to
think that the situation has changed in the late twentieth century.
Secondly, continuing his defense of minorities, Walsh argues:
'Democracy has much to tell us about the equality of moral value
of men but very little to say about the equality of intellectual
capacity. And capacity, intellectual capacity, is to be the sole
measure regulating the composition of the elite.'[8] Walsh's point is
an essential, if obvious one, and we all acknowledge the existence
and importance of intellectual elites – mathematicians, physicists,
philosophers, for example.

Yet Walsh's formulation of the criterion of the elite, 'intellectual
capacity', is not sufficiently accurate for describing Leavis's minority, for while Leavis does associate them with high intellectual
standards, they are also to be the spiritual community, and he
emphasizes the superiority of their standards of *value*: 'Upon them
depend the implicit standards that order the finer living of an age;
the sense that this is worth more than that.' Once we make
perception and awareness of value, rather than intellectual capacity, the criterion, then the conception of the minority and the
question of its relation to the rest of society become much more
problematical. Raymond Williams, who clearly has egalitarian
sympathies, challenges Leavis's – and implicitly any – emphasis on
a minority of this kind. Williams argues: 'The concept of a
cultivated minority, set over against a "decreated" mass, tends, in
its assertion, to a damaging arrogance and scepticism.'[9] Williams'
comment, however, is unfair to Leavis who rarely uses the term
masses, and whose attitude towards the working class people, whom
Williams himself writes about, is not one of 'damaging arrogance',

but of compassion and responsibility: 'It's not anything in the nature of moral indignation one feels towards *them*, but shame, concern and apprehension at the way our civilization has let them down – left them to enjoy a "high standard of living" in a vacuum of disinheritance.'[10] Moreover, on the few occasions when Leavis does refer to the 'masses' he always emphasizes how *everyone* in society is affected by the drift of civilization: 'For the industrial masses their work has no human meaning in itself and offers no satisfying interest...The civilization that has disinherited them culturally and incapacitated them humanly does nothing to give significance...to their lives, or to any lives.'[11] We are all involved in this process of civilization. In Leavis's view modern commercial and technological society, a society in which C. P. Snow can recommend, as an ultimate end, 'more jam', and in which a behaviorist psychologist can argue that there is no such thing as 'mind', impoverishes rather than enriches our sense of life and value. The essence of Leavis's case is that in this society it is mainly through the reading of literature and a knowledge of the past that one can become *aware* of values lacking in the present. The educated public are simply those who have this knowledge and awareness.

Given Leavis's analysis of modern society, it would seem imperative to get that knowledge and awareness shared as widely as possible, imperative that the cultural heritage be kept alive and that literature operate, as Leavis hopes, as 'an informing spirit in civilization, an informed, charged and authoritative awareness of inner human nature and human need.'[12] That literature and the cultural tradition *be* influential as a counter-vailing sense of human life and value – which for Leavis includes a 'religious depth of thought and feeling' – would seem to depend on the existence of an educated public.

Again, even granting the necessity for an educated public, we confront some problems. First, Leavis's minority actually involves two tiers: a tiny minority who make the judgments, and the reading, or educated public, who make them influential. He explains: 'The continuance of the literary tradition in a vigorous state depends on a tiny minority of persons of keen and articulate sensibility, and its being influential depends on a much larger reading public that respects and responds intelligently to the judgment of the elite minority.'[13] Leavis does not always consistently make this separation or distinction – in fact most of the time he simply refers to the educated public.* To the extent, however, that this distinction is involved in his conception it raises an obvious question: Who are the elite minority? How do we know who belongs to it? That there is a very small minority of people, such as Leavis himself, T. S. Eliot as critic, and perhaps Raymond Williams and Northrop Frye, who have shaped taste and influenced the way we think about literature, and possibly society, seems true enough. Yet even some of these names could be challenged, and as we move beyond them the notion of an inner 'elite minority' becomes increasingly problematical. There simply are not sufficiently clear criteria for determining who constitutes such an elite.

The more general conception of the educated public is easier to defend and it would seem easier to identify those who belong: as I have said, they are those knowledgeable about the cultural tradition and therefore capable of responding to standards. Yet difficulties arise in considering this wider educated public; in fact, there is some question as to whether it can, in any meaningful sense, even be said to exist. Certainly many critics take the absence of the educated public to be a clear fact. Northrop Frye, for instance, in *The Critical Path*, explaining that Arnold's conception of culture depends on the presence of an inner elect group which mediates the ideals and standards of society, argues that

> in the century since Arnold's book [*Culture and Anarchy*], the humanist society, which barely existed even then, has entirely disappeared. Arnold has had many successors who have followed him in his moral and judicial process of critical evaluation without noticing this fact. There are students of the humanities in universities and elsewhere, but that is not the same thing as a community of humanists. The mediating society which provides the norms for judging and evaluating literature has gone, and consequently each judicial critic can speak only for himself.[14]

* The distinction, however, is there in 'Mass Civilization And Minority Culture', where he writes: 'In any period it is upon a very small minority that the discerning appreciation of art and literature depends: it is...only a few who are capable of unprompted, first-hand judgment. They are still a small minority, though a larger one, who are capable of endorsing such first-hand judgment by genuine personal response.' *For Continuity*, pp. 13–14.

Leavis, like Frye, at times writes as if he too thought the educated public had been destroyed. In the minority-culture pamphlet he in fact states: 'there is no longer an informed and cultivated public'.[15] And the essence of his argument in the 'Two Cultures' debate is that C. P. Snow could have been taken as an authority only in an age that lacked an educated public. Yet, despite these statements, Leavis does not believe that the educated public has been wholly destroyed; it is its disintegration and dispersal that concerned and alarmed him. In the early 1930s, in the *Scrutiny* manifesto, he describes the problem in terms almost identical to those used by Matthew Arnold in 1864 in 'The Literary Influence of Academies'. Leavis writes: 'The trouble is not that such persons form a minority, but that they are scattered and unorganized... isolation makes their efforts to keep themselves informed "of the best that is known and thought in the world" unnecessarily depressing and difficult.'[16] A scattered minority does not constitute a coherent and influential public, but they represent the essential nucleus of that public. In the over forty years that passed since the beginning of *Scrutiny* Leavis did not cease to believe that this nucleus continues to exist; in his 1971 lecture on the subject he affirms that 'the educated public that Matthew Arnold's ironies, castigations and admonitions assumed hasn't yet wholly disappeared; that is why...we can fight without a sense of utter futility for the creation of a conscious public of the educated that is equipped for its responsibility, convinced of it, and therefore influential'.[17]

Frye's point, however, has not actually been answered; he could say that Leavis is simply wrong, that there is not even a potential educated public remaining. But Leavis believes that even if this were the case a new educated public could be created, and it is just this task that he sees as the wider purpose of all his work. In his introduction to the Clark lectures he explains:

> My preoccupation in the following lectures (or anywhere else) is...not with the advocacy of a university English school that should send out into the world a number of discriminating critics and a greater number of cultivated readers: to make it that – merely that – is to de-nature it. And it is not merely with literary education...Nor is it merely with education. It is with restoring to this country an educated public that shall be intelligent, conscious of its responsibility, qualified for it and influential – such

a public as might affect decisively the intellectual and spiritual climate in which statesmen and politicians form their ideas, calculate, plan and perform. It conceives the university not merely as a place of learning, research and instruction, but as itself a nucleus (one of a number) of the greater public, the spiritual community the country needs as its mind and conscience. I use the word 'spiritual' as a way of indicating that association of knowledge and political purpose with non-material ends and other-than-quantitative standards the lack of which makes the prospects for human life in this country (and elsewhere) so desolating.[18]

Leavis's educational proposals are designed to restore and develop this educated public. The function of the university, he argues, is to create a new educated public and be in relation to it a centre of concentration and a maintainer of standards. Much of Leavis's writing about the university focuses on a defence of standards and he opposes, as totally inappropriate, and as leading only to a levelling down, any attempt to apply democratic principles to the field of intellectual inquiry. Like Arnold, Leavis considers democratic levelling down as inimical to society at large, for it is the lack of standards 'which makes the prospects for human life in this country so desolating'. This attitude explains his outright hostility to the American mass-university, and to what he considers the American conception of democracy, where 'there is nothing to check the democratic principle, according to which anything in the nature of an intellectual elite is to be jealously guarded against'.[19] We should be careful not to misunderstand Leavis here. He is not suggesting that higher education should be available only to an elite group; rather, he explains: '*I'm in favor of extending higher education to the utmost*. . . [but] it's disastrous to identify higher education with the university. It's disastrous because the more you extend higher education. . .the more insidious becomes the menace to standards and the more potent and unashamed the animus *against* them.'[20]

Leavis's second key idea is that if the university is to help create the new educated public it must itself be a real centre and thus attempt to counter the increasing specialization that has, ultimately, led to the loss of a centre in society. Leavis is not denying that the university should produce specialists, but he wants to discover some way to bring them into significant relation, and, further, to train

a non-specialist public. The centre for the university, he argues,
could be created through the English school. A number of characteristics of 'English' make it suitable for this role. First, English
literature provides centuries of cultural continuity; literary history,
as Leavis frequently observes, is 'far from being concerned with the
merely *literary* (whatever that is, or could be)'.[21] Literature
provides the supreme example of a living tradition and of a creative
continuity with the past. Further, 'English' cultivates, or should,
a distinctive discipline of intelligence and sensibility that is centrally
concerned with value. This concern with value traditionally has
given the humanities their importance and it is the training of
sensibility that gives English its key place within the humanities.
For these various reasons, the training for an avowedly elite group
that Leavis outlines in *Education And The University* should, he argues

> be done by the 'literary mind',...by, that is, an
> intelligence with the sensitiveness, the flexibility and the
> disciplined and mature pre-occupation with value that
> should be the product of a literary training. It is an
> intelligence so trained that is best fitted to develop into the
> central kind of mind, the co-ordinating consciousness,
> capable of performing the function assigned to the class of
> the educated.[22]

Two points need to be kept clearly in mind here. Leavis is not
claiming that the English school, even at Cambridge, inevitably
produces this sensitive, mature intelligence. He in fact acknowledges
that 'the inquiry, pushed home, as to how far any actual English
school fulfilled this requirement would compel a recognition
humiliating for us who care. But there is no defense of English as
a university study that doesn't make the claim.'[23] He is pointing
to an ideal of what the English school *could* achieve. Nor is he
claiming that 'English' alone trains this central kind of mind;
rather, his proposed scheme, in *Education And The University*, of a
comparative analysis of modern and seventeenth-century civilization includes the study of religious, economic and social history,
political and philosophical thought. It is out of this background,
this varied training, that a 'co-ordinating consciousness' could
possibly be *developed*.

Leavis emphasizes that his proposals, aimed at a very specific
situation at Cambridge, are only one possible way of creating the
necessary centre in the university. Other ways are conceivable, and

one could question or reject the central place he gives to English, yet sympathize with his attempt to confront the problem of specialization. It is true that his idea of a centre, his conception of *liaison* is not entirely satisfactory since his own attitude to certain departments of the university is not one that encourages collaboration. He is extremely unsympathetic towards academic psychology, which is predominantly behaviourist, and, apart from his recent use of Stanislev Andreski, the social sciences, which he tends to regard as taking a Benthamite approach towards man and society. I don't know how behaviourist psychology can escape the charge of having a reductive, quantitative view of man, but certainly the social sciences, at least to the extent Weber and Durkheim are representative, present a profounder understanding of man than Leavis allows. Leavis essentially seems to discriminate between disciplines that provide centuries of cultural continuity (philosophy, history, languages) and those that do not (sociology, psychology). While he tends to reject the latter, his proposed study of the seventeenth century indicates one of the forms a *liaison* could take between English, history and philosophy, and the use he himself makes of Michael Polanyi provides an example of a constructive relation between literature and philosophy. Certainly his recent essay 'Mutually Necessary' insists on the need for an intimate connection between the English and philosophy departments.

Through this centre the university would play its part in shaping contemporary taste and creating contemporary standards. Leavis does not think that this role is the responsibility simply of the English department, but of the minority of exceptional individuals within the university at large. As he explains: 'In the university in which an English School worthy of a good scientist's respect was livingly "co-present" there would (essential to the English School itself) be a more embracing community of those qualified for mature human perception and judgment – qualified, that is, to collaborate in the formation of "educated opinion".'[24] It is this minority Leavis believes whose 'total active presence would make the university the creative centre of civilization we need.'

Leavis's attempt to restore the educated public is inseparable from his attempt to maintain standards, for, he frequently insists, standards of literary criticism have their effective presence only in the existence of an educated public. And he maintains that this truth has general application for 'the literary-critical judgment is the type of all judgments and valuations belonging to what in my unphilosophical way I've formed the habit of calling the "third realm" – the collaboratively created human world, the realm of what is *neither* public in the sense belonging to science...nor merely private and personal.'[25] In all fields then, Leavis's aim of re-grouping, re-creating the educated public would remedy what he sees as a general collapse of standards.

This matter of standards, however, is a vexed one, and Leavis's position on standards and the educated public involves him in a number of difficulties. First, he tends to present a circular argument in explaining the meaning of standards and of the educated public. On the one hand he contends that standards are 'there' only in the existence of an educated public – that is, he 'defines' standards by pointing to the educated public: 'There is no public of the cultivated to appeal to – no public representing, with effect, a general humane culture appropriate to the age; that is what is meant by "lack of standards".'[26] On the other hand, at times he defines the educated public by the fact that they represent standards. In *The Living Principle*, for example, he explains: 'Non-quantitative critical standards effectively exist only in a public which, capable of responding to them when they are critically appealed to, is in that sense "educated".'[27] Without a different description of the educated public or of standards this circular argument calls Leavis's position into question. And nothing in Leavis's work is more difficult to pin down than his use of the word 'standards'.

The problem involved here derives partly from Leavis's insistence that standards cannot be explained or defined in any abstract or theoretical manner: 'The word "standards" is not the less necessary because, like so many of the most important words in our field of discourse, its use can't be justified by the kind of definition the prompt logic of the enemy demands.'[28] The position Leavis generally takes about the need to recognize value in the concrete makes it difficult to engage in a debate about standards. For example, in his early essay 'Towards Standards Of Criticism', written as an introduction to a selection of essays from *The Calendar of Modern Letters*, he argues: 'These "standards of criticism" are assumed; nothing more is said about them. Nothing more needed to be said; for if we can appreciate – which is not necessarily to agree with – the reviewing in *The Calendar*, we know what they are, and if we cannot, then no amount of explaining or arguing will make much difference.'[29] His later attempt, in *English Literature In*

Our Time, to explain the meaning of standards provides a more concrete example of the difficulty with this view:

> The term 'standards' presents itself when there is a question of getting recognition for the justice – or the absurdity – of judgments affirming...relative value and importance...the general acceptance in England of Hemingway as a great writer...would have been possible only in a period marked by a collapse of standards. We talk about 'standards', in fact, at times when it is peculiarly hard to invoke standards with effect. And they can be 'there' to be invoked with effect by the critic only in the existence of an educated public capable of responding intelligently, and influential enough to make its response felt.[30]

I do not think that Hemingway is a great writer, but for anyone who does Leavis's judgment is not going to prove very illuminating about the meaning of standards. And his position does not lead to the discussion of fundamentals that might seem involved in a disagreement over Hemingway's stature.

In fact, Leavis apparently rejects the notion that there can be a discussion focusing on essential fundamentals. He argues that the entire enterprise of criticism is based on a shared sense of value, or, at least, a tacitly held set of common assumptions. Within this common framework diversity and disagreement are both possible and desirable:

> The collaboration that builds up the human world takes largely, as Blake, the great vindicator of human creativity, knew, the form of creative quarrelling. It is not unanimity that characterizes a real educated public, but the profound active knowledge that human nature and human need transcend the blind assumptions of technologico-Benthamism and that those assumptions are disastrous...the assumption that we have enough common ground between us to make disagreement both intelligible and profitable ...But where...the implicit ground of assumption is not there and active, difference, disagreement and controversy will hardly be creative.[31]

The passage, however, raises two further difficulties. While Leavis expresses an admirable openness here, there seems little doubt that with his judgment of Hemingway he thinks there can be no disagreement. Further, Leavis's position is stated at such an extreme level of generality – 'human nature and human need transcend the blind assumptions of technologico-Benthamism' – that it is of little use in helping us to understand the meaning of 'standards'. Surely Hemingway's work, whatever its shortcomings, transcends those 'blind assumptions'.

We are still left then with the question of from where, and how, the educated public derives its authority and the standards by which it would evaluate, say, Hemingway. Leavis answers this in two ways. In his early essay 'Towards Standards Of Criticism' he writes: 'Where the recognition of standards of criticism can be counted on, then there is more than the individual; there is also some remnant of tradition, the common mind, the something-more-than-individual.'[32] Tradition in the modern world is primarily represented by the literary tradition. While it is from here that the educated public largely derives its standards, Leavis adds: 'I put "standards" in inverted commas as a disavowal of false suggestion: the indispensable public represents the ability to modify, in response to significant creation, the implicit criteria by which it judges.'[33] This perhaps best explains why Leavis thinks standards cannot be 'defined' or stated theoretically: they are to be thought of as something flexible and growing, not as something static. Explaining this view of 'standards' Leavis observes: 'A truly great work is realized to *be* that because it so decidedly modifies – alters – the sense of value and significance that judges.'[34] This leads us into Leavis's second answer, which actually is a variation of the first, but more characteristic of the later Leavis. The mistake, which Leavis repeatedly attacks, of thinking of 'fixed standards', is, nonetheless, a common one; it betrays a radical incomprehension of standards, for, in fact, they are a representation of human creativity, of collaborative creation. In the passage where Leavis argues that Hemingway's reputation indicates a period marked by a collapse of standards, he explains: 'They depend on, they are a manifestation of, that collaborative interplay in which the poem is established as something in which minds can meet, which maintains the life of a language, which creates the essential values and significances of the human world, which creates a culture.'[35] This collaborative interplay *creates* standards. This clearly is a human centred view of cultural values, so, for instance, any loss of belief in a transcendental order does not call into question the possibility of re-awakening standards. If the educated public could be made influential we would hear no more of a collapse of standards.

For Leavis, then, the question of Hemingway's importance would be resolved by this communal dialogue, a critical collaboration of the 'This is so, is it not?' nature, which focused on a discussion not of general values but of particular examples of Hemingway's work. This dialogue is possible only through the educated public, and where it is properly influential

> the critic, even when advancing judgments that challenge the most generally accepted valuations, may hope, if he expresses his judgments cogently and aims them with sufficient address at the critical conscience, to get the weight of corroborative response with him, and so tell. But where no such public exists to be appealed to, the critic's unpopular judgments, even if he can get them printed, remain mere arbitrary assertions and offensive attitudes.[36]

Only this collaborative response can determine Hemingway's stature, and, can establish standards.

Leavis believes that the educated public and the standards they represent not only make literary criticism possible, but also have an essential part in aiding the work of creative writers. In emphasizing this aspect of the educated public's importance Leavis is following the line of argument Matthew Arnold had advanced in 'The Function Of Criticism At The Present Time'. Arnold claimed that in the periods of greatest creative achievement, in the England of Shakespeare and the Greece of Sophocles, 'society was, in the fullest measure, permeated by fresh thought, intelligent and alive; and this state of things is the true basis for the creative power's exercise'.[37] The responsibility for permeating society with fresh thought belongs to the educated public. Arnold's comment can be seen as a general statement about the conditions necessary for a healthy, creative society, and Leavis unquestionably concurs with this view. Certainly the statement's more particular meaning that the creative writer depends on the atmosphere of ideas and valuations he finds himself in – a view which T. S. Eliot also supports – Leavis accepts as 'an obvious truth'.

Leavis, however, differs in some significant ways from Arnold in his thinking about the relation between society, the educated public and the writer, and these differences reveal the weaknesses as well as the strengths of his position. It is to Arnold's advantage that he is thinking of criticism in the widest possible sense, as the general intellectual life of society. In 'The Function Of Criticism' he discusses political and religious thought at great length before turning to literature. All these matters are of necessary concern to the educated public if it is truly to permeate society with fresh thought. But Leavis, when he is thinking about the relation of the writer and the educated public, is concerned almost entirely with literary criticism. While in his *conception* of the educated public he is concerned with more than a literary minority, in most of his comments that have to do with the audience of creative writers, it is almost impossible to separate the role of the educated public from that of the literary critic.

Further, Arnold and Leavis in fact conceive of the educated public, or critics, as playing very different roles in relation to the writer. Arnold considers the role of criticism to be essentially preparatory – in an age of concentration it will make possible the creative work to come in the future. This idea invites a number of objections, but I simply want to note the critique of it made by Donald Davie, for in advancing his objection he mistakenly equates the positions of Arnold and Leavis:

> Arnold's thesis – that the creative imagination flourishes best when the critical imagination has been before it, stimulating a traffic of keen and enlightened ideas in its potential audience – seems to me not to square with the facts, so far as I can determine them, in any chapter of literary history that I have studied. It was nonetheless the crucial plank in the platform of the most influential and serious of British critical organs, Leavis's magazine *Scrutiny*. Undoubtedly it tends to establish the creative imagination and the critical intelligence dangerously near to parity, if indeed it does not make the poet virtually dependent on the critic – not indeed the critic as interpreter, but the critic as valuable forerunner.[38]

But Leavis does *not* consider criticism as preparatory, nor the critic as forerunner; rather he insists on the necessity of a *continual* collaboration between the creative writer and the educated public. Since Leavis is primarily concerned about the immediate response to the literary work it is evident that he has, in effect, narrowed the educated public to literary critics. And if Arnold's thesis does not 'square with the facts' Leavis's 'thesis' on the need for continual collaboration raises its own difficulties.

Leavis confronts this question of the relation of the artist and his public much more directly than Arnold did, and in fact he has some sound things to say about the artist's need for an intelligent public. Much of his literary criticism circles around this topic; for example he explains the decline in the later careers of Henry James and Lawrence, and the 'eccentricity' of Hopkins, by the fact that they lacked a duly responsive public. And of Blake's later prophetic books he argues that:

> in the absence, we may put it, of adequate social collaboration (the sense, or confident prospect, of a responsive community of minds was the minimum he needed) his powers of attaining in achieved creation to that peculiar impersonal realm to which the work of art belongs...failed to develop as, his native endowment being what it was, they ought to have done.[39]

Whatever one thinks of Leavis's judgment on the later career of these writers they all unquestionably suffered acutely from their isolation – James in particular bemoaned his fate and Hopkins, recall, had almost no audience but Bridges. They all would have benefited from an active and responsible public that offered recognition and confirmation of purpose. In this sense writers obviously need some kind of 'social collaboration' from their public.

If the artist needs collaboration, this means that negative criticism, as well as recognition, is often necessary. This is the main point in Leavis's treatment of W. H. Auden and the supposed 'Poetical Renascence' of the 1930s. Leavis finds in these poets a lack of development, a 'lack of that sureness of self-realization, that awareness of essential purpose, which registers itself in technique' and concludes that this lack 'is just what one would expect in the absence of an intelligent public'.[40] The way in which Leavis discerns the absence of an educated public in the very texture of the verse is rather startling to anyone with romantic ideas of creation; this kind of procedure provoked Anthony Cronin to remark flippantly: 'We now see who is responsible for good poetry when it appears; it is the audience, the trained critic, academically trained in the proper way, who is all important.'[41] This is not of course what Leavis means or says; rather he insists that only the existence of an intelligent public can provide the give and take necessary for the artist's self-realization. And his argument that Auden's artistic development was impeded by the uncritical adulation he received in the early 1930s seems, at least, plausible. Artists suffer not only from being unduly ignored, but also from being unduly acclaimed.

Yet for all that is salutary in what Leavis says there clearly are difficulties in his position. What obviously is questionable in his treatment of Auden is his tendency to reduce a very complex subject – Auden's alleged failure to develop – to a single fact: the absence of an educated public. For all the flippancy in Anthony Cronin's remark it does touch on a serious problem: if a poet's failure to develop can be attributed to the lack of a public, assumedly a poet's development *could* be attributed to the existence of such a public – and this seems as if it could be true only up to a certain point, and, with a certain kind of writer. For instance, Leavis's criticism of Auden's early poetry – for its needless obscurity and lack of organization – could perhaps have led Auden to correct certain weaknesses in his work. But beyond this pointing-out of particular failings – from which, granted, Auden might have learned – the sense in which a collaborative critical response could have led Auden to develop and become a better poet seems limited. It is surely not the critic's task, finally, to explain craft or technique to the writer. Perhaps the critic can help to develop, enrich, the poet's 'ideas'; but Leavis's own conception of poetry – and here we see his final and most important difference from Arnold – suggests that this is not the critic's role either. While Arnold, like Eliot, seems to think that the poet takes over ideas, using the ideas the philosopher discovers, Leavis regards poetry as a mode of creative, heuristic thought in its own right. Leavis, I believe, gives a better account of the nature of poetry, but his position raises much more acutely than those of Arnold and Eliot the question of the *way* in which the creative mind is dependent either on the atmosphere in which it exists or, especially, on the critic's response. On the basis of Leavis's own understanding of the nature of major creativity it would seem that the critic can be of no help to the truly significant writer. Creative genius involves a break-through into new areas of expression and new areas of human experience; *major* creativity is an exploration on the hinterland of thought and feeling. The pre-eminent creative artists educate us, rather than the other way around, and it may take some time before we adjust to the new ground they have broken.* The importance of the work of Blake

---

* This obviously applies to all of the arts, and the reception of Edward Munch's work provides a good example from painting. Munch's

and Melville, for example, was not fully recognized until a considerable change in sensibility had taken place in society. And while Leavis himself recognized D. H. Lawrence's importance as early as 1930, it took another twenty-five years before he understood, sufficiently well to write really intelligently about it, the radically innovative exploration into human experience that Lawrence's art represents. It is inconceivable that in those early years when Lawrence was writing *The Rainbow*, that Leavis, or any other critic could have given him helpful advice. We are left then with the view that while the critic may play a significant role – provide helpful collaboration – when dealing with minor talent, in the face of a writer whose creativity, originality, is major, the best the critic can do is, hopefully, recognize what is there.

On the other hand, one can grant that the major creative writer is in advance of his age – the 'antennae of the race' as Pound calls them – and still reject the purely romantic notion of the artist creating in isolation. No artist escapes being shaped – enriched or impoverished – by his environment, and Leavis's observation that while art depends on the potently creative individual, the 'work of art, we can hardly remind ourselves too often, is never a merely individual achievement', is surely valid.* The educated public, the critic, unquestionably has, or should have, a central place in shaping the environment, the intellectual atmosphere in which the artist works. Thus, if the critic cannot provide direct collaboration for the major writer he can have an indirect influence by making known the 'best that is thought and known'; in this way he can indirectly influence the creation of significant new work, for, as Arnold insisted: 'When the right standard of excellence is lost, it is not likely that much which is excellent will be produced.'[42]

exploration of the inner world and his creation of expressionist techniques were, originally, not understood; the 'critics' generally denounced his work.

* R. G. Collingwood, in his discussion of 'The Artist And The Community', takes a similar position: 'The work of artistic creation is not a work performed in any exclusive or complete fashion in the mind of the person whom we call the artist. That idea is a delusion bred of individualistic psychology...The aesthetic activity...is a corporate activity belonging not to any one human being but to a community...The artist...stands...in collaborative relations with an entire community.' *The Principles of Art*, Oxford: Oxford University Press, 1974, pp. 323–4. To Leavis as well 'individualistic psychology' is a delusion.

Leavis's commitment to this Arnoldian ideal of the 'right standard' and his belief in the crucial importance of the intellectual atmosphere lie behind his well-known attacks on the literary world. Since the early 1930s, he argues, the right standard has been lost, and the atmosphere of ideas in which an author writes is one determined not by the educated public, but by a small coterie.* Since his early essay 'What's Wrong With Criticism' (1932) (apparently written for *The Criterion* at T. S. Eliot's request and then rejected by Eliot as possibly being offensive), Leavis's attacks on the metropolitan literary world of *The Times Literary Supplement*, *The New Statesman*, the BBC, etc., focus on the claim that it controls the climate of taste and impedes the recognition and *development* of significant new work. In this battle Auden became a representative figure to Leavis, a 'portent', for his career illustrates to Leavis 'the consequences for literature of a state of affairs in which the natural tendency of a small modish literary world to impose its social-personal valuations as those of serious criticism remains unchecked. For if it is a small world, it is, as a system of personal and institutional connections, comprehensive: it virtually controls the currency of accepted valuations and the climate of taste.'[43] Leavis, it is true, had a directly personal quarrel with the 'system'; he clearly thinks that both he and *Scrutiny* had been ignored and persecuted: 'One finds arrayed against one a comprehensive system of personal relations.'[44] But it is the *general* issue involved here that preoccupied him: 'The supersession, in what should be the field of real intellectual and spiritual authority, of serious criteria by the

---

* Leavis's insistent criticism of Bloomsbury is also part of this battle against the influence of a coterie public – or at least what he regards as a coterie. Bloomsbury, of course, was more than a literary minority and it shaped many aspects of English taste. Leavis always considered the formation of Bloomsbury to be a crucial point in the history of English culture; it represented for him the usurpation of the proper authority of the educated public by a coterie, and the end of the effective presence of standards. He describes Maynard Keynes, for example, as the most formidable promoter of the coterie spirit that modern England has ever known and argues that he gave 'respectability and sanction to the natural human weakness for replacing the real standards by personal and coterie considerations.' The whole question of the accuracy of Leavis's view of Bloomsbury, however, is one that is far too large and complex to go into in this book. His comments on Bloomsbury are worth noting here simply as a way to understand the distinction he makes between the nature of a coterie and that of an authentic educated public.

power of creating publicity-values is a frightening manifestation of the way our civilization is going.'[45]

Nonetheless, Leavis's attacks on the literary world have earned him a great deal of hostility. His attitude is frequently referred to as being almost paranoid and it is claimed that this concern has seriously weakened his work. George Steiner, for example, while maintaining that 'Leavis' "necessary attitude of absolute intransigence" has had an exemplary, moving force' nonetheless contends: 'But he has sustained that attitude at a cruel psychological cost. He has had to define and, in significant measure, create for himself "the enemy". Like a fabled, heraldic monster, the Enemy has many heads. They include the Sunday papers and The Guardian.'[46] Frank Kermode rejects entirely Leavis's view of the London literary world and claims that Leavis's idea of a system 'is pure myth and such myths rapidly corrupt the health and vigor of a genuine minority position (such as that from which *Scrutiny* started) until energy is converted into rancour and criticism into shrill complaint'.[47] It is true that Leavis seems to need enemies; he appears to operate best when he has something to battle not just for, but again. The very title of *Nor Shall My Sword* reveals his characteristically embattled stance, and this aspect of his temperament (which indicates his affinity to Lawrence, Bunyan and the Protestant Nonconformist tradition) must certainly be kept in mind when considering the validity of his view of the literary world. Also, Leavis does seem to have created a rather mythologized, crisis view of the history of the literary world. Everything appears to happen in 1930 when Lawrence dies: Kingsley Martin takes over as editor of the combined *New Statesman and Nation*, Bloomsbury is in control, *The Criterion*, in the face of the 'poetical Renaissance' abdicates its critical function, and, suddenly, the coterie is dominant. While this notion of a key year serves Leavis's polemical purposes, realistically it is difficult to imagine such a sudden, and decisive, turn. And even if Leavis is right about the nature of the literary world, he surely needs to be challenged when he contends: 'There is no mystery about the barrenness of the period since the beginning of the last war, when Eliot completed "Little Gidding"...What chance had potential originality of developing after 1930? There was no *English Review*...In these days of the Arts Council and Reg Prentices as Ministers of Education, creative gifts, however charged with potentiality, don't develop.'[48] This is, again, to reduce a very complex issue to a single factor. That there are these questionable aspects to Leavis's position needs to be granted. But I do not see that his work is seriously weakened by this. For one thing, his attacks on the literary world, as a quick check of his writings will show, are not nearly as frequent as his critics suggest. Further, Kermode's claim that the system is 'pure myth' is belied by the hostile attitude the *TLS* has maintained towards Leavis, by the considerable importance given to C. P. Snow, and by what seems a natural tendency for any literary world to become enclosed and self-protecting. 'Publicity-values' *are* repeatedly created by the media. Even George Steiner acknowledges that behind Leavis's 'Enemy', 'there *is* a certain complex reality. Being geographically compact, English intellectual life is sharply susceptible to the pressures of club and cabal.'[49] Leavis has waged his battle against these very real tendencies of the literary world.

In contrast to these self-protecting tendencies of the literary world, the educated public, Leavis argues, is characterized by 'creative quarrelling'. Its importance, he insists, 'is conditioned by its diversity of presumable bent, and the lack of anything like ideological unity'.[50] Realistically one might wonder if the various centres of the educated public can maintain this diversity and openness, but Leavis has explained clearly what the educated public, ideally, should be. And from that first pamphlet in 1930 through his last book he fought consistently and intensely in an attempt to make it possible for the educated public to play its proper role in shaping contemporary taste, creating standards, and, ultimately, in acting as a directing force in modern society.

4

The Idea Of Criticism

Leavis is best known for his decisive and provocative literary judgments – for his own efforts in 'shaping contemporary taste'. What has not received wide enough attention is the fact that lying behind his judgments on literature is a very subtle and lucidly articulated idea of literary criticism. It should be recognized that Leavis's pronouncements on the function and nature of literary criticism are a central and major part of his achievement. Leavis insists that evaluation is the principal concern of criticism and, of perhaps equal importance, he insists that literary criticism is a distinct discipline with its own proper approaches and interests. In explaining and elaborating on these two focal points Leavis presents one of the most definite and coherent ideas of criticism of the twentieth century.

For nearly half a century Leavis struggled to win recognition for the central importance of the function of literary criticism in modern civilization. As Leavis conceives it this function involves, in the first place, ensuring that English literature shall be a living reality operating as an informing spirit in society, but he also gives a wider explanation of its purpose. In an early essay of the 1930s, 'Restatements for Critics', he explains that the function of criticism involves shaping the contemporary sensibility:

> And we know that, in such a time of disintegration as the
> present, formulae, credos, abstractions are extremely
> evasive of unambiguous and effective meaning and that,
> whatever else may also be necessary, no effort at
> integration can achieve anything real without a centre of

real consensus – such a centre as is presupposed in the
possibility of literary criticism and is tested in particular
judgements. But 'tested' does not say enough; criticism,
when it performs its function, not merely expresses and
defines the 'contemporary sensibility'; it helps to form
it... to persuade an effective 'contemporary sensibility'
into being.[1]

Criticism defines and organizes the contemporary sensibility – and,
as Leavis points out, 'contemporary' includes as much of the past
as there is any access to – making conscious the standards implicit
in it. In this way criticism provides the centre of value that is
necessary to guide society.

This is obviously an ambitious conception of the function of
criticism. One must keep clear, however, that, while in many ways
Leavis places criticism at the centre of the intellectual life of
civilization, he argues that criticism can have this importance only
by fulfilling its specific function. He makes this point most lucidly
in what is, perhaps, his fullest statement on the business of criticism,
in the essay entitled 'The Function of Criticism At Any Time'
(1953). In this essay he challenges the conception of criticism
advocated by F. W. Bateson, and it is entirely characteristic of
Leavis that out of this disagreement with another critic should come
a succinct presentation of his own position. Leavis's disagreements
with René Wellek and Laurence Lerner, as well as with Bateson,
have been extremely fruitful in stimulating him to clarify his own
idea of criticism. Bateson's idea, which Leavis rejects, is that the
literary critic *qua* critic has a special insight into society and that
his function is fulfilled in this social diagnosis; with the emphasis
Leavis places on the importance of literary criticism to the student
of society one might almost be led to think that Leavis agrees with
Bateson. He actually regards Bateson's view as a betrayal of
criticism, for he insists that the business of the literary critic is with
literature and literary criticism. The responsibility of the critic, as
such, is not primarily to analyse contemporary social processes but
to serve the function of criticism, which Leavis explains as follows:

The *utile* of criticism is to see that the created work fulfils
its *raison d'être*; that is, that it is read, understood and duly
valued, and has the influence it should have in the
contemporary sensibility. The critic who relates his
business to a full conception of criticism conceives himself

as helping, in a collaborative process, to define – that is, to form – the contemporary sensibility.[2]

Criticism is vindicated as a serious function by asserting its true responsibilities in the area of literature. Leavis regards Bateson's attempt to place the importance of literary criticism in a non-literary-critical function as a sign of disbelief that criticism (and literature) really matters. This point, perhaps, needs further explanation. Bateson may sound Arnoldian (criticism is not only literary criticism), but he is simply bypassing literary criticism for social criticism. On the other hand, Leavis does not deny that the literary critic, or the 'literary mind', has a concern with the health of society at large, but the critic's primary and essential concern is with literature.

Leavis goes on in the essay to contend that the function of criticism cannot be adequately discussed as a matter of critical method or theory; to understand the function one must have recourse to a concrete example. The example he gives is the achievement of *Scrutiny* in presenting a revaluation of the past of English literature and in determining the significant points in the contemporary field – 'placing' Auden, standing by Eliot while insisting on Lawrence's superiority. He explains:

> My point is that *here*, in such work, we have the *utile* of criticism (and it is *creative* work). In the creating, with reference to the appropriate criteria – the creating in an intelligent public – of a valid sense of the contemporary chart (as it were), or sense of the distribution of value and significance as a mind truly alive in the age would perceive them, 'the function of criticism at the present time' has its fulfilment.[3]

The function of criticism, then, is neither social analysis, nor the formulation of a poetics or theory of literature; it entails the specific acts of evaluation which reveal the contemporary sensibility in a concrete form. Leavis explains the peculiar importance of this idea of the function of criticism: 'Where there is steady and responsible practice of criticism a "centre of real consensus" will, even under present conditions, soon make itself felt. Out of agreement and disagreement with particular judgments of value a sense of relative value in the concrete will define itself, and without this, no amount of talk about "values" in the abstract is worth anything.'[4]

This relative sense of value which comprises the contemporary sensibility can be defined only by a collaborative process. Leavis always regarded collaboration – the interplay of personal judgments in which values are established in the concrete and a world created that is neither public nor merely private – as an essentially creative process; the function of criticism, therefore, must be seen to be a creative achievement. In order for collaboration to be effective, and creative, Leavis claims that there must be a number of good critics practising: 'The performance of that function implies a collaborative interplay, so that in a state of cultural health there would be more than one intelligent critic practising – there would be a whole corps of them.'[5] In his early 1932 essay 'What's Wrong With Criticism' he observes that for a healthy state of criticism we need not only a major critic like Eliot, but also a number of journalistic critics of the quality of Desmond MacCarthy who engage in a full collaboration. The function of criticism cannot be fulfilled by the single critic acting in isolation, but only by the concerned action of a group of critics who compose part of the educated public.

To understand Leavis's idea of criticism it is necessary to grasp both the point that he thinks of criticism as collaboration and the nature of collaboration. I think, in fact, that there is nothing more basic to an understanding of Leavis's view of the critical process than realizing that the idea of collaboration is at the centre of it. Leavis repeatedly insisted upon this, yet I continually encounter people who regard his critical position as dogmatic, absolutist and closed. A good example of this is Bernard Heyl, in his essay 'The Absolutism of F. R. Leavis'. The title of Leavis's 1952 collection of essays, *The Common Pursuit*, comes of course from Eliot's description of criticism as 'the common pursuit of true judgment'. Heyl, referring to Leavis's use of this title, claims that 'By this he seems to mean...that one, and only one, valuation of a work of art is valid or correct.'[6] Heyl then goes on to attack the absolutist theory of value. But in the very preface to *The Common Pursuit* Leavis had explained that criticism is not a matter of one absolute judgment, but of collaboration, that the critic's 'perceptions and judgments are his, or they are nothing; but, whether or not he has consciously addressed himself to co-operative labour, they are inevitably collaborative. Collaboration may take the form of disagreement, and one is grateful to the critic whom one has found worth disagreeing with.'[7] There is not one absolutely right judgment, but room for disagreement. The epigraph to *Education And The University*, it's worth noting, is 'Collaboration, a matter of differences as well as agreements.'

Leavis certainly believes in the need for decisive and firm judgment; a review he entitled 'Catholicity or Narrowness' states this basic attitude of his very forcefully:

> Discrimination is life, indiscrimination is death: I offer this as obviously a very suitable maxim for a university school of English, and it seems to me very plain that a critical habit tending to carry severity even towards "narrowness" constitutes for the student a more healthy climate than Sir Herbert Grierson's and Dr Smith's kind of catholicity – which is the kind fostered almost universally in the academic world.[8]

What needs to be emphasized in the light of this comment is that his insistence on discrimination does *not* mean that the evaluation the critic advances closes the question, allowing for no possible difference. In one of his most concise pronouncements on the nature of criticism Leavis explains that:

> A judgment is a real judgment, or it is nothing. It must, that is, be a sincere personal judgment; but it aspires to be more than personal. Essentially it has the form: 'This is so, is it not?' But the argument appealed for must be real, or it serves no critical purpose and can bring no satisfaction to the critic. What his activity of its very nature aims at, in fact, is a collaborative exchange or commerce. Without a many-sided real exchange – the collaboration by which the object, the poem (for example), in which individual minds meet and at the same time the true judgments concerning it are established – the function of criticism cannot be said to be working.[9]

Criticism does seek the true judgment, but not by the judgment of the single critic; it is determined collaboratively. Leavis clearly does not believe in critical relativism or subjectivism, but neither does he believe in 'absolutism'; they are not the only alternatives.

Leavis contends that the collaborative exchange upon which criticism depends demands a corrective and creative interplay of judgments; 'the response I expect at best will be of the form, "Yes, but -", the "but" standing for qualifications, corrections, shifts of emphasis, additions, refinements.'[10] 'Yes, but,': that is how Leavis expects a judgment to be answered, with a fully overt collaboration. It is well worth labouring this point, because it is so central, but also because Leavis is so often considered to hold a position like that of Yvor Winters. Winters does believe in absolute judgments, and when he advances his evaluations they are not open to any questioning or qualifying response; Leavis's position is both more complex and more flexible. I realize that one could try to argue ('Yes, but') that is what Leavis says in theory but it is not what he does in practice; that with his judgments on the later James or on Auden's poetry he really does think that there can be no qualifications of his view. It is difficult to deny a certain element of truth in this, particularly in the two examples I have cited; yet in the case of Auden he sought collaboration of his judgment from other writers in *Scrutiny* (a situation which raises other questions). What cannot be denied is that Leavis's idea of criticism demands that the critic's judgment be open to disagreement, qualification, and the fullest kind of collaboration.

Criticism depends on collaboration, but it begins with the discriminations made by the individual critic and Leavis repeatedly explained the nature of the process by which the critic makes his evaluation or judgment. Leavis insists that the act of making an evaluation is not to be thought of as 'imposing accepted values' or of providing 'fixed standards' with legal backing. To describe the process in that way is to reveal a complete misunderstanding of the nature of evaluation:

> So far from valuing being a matter of bringing up a scale, a set of measures, or an array of fixed and definite criteria to the given work, every work that makes itself felt as a challenge evokes, or generates, in the critic a fresh realization of the grounds and nature of judgment. A truly great work is realized to *be* that because it so decidedly modifies – alters – the sense of value and significance that judges. That is what is testified to in the commonplace that a great artist creates the taste by which he is appreciated.[11]

This is an important statement of Leavis's position and describes a critical process that is *open* to modification in a way that the attempt to judge by definite, clearly defined, criteria would not likely be.

It was René Wellek's review of *Revaluation* that stimulated Leavis to give what is his finest description of the process of evaluation. Wellek asked that Leavis define his standards, the norms by which he made his judgments, and in his reply Leavis tried to make clear that Wellek misunderstood the nature of evaluation:

> The critic – the reader of poetry – is indeed concerned with evaluation, but to figure him as measuring with a norm which he brings up to the object and applies from the outside is to misrepresent the process. The critic's aim is, first, to realize as sensitively and completely as possible this or that which claims his attention; and a certain valuing is implicit in the realizing. As he matures in experience of the new thing he asks, explicitly and implicitly: 'Where does this come? How does it stand in relation to...? How relatively important does it seem?' And the organization into which it settles as a constituent in becoming 'placed' is an organization of similarly 'placed' things, things that have found their bearings with regard to one another, and not a theoretical system or a system determined by abstract considerations.[12]

The 'norms' or 'criteria' of the critic, it is clear, are not to be considered as matters for abstract definition. Leavis continues to further explain that the critic's concern

> is to enter into possession of the given poem (let us say) in its concrete fulness, and his constant concern is never to lose his completeness of possession, but rather to increase it. In making value-judgments (and judgments as to significance), implicitly or explicitly, he does so out of that completeness of possession and with that fulness of response. He doesn't ask, 'How does this accord with these specifications of goodness in poetry?'; he aims to make fully conscious and articulate the immediate sense of value that 'places' the poem.[13]

Wellek, being largely a philosopher, thinks of the critic's business as essentially involving the abstract definition of the qualities that are looked for in good poetry; what Leavis makes clear is that the critic operates by a living sense of value. (Leavis here is very close to D. H. Lawrence's view that you can develop an instinct for life instead of a theory of right or wrong.) I think it is instructive that

Wellek should find it difficult to understand how Leavis can admire both Lawrence and Eliot, since in an abstract way their values are so different; here one can clearly see the advantage of responding, as Leavis does, from a sense of value. Wellek's position is not unlike that of Winters, who also thinks of the process of evaluation as a matter of bringing clearly formulated and defined criteria or principles to bear upon poetry. Wellek and Winters have a commitment to reason as the agent of judgment; moreover Winters has a strong distrust of emotion. Leavis's reference to a sense of value is a way of indicating that the whole being must be engaged in evaluation. And surely we must agree with Leavis on this point.

Leavis's high opinion of Arnold's literary criticism is a related matter to consider here – he ranks Arnold's achievement as a critic above that of Coleridge. This is a revealing judgment on Leavis's part, one that contrasts him with other modern critics, such as I. A. Richards, Kenneth Burke and Cleanth Brooks, who 'descend' from Coleridge and have shown less interest in Arnold. Richards and Burke of course are primarily theoreticians, if not simply philosophers, rather than strictly literary critics. The very thing occasionally seen as Arnold's limitation – his lack of a systematic theory – Leavis regards as related to his strength, which is that he, unlike Richards and Burke, essentially is a literary critic. Leavis elucidates and defends the way in which Arnold makes his evaluations (and Leavis's approach is clearly similar). In explaining Arnold's description of poetry as a 'criticism of life', Leavis writes that Arnold

> intends, not to define poetry, but...to remind us of the
> nature of the criteria by which comparative judgments are
> made...To define the criteria he was concerned with,
> those by which we make the most serious kind of
> comparative judgment, was not necessary, and I cannot
> see that anything would have been gained by his
> attempting to define them. His business was to evoke them
> effectively.[14]

This is similar to what Leavis told Wellek, that in *Revaluation* he had evoked and concretely defined the 'criteria' by which he judged poetry.

The judgments of the literary critic should be distinct not only from those of the philosopher, but also from those of the moralist. Leavis's criticism is frequently referred to as 'moral criticism';

perhaps the most notable example of this designation of his work comes from T. S. Eliot. In *To Critize The Critic*, Eliot, categorizing the various kinds of modern critics, asks: 'And where are we to place...another critic of importance, Dr F. R. Leavis, who may be called the Critic as Moralist?'[15] The implication of this view is that Leavis's work is not strictly literary criticism, but Leavis himself has consistently attempted to distinguish literary criticism from overtly moral criticism. Leavis remarks of Eliot's *After Strange Gods*, where Eliot had professed to speak as a moralist and not as a literary critic: 'I think he would have done well to remind himself that one cannot "apply moral principles to literature" without being a literary critic and engaging in literary criticism.'[16] Moral or religious criticism, Leavis insists, cannot be a substitute for literary criticism. In his essay on Samuel Johnson he observes that while Johnson is a great moralist, he is in criticism a classic *qua* critic. If we look back to the essay on Arnold, however, we find Leavis giving an explanation of the nature of judgment that does make it difficult to grasp the distinction:

> We make (Arnold insists) our major judgments about
> poetry by bringing to bear the completest and profoundest
> sense of relative value that, aided by the work judged, we
> can focus from our total experience of life (which includes
> literature) and our judgment has intimate bearing on the
> most serious choices we have to make thereafter in our
> living.[17]

From this it would seem that the judgments we make about poetry are largely identical with the judgments we make about life and are therefore essentially moral judgments. But as we read on in the essay Leavis clarifies the issue. Discussing the problem of 'genuineness' in Arnold's criticism, the problem of how the critic makes the initial recognition of life and quality which must proceed and inform all discussion of poetry, Leavis observes that 'Arnold goes on to insist...that the evaluation of poetry as "criticism of life" is inseparable from its evaluation as poetry; that the moral judgment that concerns us as critics must be at the same time a delicately relevant response of sensibility.'[18] Moral values certainly enter into the evaluation of the work of art, but they can only be invoked by the critic's sensibility bringing them in with due relevance.

The business of ensuring relevance, Leavis insists, is a difficult and delicate one; his objection to 'Christian Discrimination', for instance, is that it knows beforehand what kind of response is called for, and the application of moral principles is divorced from the critic's sensibility – there is a failure of relevance. Leavis's complete-test statement on the problem of relevance comes, quite properly, in an essay on Samuel Johnson:

> I don't think that for any critic who understands his job there are any 'unique literary values' or any 'realm of the exclusively aesthetic'. But there *is*, for a critic, a problem of relevance: it is, in fact, his ability to be relevant in his judgments and commentaries that makes him a critic, if he deserves the name. And the ability to be relevant, where works of literary art are concerned, is not a mere matter of good sense; it implies an understanding of the resources of language, the nature of conventions, and the possibilities of organization such as can come only from much intensive literary experience accompanied by the habit of analysis. In this sense it certainly implies a specially developed sensibility.[19]

The comment that Leavis's criticism is moral criticism usually assumes a clear separation of literary and moral values; Leavis considers this an unreal distinction and refuses to make it. Instead his statement of his position is: 'I don't believe in any "literary values" and you won't find me talking about them; the judgments the literary critic is concerned with are judgments about life. What the critical discipline is concerned with is relevance and precision in making and developing them.'[20] There is a tendency in thinking about Leavis's criticism to remember only the first part of this statement and to overlook the very necessary second sentence. The critic's ability to make his judgment about life demands a trained response to literature.

The way in which the critic makes his judgment can best be illustrated by contrasting Leavis's position with that of Northrop Frye. Frye of course advocates the view that evaluation is not a legitimate part of the function of criticism. He dismisses evaluative criticism as 'what belongs only to the history of taste, and therefore follows the vacillations of fashionable prejudice'.[21] Quite typically, and somewhat cynically, Frye tries to reduce judgment to the level of mere 'prejudice' – a statement which is merely a rhetorical assertion on his part. One of the main reasons for Frye's dismissal of evaluative criticism is that he thinks that a value judgment can be neither proven nor demonstrated, that, in fact, 'a writer's value sense can never be logically a part of a critical discussion'.[22] It seems that for Frye judgment is largely intuitive and one cannot go beyond merely asserting it. Leavis agrees that a value judgment cannot be proven, but he does believe that the critic can make some approach towards enforcing his judgment:

> In criticism, of course (one would emphasize), nothing can be proved; there can, in the nature of the case, be no laboratory-demonstration or anything like it. Nevertheless, it is nearly always possible to go further than merely asserting a judgment or inviting agreement with a general account. Commonly one can call attention to this, that or the other detail by way of making the nature and force of one's judgment plain.[23]

Logically enough, Frye has devised a system or method of criticism which adopts a stance back from the work looking for the similarities between it and other works, while the 'method' or approach of Leavis's evaluative criticism involves a stance close up to the work, concentrating on the 'words on the page', where the critic can distinguish its differences from other works. Of course evaluation does not finally depend on any 'method', but rather on the response of the whole man – on bringing to bear that fusion of intelligence and sensibility that, for Leavis, gives literary criticism its importance.

Leavis's efforts to restore the function of criticism involves the attempt to get literary criticism recognized as a special and distinct discipline of intelligence and sensibility. His concern to define this conception of literary criticism is related to his problem as a teacher in making the study of literature a discipline. In *Education And The University* he writes:

> There must be a training of intelligence that is at the same time a training of sensibility; a discipline of thought that is at the same time a discipline in scrupulous sensitiveness of response to delicate organizations of feeling, sensation and imagery. Without that appreciative habituation to the subleties of language in its most charged and complex uses which the literary-critical discipline is, thinking – thinking to the ends with which humane education should be most

concerned – is disabled. And the process of evaluative
judgment, implicit or explicit, that is inseparable from the
use of intelligence in that discipline is no mere matter of
'taste' that can be set over against intelligence.[24]

(In the light of Frye's relegation of judgment to a mere matter of
'taste', Leavis's last point should be particularly noted.) This kind
of discipline Leavis believes provides the best possible training for
free, unspecialized, general intelligence, for the central kind of
mind, the co-ordinating consciousness necessary for the educated
public. Literary criticism, rather than philosophy, history, or the
classics, for instance, has this central importance, because only
literary criticism trains intelligence *and* sensibility.

But just what does Leavis mean by 'sensibility' and how is it
related to 'intelligence'? When one thinks of the word 'sensibility'
the first association is with the physical senses. In *Twilight in Italy*
in the chapter 'The Theatre' Lawrence, in describing the men of
the village, uses the word in this way: 'There is a pathos of physical
sensibility and mental inadequacy. Their mind is not sufficiently
alert to run with their quick, warm senses.'[25] Sensibility and mind
are distinct here (and Lawrence's concern is for them to exist in
a proper harmony). It seems likely, though, that Leavis derives the
word from Eliot's 'dissociation of sensibility', but he uses it
somewhat differently. While Eliot is not entirely consistent in his
use, since he sometimes equates sensibility with feeling, generally
by a unified sensibility he means one where thought and emotion
work together; that is, 'sensibility' refers to the whole psyche.
Leavis on the other hand does not use sensibility in that comprehensive way, but neither, since he thinks of real intelligence as an
agent of the whole psyche, does he mean by it just 'emotion' or
'taste'. In an early essay (very significantly Leavis's first essay in
Scrutiny) entitled 'The Literary Mind', Leavis tries to clarify in
what way Max Eastman is deficient in intelligence and sensibility.
Remarking that Eastman is obviously deficient in sensibility Leavis
observes:

> There is a pervasive debility, a lack of tension, outline and
> edge, in his thinking. The point might be made by saying
> that he has none of that sensitiveness of intelligence
> without which all apparent vigour of thought is illusory.
> And when such a phrase as 'sensitiveness of intelligence'
> suggests itself it begins to appear that the relation between

'intelligence' and 'sensibility' is not the simple distinction that is readily assumed.[26]

He then argues that Eastman's defect of sensibility *is* a defect of intelligence. One cannot lack sensibility and still be truly intelligent. Leavis concludes that:

> a certain fidelity to concrete particulars *is* required of him. And it may be regarded of all thinking, however abstract, that is likely to interest those of us who are preoccupied with problems of living, that the criticism of it concerns its fidelity to concrete particulars and the quality of these. No easy distinction between intelligence and sensibility comes to hand here.[27]

In Leavis's understanding intelligence and sensibility interpenetrate each other; yet, while no simple distinction can be made, they are different and both terms are necessary.

Leavis insists on the dual emphasis in explaining his conception of criticism, for while intelligence is essential, only a trained sensibility can ensure a proper approach; it is the sensibility that is initially responsive to the subtleties of language and feeling. Leavis finds fault with Bradley's Shakespeare criticism, asserting that 'his method is not intelligent enough, and, to reverse my earlier stress, the defect of intelligence is a default on the part of sensibility; a failure to keep closely enough in touch with responses to particular arrangements of words.'[28] The idea of criticism as focused by the sensibility on the use of language is necessary, Leavis argues, not just with Shakespeare, but equally so with writers such as Wordsworth or Lawrence who 'invite the discussion of doctrine or ideas as such; by intelligence, that is, apart from sensibility, or apart, at any rate, from the trained sensibility of the literary critic'. It is only the critical sensibility that can maintain relevance of discussion. I think that we can more fully grasp the significance of Leavis's description of criticism as a discipline of intelligence and sensibility by thinking of Yvor Winters. Winters, it seems to me, frequently approaches literature by intelligence alone; in analysing the poetry of Hart Crane or Robert Frost, for example, he discusses their ideas almost totally apart from their use of language. Winters remarks that Ezra Pound strikes him as a poet of sensibility without any intelligence; and it is tempting to reply that Winters is a critic of intelligence without sensibility – or at least that his sensibility is not always fully engaged.

In 'How To Teach Reading', the early educational pamphlet, Leavis indicated the central place of analysis in the training of sensibility: 'Everything must start from and be associated with the training of sensibility. It should, by continual insistence and varied exercise in analysis, be enforced that literature is made of words and that everything worth saying in criticism of verse and prose can be related to judgments concerning particular arrangements of words on the page.'[29] This emphasis on analysis, on a method of criticism which focuses on the 'words on the page', is one of the most distinguishing aspects of Leavis's criticism and relates him to the revolution in criticism in the 1920s. I. A. Richards pioneered the training of sensibility through analysis, but Leavis has his own very distinctive formulation. He writes in *Education And The University* that 'the cultivation of analysis that is not also a cultivation of the power of responding fully, delicately and with discriminating accuracy to the subtle and precise use of words is worthless. This would seem to be obvious enough. Yet in how many languages besides one's own can one hope to acquire even the beginning of a critical sensibility.'[30] This last point is obviously of major importance in understanding Leavis's approach to literature; it is part of the explanation why, with the major exception of the essay on *Anna Karenina*, all of his criticism has been on the literature of his own language – it is only to that one can bring the full critical response. This point also determines Leavis's approach to literary education. In contrast to Northrop Frye, for whom the aim of literary study is to produce the 'educated imagination', and who does not seem to think of the growth of the imagination as necessarily related to a response to language, for Leavis, literary training should produce an 'educated sensibility' (and intelligence) and he thinks that this can only be done in response to the literature of one's own language. Leavis provides a precise description of what he means by analysis in the chapter 'Literary Studies' in *Education And The University*. He states that the training of reading capacity is of primary importance in the attempt to justify literary criticism as a distinct discipline. Analysis, he explains,

> is the process by which we seek to attain a complete
> reading of the poem – a reading that approaches as nearly
> as possible to the perfect reading. There is about it nothing
> in the nature of 'murdering to dissect', and suggestions
> that it can be anything in the nature of laboratory-method

misrepresent it entirely. We can have the poem only by an inner kind of possession; it is 'there' for analysis only in so far as we are responding appropriately to words on the page. In pointing to them (and there is nothing else to point to) what we are doing is to bring into sharp focus, in turn, this, that and the other detail, juncture or relation in our total response; or...what we are doing is to dwell with a deliberate, considering responsiveness on this, that or the other mode or focal point in the complete organization that the poem is, in so far as we have it.[31]

This is a very succinct, lucid account of the nature of analysis, and Leavis then goes on to make what I think is his most important point about analysis:

Analysis is not a dissection of something that is already and passively there. What we call analysis is, of course, a constructive or creative process. It is a more deliberate following-through of that process of creation in response to the poet's words which reading is. It is a recreation in which, by a considering attentiveness, we ensure a more than ordinary faithfulness and completeness.

I. A. Richards was largely responsible for developing the idea of practical criticism, but the description I have quoted makes clear how different Leavis's conception is. For Leavis analysis is a creative process and has nothing in common with Richards's view of it as a method amenable to laboratory technique.

For Richards (and Frye) criticism should attempt to become more scientific, more systematic; Leavis remained inveterately against any notion that criticism is or should become a science. What Lawrence says on this issue can be taken to represent Leavis's position as well: 'Criticism can never be a science: it is, in the first place, much too personal, and in the second, it is concerned with values that science ignores.'[32] In the debate on whether criticism is an art or a science Leavis in effect takes a position which rejects the either/or alternative as a false opposition. Analysis is creative, but essentially a discipline, although Leavis wants to make it clear that there is nothing technical or even remotely scientific about it:

To insist on this critical work as discipline is not to contemplate the elaboration of technical apparatus and drill. The training is to be one in the sensitive and

scrupulous use of intelligence; to that end such help as can
be given the student will not be in the nature of initiations
into technical procedures, and there is no apparatus to be
handed over – a show of such in analytic work will most
likely turn out to be a substitute for the use of intelligence
upon the text. Where help can and should be got, of
course, is in examples of good practice, wherever these can
be found.[33]

The contrast with Frye, who conceives of such an apparatus or
system, is extreme. It is not only, Leavis insists, that there is no
technical apparatus to be taken over in criticism, but the very terms
that the critic uses are not to be thought of in a technical way:

Terms must be made the means to the necessary precision
by careful use in relation to the concrete; their use is
justified in so far as it is shown to favour sensitive
perception; and the precision in analysis aimed at is not to
be attained by seeking formal definition as its tools. It is as
pointers for use – in use – in the direct discussion of pieces
of poetry that our terms and definitions have to be
judged.[34]

This is a point of considerable importance; Leavis does have a few
key terms (such as impersonality, concreteness, realization), but
there is no point in trying to define them here in the abstract. They
must be examined and understood as he uses them in the different
contexts of his actual criticism.

Leavis's view of analysis differs from that of Empson as well as
Richards. In his insistence that analysis is a discipline Leavis cites
Seven Types of Ambiguity as a warning against temptations that the
analyst must resist, for 'valid analytical practice is a strengthening
of the sense of relevance: scrutiny of the parts must be at the same
time an effort towards fuller realization of the whole, and all
appropriate play of intelligence, being also an exercise of the sense
of value, is controlled by an implicit concern for a total value-
judgment'.[35] Leavis claims that local analysis leads us to the core
of the work, that the whole of the organism is present in the part;
the part, however, must be seen as belonging to an ever widening
context and the critic must not make Empson's mistake of extrapo-
lating the part from its contexts. Moreover, Leavis's remark
clarifies a further essential distinction between his view of analysis

and that of Empson: Leavis never practices analysis for its own sake, but as a step towards a 'total value-judgment'.

Leavis's idea of analysis should also be differentiated from that of the New Critics, or at least a critic like Cleanth Brooks. The relation between Leavis's conception of criticism and that of the New Critics is occasionally made because they both direct the attention of criticism away from external, historical factors to an internal approach centering on the language of poetry, but Leavis's social and cultural concerns always remained an integral part of his criticism. I have explained his conception of 'internal' analysis, but Leavis never thought of criticism as ending there. He does not advocate the kind of practical criticism that would make it feasible to assimilate his position to that of Brooks:

> To insist that literary criticism is, or should be, a specific discipline of intelligence is not to suggest that a serious interest in literature can confine itself to the kind of intensive local analysis associated with 'practical criticism' – to the scrutiny of the 'words on the page' in their minute relations, their effects of imagery and so on; a real literary interest is an interest in man, society and civilization and its boundaries cannot be drawn; the adjective is not a circumscribing one.[36]

Education And The University is a book of particular interest in this context because it contains examples both of Leavis's analyses of poems and of his social criticism – and shows the close relation between the two.

If Leavis's method of analysis differs from those of Brooks, Empson and Richards, it is similar to, and largely derives from, the method of T. S. Eliot. In an early (1932) letter, referring to *New Bearings In English Poetry*, Leavis remarks: 'My critical approach... I have always imagined myself (as I hint in my Prefatory Note) to derive from Mr Eliot as much as from anyone.'[37] When Leavis suggests that the student can learn from examples of good criticism he refers specifically to the early Eliot; what Eliot demonstrates in the essays on Massinger and the seventeenth century, for example, is how local analysis can lead into a wider diagnosis. Leavis's own analysis, without forgetting his dictum that 'everything is done locally with words', does not stop at the analysis of texture.

There is another related aspect of Leavis's idea of criticism, of analysis, that must be understood: he argues that the sharp separation made between practical and theoretical criticism represents a false distinction. In the Introduction to *Determinations*, he writes that

> the keener one's interest in the profitable discussion of literature, the less easily does one assume sharp distinctions between theoretical and practical criticism. Some of the essays...would commonly be called 'theoretical'; they seek, that is, by defining general ideas and relations to improve the equipment of the critic...But it is particular perceptions that they generalize and relate, and without a fine capacity for particular immediate response to art there can be no good 'theoretical critic' just as the merely 'practical' critic is hardly conceivable.[38]

This statement is of great importance for a proper understanding of Leavis's actual criticism and of his idea of criticism. If one ignores the point he makes here, and considers Leavis's own criticism as well as his negative attitude towards such 'theoretical' critics as Kenneth Burke, Richards, and Wellek, it could be possible to adopt the mistaken view of Laurence Lerner in his essay on Leavis and *Scrutiny*.[39] Lerner postulated a distinct separation between practical and theoretical criticism and argued that Leavis believed only in the former; of equal interest Lerner misread Leavis's essay on Coleridge, taking it to present a flat rejection of Coleridge as a theoretical critic. Lerner's mistakes however, proved profitable because they provoked Leavis into a caustic, but extremely illuminating reply. Leavis wrote:

> What I *must* comment on is that conception of 'practical criticism' (if it can be called a conception) which Mr Lerner offers to define. The term, which I have never liked,...means, in common acceptance, elementary exercises in judgment and analysis, the specimens, in the nature of the conditions of work, necessarily being as a rule short poems or passages. One reason for my disliking it is that it encourages the kind of confusion into which Mr Lerner is led when he elaborates his antithesis of 'practical' and 'theoretical'.[40]

As Leavis explains to Lerner, in the essay on Coleridge he points out that where Coleridge's genius as a critic is evident it is impossible to disengage the dealings with principle from practical criticism, that in Coleridge's criticism principle emerges from practice and the master of theoretical criticism who matters is the completion of the practical critic. Leavis's point is that this proposition applies not just to Coleridge, but is general, and must be taken both ways: 'If I cannot imagine a great master of such critical theory as matters who is not a great critic – a great critic in critical practice, neither can I imagine a great or considerable critic who is not very much concerned with critical principle.'[41] This is the key point. Leavis insists that he, and the other *Scrutiny* critics, were in fact essentially concerned with critical principles or fundamentals and that Lerner could think they were not only because he assumes that the discussion of fundamentals must be philosophical. The issue here is of course the same as the issue between Leavis and Wellek, and Leavis contends that in his reply to Wellek he was 'so far from disclaiming any intent in defining the criteria and grounds of my criticism, I point out that they are defined in the actual process of criticism with a precision (it seems to me) that makes the kind of defining Dr Wellek favours intolerably clumsy and ineffective'.[42] His concern with principle in other words, he argues, was essentially that of literary criticism, which allows no sharp distinction between theoretical and practical criticism.

We should not slide over this point, or accept Leavis's answer too easily. Lerner is not alone in his view of Leavis's criticism, and much of the dissatisfaction expressed with Leavis's work centres on what is taken to be his indifference or even hostility to 'theoretical' enquiry. Yet it seems true to me that most of what is called 'theoretical' criticism is undertaken by philosophers, or by people whose interests are as strongly philosophical as they are literary – Richards, Burke, Wellek and Eliseo Vivas, for instance. In certain of these cases there is a tendency to make literary criticism subsidiary to philosophical enquiry, or at the very least, a tendency to move away from any engagement with specific texts. We should note that in his Introduction to *Determinations* Leavis argues that the 'theoretical' essays he includes all generalize from 'particular perceptions' and that the critics all have a 'fine capacity' for immediate response to art. Leavis himself only presents a general proposition about literature in terms of his own immediate response to a text. It is only by maintaining a fidelity to the concrete, Leavis believes, that literary criticism, as opposed to philosophy, shows its distinctive concern with fundamentals.

There is one last feature of Leavis's idea of criticism to consider, and that is its relation to literary history and scholarship. In his early dispute with F. W. Bateson Leavis made it clear that he does not think that literary history can be considered as a field distinct from literary criticism; he insists that the only possible approach to literary history is that of the literary critic. In his review of Bateson's *English Poetry And The English Language* Leavis writes:

> 'critic', one gathers, is a description that he would repudiate. The nature of the distinction that, in his opening pages, he tries to elaborate between the critic and the literary historian is not clear, but he certainly intends a separation, and he calls his book 'An Essay in Literary History'. Yet the kind of essay he undertakes could be successfully attempted only by a critic and would then be essentially literary criticism.[43]

That is, the literary historian, Leavis argues, cannot 'take over' anything; only by being a critic, making a personal response, can he determine, for instance, even questions of influence.

The argument between Bateson and Leavis was renewed in 1953. In 'The Responsible Critic: Or The Function of Criticism At Any Time', Leavis forcefully states his objections to the kind of literary history Bateson commits himself to; however, the disagreement with Bateson here belongs to the wider context of Leavis's quarrel with scholarship. Leavis begins the essay by objecting to the opposition that is usually made between scholarship and criticism: 'I do not like, let me say at this point..., the way in which scholarship is commonly set over against criticism, as a thing separate and distinct from this, its distinctive nature being to cultivate the virtue of accuracy.'[44] Accuracy, he goes on to explain 'is a matter of relevance, and how in the literary field, in any delicate issue, can one hope to be duly relevant...without being intelligent about literature?' And in answer to this question Leavis replies that 'the most important kind of knowledge will be acquired in the cultivation of the poetry of the period, and of other periods, with the literary critic's intelligence...insistence on an immense apparatus of scholarship before one can read intelligently or judge is characteristic of the academic over-emphasis on scholarly knowledge'. Leavis's quarrel with scholars runs through his entire career, and one has only to glance through the essays in *The Common Pursuit* to find frequent acerbic references to academic scholars; this quarrel must be seen as part of his battle to gain recognition for literary criticism as a distinct and essential discipline. When Eliot had occasion to remark on the special competence, as a critic, of the scholar, Leavis objected:

> The deference he exhibits towards the scholars seems to me wholly deplorable...For the purposes of criticism, scholarship, unless directed by an intelligent interest in poetry – without, that is, critical sensibility and the skill that enables the critic to develop its responses in sensitive and closely relevant thinking – is useless. This skill is not common among scholars.[45]

Part of the hostility Leavis generates comes from his intransigent opposition to scholarship, 'work on', about and around the great works of literature, which is not directed by a serious and relevant critical interest. The counter-charge is often levelled against him (for example by George Watson) that he is guilty of poor scholarship, but I know of only one concrete instance where it has been shown that he lacked the necessary knowledge.[46]

To return to 'The Responsible Critic', Leavis objects to Bateson's concept of 'contextual reading', the idea that in order to achieve a correct reading of a poem one must put it back into the 'total context' of its world. But, Leavis argues, Bateson's total social context is an illusion, the '"context", as something determinate is, and can be, nothing but his postulate'.[47] On the other hand, the poem 'is a determinate thing; it is *there*; but there is nothing to correspond – nothing answering to Mr Bateson's "social context" that can be set over against the poem...and there never *was* anything'. Bateson's approach would make literary criticism completely dependent on extra-literary studies in a way that is anathema to Leavis, who insists that the inordinate apparatus or contextual aids which Bateson deploys are unnecessary to the critic. Leavis of course assumes that the critic will have an understanding of the civilization that the poem is written out of, but his point is that no total social context could be established, and that Bateson is setting the student, and critic, after something no study could yield. Moreover, knowing about the civilization does not explain the poem in any direct manner. I think the crucial point in this argument is that made by Leavis in his rejoinder. After repeating that the essential knowledge the critic needs can come only from the reading of poetry and not from background knowledge, Leavis remarks: 'Some of the essential meanings that one has to recognize are *created* by the poet, but this possibility...Mr Bateson cannot permit himself to entertain.'[48] To pass directly from, say, the meaning in an emblem book to the meaning of a poem is to ignore the creative achievement of the poet. This is the gist of Leavis's reply to Bateson about the nature of Marvell's 'A Dialogue Between the Soul and Body':

> To call it an allegory at all can only mislead, and to say, as Mr Bateson does, that it 'dresses up' a 'more or less conventional concept' in some 'new clothes' (these being the 'real *raison d'être*') is to convey the opposite of the truth about it. For it is a profoundly critical and inquiring poem, devoted to some subtle exploratory thinking, and to the *questioning* of 'conventional concepts' and current habits of mind.[49]

This creative exploration and questioning is precisely what gives literature its importance for Leavis, and neither scholarship nor literary history is fully adequate to grasp the nature of the poet's enquiry; only the discipline of literary criticism can properly come to terms with the poet's work.

Much of Leavis's own work is devoted to expounding and defending the idea of criticism that I have outlined – and it seems to me that Leavis states his position with a compelling clarity and precision. He continually asserted that literary criticism, as well as literature, is of the utmost importance in any attempt to restore cultural health to society. As he writes in 'Towards Standards of Criticism':

> Literary criticism provides the test for life and concreteness; where it degenerates, the instruments of thought degenerate too, and thinking, released from the testing and energizing contact with the full living consciousness, is debilitated, and betrayed to the academic, the abstract, and the verbal. It is of little use to discuss values if the sense for value in the concrete – the experience and perception of value – is absent.[50]

In his poetry and novel criticism, and especially in his work on D. H. Lawrence, Leavis presents his perception of value: his sense of those sources of value and wisdom that he believes are urgently needed in modern civilization.

*PART TWO: LEAVIS'S CRITICISM OF
POETRY AND THE NOVEL*

5

From Poetry Criticism To Novel Criticism

i. Leavis and Eliot

F. R. Leavis's achievement as a critic of poetry is unquestionably a remarkably distinguished one. Certainly *New Bearings in English Poetry* and *Revaluation*, both written in the early 1930s, are central works of the modern critical revolution. Further, the essays on poetry in *The Common Pursuit*, the three essays grouped as 'Notes In The Analysis Of Poetry', and the long critique of T. S. Eliot's *Four Quartets* in *The Living Principle* – all these constitute an outstanding and impressive body of work. Nonetheless, I believe that what Leavis achieved here is of less importance than his accomplishments in writing on the novel. The position taken by George Steiner in *Language And Silence* strikes me as being fundamentally sound:

> Undoubtedly, Leavis' principal achievement is his critique of the English novel. *The Great Tradition* is one of those very rare books of literary comment (one thinks of Johnson's *Lives of the Poets* or Arnold's *Essays in Criticism*) that have re-shaped the inner landscape of taste. Anyone dealing seriously with the development of English fiction must start, even if in disagreement, from Leavis' proposals. Whereas much of what Leavis argued about poetry, moreover, was already being said around him, his treatment of the novel has only one precedent – the essays and prefaces of Henry James. Like James, but with a more deliberate intent of order and completeness, Leavis has brought to bear on the novel that closeness of reading and expectation of form reserved previously for the study of poetry or poetic drama.[1]

Steiner further argues: 'The assertion that...the prose novel has concentrated the major energies in Western literature...is now a commonplace...More than any man except James, Leavis has caused that revolution.'[2] I disagree with Steiner only in thinking that Leavis's novel criticism has had an even deeper impact than James's, whose specific critical evaluations, centred so often on the French novelists, have been of less interest, certainly to English critics, than Leavis's judgments.

One central reason for considering Leavis's work on poetry less important than his work on the novel is that given by Steiner: much of what Leavis argued about poetry – at least in the early part of his career, in the 1930s – was already being said around him, and most of it was due to the influence of T. S. Eliot. Edmund Wilson, in *Axel's Castle*, published in 1931, that is before *New Bearings in English Poetry* and *Revaluation*, remarked:

> The extent of Eliot's influence is amazing: these short essays...are even by way of establishing in the minds of the generation now in college a new set of literary clichés. With the ascendancy of T. S. Eliot, the Elizabethan dramatists have come back into fashion, and the nineteenth-century poets gone out. Milton's poetic reputation has sunk, and Dryden's and Pope's have risen. It is as much as one's life is worth nowadays, among young people, to say an approving word for Shelley or a dubious one about Donne.[3]

In *Revaluation*, of course, Leavis severely criticized Milton and Shelley, while praising the poets in the 'Line of Wit', especially Donne and Pope. It is generally assumed that, particularly in *Revaluation*, Leavis rather slavishly supported Eliot's judgments. René Wellek describes *New Bearings in English Poetry* as 'the exposition, development and application of Eliot's point of view' and contends that *Revaluation* 'can be described as an application of Eliot's methods and insights to the history of English poetry. It is the first consistent attempt to re-write the history of English poetry from a twentieth-century point of view.'[4] While seeing the dependence of Leavis's book on Eliot's work, Wellek at least grants that the book has its own distinction. Bernard Bergonzi, however, argues more strongly that Leavis showed complete discipleship: 'The evaluations that Eliot puts forward,...were systematized by F. R. Leavis in *Revaluation*, a book which is largely an expansion of hints offered in Eliot's essays on Marvell and the Metaphysical poets.'[5] There would, I think, be no point in denying the large element of truth in this description, yet this position is not entirely fair to Leavis, and it is worth briefly examining his dependence on Eliot to show that he also differs in some ways.

At the very beginning of *New Bearings in English Poetry* Leavis tells us:

> This book...starts from certain general considerations about poetry and, in particular, the relation of poetry to the modern world. How little I suppose these considerations to be original the book will make plain: it is largely on acknowledgement, vicarious as well as personal, of indebtedness to a certain critic and poet. Indeed they have been common-places of some years.[6]

The 'critic and poet', of course, is Eliot, and Leavis's indebtedness is immediately apparent in the opening chapter where he attacks the nineteenth-century idea of the poetical. The 'poetical' is rejected for showing a separation of thought and feeling and a divorce from the actual world. Leavis describes nineteenth-century poetry as preoccupied with the creation of a dream world and acknowledges that it was Eliot who had pointed this out in *Homage to John Dryden*. Leavis gives a curt dismissal of the Victorian poets and in a later essay informs us that 'the critic has every ground for judging the Victorian poetic tradition to have been unsatisfactory...It was Mr Eliot who made us fully conscious of the weaknesses of that tradition.'[7]

Eliot's influence is further apparent both in specific judgments, and in terms of the general concern of both books, that of relating individual poets to tradition and discriminating between the strong and weaker traditions. In the essay 'Literature And Society', written in 1943, Leavis explains how Eliot's criticism directed his own thinking on the matter of tradition:

> No one interested in literature who began to read and think immediately after the 1914 war – at a time, that is co-incident with the early critical work of T. S. Eliot – can fail to have taken stock, for conscious rejection, of the Romantic critical tradition (if it can be called that): the set of ideas and attitudes about literary creation coming down through the nineteenth century. That tradition laid

all the stress on inspiration and the individual genius.
How do masterpieces arrive? Gifted individuals occur,
inspiration sets in, creation results. Mr Eliot, all of whose
early prose may be said to have been directed against the
Romantic tradition, which till then had not been
effectively challenged, lays the stress on other things (or
some of them) besides individual talent and originative
impulse...

Something like the idea of Tradition so incisively and
provocatively formulated by him plays, I think, an
essential part in the thinking of everyone today who is
seriously interested in literature. If I say that idea
represents a new emphasis on the social nature of artistic
achievement, I ought to add at once that the word 'social'
probably doesn't occur in the classical essay, *Tradition and
the Individual Talent* (the word that takes Mr Eliot's stress is
'impersonal').[8]

Leavis, of course, in his later years no longer regarded 'Tradition
and the Individual Talent' as a 'classical' essay, in fact, he
repeatedly attacked it, but we can clearly see the impact it had on
his two early books on poetry. The impact is perhaps most obvious
on *Revaluation*, which is subtitled 'Tradition And Development In
English Poetry', but the relation to *New Bearings in English Poetry*
– where Leavis argues that modern poetry has escaped the weaknesses of the nineteenth-century tradition partly by opening up
lines with the seventeenth-century poetry of wit – is apparent
enough.

Leavis's debt to Eliot in general procedure and judgments is
obvious; yet, in recent years Leavis referred to *New Bearings in
English Poetry* as a 'pioneering book'[9] and there is a considerable
amount of justice in this claim. The pioneering lies both in the
content of the book – the bringing together of this particular group
of poets – and in the application of consistent standards to their
work. And much of the assessing was done independently of Eliot.
At the centre of the book is the section on Eliot's poetry, attempting
to establish Eliot as the central modern poet, and Leavis obviously
could not depend on Eliot the critic here. There were, of course,
earlier critiques of Eliot's poetry, most notably by I. A. Richards
and Edmund Wilson, but Leavis provides a more literary-critical
orientation to the then extant body of Eliot's work. Eliot had

written on Pound, but Leavis engages Eliot's views mainly to dispute them. He rejects both Eliot's distinction between technique and content in poetry and his high valuation of *The Cantos*, insisting that *Hugh Selwyn Mauberley* is Pound's major achievement. And the central importance Leavis gives to Hopkins finds no parallel in Eliot's writing; it is an independent assessment. (It must be acknowledged that in Leavis's later, 1944, essay on Hopkins he revises his earlier laudatory judgment and writes: 'In assenting, half-protestingly, to Mr Eliot's description of him as a "nature poet" one is virtually recognizing that a significant limitation reveals itself.'[10] This is the only instance I know of where Leavis reverses a later judgment in accord with Eliot's; generally his disagreements are stressed.) Further, Leavis's appreciative comments on Yeats, Hardy, and Edward Thomas have no precedent in Eliot's early criticism. And Leavis's discussion of Yeats in particular deserves high praise for having pointed out so clearly the influences on Yeat's work, the nature of his development – the change in his style – and the strengths and limitations of his work. There is then a fair amount of 'pioneering' in *New Bearings in English Poetry* and it has retained its value as living criticism in a way that Wilson's *Axel's Castle* has not. I think this point is worth making because Graham Hough has dismissed both books as now being only of 'historical value'; this is very unfair to Leavis's study. Despite this, it is in many ways a dependent work, influenced by William Empson and I. A. Richards as well as Eliot – much is made of 'ambiguity' in Eliot and Hopkins, and while Leavis tells us that Hardy's greatness rests on a dozen poems, of the six he mentions, four had been earlier selected by Richards; this is a minor point, assuredly, but it has always struck me as curious. It is difficult, in a short space, to give a proper assessment of *New Bearings in English Poetry*, but, for all its merits, this is not the book I would send someone to if I wanted to convince them that Leavis is a great or profoundly original critic.

Revaluation is a more impressive book in many ways. The improvement is possibly due just to the fact that Leavis wrote it later, but it may be that in writing on established poets he was able to give a fuller analysis than he could in making a 'case' for contemporary poets. The indebtedness to Eliot is again apparent, especially in the first two chapters and the evaluation of Shelley. Leavis opens chapter one, on 'The Line of Wit' by remarking: 'The work has been done, the re-orientation effected: the heresies of ten

years ago are orthodoxy. Mr Eliot's achievement is a matter for
academic evaluation, his poetry is accepted, and his early observations on the Metaphysicals and on Marvell provide currency
for university lectures.'[11] Leavis follows Eliot in describing the line
of wit, but has some minor points of disagreement about the lack
of the quality of wit in Cowley and Milton's *Comus*. The topic of
the 'dissociation of sensibility', introduced here, Leavis of course
takes over from Eliot. The essay on Milton's verse also begins by
acknowledging Eliot's influence: 'Milton's dislodgement, in the
past decade, after his two centuries of predominance, was effected
with remarkably little fuss. The irresistible argument was, of course,
Mr Eliot's creative achievement: it gave his few critical asides –
potent, it is true, by context – their finality, and made it unnecessary
to elaborate a case.'[12] This essay is certainly the most famous in
the book, and it is perhaps the most controversial essay Leavis has
ever written, provoking a heated debate that still goes on.* (In
terms of being controversial and provocative only the opening essay
in *The Great Tradition* and the chapter on Dickens's *Hard Times* can
compare in the impact they have had.) The point that needs to be
made here, though, is that even if Eliot's negative judgment on
Milton was prior, it was Leavis who fully stated the 'case' and
whose statement of the case has engaged other critics. Shelley also
comes under Leavis's fire, but Leavis criticizes his verse, and not,
as Eliot does, his ideas. Leavis's essay on the Augustan Tradition
does not state any debt to Eliot, but Leavis always considered
Eliot's essay on eighteenth-century poetry one of his finest pieces
of criticism, and a comparison shows that while Leavis gives greater
emphasis to the work of Johnson and Crabbe, his argument is partly
dependent on Eliot's.

Leavis's revaluations of Pope, Wordsworth and Keats, however,
were made indepedently of Eliot. Against the exaltation of Dryden
in *Homage To John Dryden* Leavis argues the case for the superiority
of Pope. It is true, however, that the grounds on which Leavis
praises Pope – for the Metaphysical element of his poetry, his 'wit'

---

* Given the false picture of Leavis's views on Milton that is often put forth,
it is worth noting that the 'dislodgement' that Leavis refers to was, of
course, the removal of Milton as an effective model for currently
practising poets. He was not dismissing Milton from the reading of
students, but pointing out that Donne and the line of wit, rather than
Milton and the line of grandeloquence, were now important to modern
poets.

– are essentially derived from Eliot. The essay provides one of Leavis's most concise statements of what he means by 'wit': 'The changes of tone and attitude imposed on the reader...result in an alertness; a certain velleity of critical reserve in responding; a readiness for surprise that amounts in the end to an implicit recognition, at any point, in accepting what is given, of other and complementary possibilities.'[13] Behind these remarks clearly lies Eliot's description of 'wit' in Marvell. Leavis's revaluations of Wordsworth and Keats, on the other hand, reveal his own distinctive concerns and criteria. The assessment of Wordsworth, with its emphasis on his social–moral centrality, provides a very 'Leavisite' view of the poet, but what one could not have predicted from Leavis's other poetry criticism was the emphasis he lays on the 'religious' quality of Wordsworth's poetry; in this interpretation of and emphasis on the importance of a 'religious sense' Leavis differs considerably from Eliot. And the praise of Keats's poetry for its 'native English strength', particularly as it manifests itself in *To Autumn*, is distinctly Leavis's.

Much as with *New Bearings in English Poetry*, then, we find in *Revaluation* a heavy dependence on Eliot, but also the evidence of an individual, personal critical sense in operation, achieving enough to give Leavis a distinguished place among modern poetry critics. It was not only, as Wellek observes, the first consistent attempt to re-write the history of English poetry from a twentieth-century point of view, but it remains the classic statement of that view. And even those who disagree with Leavis about Milton, or even about Shelley, must surely agree that Leavis's positive appreciations in this book – particularly those on Pope, Wordsworth, and Keats – provide a superb and often independent orientation towards these poets.

In the course of his critical career Leavis moved further and further away from Eliot's critical influence, and the essay 'Mr Eliot and Milton', 1949, which provides one of the clearest demarcations of this break, Leavis considered important enough to print as the first essay in *The Common Pursuit*. While Leavis's changing relationship to Eliot is worked out largely in terms of D. H. Lawrence, Eliot's 'supposed' recantation on Milton also made Leavis more critical of him. Nonetheless, Leavis's 'break' from Eliot was never absolute and he always had high praise for Eliot's essays on Marvell and the Metaphysical poets – and for his insights into the 'dissociation of sensibility'. And however great the gap between Leavis and Eliot grew to be, there can be no doubt that in writing his two major books on poetry, Eliot was the dominating influence.

Fortunately, on a number of occasions Leavis wrote explicitly about the nature and importance of Eliot's influence. One of Leavis's earliest published works, on 8 Feb. 1929, in *The Cambridge Review*, was entitled: 'T. S. Eliot – A Reply to the Condescending'. The essay was written to defend Eliot and to acknowledge, at that early date, Leavis's own debt to him. In fact Leavis writes here very much as a complete disciple, even defending and praising 'For Lancelot Andrewes', which is so often taken as the watershed in Eliot's critical career. On two much later occasions Leavis explained the nature and degree of his debt to Eliot. In a review entitled 'Approaches to T. S. Eliot', written in 1947, Leavis informs us:

> It is a debt that I recognize for myself as immense. By some accident (it must have been – I had not come on Mr Eliot's name before) I bought *The Sacred Wood* just after it came out, in 1920. For the next few years I read it through several times a year, pencil in hand. I got from it, of course, orientations, particular illuminations, critical ideas of general instrumental value. But if I had to characterize the nature of the debt briefly I should say that it was a matter of having had incisively demonstrated, for pattern and incitement, what the disinterested and effective application of intelligence to literature looks like, what is the nature of purity of interest, and what is meant by the principle (as Mr Eliot himself states it) that 'when you judge poetry, it is as poetry you must judge it and not as another thing'.[14]

Eliot's writings powerfully represented the idea of literary criticism as a discipline of intelligence to Leavis, and this was their great attraction for him. His later statement in the review entitled 'T. S. Eliot As Critic', written in 1958, gives us an illuminating insight into the manner in which Eliot's influence operated. Leavis, in reviewing *On Poetry And Poets*, remarks:

> The author of this volume was at one time so unquestionably a major critical influence...I recall that I bought my copy of *The Sacred Wood*...in 1920...In those early years after the great hiatus...it was Santayana...

and Matthew Arnold who really counted. (Let me say at once that I didn't, and don't, find Santayana fundamentally congenial; indebtedness to an influence needn't mean radical sympathy or approval – the generalized observation has, perhaps, its point in a note on T. S. Eliot's place in criticism.)[15]

At this later date, Leavis distances himself from Eliot, at the same time as he acknowledges his debt. Leavis then explains:

> *The Sacred Wood*, I think, had very little influence or attention before the Hogarth Press brought out *Homage to John Dryden*...It was the impact of this slender new collection that sent one back to *The Sacred Wood* and confirmed with decisive practical effect one's sense of the stimulus to be got from that rare thing, a fine intelligence in literary criticism...And the nature of the peculiar force of the criticism – the condition of the authority with which it claimed one's attention – was now plain...Eliot's best, his important, criticism has an immediate relation to his technical problems as the poet who, at that moment in history, was faced with 'altering expression'.
>
> Never had criticism a more decisive influence...it was the poetry that won attention for the criticism, rather than the other way round. What the criticism did was to insure that recognition of the poetry should be accompanied by a general decisive change, not only of taste, but of critical idea and idiom, of critical approach to questions of 'poetic', and of the sense of the past of English poetry, and of the relation of the past to the present.[16]

These are long quotations from both reviews, but despite a certain repetition they are complementary to each other, and they are immensely important in giving us an explicit statement of one aspect of the relation between the two major English literary critics of the twentieth-century. They reveal Leavis's awareness of how deeply Eliot had influenced his thinking about poetry. It is Eliot (granted, along with Richards) who is responsible for the modern critical revolution centred on poetry, and Eliot deserves to be recognized as the most important critic of poetry – certainly that dealing with the past – in our time. Leavis's writings on Eliot's own poetry, it is true, are not indebted (at least directly) to Eliot the writer, and his writings on *Four Quartets* in particular – which I deal with in chapter twelve – give Leavis a strong claim to a position of pre-eminence as a critic of modern poetry. Nonetheless, his greatest achievement lies elsewhere – in his writings on the novel.

ii. The Poetic–Creative Use of the English Language

There is, however, a further aspect of Leavis's poetry criticism that it is essential to discuss here: his views on language. While his views on poetic language apply to all of his criticism – he argues, for instance, that in the nineteenth century the poetic strength of the English language went into prose fiction – those views are spelled out almost entirely in his writings on poetry. Leavis's understanding of the nature of poetic language differs considerably from Eliot's, and his various statements on the language of poetry do, in fact, add considerably to his stature as a critic of poetry.

The notion of the poetic–creative or Shakespearian use of the English language is at the heart of Leavis's thinking about literature and involves three main points: first, a view of the proper relation between poetry and the spoken English language; secondly, the claim that the quality of concrete realization characterizes the essentially Shakespearian use; and finally, and most importantly, an insistence that poetic language is ultimately exploratory-creative. This view of poetic–creative language is Leavis's cardinal criterion for evaluating poetry and it is both invoked implicitly in many of his judgments and written about explicitly in certain key essays.

Leavis repeatedly argues that the richest poetic language is closely tied to the spoken language, and he has what, at times, almost seems to be a mystique about the power of the spoken, idiomatic English language. Both Hopkins and Keats are particularly praised for their use of the resources of the English language. Of Hopkins Leavis writes:

> It is not that he derives from Shakespeare...We cannot
> doubt that he knew his Shakespeare well, but if he profited
> he was able to do so because of his own direct interest in
> the English language as a living thing...The similarities
> arise out of a similar exploitation of the resources and
> potentialities of the language. Hopkins belongs with
> Shakespeare, Donne, Eliot, and the later Yeats as opposed
> to Spenser, Milton, and Tennyson. He departs very widely

from current idiom (as Shakespeare did), but nevertheless
current idiom is, as it were, the presiding spirit in his
dialect, and he uses his medium not as a literary but as a
spoken one. That is the significance of his repeated
demand to be tested by reading aloud.[17]

This is an important statement of Leavis's view that literature
should use a spoken and not a literary medium, but it does not
particularly enlighten us on what constitutes the strength of the
spoken English language; however, in the same essay he goes on
to insist:

In comparison with such a poem of Hopkins as this [*Spelt
from Sibyl's Leaves*], any other poetry of the nineteenth
century is seen to be using only a very small part of the
resources of the English language. His words seem to have
substance, and to be made of a great variety of stuffs.
Their potencies are correspondingly greater for subtle and
delicate communication. The intellectual and spiritual
anemia of Victorian poetry is indistinguishable from its
lack of body.[18]

It is this 'body', 'substance', which is of the language, that Leavis
is praising. Keats earns a similar praise for his use of language, and
in *Revaluation* Leavis claims:

That 'moss'd cottage-trees' represents a strength – a native
English strength – lying beyond the scope of the poet who
aimed to make English as like Italian as possible. So too
with the unpoetical 'plump'; its sensuousness firmness – it
introduces a tactual image – represents a general concrete
vigour such as is alien to the Tennysonian habit, and such
as a Tennysonian handling of the medium cannot breed.
This English strength pervades the ode.[19]

In his novel criticism as well Leavis discerns essentially 'English'
qualities which he praises, but in poetry it is the 'English' use of
language. In the essay on 'Mr Eliot and Milton' he gives us a
clearer idea of the nature of this English strength:

And to take from Keats one more illustration of an
un-Miltonic effect, it seems to me that we have a very
obvious non-visual image here:

> And sometimes like a gleaner thou dost keep
> Steady thy laden head across a brook...

As we pass across the line-division from 'keep' to 'steady' we are made to enact, analogically, the upright steadying carriage of the gleaner as she steps from one stone to the next. And such an enactment seems to me properly brought under the head of 'image'. This effect, I say, is un-Miltonic: the rhythmic habit of Milton's verse runs counter to such uses of stress and movement. And Milton's preoccupation with 'music' precludes any strength in the kinds of imagery that depend on what may be called a realizing use of the body and action of the English language – the use illustrated from Keats.[20]

As these quotations show, Leavis thinks Milton's verse does not use the strength of the English language; in fact, much of his objection to Milton is that he creates a medium divorced from the spoken language. In *New Bearings* Leavis comments that 'Milton is using only a small part of the resources of the English language. The remoteness of his poetic idiom from his own speech is to be considered here...A man's most vivid emotional and sensuous experience is inevitably bound up with the language that he actually speaks.'[21] This brings into sharper focus the reason why Leavis considers the spoken language so important, and the point is made in more detail in his essay on Milton's verse:

> The extreme and consistent remoteness of Milton's medium from any English that was ever spoken is an immediately relevant consideration. It became, of course, habitual to him; but habituation could not sensitize a medium so cut off from speech – speech that belongs to the emotional and sensory texture of actual living and is in resonance with the nervous system; it could only confirm an impoverishment of sensibility. In any case, the Grand style barred Milton from essential expressive resources of English that he had once commanded.[22]

In the remainder of the essay Leavis attempts to explain what Milton forfeits by departing from the life of idiom, the pressure of speech. Leavis is claiming that there is a strength in the language – certain expressive resources – and certainly is committed to the view that a special 'poetic diction' or literary language is a

weakness. Further, he maintains that only by drawing on the
subtleties of the living language can the texture of experience be
rendered or expressed. He always insisted that it was T. S. Eliot's
creative achievement that brought home to him most clearly the
limitations of Milton's use of language, and in his recent essay on
Eliot's 'classical standing', he indicates why:

> But when I speak of 'rhythmic life' it is the essential
> characteristics of the poem that are really in question –
> the characteristics that make it something new in poetic
> experience. . .For in that life, which is both strong and
> subtle, of the rhythm the changing subtleties of tone
> clearly play a large part. . .And the poet can command
> such a play only in a medium that can suggest (as a
> Miltonic or Tennysonian or Swinburnian medium cannot)
> the subtleties of living speech. . .
>
> With this use of language goes a new freedom of access
> to experience, and a closeness to its actual texture,
> together with a flexibility of tone inconceivable in serious
> poetry ('genuine poetry') while the Arnoldian canons
> prevailed.[23]

Again, Leavis contends that only a certain use of language allows
the exploration of the full range of human experience.

It is, of course, Shakespeare's use of language that, for Leavis,
presents the fullest grasp of human experience; his language *is* the
poetic use. Leavis, however, did not write any separate essay on
Shakespeare's poetry; his handling of language is usually discussed
by Leavis in essays on other writers. Perhaps the best explanation
of the Shakespearian use of language is given in two articles Leavis
wrote in 1933: 'Joyce and "The Revolution of the Word"' and
'Milton's Verse'. Leavis's critique of Milton's use of language,
which he contrasts unfavourably with Shakespeare's, is well known
– and this either/or choice of Shakespeare or Milton in poetry is
similar to the either/or choice of Lawrence or Joyce he offers us
in the novel – but his analysis of Joyce's use of language has not
received much attention. Leavis's objections to Joyce's later work
resemble those he makes about Milton:

> Mr Joyce's liberties with English are essentially unlike
> Shakespeare's. Shakespeare's were not the product of a
> desire to 'develop his medium to the fullest,' but of a

pressure of something to be conveyed. One insists, it can hardly be insisted too much, that the study of a Shakespeare play may start with the words; but it was not there that Shakespeare – the great Shakespeare – started: the words matter because they lead down to what they came from...in the mature plays, and especially in the late plays...it is the burden to be delivered, the precise and urgent command from within, that determines expression – tyrannically. That is Shakespeare's greatness: the complete subjection – subjugation – of the medium to the uncompromising, complex and delicate need that uses it. Those miraculous intricacies of expression could have come only to one whose medium was for him strictly a medium; an object of interest only as something that, under the creative impulsion, identified itself with what insisted on being expressed: the linguistic audacities are derivative.[24]

Leavis's objection to *Work in Progress* is that Joyce is interested primarily in the words, his medium, and not in what he had to express. (Leavis's criticism of W. H. Auden is made on similar grounds.) Further, with Shakespeare 'the essential is that the words are servants of an inner impulse or principle of order; they are imperiously commanded and controlled from an inner centre...In the *Work in Progress*, even in the best parts, we can never be unaware that the organization is external and mechanical.'[25] Whether in poetry or the novel Leavis looks for signs of this inner principle of order.

In the Milton essay Leavis argues that the pattern of Milton's verse has no particular expressive work to do; rather, he insists:

It needs no unusual sensitiveness of language to perceive that, in this Grand Style, the medium calls pervasively for a kind of attention, compels an attitude towards itself, that is incompatible with sharp, concrete realization; just as it would seem to be, in the mind of the poet, incompatible with an interest in sensuous particularity. He exhibits a feeling *for* words rather than a capacity of feeling *through* words: we are often, in reading him, moved to comment that he is 'external' or that he 'works from the outside'.[26]

As with Joyce, that is, the handling is external. Leavis rejects Milton's use of language because, in complete contrast to Shakespeare, he finds no pressure behind his words; instead of the tension of something precise to be defined and fixed, he detects only a concern for mellifluousness.

The term 'concrete realization', introduced above in the description of Milton's medium, is one of Leavis's central criteria; for poetry it is perhaps *the* criterion. Leavis uses the terms 'realization', 'concreteness', and 'concrete realization' almost interchangeably, and they always indicate something grasped from within, possessed imaginatively from a deep centre. He argues that the superiority of Shakespeare's verse over both Dryden's and Shelley's can be seen in its greater 'concrete realization'. In the comparison he makes between *Antony and Cleopatra* and *All For Love*, Leavis praises the superiority of the 'life' of the verse – superiority in concreteness – in Shakespeare's play, and claims that 'eloquence' instead of 'life' is the proper word for Dryden's verse. In contrast to Dryden's eloquence – talking *about* – Shakespeare's verse, he insists, enacts its meaning. 'Enact' here is almost being identified with 'realized' and Leavis explains:

> The characteristic Shakespearian life asserts itself in Enobarbus's opening lines:
>
>> The barge she sat in, like a burnish'd throne
>> Burn'd on the water...
>
> – The assonantal sequence, 'barge' – 'burnish'd' – 'burn'd', is alien in spirit to Dryden's handling of the medium...The effect is to give the metaphor 'burn'd' a vigour of sensuous realization that it wouldn't otherwise have had; the force of 'burn' is reflected back through 'burnish'd' (felt now as 'burning' too) upon 'barge', so that the barge takes fire, as it were, before our eyes: we are much more than merely told that the barge 'burned'.[27]

Leavis very clearly here describes what he means by 'realization' in poetry, the power of making language create and enact, instead of merely saying. In contrast, Leavis insists, Dryden's habit of expression, his use of language:

> manifests plainly the external approach, the predominance of taste and judgment. It is an approach equally apparent in the treatment of emotion in what are meant to be the especially moving places...The emotion doesn't emerge from a given situation realized in its concrete particularity;

it is stated, not presented or enacted. The explicitness is of
the kind that betrays absence of realization.[28]

Leavis's contrast of Shakespeare and Shelley provides an equally
clear description of concrete realization. In *Revaluation* Leavis
contrasts Shelley's play *The Cenci* with Shakespeare's *Measure For
Measure*: 'The juxtaposition is enough to expose the vague, gener-
alizing externality of Shelley's rendering. Claudio's words spring
from a vividly realized particular situation; from the imagined
experience of a given mind in a given critical moment that is felt
from the inside – that is lived – with sharp concrete particularity.'[29]
That is, the concrete particularity of the language reveals that
something was felt from the inside – or realized. In the comparison
of the plays Leavis contends:

> The point has been sufficiently enforced that, though this
> vivid concreteness of realization lodged the passage in
> Shelley's mind, to become at the due moment
> 'inspiration', the passage inspired is nothing but wordy
> emotional generality. It does not grasp and present
> anything, but merely makes large gestures towards the
> kind of effect deemed appropriate. We are told
> emphatically what the emotion is that we are to feel;
> emphasis and insistence serving instead of realization and
> advertising its default.[30]

As we shall see, this is almost identical with Leavis's description of
the poetic use of language, and I quote it here mainly to illustrate
the point that in Leavis's terminology 'concrete realization' and
'poetic' are nearly identified. There is also the phrase 'wordy
emotional generality' to consider: Leavis consistently thinks of
emotion as associated with wordiness and generality, and associates
intelligence with precision and particularity. He concludes by
remarking: 'As so often in bad poetry (the lack of realizing grasp
being commonly manifested in both these ways at once), vagueness is accompanied by excessive – a betraying excessive –
explicitness.'[31] This is an unusually explicit statement of Leavis's
criteria in evaluating poetry, and almost sounds like a theoretical
'standard'. The essays on Shelley and Milton are among Leavis's
best known efforts at negative criticism, and it is instructive to note
that in the work of both of these poets he deplores the lack of
concrete realization – the very quality that he finds pre-eminently
in Shakespeare.

The most important aspect of the poetic or Shakespearian use of the English language, however, is its quality of exploratory-creation. Leavis's main explanations of the poetic–creative use of language occur in three essays, all written about the same time, in which he is dealing with critics who have failed to grasp its nature; two essays on Samuel Johnson, 'Johnson As Critic', 1944, and 'Johnson And Augustanism', 1946, as well as the essay 'Tragedy And The "Medium"', 1944, which begins in a dispute with Santayana. Leavis clearly holds a definite view of what takes place in the creative process to account for the poetic–creative use of language; he believes there is a very particular relation between thought and language. He quotes approvingly D. W. Harding's comment on Rosenberg's handling of language as an apt description of the Shakespearian, the essentially poetic use:

> He – like many poets in some degree, one supposes – brought language to bear on the incipient thought at an earlier stage of its development. Instead of the emerging idea being racked slightly so as to fit a more familiar approximation of itself, and words found for *that*, Rosenberg let it manipulate words almost from the beginning, often without the controls of logic and intelligibility.[32]

The total contrast of this use of language, or kind of creative process, with the Augustan use is obvious. (The contrast with the use of language by a modern poet like E. A. Robinson, whom Yvor Winters admires so greatly is equally apparent; the difference in Winters' and Leavis's view of poetry is implicit here – there is no place for the kind of rational (conceptual) evaluation of experience, which Winters demands, in the poetic use of language.) In the Augustan use of language the thought is known and language is used, as simile, to dress it up. Leavis, in commenting on Harding's remark, explains:

> Shakespeare's 'thoughts', concretely realized moments in the development of the dramatic poem (itself a marvellous concrete and complex whole), are apt to be highly specific, and, so, highly complex – which is to say, compressed and licentious in expression: hence the occasions for Johnson's vigours and rigours of censure. The Augustan can not conceive the need for such a use of language. The ideas he

wants to express are adequately provided for – and this is
true of poetry as of prose – in the common currency of
terms.

In his 1946 essay on Johnson Leavis again draws this contrast
between the poetic and the Augustan use of language:

> Every word in a piece of Augustan verse has an air of
> being able to give the reasons why it has been chosen, and
> placed just there. The thoughts that the Augustan poet,
> like any other Augustan writer, sets himself to express are
> amply provided for by the ready-minted concepts of the
> common currency... The exploratory-creative use of words
> upon experience, involving the creation of concepts in a
> free play for which the lines and configurations of the
> conventionally charted have no finality, is something he
> has no use for... So that even when he is Johnson... he
> cannot securely appreciate the Shakespearian
> creativeness.[33]

This is a view of poetry as a creative mode of thought, and it is
also an insistence on the dramatic nature of poetic language. That
is, Leavis argues that the poetic use of language is not a matter of
stating or telling but of presenting experience to speak and act for
itself, of enactment. He points out, in this essay, that Shelley's use
of language, for all its differences from Johnson's, is equally
un-Shakespearian and unpoetic by being undramatic; instead of
creating a situation which would produce an emotional effect,
Shelley tells us what his emotions are. Statement, Leavis insists,
whether for an intellectual purpose like Johnson's, or an emotional
purpose like Shelley's, is not the poetic use of language.

Leavis's essay 'Tragedy And The "Medium"' provides perhaps
his most important statement on the poetic–creative use of language. He begins by asserting that Santayana, like Johnson, fails
to grasp the poetic, that is essentially dramatic, use of language
exemplified by Shakespeare. Leavis states that 'to demand that
poetry should be a "medium" for "previously definite" ideas is
arbitrary, and betrays a radical incomprehension. What Mr
Santayana calls "Shakespeare's medium" creates what it conveys;
"previously definite" ideas put into a "clear and transparent"
medium wouldn't have been definite enough for Shakespeare's
purpose.'[34] Leavis goes on in the essay to explain his view of the

relation between tragic experience and impersonality, in this context, his term for a religious sense of a dimension of experience which transcends the individual. This idea of impersonality is central to Leavis's religious conception and it clearly involves a metaphor of depth since it can only be reached by freeing oneself from the confines of the ego. For my immediate purposes the main point is that he goes on to argue: 'The attainment in literature of this level, and of organization at this level, would seem to involve the poetic use of language, or of processes that amount to that.'[35] By way of contrast Leavis explains that a mind tied to the use of language as a medium in which to put 'previously definite' ideas issues in an attitude that 'is really an exaltation of the established ego'. Only the exploratory-creative use of language – coming from the depths of the self – allows the attainment of the level of experience at which the emancipation from the 'ready-defined self' is achieved.

This 'depth' often has a religious connotation in Leavis's writings, and his comments on the 'religious sense' are frequently associated with remarks on the poetic use of language (I take this up in the next section); in fact, the expression of a religious sense in literature is inseparable from a poetic use of language. It is also worth noting that Leavis's description of the level of experience that is reached by the poetic use of language is strikingly Laurentian; what Leavis is praising is essentially a transcendence of the ego – of the realm of the *known* – and of all attitudes of self-assertion. To relate the access of this level of experience to a certain use of language is, of course, very un-Laurentian.

The heart of the matter, then, and what gives literature its great importance to Leavis, is that with the essentially poetic use of language there is exploratory creation. Leavis thinks of artists as the master explorers of human experience and of literature as a manifestation of the highest creativity of life; but this creativity only occurs, in literature, with the poetic use of language. Leavis contends that Eliot's theory of the 'dissociation of sensibility' points to the fact that between the time of Shakespeare and the eighteenth century there occurred

the loss of any essential distinction between a poetic use of language and the prose use. The eighteenth century knew only one kind of use for language: you get your ideas clear, then, with the aid of judgment, you find *les mots justes* for

them...'the positiveness' of the culture amounted to a
blank denial of creativity – creativity as an inescapable
fact of life. It eliminated the creative function.[36]

The supreme importance of literature lies in the creativity it
represents, and for Leavis the great significance of William Blake,
writing in the late eighteenth century, was that he reasserted the
creative nature of life – by a distinctive employment of the poetic
use of language.

iii. The Distinction Between Leavis's Criticism of the Novel and Poetry
Leavis insists that the poetic–creative use of language is found in
major novelists as well as in major poets; while this undoubtedly
is the case, his own *statements* on the nature of poetic language are
made only in his writings on poetry. In his novel criticism he neither
explains nor analyses this poetic language; this indicates, I think,
that his novel criticism is sufficiently distinct from his work on
poetry, and deals with sufficiently different issues, that in any
attempt to analyse Leavis's work, the novel criticism should be
given separate treatment. The most obvious way, of course, of
differentiating Leavis's criticism on poetry and the novel is by
chronology: there was a gradual shift in his interest towards fiction.
I don't think it is fully realized just how long it took before Leavis
began to centre his attention on the novel. Apart from his work
on D. H. Lawrence, his only comments on novelists in the early
1930s came in reviews of John Dos Passos, William Faulkner and
James Joyce. His first formal essay on a novelist was that on late
James (reprinted in *The Great Tradition*), written in 1937, just after
the completion of *Revaluation*. But it can't really be said that this
essay marks the change in Leavis's interests. The following year he
wrote the essay on E. M. Forster and that finished his work on the
novel in the 1930s. And in the early 1940s his contribution to novel
criticism was not much greater. In fact, there was only the
revaluation of Conrad – two essays – and a review of Virginia
Woolf. But late in 1945 Leavis also began his revaluation of George
Eliot – a series of four essays – and from this point the novel is at
the centre of his critical interest. The reasons for the change seem
fairly obvious: on the one hand Leavis had apparently said nearly
all that he wanted to say about poetry – with the notable exception

of Blake (whom he had referred to only briefly in *Revaluation*), he never took up the work of any poet not discussed in those early years – and the novel is better suited to his social and moral concerns; but this is to anticipate.

This chronological shift is of considerable interest, but by itself is not sufficient ground for claiming that Leavis's novel criticism needs separate examination from the poetry criticism. And Leavis's earliest statements on the question of the proper approach to the novel lend at best slight support to any such distinction. In *How To Teach Reading*, it is true, he does give some backing to the view that the novel requires a different approach than poetry. Having explained the proper method for dealing with poetry and Shakespeare, he comments:

> Prose demands the same approach, but admits it far less readily – it is not for nothing that criticism of the novel has hardly yet begun. With the novel it is so much harder to apply in a critical method the realization that everything that the novelist does is done with words, here, here and here, and that he is to be judged an artist (if he is one) for the same kind of reason as a poet is. Poetry works by concentration; for the most part, success or failure is obvious locally, in such passages as can be isolated for inspection. But prose depends ordinarily on cumulative effect, in such a way that a page of a novel that is as a whole significant may appear undistinguished or even poor.[37]

Here, in effect, Leavis is conceding that there is a distinction between poetry and the novel, and that the same approach cannot be rigorously applied to both. However, his other early statement on novel criticism, which appears in the essay 'Towards Standards of Criticism', 1933, argues more insistently for the same approach to poetry and the novel. Leavis contends that apart from a few hints from Henry James, the only help with 'principles' in criticizing fiction that can be found is C. H. Rickword's 'A Note on Fiction' in *The Calendar of Modern Letters*. Rickword's position is that 'the problem of language, the use of the medium in all its aspects, is the basic problem of any work of literature'.[38] And Leavis comments: 'All preoccupation with "form", "structure", "method", "technique", that is not controlled by this axiom must be more or less barren.' The close analytical attention to the workings of language is what, more than anything else, characterizes modern criticism of poetry, and Leavis goes on to explain:

> A novel, like a poem, is made of words; there is nothing else one can point to. We talk of a novelist as 'creating characters', but the process of 'creation' is one of putting words together. We discuss the quality of his 'vision', but the only critical judgments we can attach directly to observable parts of his work concern particular arrangements of words – the quality of the response they evoke. Criticism, that is, must be in the first place (and never cease being) a matter of sensibility, of responding sensitively and with precise discrimination to the words on the page. But it must, of course, go on to deal with larger effects.

The last sentence indicates Leavis's awareness of the problem involved with this emphasis, but his theoretical focus is on language, the 'words on the page', and certainly the neo-Aristotelians, for instance, would object that the 'larger effects' – form, structure – are not receiving adequate consideration. (Leavis's later notion of 'moral pattern' does in fact take full account of the 'larger effects'.) Leavis then argues:

> This bringing together of fiction and poetry is the more richly suggestive because of the further assimilation it instigates. The differences between a lyric, a Shakespeare play, and a novel, for some purposes essential, are in no danger of being forgotten; what needs insisting on is the community. And this for the sake not merely of critical principle, but of immediate profit in critical technique.[39]

The way this is worded, this position is acceptable enough, although a frequent objection that has been made against the New Criticism is that it did ignore the differences between genres and treated all works as a lyric poem. In concluding Leavis asserts:

> If one is not intelligent about poetry one is unlikely to be intelligent about fiction, and the connoisseur of fiction who disclaims an interest in poetry is probably not interested in literature. And the proposition holds as essentially of novels where the staple medium appears to be much like

that of the essayist or the historian as of those which C. H. Rickword...has in mind here: '...rely for their effects...on the poetic properties of words'.[40]

This seems an extreme position, and much of the statement can be challenged. There have been many excellent critics whose critical abilities were limited to either the novel or poetry. Both Conrad and James were perceptive critics of the novel, but neither was particularly interested in nor intelligent about poetry. And Eliot's and Arnold's intelligence about poetry failed to make them perceptive critics of the novel. Leavis may not have meant his statement to apply to writers – who, as critics, are notably confined to their own genre – but I see no reason why it should not be tested by applying it to them. Further, it is difficult to support the view that the language of the novel is as important as the language of poetry; certainly with novels whose medium is 'much like that of the essayist or historian', but even with 'poetic novels', it does not seem that the language of the novel deserves as much attention as the language of poetry. As Leavis indicated in *How To Teach Reading* a novel simply does not depend on concentration as much as a poem does. Leavis intended the essays from *The Calendar Of Modern Letters*, and his introduction ('Towards Standards Of Criticism'), to serve a pedagogical purpose, and I think this helps to explain why he states his position in an extreme way – certainly in the early 1930s it was instructive and necessary to insist that the language of the novel deserved close attention.

Leavis made this statement about the proper approach to the novel when he was essentially concerned with poetry, and as we would expect it reflects this concern. But it cannot be said that in his novel criticism he ever fully followed that approach: the problem of language, the use of the medium, is not in fact his controlling interest in his dealings with the novel. It is true that Leavis's concept of the novel as dramatic poem, first advanced in his essay on *Hard Times*, in 1947, would seem to support his position in 'Towards Standards Of Criticism'; it seems to indicate that he is assimilating the novel to poetry and directing our attention to the language of the novel. However, David Lodge, in his book *The Language of Fiction*, makes the point that in part three of *Education And The University*,

> Dr Leavis comes unusually near to stating his critical principles. That essay, however, draws its illustrations

exclusively from poetry and poetic drama; and it seems to
me that the critical movement associated with the name of
Leavis has, despite its slogan, 'The novel as dramatic
poem', shared the tendency of most modern criticism to
accord the language of the novel less importance than the
language of poetry.

Dr Leavis has two distinct 'images' as a critic: he is the
critic of close analysis, of 'the words on the page'; and he
is the 'moral' critic *par excellence*, insisting on the responsibility of literature to be 'on the side of life'. These
two images are not irreconcilable – and both can be traced
to some extent in everything Leavis has written. But is it
not true that we think principally of his work on poetry in
connection with the first image, and of his work on the
novel in connection with the second? Poets (Milton, for
instance) are assessed according to their awareness of the
possibilities of language; novelists according to their
awareness of 'the possibilities of life'.[41]

As a general distinction this is largely true, but it needs to be
qualified in at least one way. Even though in his novel criticism
Leavis does not give the same attention to language as he does in
his poetry criticism, his focus is still directed to 'words on the page'.
Leavis quotes as extensively as any major critic I know of and his
comments usually relate to the passage he has placed in front of
us – to the 'words on the page'. But the comments he makes on
novels are less about the quality of the language than about the
quality of the novelist's moral imagination making discriminations
and judgments about his characters.

In fact, even where Leavis's discussion of novelists seems closest
to his work on poetry – in his frequent praise of novelists as poets
– we find that the distinction Lodge makes largely holds true:
Leavis is essentially concerned not with the novelist's handling of
language, but with his response to life. The difference is apparent
the very first time Leavis uses the term 'poet-novelist' – in *The Great
Tradition* where he applied it to Henry James: 'It was the profundity
of the pondering that I had in mind when I referred to him as a
"poet-novelist": his "interests" were not of the kind that are
merely written *about*.'[42] The point made here makes sense in light
of Leavis's view that poetry involves enactment, not statement, but
Leavis then explains:

In calling him 'poet-novelist' I myself was intending to
convey that the determining and controlling interests in
his art engages what is 'deepest in him' (he being a man
of exceptional capacity for experience), and appeal to
what is deepest in us...The qualities of his art that derive
from the profound seriousness of his interest in life – it is
these in general that one stresses in calling him a poet...
When these qualities are duly recognized it becomes
ridiculous to save the word 'poet' for the author of *The
Waves* and *The Years* – works that offer something like the
equivalent of Georgian poetizing.[43]

The distinction Leavis makes between James and Woolf – with her
'poetic prose' – is instructive, but there is a clear difference
between the description of the poet here, and that offered at the
beginning of *New Bearings*: there the response to life and to language
were given equal stress, here Leavis is really emphasizing just the
response to life – it is the depth and seriousness of that which makes
James a poet. In itself this is obviously an unsatisfactory definition
or description of what 'poet' means.

In *The Great Tradition* neither Conrad nor George Eliot is referred
to as a 'poet' or 'poet-novelist'; it is Dickens, in the essay on *Hard
Times*, who is extolled as a poet. Leavis praises the range of tones
in the novel, then comments:

To the question how the reconciling is done – there is
much more diversity in *Hard Times* than these references to
dialogue suggest – the answer can be given by pointing to
the astonishing and irresistible richness of life that
characterizes the book everywhere. It meets us
everywhere, unstrained and natural, in the prose. Out of
such prose a great variety of presentations can arise
congenially with equal vividness. There they are,
unquestionably 'real'. It goes back to an extraordinary
energy of perception and registration in Dickens...His
flexibility is that of a richly poetic art of the word. He
doesn't write 'poetic prose'; he writes with a poetic force
of evocation, registering with the responsiveness of a genius
of verbal expression what he so sharply sees and feels. In
fact, by texture, imaginative mode, symbolic method, and

the resulting concentration, *Hard Times* affects us as
belonging with formally poetic works.[44]

Here both criteria of what constitutes a poet, his response to life
and to language, are invoked to some degree. But Leavis does not,
in fact, analyse Dickens's use of language; rather he goes on to
discuss the nature of Dickens's positive response to life. In his
concluding insistence on Dickens's achievement as a poet Leavis
maintains:

> But the packed richness of *Hard Times* is almost incredibly
> varied, and not all the quoting I have indulged in suggests
> it adequately. The final stress may fall on Dickens'
> command of word, phrase, rhythm, and image: in ease
> and range there is surely no greater master of English
> except Shakespeare. This comes back to saying that
> Dickens is a great poet: his endless resource in felicitously
> varied expression is an extraordinary responsiveness to
> life.[45]

Dickens is praised here for his handling of language – 'no greater
master of English except Shakespeare' – yet his mastery of language
is simply reduced to his response to life.*

In his later writings Leavis continues to describe novelists as
poets, and in his essay on *The Shadow Line* he has high praise for
Conrad's handling of language. He argues that Conrad's decision
to write in English rather than French was actually as inevitable
as if he had been born to the language:

> Conrad's English, as we read his supreme things, compels
> us to recognize it as that of a highly individual master,
> who has done his creative thinking and feeling – explored
> most inwardly the experience moving him to creation – in
> that language...The point I am making is that, as a
> writer, he had to English the relation we think of as that
> of the distinguished poet. He used it to bring to definition
> an intensely personal sense of life, and did this with a

---

* This comparison with Shakespeare is almost the highest praise Leavis
  could bestow, and it's worth pointing out that he did think this highly of
  Dickens in 1947, since it is primarily his dismissal of Dickens as an
  'entertainer' that is remembered; Leavis's recent acclaim of Dickens is
  not at all surprising in light of such a description as this.

> responsiveness to the finer potentialities of language so
> vital and delicate that he stands among those writers
> whom (if we do them justice) we see as pre-eminently its
> maintainers.[46]

Leavis here comes closest to describing a novelist as a poet *and*
praising him mainly because of his response to the potentialities of
language rather than life, so according him the poet's function of
'purifying the dialect of the tribe'. But nowhere in the essay does
Leavis go on to analyse Conrad's use of language; rather he
discusses the values enacted by the characters, and, Conrad's 'sense
of life'.

Many of the critics who have written on Leavis – René Wellek,
Vincent Buckley, John Casey, for example – have discussed his
criticism as a whole, drawing examples from both the poetry and
novel criticism. Michael Tanner, in a review-article on John
Casey's *The Language of Criticism* is severely critical of Casey's
procedure of assimilating Leavis's work on the novel to his work
on poetry:

> He concentrates very largely on Leavis's criticism of
> poetry, and is therefore able to assimilate his work to the
> expressionist tradition in a way that produces, finally, a
> very unbalanced account of Leavis's total position. I am
> not the first to note the changing emphasis in Leavis's
> criticism from poetry to the novel. That he should have
> developed in this way is a matter of profound interest. In
> this context its significance is that the stress on emotion in
> literature, characteristic of expressionism, goes much more
> naturally with poetry, and with certain kinds of poetry,
> than with the novel. The issues raised by Leavis's dealings
> with the novel cannot be explained by concentrating on
> his treatment of poetry.[47]

The terminology of Leavis's poetry criticism is deeply expression-
istic, and poetry is repeatedly described as the 'expression of
sensibility'. Of Pound's *Mauberley* Leavis writes that 'we feel a
pressure of experience, an impulsion from deep within. The verse
is extraordinarily subtle, and its subtlety is the subtlety of the
sensibility that it expresses.'[48] Leavis does use this expressionist
language in his novel criticism and one doesn't have to look very
far in *The Great Tradition* or *D. H. Lawrence: Novelist* to find an

example of it: 'That tone, so characteristic of Lawrence... expresses an extraordinary poise and completeness of attitude.'[49] Nevertheless, the language of expressionism is not nearly as pervasive in Leavis's novel criticism as it is in his dealings with poetry.

The central term in expressionist criticism is probably 'sincerity', indicating the honesty or truthfulness of the poet to his emotions and experience, and while this is a key term of Leavis's poetry criticism it is not a term he uses in writing on the novel.[50] Perhaps the only notable exception in his novel criticism is his judgment that D. H. Lawrence's *The Plumed Serpent* is 'insincere'; otherwise this criterion is not applied to novels or novelists. (There's some incidental use in his essay on Tolstoy.) On the other hand one of his central essays on poetry is entitled simply 'Reality And Sincerity' and much of his criticism of T. S. Eliot's poetry is focused on explaining the nature of the sincerity of his work: 'It is impossible not to see in it a process of self-scrutiny, of self-exploration; or not to feel that the poetical problem at any point was a spiritual problem, a problem in the attainment of a difficult sincerity.'[51]

Even when Leavis does use expressionist language in his writings on fiction, there is a difference between what he characteristically describes as being expressed by a poet and by a novelist: a poet expresses his sensibility, while a novelist expresses his moral sense or sense of life. The distinction between these two sets of terms is not entirely clear, especially since Leavis frequently speaks of the novelist's 'ethical sensibility' – and I suppose this is what the poet expresses – but it is, nonetheless, a distinction that runs through his criticism. Perhaps the best way of illustrating this difference is by comparing what are two of Leavis's central and characteristic statements of position, first with regard to poetry, then on the novel. In *How To Teach Reading* Leavis engages in a dispute with Ezra Pound over the concept of technique in poetry. Pound considers technique as a separate, 'aesthetic' matter and Leavis retorts that this reveals the common, disastrous misconception of 'technique':

> The misconception illustrates the dangers attending these
> processes of abstraction which are inevitable in all
> criticism. We have to speak of 'technique' as something
> distinct from 'sensibility', but technique can be studied
> and judged only in terms of the sensibility it expresses. The
> 'technique' that is not studied as the expression of a given

particular sensibility is an unprofitable abstraction, remote
from any useful purpose of criticism.[52]

This is an important statement for understanding Leavis's poetry
criticism; technique subserves sensibility, and the critic assesses that
sensibility. This refusal to separate technique from sensibility in
poetry becomes a refusal to separate form from moral sense or moral
interest in the novel. In a similar disagreement with another
American critic, Henry James, Leavis states his position on the
novel: 'Is there any great novelist whose preoccupation with
"form" is not a matter of his responsibility towards a rich human
interest, or complexity of interests, profoundly realized? – a responsibility involving, of its very nature, imaginative sympathy,
moral discrimination, and judgment of relative human value?'[53]
Leavis doesn't actually use the terms 'moral sense' or 'sense of
life' here, but a quick glance through his essay on the late James
in *The Great Tradition* will illustrate my point that, in the novel,
Leavis thinks of technique subserving not sensibility but 'moral
fineness'. Finally, the point should be made that Leavis combines
any 'theory' of expressionism he might hold with a sense of the
mimetic quality of fiction. One only has to think of his essay on
The Rainbow, or the recent one on *Adam Bede*, stressing the historical
dimension of these books to realize that Leavis very much thinks
of the novel as a 'mirror'.

The distinction between Leavis's criticism of the novel and
poetry should be made carefully. Tanner, in his review, speaks
critically of Casey's

> assimilating Leavis's criticism of the novel to his dealings
> with poetry, whereas it is surely obvious that on the whole
> Leavis employs strikingly different methods in the two
> fields; the kind of 'close reading' which is exemplified by
> his treatment of the *Ode to the Nightingale*, for instance, is
> something that we don't find in *The Great Tradition* or
> *D. H. Lawrence: Novelist*. Leavis has the tact and flexibility
> to realize that the methods appropriate to dealing with
> poetry, and especially short poems, are not likely to be
> those most suited to dealing with extended prose works.[54]

Yes, but...My qualification here is similar to the one I made about
Lodge's remark. Much of Leavis's novel criticism is focused on the
analysis of tone in the novel and the analysis of tone we usually

associate with poetry criticism. Tanner is being a little too extreme in the separation he makes. My point is not that there are no points of contact between Leavis's novel and poetry criticism – in fact there are many – but that despite this we best understand Leavis's criticism by examining them separately. The crucial difference is Leavis's concern with moral interest in the novel, with 'moral pattern' and the 'moral fable' and his examination of novelists in terms of their awareness of the 'possibilities of life'; these distinguishing features are the subject of the following chapter.

6

The Basic Concepts Of Leavis's Novel Criticism

At the centre of Leavis's thinking about the novel are two firmly held ideas: first, that there is a particularly close connection between the novel and morality; secondly, that great novels represent an affirmation of life. Leavis's thinking about the moral dimension of fiction is especially complex and revolves around a number of closely related ideas: a definite concept of form in fiction, the concepts of the novel as moral fable and dramatic poem, and a notion of moral enactment and moral exploration. While Leavis does not give an explicit or theoretical explanation of these ideas, they are implicit in all his fiction criticism, underlying his specific judgments on novelists. And added to these basic concepts is, of course, Leavis's idea of the great tradition of the novel.

i. The Novel and Morality

One of Leavis's central contentions is that great novelists show an intense moral interest in life and that this moral interest determines and conditions the nature of their preoccupation with form in fiction. In the opening chapter of *The Great Tradition* Leavis attempts to set out what he considers to be the proper relation between form (or 'composition') and moral interest, or art and life. He contends that:

> Jane Austen's plots, and her novels in general, were put together very 'deliberately and calculatedly'...But her interest in 'composition' is not something to be put over against her interest in life; nor does she offer an 'aesthetic'

value that is separable from moral significance. The
principle of organization, and the principle of
development, in her work is an intense moral interest of
her own in life that is in the first place a preoccupation
with certain problems that life compels on her as personal
ones.[1]

Leavis refuses to separate art from life, the aesthetic or formal from
the moral. He insists:

> When we examine the formal perfection of *Emma*, we find
> that it can be appreciated only in terms of the moral
> preoccupations that characterize the novelist's peculiar
> interest in life. Those who suppose it to be an 'aesthetic
> matter', a beauty of 'composition' that is combined,
> miraculously, with 'truth to life', can give no adequate
> reason for the view that *Emma* is a great novel, and no
> intelligent account of its perfection of form.[2]

Leavis's view of the proper relation of form and moral interest in
fiction has proven to be as contentious an issue as certain of his
evaluations; the statement above is frequently quoted and argued
with. David Lodge, for instance, in *Language of Fiction*, reverses
Leavis's terms and suggests that the 'moral preoccupations' of
Emma can be appreciated only in terms of 'the formal perfection'
of the novel.[3] It is a dogma of modern criticism that the moral and
the formal in a successful work of art are one – what Eliseo Vivas
calls 'informed substance' – and it is a tenet that Leavis would
subscribe to. But Leavis's formulation *seems* to bring the two apart
by regarding the moral as prior to the formal, and certainly as the
more important. (This may not be quite fair to Leavis; his insistence
is that the preoccupation with form is inseparable from moral
concern, not that it is less important.) We should nonetheless
consider whether Leavis does not give us a proper understanding
of the nature of form in major works of fiction, as opposed to the
more rigid, stylized kind of form found in the use of, say, the sonnet.

We can further consider Leavis's position by examining the
criticisms he makes of Henry James's notion of form. James's
position is a more formalist one than Leavis's, and the word
'composition' or 'form' is often used as an important criterion in
his criticism. For example, James complains that for George Eliot
the novel was 'not primarily a picture of life, capable of deriving

a high value from its form, but a moralized fable, the last word of a philosophy endeavouring to teach by example'.[4] Leavis objects strenuously to what he calls the 'misleading antithesis' of James's position: 'What, we ask, is the "form" from which a "picture of life" derives its value?'[5] And he insists that a great novelist's preoccupation with form is a matter of his responsibility towards a rich moral interest. Leavis is not denying that there are works of art with a limited formal concern, but his point is that they are not the greatest kind of fiction. This point is made most clearly, perhaps, in his essay on Tolstoy's *Anna Karenina*. In this essay Leavis attempts to 'confute' James's critical censures and to show the nature of the composition that makes *Anna Karenina* a great work of art. James found Tolstoy's novel lacking in composition and architecture, and Leavis answers that whereas a limited and clearly concerned interest determined the 'composition' of a Jamesian novel,

> the relation of art to life in Tolstoy is such as to preclude this kind of narrowly provident economy. It is an immensely fuller and profounder involvement *in* life on the part of the artist, whose concern for significance in his art is the intense and focused expression of the questing after significance that characterizes him in his daily living...Tolstoy might very well have answered as Lawrence did when asked, not long before his death, what was the drive behind his creating: 'One writes out of one's moral sense; for the race, as it were.'[6]

Leavis makes almost the same point in explaining, in *The Great Tradition*, why Conrad is a greater novelist than Flaubert. Leavis's statement offers a further elaboration of his view of the proper relation between form and moral interest, and it serves to introduce the topic of the moral fable. He claims:

> James would have testified to [Conrad's] intense and triumphant preoccupation with 'form'. He went to school to the French masters, and is in the tradition of Flaubert. But he is a greater novelist than Flaubert because of the greater range and depth of his interest in humanity and the greater intensity of his moral preoccupation: he is not open to the kind of criticism that James brings against *Madame Bovary*. *Nostromo* is a masterpiece of 'form' in

senses of the term congenial to the discussion of Flaubert's
art, but to appreciate Conrad's 'form' is to take stock of a
process of relative valuation conducted by him in the face
of life: what do men live by? – what *can* men live by? –
these are the questions that animate his theme. His
organization is devoted to exhibiting in the concrete a
representative set of radical attitudes, so ordered as to
bring out the significance of each in relation to a total
sense of human life. The dramatic imagination at work is
an intensely moral imagination, the vividness of which is
inalienably a judging and a valuing. With such economy
has each 'figure' and 'situation' its significance in a taut
inclusive scheme that *Nostromo* might more reasonably
than any of George Eliot's fictions except *Silas
Marner*. . . be called a 'moralized fable'.[7]

There can be no significant form apart from this kind of radical
moral inquiry into life, and the organization that results – the
inclusive scheme – is that of the moral fable or moral pattern.

It is *Hard Times* which perhaps is best known as the example of
what Leavis means by the novel as moral fable, but in fact most
of the novels he praises in *The Great Tradition* – *The Secret Agent* as
well as *Nostromo*, *The Europeans* and *The Portrait of a Lady*, *Silas
Marner* – are described as being, essentially, 'moral fables'. Under
this heading Leavis attempts to define a distinct concept of the
novel and to reject the conventional view. In discussing *Hard Times*
he criticizes the traditional approach to 'the English novel':

> The business of the novelist, you gather, is to 'create a
> world', and the mark of the master is external abundance
> – he gives you lots of 'life'. The test of life in his characters
> (he must above all create 'living' characters) is that they
> go on living outside the book. Expectations as unexacting
> as these are not, when they encounter significance, grateful
> for it, and when it meets them in that insistent form where
> nothing is very engaging as 'life' unless its relevance is
> fully taken, miss it altogether. This is the only way in
> which I can account for the neglect suffered by Henry
> James's *The Europeans* which may be classed with *Hard
> Times* as a moral fable. . .Fashion, however, has not
> recommended his [James's] earlier work, and this. . .still
> suffers from the prevailing expectation of redundant and
> irrelevant 'life'.

I need say no more by way of defining the moral fable
than that in it the intention is peculiarly insistent, so that
the representive significance of everything in the fable –
character, episode, and so on – is immediately apparent as
we read...[an] inclusive significance that informs and
organizes a coherent whole.[8]

It may seem paradoxical to find Leavis speaking of 'redundant and
irrelevant life' in a novel, but, as this passage reveals, the 'life' that
he values in a novel must be controlled art. One obvious problem
which arises with the conception of the novel as moral fable is that
of deciding how much 'irrelevant life' can be sacrificed to the
inclusive significance. A. J. Waldock, writing about Leavis's analysis of *Hard Times*, objects that it 'remains a highly questionable
point whether a novelist is entitled to secure his "significance" at
the cost of jettisoning his life.'[9]

We get a fuller understanding of what Leavis means by 'moral
fable' by considering his remarks on James's novel *The Europeans*.
Leavis writes: 'In fact, all the figures in the book play their parts
in this business of discriminating attitudes and values, which is
performed with remarkable precision and economy... *The Europeans* (as the very names of the characters suggest) is a moral
fable.'[10] Leavis again insists on the concentrated, or inclusive,
significance as the distinguishing feature, and the characters in the
novel are limited to their place in this scheme. It seems to me that
the difficulty with this concept is that it is too centered on the
scheme of values, and slights the novelist's achievement in creating
character. The desire to present and explore the full complexity of
the individual character may not be fully compatible with the
intent to create a work of art where the representative significance
is 'immediately apparent'. In discussing James's novel, Leavis
argues that the two Europeans 'stand for different things: they
have, in their symbolic capacities, different – even conflicting –
values'.[11] This is typically the way in which Leavis deals with
character in fiction, by referring to the values they 'stand for' or
'represent'. James perhaps achieves a satisfactory balance between
character and value in *The Europeans*, but in Dickens's *Hard Times*
the emphasis is too heavily on the values represented. Leavis
contends that in this novel Dickens is for once possessed by a
comprehensive vision in which the inhumanities of Victorian
civilization are seen as fostered by the hard philosophy of utilitarianism. The philosophy, Leavis claims, is represented in the novel

by Gradgrind, who 'stands for' one aspect of it, and Bounderby, who *is* 'Victorian rugged individualism'. Surely to be able to say that Gradgrind 'stands for' and Bounderby 'is' an aspect of a philosophy or ethos indicates that the characters are simplified, almost conceptual. They are perhaps suitable for fulfilling their part in a moral fable, but not for embodying the full creation and complexity of art. We finally value novels for their exploration of character as well as values, and both must be given their due.

Both *Hard Times* and *The Europeans* are short novels and Leavis's praise of them alone might raise questions about the possibility of extending the concept of the moral fable to longer, more complex works; but he insists that the major novels of James and Conrad have a similar organization. He writes of *The Portrait of a Lady*:

> Though Pansy serves obvious functions as machinery...her presence in the book has, in addition, some point. As a representative figure...she brings us, in fact, to the general observation that almost all the characters can be seen to have, in the same way, their values and significances in a total scheme. For though *The Portrait of a Lady* is on so much larger a scale than *The Europeans*, and because of its complexity doesn't invite the description of 'moral fable', it is similarly organized: it is all intensely significant. It offers no largesse of irrelevant 'life'; its vitality is wholly that of art.[12]

Again we have the clear – if surprising – distinction between art and life: the organization and total significance is one of art. It is true that, because of its greater complexity, Leavis does not actually classify *The Portrait of a Lady* as a moral fable, but his praise of the novel depends on its presentation of a 'total scheme' of values.

A similar term to moral fable is moral pattern and in describing Conrad's greatest works Leavis singles out this aspect of the novels. His high praise of *Nostromo* is based on the claim that the whole book forms a rich and subtle but highly organized pattern of moral significances. And of *The Secret Agent* he claims: 'The theme develops itself in a complex organic structure. The effect depends upon an interplay of contrasting moral perspectives, and the rich economy of the pattern they make relates *The Secret Agent* to *Nostromo*: the two works, for all the great differences between them in range and temper, are triumphs of the same art.'[13] The essays on Conrad in *The Great Tradition* were written before Leavis advanced the phrase 'moral fable', but it is apparent that 'moral pattern' involves the same concept of the novel. The presence of this controlling moral pattern constitutes the greatness of a novel for Leavis. Graham Hough, however, asserts that the 'moral' approach Leavis takes 'can only throw a limited illumination on the art of the novel, for no novel worth the name can be pared down to a structure of moral significances.'[14] Hough seems to imply – in 'pared down' – that 'a structure of moral significances' excludes 'life', but in fact one of Leavis's central criteria for a novel is its adequacy to the complexities of the real, or to life. For example, he praises George Eliot over Henry James for the greater specificity – the fuller reality – of her art. Nonetheless there probably is a certain difficulty in thinking of a novel in this way, and it does suggest at least the possibility that a clearly presented pattern of moral concepts may be too readily granted the status of fully achieved art.

Whatever the difficulties with the concept of the novel as moral fable, we should be careful not to misconstrue Leavis's critical procedure, nor his view of how a novel presents its moral significances. Hough objects to what he considers the standard method of Leavis – and other 'moral' critics – in dealing with the novel: 'His procedure is to extract a moral essence – with our traditional novelists not a very arduous task – and then to seal it with his approval.'[15] I want to show that Hough misrepresents Leavis's normal procedure, but first to consider an instance where the description is applicable. One of the few places where Leavis approves of the 'moral' of the work is in his essay on *Hard Times*. He writes: 'And there follows the solemn moral of the whole fable, put with the rightness of genius into Mr Sleary's asthmatic mouth',[16] and on the following page asserts: 'Here is the formal moral.' Here Leavis is, in effect, extracting a moral which he approves of, and his treatment of the entire novel comes very close to reducing it to a battle of conflicting values, one which he approves and the other rejects. There are other instances where we find Leavis discussing the conflicting values within the novel in such a way as to indicate not only that he is writing as a moral critic in the manner Hough deprecates, but also that he is considering the novelist primarily as a moralist. Yet this is not characteristic of Leavis's thinking; he usually insists that the moral value of a work depends on its being art. In discussing *Felix Holt* he makes the point that 'to speak of George Eliot here as a moralist would, one feels, be to misplace a stress. She is simply a great artist – a great novelist, with a great novelist's psychological insight and fineness of human valuation.'[17] And in a further description of that novel he insists: 'There is no touch of the homiletic about this; it is dramatic constatation, poignant and utterly convincing, and the implied moral, which is a matter of the enacted inevitability, is that perceived by a psychological realist.'[18] That is, Leavis thinks of a novelist primarily as a novelist, not as a moralist, and in his criticism does not treat novels like moral tracts. Hough, in fact, is trying to make it appear that Leavis approaches the novel much as Samuel Johnson approaches Shakespeare, and this is not so – as an examination of Leavis's use of the concept 'the novel as dramatic poem' will clarify.

If we look at Leavis's discussion of James's *The Europeans* and Conrad's *The Shadow-Line* – both essays are in *Anna Karenina and Other Essays* – we shall see how little he 'extracts' a moral essence from the novels. The essay on *The Europeans* is one of Leavis's finest and most convincing; it is also of great importance in being the second essay he wrote under the headings moral fable and dramatic poem. He interprets the novel as a comparative enquiry, enacted in 'dramatic and poetic terms', into the criteria of civilization and its possibilities. The two Europeans – Felix Young and the Baroness – he explains, stand for conflicting values, but these values are brought out dramatically and poetically; that is, these values are not simply stated, but we determine what they are from the whole novel. In explaining how these values are established Leavis writes:

> But perhaps it would be better not to refer, in this way, to James himself. When we elicit judgements and valuations from the fable – which is perfectly dramatic and perfectly a work of art – we don't think of them as coming from the author. It is a drawback to the present kind of commentary that it tends in some ways to slight this quality of art, this creative perfection; it doesn't suggest the concrete richness and self-sufficiency of the drama, or the poetic subtlety of the means by which the discriminations are established. No instancing can convey the variety and flexibility of these means.[19]

What Leavis is approving of is not a 'moral essence' but the enacted moral quality expressed by the whole novel.

This point is made more explicitly in Leavis's essay on *The*

Shadow-Line – which is also one of his finest studies of a single novel. He asks about *The Shadow-Line*:

> Is the moral of the tale that one must achieve a maturity for which the 'boredom' of the jaded, adult, settled-down routine of life must be accepted...Nothing so simple, I think. In fact, I don't think the tale is a simple enough kind of thing to have what can be called a 'moral', or the ordeal a simple enough kind of thing to have an easily summarizable outcome or significance. What one *can* do is to point to some of the major elements, themes, and insistences that work together in the delicate complexity of the total effect; the tale, as I suppose I've by now virtually said, being a kind of dramatic poem that communicates a meaning such as couldn't have been communicated in any other way.[20]

I want to emphasize the last observation, that the meaning 'couldn't have been communicated in any other way.' Much of modern poetry criticism, particularly the New Criticism of the 1930s, was concerned with the problem of explaining how poetry communicates what cannot be expressed in any other way; one of Leavis's many distinctions is to have provided a comparable explanation of how a novel functions. The work as a whole, he insists, conveys the moral quality:

> You may say that the moral is given in the final 'There's no rest for me till she's out in the Indian Ocean and not much of it even then'...The point I have to make is that the significance of the kind of creative work ('dramatic poem', I have called it) we have in *The Shadow-Line* is such that it can't be represented by any moral. I have spoken of 'symbolism': I have not meant to suggest that *The Shadow-Line* is symbolic in such a way as to admit of a neat and definitive interpretation.[21]

Leavis explains that even Conrad couldn't have provided a summing-up of the tale's significance, and that the critic's procedure is not to abstract a message but to balance one suggestion against another until one's sense of the tale has settled into an inclusive poise.

It should be clear from this that for Leavis the whole work is moral, and that as a critic he assesses the entire work, and not its moral essence. A reference here to Leavis's essay on Samuel Johnson may help to clarify the point I am making. Johnson's criticism is also known for its uncompromising association of literature and morality, but Leavis's objection to Johnson's central position brings out their clear difference on this matter. Leavis argues:

> Johnson was representative in his inability to appreciate the most profoundly creative uses of language. He cannot appreciate the life-principle of drama as we have it in the poetic-creative use of language – the use by which the stuff of experience is presented to speak and act for itself.
>
> This disability has its obvious correlative in Johnson's bondage...to moralistic fallacy...Johnson cannot understand that works of art *enact* their moral valuations. It is not enough that Shakespeare, on the evidence of his works, 'thinks' (and feels), morally; for Johnson a moral judgement that isn't *stated* isn't there. Further, he demands that the whole play shall be conceived and composed as statement. The dramatist must start with a conscious and abstractly formulated moral and proceed to manipulate his puppets so as to demonstrate and enforce it.[22]

For Johnson, then, literature is moral by being didactic – it enforces values that exist prior to the work; but Leavis does not hold a didactic view at all, for he thinks of the creative use of language as involved in the exploration and creation of values – not their enforcement. We should recall that his recent harsh criticism of *Lady Chatterley's Lover* is based on the view that it is a didactic novel, one where Lawrence writes with a willed purpose to enforce his moral. In a successful work, Leavis insists, values are not stated but *enacted* by the whole work; the concept of 'enactment' is at the centre of Leavis's thinking about morality and the novel. He praises, for instance, *Women in Love* because 'an experimental process of exploring, testing, and defining does seem really to be enacted, dramatically, in the "tale"; so little are we affected as by any doctrine formulated in advance, and coming directly from Lawrence'.[23] The morality of a novel is inseparable from its integrity as art.

Leavis's concept of 'enactment' is closely related to his insistence that literature is an 'exploration' of values. At times he seems to prize literature primarily for the search for values it embodies, for creative questioning and exploration. One of the clearest examples of this is in his lecture on C. P. Snow, 'Two Cultures', where Leavis writes: 'what for – what ultimately for? What, ultimately, do men live by? These questions are in and of the creative drive that produces great art in Conrad and Lawrence.' He praises the 'urgent creative exploring' represented by their works and then declares:

> Of course, to such questions there can't be, in any ordinary sense of the word, 'answers', and the effect of total 'answer' differs as between Conrad and Lawrence, or as between any two great writers. But life in the civilization of an age for which creative questioning is not done and is not influential on general sensibility tends characteristically to lack a dimension; it tends to have no depth.[24]

The notion of 'creative exploring' or 'creative questioning' should make it completely obvious that Leavis's view of literature is the antithesis of a didactic one.

ii. The Novel as an Affirmation of Life

Leavis, of course, does not describe literature just as an exploration of life or values, but more characteristically as an affirmation of the possibilities of life, and I now want to examine this aspect of his criticism. It is, however, essential to remember that for Leavis literature is an affirmation only by first being an exploration; this is the central point he makes in discussing Tolstoy's novel, *Anna Karenina*: 'While what makes itself felt as we read *Anna Karenina* is decidedly a positive or creative nisus, it affects us as an exploratory effort towards the definition of a norm.'[25]

Perhaps Leavis's best-known statement about the writer's affirmation of life is that given at the opening of *The Great Tradition* where he outlines his criteria for selecting the great novelists:

> It is necessary to insist, then, that there are important distinctions to be made, and that far from all of the names in the literary histories really belong to the realm of significant creative achievement. And as a recall to a due sense of differences it is well to start by distinguishing the few really great – the major novelists who count in the

same way as the major poets, in the sense that they not only change the possibilities of the art for practitioners and readers, but that they are significant in terms of that human awareness they promote; awareness of the possibilities of life.[26]

The influence of D. H. Lawrence's criticism is apparent here in examining literature in terms of the 'possibilities of life', but there are in fact two criteria annunciated – possibilities of art, as well as life – and it is frequently remarked that Leavis really only considers the latter. In a way this is true, yet as a criticism it is misleading. For example, both Joyce's *Finnegans Wake* and the later novels of James are obvious examples of works which appear to extend the possibilities of art, and Leavis judges both harshly. In fact, what those works exemplify, to Leavis, is an innovation and extension only of 'technique', involving a separation between life and art, that does not enhance the possibilities of art. In effect, in Leavis's thinking, to extend the possibilities of art and the possibilities of life are almost the same thing; art cannot be reduced to technique.

Leavis provides a completer statement of his demand that great novelists promote awareness of the possibilities of life in his essay 'James As Critic':

Art is a manifestation of life or it is nothing. The creative writer's concern to render life *is* a concern for significance, a preoccupation with expressing his sense of what most matters. The creative drive in his art *is* a drive to clarify and convey his perception of relative importances. The work that commands the reader's most deeply engaged, the critic's most serious, attention asks at a deep level: 'What, at bottom, do men live for?' And in work that strikes us as great art we are aware of a potent normative suggestion: '*These* are the possibilities and inevitablenesses, and in the face of them, *this* is the valid and wise (or the sane) attitude.[27]

Thus, only affirmative art, or, as he calls it here, normative art, can be considered great. It is worth emphasizing again that Leavis's concept of affirmation is much more explicit in his writings on the novel than in his poetry criticism. While he does judge poets by their attitudes to life – and criticizes Eliot for his negative, life-rejecting attitudes – he is more concerned with the question of a poet's 'sincerity'. The notion of literature as an affirmation of life can be worked out more fully in the novel where characters can represent aspects of life that the novelist – and Leavis – value.

Lawrence, of course, has his pre-eminence for Leavis because of the affirmative nature of his fiction, but also in Leavis's writings on the novel collected in *Anna Karenina And Other Essays* it is particularly apparent that his praise for a novel is tied to his sense of the affirmation the work is making. In discussing Tolstoy's novel he emphasizes 'that Kitty and Levin have...a clear normative significance – that they represent...the especially clear affirming presence of the normative spirit that informs the whole work'.[28] And in both of the essays on James it is clearly the affirmative nature of the art that wins Leavis's admiration. Of *The Europeans* he writes: 'The informing spirit of the drama is positive and constructive: James is unmistakably feeling towards an ideal possibility that is neither Europe nor America.'[29] He is even more explicit in praising *What Maisie Knew* for the affirmation he insists it makes: 'The strength of the pathos, as of the comedy in which it finds its felicitous definition, is the strength of the affirmation of positive values that it conveys. We have it here, the affirmation; the normative concern with a concept of an essential human goodness.'[30]

The difficulty with this position is obvious: Leavis can praise only those writers whose response to life is unquestionably positive, and who affirm – even if in an exploratory manner – positive values. This would seem to rule out, almost automatically, such a writer as Samuel Beckett, makes it very difficult to be fair to Thomas Hardy, and I'm not sure how Melville can be saved. Melville and Hardy, it is true, both affirm certain values, but the affirmation is qualified. Melville's paradisal vision of the grand armada is offset by his sense of the constant presence of the sharks; his response to life is balanced between affirmation and rejection. In Hardy's vision of life the positive forces of life are almost inevitably destroyed; one can't describe his response as essentially affirmative. I don't want to give a distorted view of Leavis's position: by affirmative he does not mean simply 'with a happy ending'. He insists that *The Portrait of a Lady* is tragic, but that nonetheless certain possibilities of life are convincingly affirmed by James – and Leavis generally focuses his attention on the affirmation contained in the work.

Leavis's dealings with both Conrad and Mark Twain are

instructive on this issue. One of the things that makes Leavis's writings on Conrad in *The Great Tradition* so interesting is the difficulty he has in convincing us (and possibly himself) that Conrad is an affirmative – and therefore, great – writer. Conrad is frequently thought of as being as much of a pessimist as Hardy, and there would seem to be some grounds for regarding his response to life as despairing and bleak, at moments almost nihilistic. D. H. Lawrence's judgment of Conrad is interesting and representative in this matter: 'The Conrad, after months of Europe, makes me furious – and the stories are *so* good. But why this giving in before you start, that pervades all Conrad and such folks – the Writers among the Ruins. I can't forgive Conrad for being so sad and for giving in.'[31] This is an interesting evaluation, for while Lawrence rejects Conrad's lack of affirmation, he still praises his work; I do not think Leavis ever gives us a similar kind of response. In writing on Conrad in *The Great Tradition* Leavis struggles to present him as an affirmer of life, but it is an unconvincing argument. Leavis regards *Nostromo* as Conrad's masterpiece but is hard put to interpret it as an affirmation, or to find *any* positive values in it. Leavis writes of the novel: 'It will probably be expected, after so much insistence on the moral pattern of *Nostromo*, that something will be said about the total significance. What, as the upshot of this exhibition of human motive and attitude, do we feel Conrad himself to endorse? What are his positives? It is easier to say what he rejects or criticizes.'[32] In *Nostromo* there are not any clear positives Leavis can point to, as there are in so many of the other novels he praises. This presents a distinct difference from James's *The Portrait of a Lady*, where James clearly endorses the fineness represented by Isabel Archer. Whatever spiritual values are presented in *Nostromo* are submitted to a severely ironic testing, and the background of the mountain and gulf dwarfs the lives of the characters and their supposed values. Leavis observes that this negative sense of life corresponds to something radical in Conrad, then leaves the case for *Nostromo* up in the air; we can only assume that on the evidence of his 'greatest' work Conrad is not an affirmative writer. The question here, of course, is whether, supposing that *Nostromo* is a totally ironic novel, this means it can not be considered a great novel.

Leavis makes Conrad appear to be more of an affirmative writer than he actually is only by leaving his questions about *Nostromo* unanswered and shifting his discussion to *Victory*. This novel, he argues, presents a 'victory over scepticism, a victory of life', although, he notes, Conrad is no simple yea-sayer and Heyst's irony merges into the author's own. Despite the ambiguity in the irony of the book, it is clear that the novel advocates an acceptance of life: much as Gradgrind's utilitarian philosophy is proven inadequate in the face of life, so is Heyst's scepticism. The difficulty is that Leavis has put this discussion of *Victory* at the centre of his study of Conrad and it does not belong there. The novel is a late work of Conrad's and is not his major work (the thinness of texture and the schematic quality of the book – the use of almost allegorical figures – weaken it); the presence of a more positive attitude that we find in this work can not be taken to represent the attitude to life that Conrad conveys in those novels – *Nostromo* and *The Secret Agent* – which Leavis takes to be his greatest works. *The Secret Agent* in particular seems to present a negative view of life – it is after all a story of despair and suicide; Leavis has praised this novel, but it doesn't seem to accord with his basic criteria. (It may be possible to argue that *The Secret Agent* is actually about the futility of the nay-sayers, but this doesn't leave us with much more of a direct presentation of a positive sense of life.)

In his two later essays on Conrad, however, Leavis does make a very convincing case for him as a positive writer, affirming certain potentialities of human experience. Writing about *The Secret Sharer*, Leavis praises the 'insistence on the inescapable need for individual moral judgment, and for moral conviction that is strong and courageous enough to forget codes and to defy law and codified morality and justice.'[33] Further, he insists that the captain of the ship, in aiding the swimmer, 'acts on his full human judgment. A man's supreme obligation is to recognize his own moral responsibility – to have the courage to recognize it and to act on it.'[34] The tale definitely centres on the need for moral responsibility, but I get the impression that Leavis is using the story, and his essay, to make his own assertion of the necessity of moral responsibility. In *The Shadow-Line* it is not the presentation of a specific moral quality that Leavis praises, but the affirmative sense of life Conrad conveys: 'You have the added life-dimension Captain MacWhirr can never have known, that which is given in the young captain's response to the ship's beauty: it is good to be alive in a world in which such things exist. The beautiful ship, of course, is representative and symbolic in this matter.'[35]

Mark Twain provides another revealing test case of Leavis's

critical procedure, and further, the essay on *Pudd'nhead Wilson* indicates quite clearly his negative response to satire. Twain is occasionally regarded as a pessimistic, even cynical or misanthropic writer – that is, anything but affirmative. D. H. Lawrence, for example, holds this view of Twain, regarding him essentially as a satirist. In the preface to *Max Havelaar* Lawrence writes: 'The book isn't really a tract, it is a satire. Multatuli isn't really a preacher, he's a satirical humorist. Straight on in the life of Jean Paul Richter the same bitter, almost mad-dog aversion from humanity that appeared in Jean Paul appears again in Multatuli, as it appears in the later Mark Twain.'[36] Further, Lawrence insists that the 'great dynamic force' in Multatuli and Mark Twain is 'hate, a passionate honourable hate'. This diverges considerably from Leavis's position, for Lawrence is not asking for any clear positives in the work, any affirmation; he is quite willing to praise satire and literature whose main purpose is to repudiate all that has gone dead.

Leavis's response towards Mark Twain and satire is quite different. Leavis insists that the attitude conveyed in *Pudd'nhead Wilson* is remote from cynicism or pessimism, and that the book shows neither contempt for human nature nor a rejection of civilization; that is, it does not reveal an attitude of 'passionate hate'. Leavis seems to regard satire – or the satiric attitude – as a rather straightforward rejection of life and thus he insists: 'Astringent as is the irony of *Pudd'nhead Wilson*, the attitude here has nothing of the satiric in it (the distinctively satiric plays no great part in the work as a whole).'[37] Leavis takes great pains to insist that those writers he considers great are not satiric – part of his discussion of George Eliot's *Middlemarch* is centered on demonstrating that she is not a satirist because she treats mankind with compassion rather than contempt; conversely, Leavis gives bent to his own contempt in dismissing a writer like Samuel Butler who is primarily satiric. Twain's novel earns Leavis's praise – not as it might earn Lawrence's for its repudiatory force – but for its affirmation; Leavis typically focuses his praise on a character who, he claims, represents 'life':

> We are not, by way of dismissing the suggestion of any
> general contempt, confined to adducing Wilson
> himself...Most impressively, there is Roxy...We feel her
> dominating the book as a triumphant vindication of life.

Without being in the least sentimentalized, or anything
but dramatically right, she plainly bodies forth the qualities
that Mark Twain, in his whole being, most values –
qualities that, as Roxy bears witness, he profoundly
believes in as observable in humanity, having known them
in experience.[38]

Here Leavis very plainly praises the qualities of a character in a
novel just as he would praise a person in life; he also gives a further
explanation of the nature of the life that Roxy embodies:

She is the presence in the book of a free and generous
vitality, in which the warmly and physically human
manifests itself also as intelligence and spiritual strength. It
is this far-reaching associative way in which, so dominating
a presence, she stands for – she *is* – triumphant life that
gives the book, for all its astringency and for all the chilling
irony of the close, its genial quality.[39]

It is essentially this positive assertion of life that earns Leavis's
praise. But despite this description of Roxy, to speak of 'affirmation
of life' is still vague, and leaves the sense of 'life', and of the positive
values associated with it, undefined. We get a better idea of the
sense of life and of the positive qualities Leavis approves of by
examining his writings on D. H. Lawrence and Charles Dickens.

I am devoting a separate section to Leavis on Lawrence, who,
of all writers in the modern period, most fully affirms 'life' in a
manner Leavis endorses, but his writings on Dickens are also
illuminating in this matter. In fact, by examining Leavis's writings
on Dickens we can see, first, how Leavis extends his criterion of
'affirmation', second, his completest explanation of how a novel
presents its affirmation of life, and finally, a further definition of his
use of 'life'. While Leavis generally speaks of literature as an
affirmation of life, he occasionally refers to it, like Arnold, as a
criticism of life. (To be more exact, Leavis's phrase is usually 'a
criticism of civilization'.) For example, Leavis praises *Hard Times*
for its comprehensive criticism of Victorian civilization, and much
of his analysis is devoted to the criticism of Gradgrind's philosophy
that the novel is making. But literature for Leavis is a criticism of
life only by also being an affirmation; he writes of Dickens's
presentation of positive values: 'The virtues and qualities that
Dickens prizes do indeed exist, and it is necessary for his critique

of Utilitarianism and industrialism, and for (what is the same thing) his creative purpose, to evoke them vividly.'[40] And in discussing *Hard Times* Leavis isolates for praise the characters who represent positive qualities – Sissy Jupe and Sleary's Horse-Riding Circus. He comments on Sissy:

> What may, perhaps, be emphasized is that Sissy stands for vitality as well as goodness – they are seen, in fact, as one; she is generous, impulsive life, finding self-fulfilment in self-forgetfulness – all that is the antithesis of calculating self-interest. There is an essentially Lawrentian suggestion about the way in which the 'dark-eyed and dark-haired' girl, contrasting with Bitzer, seemed to receive a 'deeper and more lustrous colour from the sun', so opposing the life that is lived freely and richly from the deep instinctive and emotional springs to the thin-blooded, quasi-mechanical product of Gradgrindery.[41]

It is instructive that here, where Leavis is giving what is perhaps his most explicit statement of 'life' as a value term in *The Great Tradition*, he invokes Lawrence. He praises the life that is lived from the deeper 'springs', and we should also note the equation of impulsive life-vitality-goodness, an equation Leavis frequently makes. The presentation of these positive qualities gives the criticism in the novel its force.

There is, however, a question that arises with regard to Leavis's praise of art as a 'creative criticism of civilization', and that is whether this describes what all great literature does. J. R. Harvey raises this point in his review of *Dickens the Novelist*, and suggests that it does not apply to Shakespeare. He then asks, 'If *Lear* can be superior to *Little Dorrit* while being so inferior to it as a criticism of civilization, what relative importance does belong to the criticism of civilization in the total economy of criteria.'[42] The problem here is partly that Harvey is comparing a Renaissance play with a Victorian novel, and there is no doubt that the nineteenth-century novel is more involved with presenting a critical reaction to society – to the new society created by industrialism – and in this sense Leavis's criterion seems more applicable to the novel than to Shakespeare's play. The kind of enquiry being made in *King Lear* is not only, or primarily, about man's relation to society, but about man's relation to his fate, the universe, God; there is a metaphysical concern in the play that is not encompassed by Leavis's criteria.

While this reveals a certain limitation in his criteria for approaching literature as a whole, the novel as a genre, with only a few exceptions (*Moby Dick* would be an obvious one), does not centrally express a metaphysical concern, but examines man in society; for dealing with this, Leavis's criteria are entirely satisfactory.

Leavis's study of *Little Dorrit* is a *locus classicus* for a discussion of his view of the novel as an affirmation of life. In the essay Leavis pellucidly explains the nature of the artist's exploration and definition of values and criteria. He begins by praising the novel as a criticism of Victorian civilization: 'He conveyed his criticism of Victorian civilization in a creative masterpiece...What, at a religious depth, Dickens hated about the ethos figured by the Clennam house was the offense against life, the spontaneous, the real, the creative, and, at this moment preceding the collapse of the symbolic house, he represents the creative spirit of life by art.'[43] While showing us how Dickens intimates his own sense of life, Leavis is, in effect, giving us his own creative definition of 'life' – 'the spontaneous, the real, the creative.' He continues his explanation of the novel as a criticism of life:

> For Arthur Clennam the ethos is that which oppressed his childhood...It is the beginning of the sustained criticism of English life that the book enacts. For Clennam himself it is the beginning of an urgently personal criticism of life in Arnold's sense – that entailed in the inescapable and unrelenting questions: 'What shall I do? What *can* I do? What are the possibilities of life – for me, and, more generally, in the very nature of life? What are the conditions of happiness? What is life for?...he can't but find himself with such a criticism of life as his insistent preoccupation.[44]

This is perhaps the best statement of how Leavis adapts Arnold's description of literature as a criticism of life; but, as I've argued, what finally gives literature its importance to Leavis is not just this criticism or questioning, but the presentation of norms or 'answers'. He explains the kind of 'answer' the novel gives:

> Clennam...opens, out of a particular situation and the pressure of a personal history, the critique of Victorian civilization. The questioning, so largely for him a matter of self-interrogation that implicitly bears on the criteria for judgement and value-perception, starts in that reverse of

theoretical way, but – or so – with great felicity. The answer implicit in *Little Dorrit* is given creatively by the book, and it is not one that could have been given by Clennam himself. Not only is it something that can't be stated; the Clennam evoked for us is obviously not adequate to its depth and range and fullness, his deficiency being among the characteristics that qualify him for his part in the process by which the inclusive communication of the book is generated. Each of the other characters also plays a contributory part, inviting us to make notes on his or her distinctive 'value' in relation to the whole.[45]

That is, literature does provide an 'answer' to this questioning, though it is not a simple, abstractable – one might say paraphrasable – answer. The entire book presents the answer and each character stands for certain aspects of life. Particularly in this novel Leavis thinks of the enquiry, or criticism of life, as demanding an answer because of the challenging presence of Henry Gowan, who represents not just irresponsibility but a negation of life. The full answer to Gowan that the book gives involves an explanation of basic criteria and values – in fact, an evaluative definition of life.

Leavis gives one of his most important explanations of how Dickens – or any novelist – provides a creative definition of 'life', and concurrently gives a lucid statement of his own use of the word 'life':

> 'Life', it may be commented, is a large word. Certainly it is a word we can't do without and unquestionably an important one, and the importance is of a nature that makes it obviously futile to try to define abstractly, by way of achieving precision, the force or value it has as I have just used it. We feel the futility the more intensely in that, as we consider Dickens's art in *Little Dorrit*, we see very potently at work a process that it seems proper to call definition by creative means.[46]

It is this kind of creative defining of life in the concrete that gives literature its importance, and Leavis emphasizes that the process of definition the artist provides is a very real form of thought (if not the *only* real form) – anti-theoretical. He insists that Dickens's capacity for effective thought about life is indistinguishable from his genius as a novelist. Leavis then explains:

> There are other important words, so clearly associated –
> as, prompted by *Little Dorrit*, we find we have to evoke
> them – with 'life' that we judge them to be equally
> unsusceptible of what is ordinarily meant by definition;
> and these we unquestionably see getting a potent
> definition in the concrete...what the prompted words in
> association portend gets *its* definition as the creative work
> builds up. Dickens's essential 'social criticism', his inquest
> into Victorian civilization is inseparable from this
> process.[47]

The affirmation of life is largely a matter of bringing out the significance of these other words, or criteria, as Leavis goes on to explain:

> My obvious next move is to record some of the notes that
> one finds oneself jotting down, as one reads, regarding the
> criteria implicit in Dickens's critique of civilized England.
> When one has noted the set of indicative, or focal, words
> one is prompted to seize on, the words to which I have
> just referred, and made the essential commentary on them,
> one has at the same time done a lot to explain the force of
> calling *Little Dorrit* an 'affirmation of life'. But to say that
> is to point to the difficulty; the words are focal, and the
> aboundingness...was not redundant. So I must make it
> plain at once that there can be no neat and systematic
> exposition.[48]

This is possibly the clearest explanation Leavis gives of how the critic goes about explaining a novel as an affirmation of life. While the explanation of 'life' given can not be systematic, it can, nonetheless, have its own precision.

In elaborating the focal words associated with 'life' Leavis concentrates on the qualities that each character embodies. He particularly focuses on Little Dorrit and the normative human possibility she represents. He compares her to James's Maisie and contends that the affinity between them is that they both prompt the characterizing notes 'ego-free love', 'disinterestedness', and 'innocence'; these are the qualities that Dickens, and Leavis, mean by 'life'. But what Leavis finds in *Little Dorrit* and Maisie is not all that is involved in his understanding of life, and he points to the importance of Daniel Doyce, who represents an indefeasible 'responsibility towards something other than himself'. It is the impersonality of Doyce's response to life that Leavis praises. Further, Leavis insists on the essentially creative nature of life, and on the importance of art as the highest manifestation of that creativity. He emphasizes the affinity of Dickens and Blake on these grounds:

> I have in mind, of course, the way in which the irrelevance of the Benthamite calculus is exposed; the insistence that life is spontaneous and creative, so that the appeal to self-interest as the essential motive is life-defeating; the vindication, in terms of childhood, of spontaneity, disinterestedness, love and wonder; and the significant place given to Art – a place entailing a conception of Art that is pure Blake.[49]

Leavis convincingly shows how – through Doyce, Flora Casby, and Pancks – Dickens makes the creativity of the artist and the creativity of life present in *Little Dorrit*. When Leavis concludes that 'reality, courage, disinterestedness, truth, spontaneity, creativeness – and, summing them, life: these words, further charged with definitive value, make the appropriate marginal comment',[50] he has succeeded in fully showing us the presence of these values in Dickens's novel and has clearly explained the way in which a novel enacts an affirmation of life.

In the course of elucidating Dickens's novel, Leavis's own criticism has been a process of exploration and definition of values. That is, what Leavis offers us is a creative exploration of its own – a radical enquiry into values and criteria. When he states that 'life always has to be defended, vindicated and asserted against Government, bureaucracy and organization – against society in that sense. The defence and assertion are above all the business of the artist',[51] we know quite vividly, by this time, what he means by 'life'. René Wellek's central objection to Leavis's criticism is the use he makes of the term 'life': 'I am, I fear, too much of a theorist not to feel strongly the ambiguity, shiftiness, and vagueness of Leavis's ultimate value criterion, Life.'[52] It seems to me that, particularly in the light of such an example as Leavis's essay on *Little Dorrit*, Wellek's complaint is unfounded. As we have seen, Leavis does not use the term vaguely; he practices a form of criticism that allows him to use the term and to bring it to a fairly precise and concrete 'definition'. Wellek wants a theoretical definition, but

Leavis demonstrates that critics, as well as artists, can convincingly offer other kinds of explanations.

Leavis is not what we consider a theoretical critic, but nonetheless he has presented in his work an extremely cogent and full conception of the novel. In his thinking on the very central issues of the relation of the novel and morality and in his conception of the novel as an affirmation and criticism of life, Leavis has decisively influenced modern views of fiction as a major art. As George Steiner argues, 'our sense of the novel as form, of its responsibility to moral perception and "vivid essential record", is that defined by Leavis' treatment'.[53] Among other critics of the novel only Henry James and D. H. Lawrence can be considered to have done so much to help us understand the nature and the possibilities of prose fiction – to say which is a way of indicating the importance of Leavis's achievement.

iii. The Idea of the Great Tradition

Leavis's view of the novel as moral fable, as dramatic poem, and as an affirmation of life, is supported by another central, and influential concept, one about the history of the novel: the idea of the great tradition. Leavis first presented the idea of 'the great tradition' in the opening chapter of his book *The Great Tradition*; since there is no previous mention it was apparently conceived around 1947. Leavis argues that the great tradition consists of the 'few really great', the major novelists who change the possibilities of life. In other words, Leavis offers us a concept of tradition that is partly identical with greatness; to be great is to belong to the tradition:

> To insist on the pre-eminent few in this way is not to be
> indifferent to tradition; on the contrary, it is a way
> towards understanding what tradition is...To distinguish
> the major novelists in the spirit proposed is to form a more
> useful idea of tradition (and to recognize that the
> conventionally established view of the past of English
> fiction needs to be drastically revised). It is in terms of the
> major novelists, those significant in the way suggested, that
> tradition, in any serious sense, has its significance.[54]

Leavis had also been concerned about tradition – the line of wit – in his poetry criticism, but in a different way. There he argued

that a minor poet, such as Carew, could be representative of the
tradition, while a major poet develops it; here the tradition is
constituted by greatness.

The description Leavis gives of Jane Austen's part in this
tradition makes it obvious where much of his idea of tradition
derives from:

> Here we have one of the important lines of English literary
> history – Richardson – Fanny Burney–Jane Austen. It is
> important because Jane Austen is one of the truly great
> writers...In fact, Jane Austen, in her indebtedness to
> others, provides an exceptionally illuminating study of the
> nature of originality, and she exemplifies beautifully the
> relations of 'the individual talent' to tradition. If the
> influences bearing on her hadn't comprised something
> fairly to be called tradition she couldn't have found herself
> and her true direction; but her relation to tradition is a
> creative one. She not only makes tradition for those
> coming after, but her achievement has for us a retroactive
> effect: as we look back beyond her we see in what goes
> before, and see because of her, potentialities and
> significances brought out in such a way that, for us, she
> creates the tradition we see leading down to her. Her
> work, like the work of all great creative writers, gives a
> meaning to the past.[55]

T. S. Eliot's concept of tradition is too well known to need to be
quoted to bring out the deep indebtedness Leavis's own concept
owes to it here. In fact, one of the striking features of the book *The
Great Tradition* is the way in which T. S. Eliot's critical influence
still manifests itself in Leavis's work, even where he is moving closer
to the position of D. H. Lawrence by making the 'possibilities of
life' his central criterion. But if his concept of tradition derives from
Eliot, his concept of the form displayed by the novelists in this
tradition derives from Lawrence. Leavis declares that

> it would certainly be reasonable to say that 'the laws
> conditioning the form of Jane Austen's novels are the same
> laws that condition those of George Eliot and Henry
> James and Conrad'. Jane Austen, in fact, is the inaugurator
> of the great tradition of the English novel – and by 'great
> tradition' I mean the tradition to which what is great in
> English fiction belongs.[56]

(This concluding remark is not very helpful, in fact, it's tautological; Leavis isn't often guilty of such pointless rhetoric.) He then adduces Lawrence to explain the form of the novels:

> The great novelists in that tradition are all very much concerned with 'form'; they are all very original technically...But the peculiar quality of their preoccupation with 'form' may be brought out by a contrasting reference to Flaubert. Reviewing Thomas Mann's *Der Tod in Vanedig*, D. H. Lawrence adduces Flaubert as figuring to the world the 'will of the writer to be greater than and undisputed lord over the stuff he writes.'

Where Flaubert seeks form and style as ends in themselves, to the writers in the great tradition, in the English tradition, they serve a deep moral interest in life.

Leavis praises the novelists in the great tradition for possessing a 'vital capacity of experience, a kind of reverent openness before life, and a marked moral intensity', then he states:

> It might be commented that what I have said of Jane Austen and her successors is only what can be said of any novelist of unqualified greatness. That is true. But there *is* – and this is the point – an English tradition, and these great classics of English fiction belong to it; a tradition that, in the talk about 'creating characters' and 'creating worlds', and the appreciation of Trollope and Mrs Gaskell and Thackeray and Meredith and Hardy and Virginia Woolf, appears to go unrecognized. It is not merely that we have no Flaubert...Positively, there is a continuity from Jane Austen.[57]

It is this assertion of the existence of a continuity between these writers that makes Leavis's position so problematical and contentious. 'Continuity' could mean that there is an affinity between these writers, or, that there are clear traces of influence and indebtedness among them. The difficulty with Leavis's position is that at times he seems to mean all of these things – and at other times none of them. He immediately proceeds from the remark above to make it appear that he is concerned to establish influence:

> There is evidence enough that George Eliot admired her work profoundly...What one great original artist learns

from another, whose genius and problems are necessarily very different, is the hardest kind of 'influence' to define, even when we see it to have been of the profoundest importance. The obvious manifestation of influence is to be seen in this kind of passage.

Having quoted a passage from Jane Austen, and one from George Eliot for comparison, Leavis comments:

> The kind of irony here is plainly akin to Jane Austen's – though it is characteristic enough of George Eliot...And here we come to the profoundest kind of influence, that which is not manifested in likeness. One of the supreme debts one great writer can owe another is the realization of unlikeness (there is, of course, no significant unlikeness without the common concern – and the common serious- ness of concern – with essential human issues). One way of putting the difference between George Eliot and the Trollopes whom we are invited to consider along with her is to say that she was capable of understanding Jane Austen's greatness and capable of learning from her. And except for Jane Austen there was no novelist to learn from – none whose work had any bearing on her own essential problems as a novelist.[58]

Leavis's definition of influence or indebtedness – that it includes the 'realization of unlikeness' – seems of questionable value; at the very least, it makes the grounds for establishing influence too wide and vague, if not misleading. What's to prevent Leavis from claiming that D. H. Lawrence was 'influenced' by Jane Austen because he realized how unlike her he was?

The whole matter of tracing the influence of one author upon another can seem at times a rather unimportant academic pastime, but for Leavis it is a way of establishing not just the existence of the great tradition, but of 'English literature'. In his recent essay on *Adam Bede*, he argues that in this novel we see

> an illuminating case of one of the major original artists learning from predecessors. For George Eliot is widely and deeply rooted in the literature of the past as well as decisively influential on major novelists succeeding her – e.g. James, Hardy, and Lawrence. She is at the centre of the creative achievements of the English language in the

phase of its history to which we still belong, and incites to
pregnant reflections on vital continuity in art: we see that
there is indeed an English literature – something more than
an assemblage of individual masterpieces or separate
authors.[59]

Leavis is still concerned with continuity in this essay, but nowhere
does he mention the influence of Jane Austen on George Eliot. He
instead describes Scott as 'the master from whom she herself had
learnt to be a novelist' and insists on her deep affinities with him,
especially in the treatment of the remembered past. The only other
novelist Leavis mentions as influencing her is Hawthorne; otherwise
he points to the influence of Greek Tragedy, Shakespeare and
Wordsworth. Leavis possibly is just supplementing his earlier
comments on Jane Austen's influence on George Eliot, or perhaps
he is thinking only of the influences operating on *Adam Bede*, and
would argue that Jane Austen's influence operates on a novel of
'civilization' like *Middlemarch*. Nonetheless, in the later essay the
whole concept of the great tradition, and of George Eliot's place
in it, appears to have been curiously abandoned.

When he comes to Henry James, Leavis merely asserts that James
admired Jane Austen and that here influence could be shown by
quotation; Leavis later argues that *The Europeans* is a development
in the line of *Emma* and *Persuasion*, and shows that James descends
from her, but on the whole very little is made of this relation. It
is primarily on the basis of James's relation to George Eliot that
Leavis argues for his place in the great tradition:

> For it can be shown, with a conclusiveness rarely possible
> in these matters, that James did actually go to school to
> George Eliot.
> That is a fair way of putting the significance of the
> relation between *The Portrait of a Lady* and *Daniel Deronda*
> that I discuss in my examination of the later book. That
> relation demonstrated, nothing more is needed in order to
> establish the general relation I posit between the
> two novelists.[60]

It is open to some question whether the kind of tradition Leavis
wants to establish can be claimed simply on the basis of the relation
between these two novels. James, in his essays on George Eliot, is
revealingly critical of her, and whatever influence she had, he was

aware that certain of his aims were different – he was more concerned with form and less with history. In his review of *Middlemarch* James makes his well-known criticism that 'it is an indifferent whole'; equally famous, and revealing of James's different intentions, is his concluding remark: 'It sets a limit, we think, to the development of the old-fashioned English novel...If we write novels so, how shall we write History?'[61] When James shows so clear a perception of the difference between his own art and George Eliot's, some doubt must be cast on the view of a close relationship between their work. Leavis admits there is a certain problem when he comments:

> Along the line revealed by the contrast between the two novels James develops an art so unlike George Eliot's that, but for the fact (which seems to have escaped notice) of the relation of *The Portrait of a Lady* to *Daniel Deronda*, it would, argument being necessary, have been difficult to argue at all convincingly that there was the significant relation between the novelists.[62]

Leavis is later to argue that the influence of Eliot's *The Mill On The Floss* is apparent in Lawrence's *The Rainbow*; in other words, in these instances he is not arguing for any pervasive impact of one author (George Eliot) upon the other two, but for the influence of a particular novel upon another novel – and this is surely a peculiarly limited kind of influence. In fact Leavis goes on to maintain of Eliot and James:

> And I had better insist that I am not concerned to establish *indebtedness*. What I have in mind is the fact of the great tradition and the apartness of the two great novelists above the ruck of Gaskells and Trollopes and Merediths. Of the earlier novelists it was George Eliot alone (if we except the minor relevance of Jane Austen) whose work had a direct and significant bearing on his own problem. It had this bearing because she *was* a great novelist...Her moral seriousness was for James very far from a dis- qualification; it qualified her for a kind of influence that neither Flaubert nor the admired Turgenev could have.[63]

If Leavis is *not* concerned to establish indebtedness, where, then, does the idea of tradition enter into this relation?

Leavis's argument is that James belongs primarily in the tradition of the English, not of the French novel, which, with its aestheticism and naturalism, Leavis considers inferior. James himself is generally more critical of the French than of the English novel, but he is far more appreciative of it than Leavis is. In the essay on 'James As Critic' Leavis suggests that James's role as George Eliot's successor is fully implied in his critique of Flaubert 'inexorable in its limiting judgment' and further that those who consider 'that Balzac is pre-eminently the master from whom he descends should consider how he deals with *La Comédie Humaine*...the upshot of James's critique is a drastic limiting or privative judgment'.[64] There is certainly justice in this, but James's criticism of George Eliot's lack of form must be partially set over against his objections to Flaubert's deficiency of moral interest. As for Balzac, Leavis is referring to James's essay of 1902, but the lecture James gave in 1905, 'The Lesson Of Balzac', is far more appreciative – and also contains his very critical remarks on Jane Austen, suggesting her popularity and value had risen higher than she merited. In contrast to this curt dismissal of Jane Austen, James can hardly be laudatory enough about Balzac. James in fact states that his *indebtedness* to Balzac is greater than his debt to any other novelist: 'I speak of him, and can only speak, as a man of his own craft, an emulous fellow-worker, who has learned from him more of the lessons of the engaging mystery of fiction than from anyone else, and who is conscious of so large a debt to repay that it has had positively to be discharged in installments.'[65] One might argue that the novels prove differently, but, unless 'lessons' is to be interpreted narrowly, what James proclaims here is clear enough.

The other difficulty with placing James in the great tradition – certainly as Leavis first formulates it – is that James is, of course, an American writer. Leavis acknowledges this obvious fact and also suggests that Hawthorne is *the* major influence on the early writing; but Leavis seems to think that James fits properly into the American and English tradition. I think one must answer, yes, but...; that is, (despite the accolade given to Balzac) James is first and foremost an American writer and some of the objections Leavis makes to his writing – its lack of specificity – apply more generally to the American than to the English novel. The impulse towards romance that characterizes the American novel is a feature of James's writing, and not one Leavis takes proper cognizance of.

With Conrad, Leavis does not present us with any argument at all about his affinity with, or the influence of, the other novelists in the great tradition. He admits that 'when we come to Conrad we can't, by way of insisting that he is indeed "in" the tradition – in and of it, neatly and conclusively relate him to any one English novelist. Rather, we have to stress his foreignness.'[66] Leavis then argues:

> Here, then, we have a master of the English language, who chose it for its distinctive qualities and because of the moral tradition associated with it, and whose concern with art – he being like Jane Austen and George Eliot and Henry James an innovator in 'form' and method – is the servant of a profoundly serious interest in life. To justify our speaking of such a novelist as in the tradition, that represented by those three, we are not called on to establish particular relations with any one of them[67]

At this point it becomes difficult to see what use there is in, or what grounds there are for, speaking of this as a tradition. This description of Conrad is acceptable, and we can agree that he is similar to the others, but this similarity does not constitute a tradition. There is some justice in John Gross's irritation with the whole concept:

> Roughly speaking, a literary tradition means one of two things. There is the loose broad historical continuity provided by the common culture shared by writers of the same language or region or social class. Leavis's Great Tradition is obviously not of this type. Alternatively, there are specific relationships between a group of writers in terms of influence, direct borrowing, strongly marked affinities, the use of similar forms and themes, and so on. Given that only five authors qualify for an assured place in the Leavis tradition, the comparative tenuousness of such relationships between them is rather striking...With George Eliot's influence on James Leavis is on much firmer ground...But then what about the influence of James on Lawrence, or of Jane Austen on Conrad? No wonder Leavis...is forced to insist...that he is not concerned to establish *indebtedness*...But we are talking about tradition; and if tradition is not a matter of historical continuity, nor of indebtedness, then what exactly is it?...he thinks they are immeasurably better

than other novelists, and he is fully entitled to say so at the top of his voice. But to dress up a list of one preferences as a *tradition* is another matter all together.[68]

Gross is really dismissing the entire concept, and I don't intend to go that far, but it is unsatisfactory and perplexing in many ways.

There is some difficulty in trying to establish Conrad as part of the English tradition, for, as Leavis himself says: 'In *Nostromo* Conrad is openly and triumphantly the artist by *métier*, conscious of French initiation and of fellowship in craft with Flaubert. The French element so oddly apparent in his diction and idiom throughout his career...here reveals its full significance, being asociated with so serious and severe a conception of the art of fiction.'[69] Conrad has an interest in the 'technique' of the novel – in point of view, the handling of chronology, the search for the right word or 'style' – that partly aligns him with Flaubert (and James) rather than with George Eliot. (I do not mean to imply that she shows no interest in technique; my point is that Conrad, at times, shows a much greater interest in what seem to be purely technical matters.) Conrad undoubtedly is a moralist in a way that finally associates him with Eliot rather than Flaubert, but certain features of his work do not fit completely into the moral tradition of English fiction. As for the question of the 'continuity' between him and the others, Leavis could have established Conrad's relation to James; there is the very laudatory essay by Conrad on James to point to, where Conrad describes him as 'the historian of fine consciences' and focuses not on the technical, but on the moral interest of James's work, praising it, in effect, for its moral fineness. But Leavis rejects this association: 'As being technically sophisticated he may be supposed to have found fortifying stimulus in James, whom he is quite unlike...But actually, the one influence at all obvious is that of a writer at the other end of the scale from sophistication, Dickens.'[70]

At the time of writing *The Great Tradition* Leavis offered only five novelists as forming the tradition, but by 1952 he was explaining 'that in Jane Austen, Dickens, Hawthorne, Melville, George Eliot, Henry James, Conrad and D. H. Lawrence we have the successors of Shakespeare'.[71] The American novelists are now seen as part of the tradition and Dickens has been more fully accepted. Leavis also claims: 'I do not mean my list as exhaustive of the writers who might relevantly be adduced. (And, not irrelevantly, I do not like

Mr Brooks's bracketing of Dickens with Thackeray.)' In fact, on the basis of Leavis's critical writings, the only other novelist we could add to the list is Mark Twain, but I want to focus on D. H. Lawrence's place in the great tradition, and on the implications of Leavis's revaluation of Dickens.

In *D. H. Lawrence: Novelist* Leavis places Lawrence in a line of English fiction that includes not only Jane Austen, George Eliot, James and Conrad, but also Dickens, Hawthorne, Melville, and Twain. The sense in which Lawrence can be said to have an affinity with these writers – especially with Jane Austen and Henry James, both of whom he obviously differs from – may not seem self-evident, but Leavis has not, as he is often accused of, selected a moral tradition of writers who hold the same values. Lawrence's values are not identical to those of Jane Austen or James or Conrad, and Leavis never said they were; what he rightly claimed is that the presentation of human experience in their work has a profound seriousness, and a corresponding depth, range and subtlety. He does not maintain that these writers present the same 'answers' to life in their fiction, but that their work embodies a response to life that is both complex and profound. In this sense, Lawrence belongs primarily in this context. Leavis's criteria of depth and range, it is true, apply at least as well to Dostoyevsky and Tolstoy, and, as Lawrence was certainly influenced by them, it might seem possible to object that *this* context was equally important for his work. It seems more likely, however, that Lawrence, or any writer, would be influenced primarily by the other writers in his own language. And in the case of Lawrence we can point to his own remark that Leavis uses as an epigraph to *D. H. Lawrence: Novelist:* 'And I am English, and my Englishness is my very vision.'

Leavis's recent reassessment of Dickens has the paradoxical effect of making it appear that he abandoned (or at least seriously modified) the idea of the great tradition and yet it makes the idea all the more plausible. In *The Great Tradition* Leavis convincingly demonstrated the influence of Dickens on Conrad and on James; with his revaluation of Dickens he would be on much better grounds for arguing that there is a relation or continuity between these writers. When we consider Dickens's influence on James and Conrad, along with his deep affinity with D. H. Lawrence (an affinity Leavis recently tried to establish in remarking on Dicken's affinity to Blake as well), then the case for the English tradition has strong support. I see no reason why it should be insisted that there

be associations or influences among all of the writers, as long as
certain key relations are established, and with Dickens as presiding
genius this is easy enough to do. (The omission of Hardy is a
problem because of the continuity of the line George Eliot–
Hardy–Lawrence.)

I simply raise the question of whether Leavis abandoned the
concept of the great tradition because of the contexts in which he
places Dickens. Dickens cannot be related to Jane Austen, so in
writing on *Dombey And Son* Leavis relates him to Shakespeare, but
more particularly to Hogarth: 'Hogarth was one of the sources of
life and shaping inspiration from the English past that gave
Dickens, as a novelist in the English tradition, such immense
advantage over any French contemporary.'[72] This is no longer an
argument about the great tradition, but as Leavis says about
'English tradition', and it is really English civilization that Leavis
is praising. In his essay on *Little Dorrit* Leavis at least returns to
literature to establish Dickens's continuity with the past, but here
again the relation is not with a novelist, but a poet, William Blake.
Here Leavis is concerned to establish affinity, not influence or
indebtedness, and it's worth noting his comments on this matter:

> To make the last point, of course, is to recognize that
> Dickens and Blake, significant as the affinity is, are also
> very different...there is no Swedenborg and no Boehme
> in Dickens's case. That fact certainly constitutes a
> difference; but it is not radical in the sense that it makes
> the recognition of an affinity absurd...[Blake] owed more
> to Shakespeare than to the 'perennial philosophy'...his
> importance [is] as the great enemy of spiritual philistinism.
> Dickens is in the same sense as Blake a vindicator of the
> spirit – that is, of life.[73]

After elaborating some of the differences between Blake and
Dickens Leavis writes:

> I need say no more about the differences. The point of
> establishing affinities between two great writers is that they
> *are* great writers, and therefore in essential ways very
> different. The importance of the affinity depends on that
> – I mean, the peculiar importance for us now. With Blake
> and Dickens I associate Lawrence, so that we have a line
> running into the twentieth century.[74]

Granting this view of affinity where there are deep differences, the addition of Blake means that this is no longer a line of novelists, and there are surely greater difficulties in relating a poet to a novelist, than in relating two novelists.

Even if we interpret this as an extension, and not an abandonment, of the concept of the great tradition there is still Leavis's summing-up to consider. Commenting on his list of great writers which includes Dickens, Melville and Hawthorne, he writes:

> I confine myself to those who present themselves as the great compelling instances when this judgement is being advanced, the justice of which seems to me so obvious: if depth, range, and subtlety in the presentment of human experience are the criteria, prose fiction in English literature between Jane Austen and D. H. Lawrence has a creative achievement to show that is unsurpassed – unsurpassed by any of the famous great phases or chapters of literary history.[75]

This is, of course, a very large claim to make, and Leavis explains more precisely what he intends by it:

> I am not suggesting that there is any equal to Tolstoy among the novelists of the English language; it is the richness of the whole "chapter"; the array in it of varied yet related great writers, that gives it its pre-eminence. And they *are* related, even if nothing simple that includes them all can be said about the relatedness, except that they are all of the English language.

The idea of relatedness perhaps never can be firmly or definitively established, yet for all the questions we may raise, Leavis has pointed out a number of important associations. Of greater importance is Leavis's proposition about the pre-eminence of the whole chapter of novelists. This claim – at least in terms of English literature – is surely not open to serious question, and to have done so much to win proper recognition for this phase of prose fiction is perhaps Leavis's prime distinction as a critic.

7

Judgments And Criteria

i. Leavis on the Novel: Problems in Evaluation

F. R. Leavis has been as decisive and influential in shaping modern views of English fiction as T. S. Eliot has been in shaping modern views of English poetry. The independence and conviction of Leavis's specific evaluations of novels and novelists have given his fiction criticism this central position. Although Leavis's achievement here is undeniable, some serious problems are raised by the *kinds* of judgments he makes. Indeed, his criticism is weakened in two essential ways. First, the reasons he presents to support his evaluation of a novel are occasionally inappropriate or at least questionable. The second, more disturbing problem, is his failure at times to state *any* reasons for his judgment and, allied to this, his tendency to offer rhetoric in place of reason. We can establish a clear hierarchy for assessing these different kinds of judgments. Where Leavis states the grounds – however questionable – of his evaluation, it is at least possible to engage in critical discourse, collaboration, the 'Yes, but...' response that is essential to critical discussion. Leavis's mere assertion of a judgment, on the other hand, makes a critical response impossible.

Before considering these problems, however, the real originality of Leavis's evaluations of prose fiction needs to be emphasized fully. *The Great Tradition*, it should be remembered, was written with the explicit purpose of drastically revising the conventionally established view of the past of English fiction. If the view that Jane Austen, George Eliot, Henry James, Joseph Conrad, D. H. Lawrence, and Charles Dickens are the great novelists now seems somewhat matter of fact, it is Leavis's judgment that largely has made it so. He did almost as much to revive George Eliot's reputation as he has done to win recognition for D. H. Lawrence. Leavis's assessments of these writers are fiercely independent, and, even today, his views on the specific *novels* that constitute their greatness remain challenging and controversial.

In *The Great Tradition* Leavis presents 'negative' criticism on much of the work of George Eliot, as well as that of James and Conrad. His approach in this book is thus quite different from his approach in *D. H. Lawrence: Novelist* where, attempting to make a 'case' for Lawrence, he is almost entirely laudatory; in *The Great Tradition* Leavis is attempting a 'revaluation' which means restating, restressing the claims on which the greatness of these novelists rests. With his praise of George Eliot's *Felix Holt* and *Daniel Deronda*, and Conrad's *Nostromo* and *The Secret Agent*, Leavis was involved in – as in so much of his novel criticism – a kind of rescue work of unjustly neglected novels. At times it almost seems as if Leavis prefers works which have not been appreciated, such as *Hard Times* and *St. Mawr*. In the collection *Anna Karenina And Other Essays* (1967) we find the familiar claim that *The Europeans* and *Puddn'head Wilson*, for example, are great novels whose greatness has gone unrecognized. Leavis's work on the novel is further extended, of course, in *Dickens the Novelist*; while Dickens was obviously an established genius without any help from Leavis, Leavis added a new dimension to our understanding of Dickens's achievement with his recent insistence on the supreme intelligence and the religious sense evident in the novels.

These judgments on novelists are at the centre of Leavis's work and are of great interest in themselves, but his characteristic approach to, and concept of, the novel often leads him into giving inappropriate reasons to support these judgments. Leavis's 'method' is to quote extensively from parts of the novel and to comment about the qualities observable from the 'words on the page'; an approach, that is, which concentrates more on texture than on structure. His primary assumptions about the nature of prose fiction largely reinforce this tendency. As we have seen, he argues that moral interest determines form: 'When we examine the formal perfection of *Emma*, we find that it can be appreciated only in terms of the moral preoccupations that characterize the novelist's peculiar interest in life.'[1] The difficulty we might expect to find with a critic holding such a view of the relation of form and content, and using such an approach, is that he does not give sufficient attention to the 'formal' nature of the work, to the primary question, from a formalist point of view, of the unity of the novel. Although Leavis shows some concern about the unity of a novel it cannot be regarded as one of his central interests. His judgment of *Adam Bede* is to a certain extent uncharacteristic: 'The point can perhaps be made by suggesting that the book is too much the sum of its specifiable attractions to be among the great novels – that it is too resolvable into the separate interests that we can see the author to have started with.'[2] Leavis further argues: 'Satisfactory at its own level as the unity is that the author has induced in her materials, there is not at work in the whole any pressure from her profounder experience to compel an inevitable development.'[3] This is an admirable statement of Leavis's view that the form of a work derives not from literature but from the pressure of the author's experience. The novel fails by lacking this kind of 'inevitable' unity. But in Leavis's fiction criticism generally, and certainly in his writings on George Eliot, he is less concerned with the success of the whole novel than with the qualities present in certain parts. For Leavis a novel can lack unity, form, wholeness, and still be a great work. His treatment of *Felix Holt* is a good example of this: he dismisses all that is associated with Felix Holt, yet pronounces it a great novel on the basis of the impersonality and maturity of the Transome theme. The major example of this procedure, though, is his judgment of *Daniel Deronda* in which he separates out the presentation of Gwendolen Harleth, praising the specificity in Eliot's depiction of her; the strength of the novel is that of a part, not of the whole.

This tendency to value novels on the basis of parts helps to account for Leavis's praise of *Hard Times* as well; he locates the strength in Sissy and the Horse-riding circus, while dismissing the portrayal of Stephen Blackpool as being sentimental. However, much of the novel centres on Stephen Blackpool and if we evaluate it as a whole, not just on the basis of its good parts, I doubt if our judgment can be as favourable as Leavis's. Leavis praises both Sissy and the Horse-riding circus because they represent 'life', and it is especially where he finds the presentation of 'life', which he endorses, in a part of a work, that he tends to ignore questions of unity. His praise of *Dombey And Son*, for instance, centres on the part dealing with Toodles, who also represent 'life'; here, however, Leavis has a clearer sense of the weakness of the novel as a whole. While this praise of parts of novels rather than of the whole novel is characteristic of Leavis, it should be noted that in works he considers to be of the very highest achievement, such as *Little Dorrit* and *Women in Love*, he insists that the entire novel is unified and informed by a controlling significance. His frequent slighting of form, however, leads to further shortcomings in his judgments.

Graham Hough makes the point that 'literature presents us with moral and social material. But this material is presented in certain formal structures. If we consider the moral-social material without considering the formal structure in which it is realized we are not really considering literature at all; we are considering history, sociology, ethics.'[4] This is clearly true, and Leavis is guilty of doing just this on certain occasions. One of the most extraordinary examples of this occurs in a comment he makes on *Silas Marner*:

> I think now that I have done less than justice to *Silas Marner*, and that my stresses on 'minor' and 'fairy-tales' are infelicitous. Certainly a fair comparison would show *Silas Marner* to have advantages over *Hard Times*...that I have not suggested; notably in George Eliot's treatment of religion, and her insight into the crucial part played by non-conformist religion in early industrial civilization.[5]

This is not a literary judgment; as an argument about history or religion it may be of some interest, but it has little to do with the merits of these two novels. I see little difference between this kind of judgment and that of a Marxist critic who commends or criticizes a novel on the basis of its treatment of the working class. What is particularly disturbing is the sense that Leavis offers this judgment without, seemingly, having any idea that it is inappropriate.

There are clear instances where Leavis the literary critic is replaced by Leavis the historian, and he values novels not as literature but as historical documents. This is true of much of his commentary on *The Pilgrim's Progress* and *Adam Bede* (both essays in *Anna Karenina And Other Essays*) and this problem also comes up in his discussion of *The Rainbow*. For example, he commends George Eliot for being an 'incomparable social historian' and contends:

> The historical value of *Adam Bede*...lies in her novelist's creation of a past England – of a culture that has vanished with the triumph of industrialism. The England preserved for us in George Eliot's art, the England of before the railway, was locally rooted and, to an extent very remote from our experience, locally self-sufficient. This we all

> know in a theoretical kind of way, but *Adam Bede* brings
> home to us what it meant in actual living – the feel and
> texture of daily life. There is a sense in which,
> paradoxically, the inhabitants of that so provincial
> England live in a larger world than their successors.[6]

Leavis describes this as the 'historical value' and we could agree
that a novel has historical value as well as other values of depth,
unity, concreteness, etc. And, to be fair to Leavis, we should realize
that he implies a distinction between what George Eliot
accomplishes and what a historian might do. Her record, Leavis
insists, is a 'novelist's creation' and more specifically that she
'brings home' to us 'the feel and texture of daily life'. She makes
the past actual and concrete for us. Nonetheless, particularly when
we remember his earlier judgment that *Adam Bede* lacks an
inevitable unity, it becomes plain that Leavis is really saying that
the value of the novel *is* the historical value – it supports his view
of the past and history. While it is true enough that if a novelist
sets out to recreate the past his or her success in doing so is relevant
to our assessment of the book, to value it primarily for the picture
of history it presents is, finally, to make a judgment about history,
rather than about literature.

While the places where Leavis values the novel as an historical
document can clearly be seen, it is not easy to isolate places where
he bases his evaluation simply on the 'ethics' of the novel. In fact,
I think it is necessary to insist that Leavis's judgments characteristically are *not* simply 'ethical'; rather, the strength of his criticism
lies in his ability to bring moral concerns to bear while still being
fully attendant to the question of artistic, realized, value. One can,
it is true, find certain *instances* where he is more concerned with
ethics than with art – his praise of *Hard Times* is, I think, the clearest
example – but this is not typical. In any case, I want to postpone
discussion of this matter until the second part of this chapter, when
I will take up in detail the crucial question of the moral dimension
of Leavis's criticism.

The instances where Leavis presents debatable grounds for his
judgment, however, are less troubling than those places where
he neglects to advance any reasons at all. In many cases Leavis
does argue convincingly about his judgments – establishing that a
defensible evaluative criticism certainly is possible – but in others
he fails to argue his case persuasively or is unable to demonstrate

what he asserts. In *The Great Tradition* it is particularly in his argument on James and Conrad that he has difficulty in making a case for their greatness. This failure occurs because Leavis takes away so much that one can't accord with his final judgment, and because, at times, his argument simply is unsubstantial.

Leavis maintains that *The Portrait of a Lady* is James's greatest novel, yet in comparing it with George Eliot's *Daniel Deronda* he is so severely critical of the novel that he comes close to discrediting any view of it as a profound work:

> We see that James' marvellous art is devoted to contenting us with very little in the way of inward realization of Isabel, and to keeping us interested, instead, in a kind of psychological detective work...we find that the constructions to which we are led are of such a kind as not to challenge, or to bear with comfort, any very searching test in terms of life. The difference between James and George Eliot is largely a matter of what he leaves out.[7]

And he adds:

> Isabel Archer, for all James' concern (if Mr Winters is right) to isolate in her the problem of ethical choice, has neither a more intense nor a richer moral significance than Gwendolen Harleth; but very much the reverse...James' lack of specificity favours an evasiveness, and the evasiveness, if at all closely questioned, yields inconsistency of a kind that partly empties the theme of *The Portrait of a Lady* of moral substance.[8]

Leavis qualifies his criticism of the novel – 'partly empties' – yet even so this surely takes away more than can be conceded if Leavis is to put forward *The Portrait of a Lady* as a major novel. His fuller discussion of the novel in his essay on James is convincing enough, so here we have an instance where Leavis states the case both for and against a novel.

This problem arises in a more acute form in Leavis's discussion of *Nostromo*, for while offering it as a great work he seems to have trouble in convincing even himself that it is one. On Leavis's criteria a great novel is an affirmative one, and, as he himself grants, *Nostromo* seems to affirm very little. Leavis is hard pressed in *The Great Tradition* to explain what else might constitute the greatness of this novel:

A negative point had better be made by way of stressing the distinctive nature of the impressiveness of *Nostromo*. The impressiveness is not a matter of any profundity of search into human experience, or any explorative subtlety in the analysis of human behavior. It is a matter rather of the firm and vivid concreteness with which the representative attitudes and motives are realized, and the rich economy of the pattern that plays them off against one another.[9]

Concreteness, realization, and pattern are Leavis's central 'literary' criteria in his writings on the novel, yet the presence of these qualities alone in a novel are not enough to make it a great work. The value of what is realized and organized surely depends on the depth and quality of human experience presented, and a novel which does not display 'any profundity of search into human experience' cannot, it seems to me, be considered great. One would assume that this is Leavis's normal position as well, and in fact the severity of his concluding judgment seems to take away the grounds of his praise: 'At any rate, for all the rich variety of the interest and the tightness of the pattern, the reverberation of *Nostromo* has something hollow about it.'[10]

Leavis's claims for what he judges to be the other two great novels of James and Conrad – *The Bostonians* and *The Secret Agent* – raise the more central problem in his evaluative criticism. I do not think that either of these novels deserves to be valued as highly as Leavis does, so it is particularly here, where I disagree, that I need to be convinced by Leavis that his judgment has a real basis; and in both instances he seems to me singularly unsuccessful in stating the reasons for his evaluation. In his discussion of *The Bostonians* Leavis spends a great deal of time exalting James over Dickens and insisting on the subtlety and maturity of James's art, but he leaves us very much in the position of having to take the passages he quotes as proof of the novel's greatness, and I do not find this enough. He concludes:

> *The Bostonians* is a wonderfully rich, intelligent and brilliant book. I said that it is an acknowledged masterpiece, but I don't in fact think that it has anything like the reputation it deserves. It could have been written only by James, and it has an overt richness of life such as is not commonly associated with him. It is incomparably witty and completely serious, and it makes the imputed

classical status of all but a few of the admired works of
Victorian fiction look silly. It is one of James's major
classics, and among the works that he devoted to
American life it is supreme.[11]

I think that the import of this judgment, to offer *The Bostonians* as
a great novel, is mistaken, but my main point is that it is unearned.
Actually that's not quite a fair way of putting it, for Leavis does
give some reasons for his praise of the book, such as the critical
attitude it reveals towards American civilization, in contrast to
James's exaltation of America in other works, but this is not an
adequate reason for thinking it a great novel. The ability to 'place'
American civilization is not equivalent to the radical critique of
society we get in Dickens' *Little Dorrit* or Lawrence's *Women in Love*.

Again it is in making his claims for Conrad that the problem
arises in its acutest form, for I find Leavis's argument about *The
Secret Agent* unconvincing. I strongly disagree with his position that
The Secret Agent is superior to *Lord Jim*, and he does far too little
to demonstrate the supposed superiority. (Besides being more
complex, *Lord Jim*, it seems to me, has a much richer moral
interest.) Leavis praises the moral pattern of *The Secret Agent*, as well
as the maturity of attitude and the consumateness of the art in
which this finds expression, but apart from this what he offers is
not much more than summary, quotation, and rhetoric: 'There
follows one of the most astonishing triumphs of genius in fiction,
the final scene between Verloc and his wife.'[12] This discussion of
The Secret Agent is probably the weakest section in *The Great
Tradition*; of the ten pages Leavis devotes to this novel at least half
are quotations, and for all that is said about the ability to quote
aptly, this is not enough. Leavis has not established that the
qualities he admires inhere in the art of *The Secret Agent*.

If Leavis at times fails to be convincing about novels which he
praises, there are also instances where he fails to give satisfactory
reasons for his dismissal of novels and novelists. For example, he
tells us that *Lord Jim* does not deserve the position of pre-eminence
among Conrad's works often assigned to it and that it is hardly one
of the most considerable. That, by itself, is too vague to be of much
use; Leavis more specifically claims that the second half of the book
– Jim's experience in Patusan – has no inevitability and is decidedly
thin. Yet, even if we grant this, especially when we consider Leavis's
frequent praise for parts of novels, particularly *Daniel Deronda*, this

is not cogent enough to discredit the view that *Lord Jim* is a great novel.

To turn to the question of Leavis's dismissal of a novelist, his response to Hardy must be judged to be totally inadequate. He writes:

> On Hardy (who owes enormously to George Eliot) the appropriately sympathetic note is struck by Henry James: 'The good little Thomas Hardy has scored a great success with *Tess of the d'Urbervilles*, which is chock-full of faults and falsity, and yet has a singular charm.'[13]

This tells us nothing about Leavis's reasons for disliking Hardy; perhaps the only thing it tells us is that Leavis (and James) are inept critics of Hardy. It is not satisfactory to say that we can deduce or surmise Leavis's reasons for rejecting Hardy from the criteria in the rest of his criticism – that, say, Hardy handles language poorly in places, or that he has a pessimistic vision of life; the fact remains that Leavis has not made any 'case' against Hardy. The point that Leavis's response to Hardy is a failure in criticism can be made more clearly by contrasting it with the negative assessment he gives of Virginia Woolf. He contrasts her with Conrad:

> The contrast brings out how little of human experience – how little of life – comes within Mrs Woolf's scope.
>
> The envelope enclosing her dramatized sensibilities may be 'semi-transparent'; but it seems to shut out all the ranges of experience accompanying those kinds of preoccupation, volitional and moral, with an external world which are not felt primarily as preoccupation with one's consciousness of it. The preoccupation with intimating 'significance' in fine shades of consciousness, together with the unremitting play of visual imagery, the 'beautiful' writing, and the lack of moral interest and interest in action, gives the effect of something clearly akin to a sophisticated aestheticism.[14]

Here we have not only the jugment, but very precisely stated the grounds of the judgment; we may disagree with Leavis, but we cannot complain that he has not stated his case. But nothing of what he objects to in Woolf applies to Hardy – who does write with a serious moral intent, and who has an interest in human action and a range of human experience. Hardy may not belong in the great tradition, but Leavis has failed to explain his reasons for excluding him.

I recognize that, possibly unfairly, I am asking a great deal of Leavis since the judgment on Hardy comes in the first chapter of *The Great Tradition*, which offers a sweeping survey of the history of English fiction – surely the most challenging assessment of the English novel we have – and that the comprehensiveness of Leavis's purpose doesn't allow him time for much detail. Yet the precise judgment on Virginia Woolf is set forth in a very short review, which indicates that it is at least possible to state the grounds of a judgment in a limited space. The same issue arises when considering what I take to be Leavis's failure to make a full case for the greatness of James and Conrad in *The Great Tradition* – it is obviously exceptionally difficult in a survey. The grounds on which he praises them are clarified in his later essays on James's *The Europeans* and *What Maisie Knew* and Conrad's *The Secret Sharer* and *The Shadow-Line*. We come away from these essays with no doubts about why Leavis considers James and Conrad major novelists; this perhaps indicates that evaluative criticism is easier to write when it is focused on individual works. But even here a problem occasionally arises, for if Leavis fails to make his case in certain instances, there are other instances where he makes it too well. That is, his discussion of certain novels – *Hard Times*, *Pudd'nhead Wilson* – makes them sound more successful than they are. J. M. Newton makes this point in his review of *Anna Karenina And Other Essays*: 'A result of reading one or two of Professor Leavis's most compelling pieces on novels which he admires is some disappointment when we read or reread the novels. . . his essay on a novel, on *Hard Times* or. . . on *The Europeans* or on *What Maisie Knew*, is more gripping than the novel itself.'[15] That is, in one way, admirable praise for Leavis's own power as a critic, but it suggests a certain failure or deflection in his critical judgment.

Leavis's failure to provide the reasons that would support his evaluations is most obvious in his frequent use of rhetoric. While Leavis insists that an evaluation cannot be 'proven' or demonstrated, that one can only offer reasons for a judgment in the spirit of 'This is so, is it not?', and hope for agreement, there are places in his criticism where he depends mainly on rhetoric to convince us. In fact, at times, it appears that at just those places where he lacks valid reasons to support his judgment that his use of rhetoric becomes excessive.

His reliance on rhetoric is notably more pronounced in *D. H. Lawrence: Novelist* than it is in *The Great Tradition*, and, in the Lawrence book, more pronounced in the discussion of the tales than of the novels. He is, of course, openly making a case for the tales – in contrast with his argument about the lesser novels – trying to win agreement with his high assessment of them. Much of his argument is based on quotation and demonstration, pointing to qualities which he values and which he contends are part of Lawrence's work. But Leavis gives the stories lavish praise, and the way in which he does this is part of the rhetoric of his argument. We should try to keep in mind one of the particular problems Leavis faced. Modern literature has not on the whole been a literature of affirmation, and the positive values that are presented are often qualified by an ironic point of view; consequently, modern critics tend to emphasize simply the questioning or exploration of values in the work. Lawrence is something of an exception since the qualities he values are presented fairly straight-forwardly. The problem for the critic here becomes one of deciding whether the values or attitudes are sentimental or real. To win our assent with his view of Lawrence's values, Leavis must frequently attempt to convince us that the presentation is not marred by sentimentality. In discussing *The Daughters of the Vicar*, for instance, he asserts that Louisa's love for Alfred is presented with 'a total truth that leaves no possibility of the sentimental' and that the contrast between the bright cottage and the gloomy vicarage 'has nothing sentimental about it'. Leavis's repeated denial of sentimentality is part of the necessary rhetoric of criticism dealing with affirmative literature; it is not something he can prove, but he can state his position and hope to gain our assent.

Nonetheless a difficulty arises from Leavis's habit of arguing that something which is not sentimental is 'real'. The word 'real' has an importance in Leavis's criticism second only to the word 'life', but his use of this term at times is anything but helpful. In his discussion of *The Daughters of the Vicar* he remarks:

> 'Reality' and 'life' have both taken on a further defining charge when we say to ourselves at this point that the class-superiority for which Mary has renounced life is indeed unreal. It is an unreality that at the same time makes us recognize its sinister power: in its presence Alfred denies the reality in himself, assuming an unreal

inferiority. And we may note here that real superiority, the reality of life to which Louisa has just paid, mutely, her tribute, is seen... as associated with certain working-class conditions... There is no sentimentalizing of the miner's life.[16]

'Real', 'unreal', 'reality', and 'unreality' – this almost reads like a parody. This is the worst example of this kind of excessive repetition of a key word that occurs in the Lawrence book, but it indicates a propensity on Leavis's part to use rhetoric, a constant repetition and insistence, as a substitute for precise definition and explanation.

The central problem involved with much of Leavis's rhetoric can be illustrated easily. He makes very high claims for the story *Mother and Daughter*:

> The distinction of *Mother and Daughter* is that it exhibits its particular mode so perfectly; it keeps to its given limits and achieves perfection with them. Its range, of course, is less than that of *St. Mawr*, but not so much less as may appear at first sight, and the advantage it gains is the unquestionable, the immediately convincing, perfection.[17]

Leavis attempts practically to overwhelm us by repeating 'perfectly', 'perfection', 'convincing perfection', and by telling us that the advantage is 'unquestionable'. Of the opening scene of *The Captain's Doll* he writes:

> Once again we are made to reflect, with a fresh wonder, that never was there a greater master of what is widely supposed to be the novelist's distinctive gift: the power to register, to evoke, life and manners with convincing vividness... To say that he exercises it incomparably over the whole social range doesn't suggest the full marvel. The women in the opening... are there, in their intimate encounter, authentic and real beyond question done – established and defined in our sense of them – by an economy of art that looks like casualness.[18]

Leavis doesn't allow for the possibility of disagreement here, it is 'beyond question' – an assertion he frequently makes, and the entire description is heavily overloaded with rhetorical terms. He tries to convince us that what 'looks like casualness' is in fact fully

achieved art, a claim he is forced to make several times in the
Lawrence study. There is the simple *insistence* that the women are
'authentic and real'; moreover, Leavis insists that the women 'are
there' and he frequently relies on this italicized adverb to carry the
weight of his judgment. A term like 'convincing vividness' is a
legitimate part of evaluative criticism, but phrases like 'fresh
wonder', 'incomparably', and 'full marvel' are mainly exclama-
tions of feeling offered instead of a demonstration. Leavis wants to
praise Lawrence and I am not trying to deny him that right, but
these rhetorical terms are an inadequate substitute for the detailed,
reasoned judgment we should expect.

In addition, Leavis's use of rhetoric often undercuts any critical
discussion. Much of his analysis of *The Virgin and the Gypsy* is a kind
of descriptive rhetoric and provides a good example of this. He
asserts that 'the genius must be apparent to any reader in the ease
and economy with which the rectory household is established'.[19]
He describes the tale as a reverent study of young life and as such
'it seems to me unsurpassable, and it has certainly never been
surpassed'.[20] Some of Leavis's rhetorical devices are unobjection-
able, asking for agreement, but others, like the ones I have just
cited, are designed to compel our agreement – 'one must' – and
tend to close off any possibility of disagreement. This kind of
rhetoric is inimical to the process of collaborative judgment as
Leavis himself defines it.

All of the difficulties that I have been examining can perhaps
be summed up by considering one final problem. Leavis's original
dismissal or exclusion of Dickens from the great tradition had been
taken to reveal the limitations of his evaluations of the novel, but
Leavis's reassessment of Dickens removes that objection. However,
this reassessment directly raises an important question about
Leavis's criticism – and about evaluative criticism generally. It is
not simply that Leavis changed his mind about Dickens that causes
the problem, but that, on the whole, the change has been so great.
In the first chapter of *The Great Tradition* Leavis remarks: 'That
Dickens was a great genius and is permanently among the classics
is certain',[21] but Leavis immediately proceeds to dismiss him from
consideration as a serious writer: 'But the genius was that of a
great entertainer, and he had for the most part no profounder
responsibility as a creative artist than this description suggests.' In
his recent book on Dickens Leavis insists that Dickens represents
supremely the profound responsibility of the creative artist. Leavis

definitely has the right to change his mind, but a change of this magnitude certainly demands a fuller explanation than Leavis ever offers; moreover, the change calls into question the manner of argument he typically uses. Leavis frequently disparages one writer while he praises another; in *The Great Tradition* it is Dickens who suffers in this way. Describing *Victory* Leavis refers to 'that aspect of Conrad's art which makes us think of Dickens – a Dickens qualified by a quite un-Dickensian maturity'.[22] And even of D. H. Lawrence's *The Lost Girl* Leavis argues: 'The ironic humour, and the presentation in general, in the first part of that book bear a clear relation to the Dickensian, but are incomparably more mature, and belong to a total serious significance.'[23] The limitations of this form of criticism can best be seen by examining Leavis's treatment of James and Dickens.

In *The Great Tradition* Leavis argues that Dickens's *Martin Chuzzlewit* influenced James, but it appears that Leavis points to this relation almost as much to deprecate Dickens as to praise James. It is worth looking at these comments in detail. Leavis remarks of a passage in *Roderick Hudson*:

> The influence of Dickens is plain here. It is the Dickens, not, as in *The Princess Casamassima*, of *Little Dorrit*, but of *Martin Chuzzlewit*. This passage of *Roderick Hudson*, of course, couldn't possibly have been written by Dickens: something has been done to give the Dickensian manner a much more formidable intellectual edge. We feel a finer and fuller consciousness behind the ironic humor, which engages mature standards and interests such as Dickens was innocent of.[24]

Leavis finds further evidence of the same influence in *The Bostonians*, in James's 'placing' of American civilization, and continues his praise of James at Dicken's expense: 'What we have now, though, is pure James. And, as we find it in the description of Miss Birdseye, the un-Dickensian subtlety – the penetrating analysis and implicit reference to mature standards and interests – is pretty effectually dissociating.'[25] He contends that James's rendering of American civilization gives us *Martin Chuzzlewit* redone by an 'enormously more intelligent and better educated mind' and that the presentation of the American newspaperman in the novel 'is rendered with a force so much surpassing Dickens's (we remember the theme in *Martin Chuzzlewit*) because of the so much greater subtlety of

James's art'.[26] There is even more of this kind of denigration of Dickens, but this is enough to indicate how completely Leavis, in 1948, considered James the greater writer. (Leavis, it is true, is referring only to *Martin Chuzzlewit*, but he conveys the sense that subtlety, maturity, and an intellectual edge are generally lacking in Dickens's work.)

Now for a total contrast to Leavis's stance in *The Great Tradition* we can turn to his later remarks in *Dickens the Novelist*. Here again he points to an instance of Dickens' influence on James, that of *David Copperfield* on *What Maisie Knew*, a novel of James's that Leavis admires greatly. However his purpose here is reversed: 'I challenge the Jamesian critical attitude towards Dickens...James's assured critical bent is that of the decidedly less great artist. – My concern is not to depreciate James, but to vindicate the genius of Dickens.'[27] Later in the same essay Leavis gives us a fuller statement of his grounds for now preferring Dickens over James:

> There are in fact the strongest reasons for calling the art of the great Dickens Shakespearian. This is the emphasis one might very well resort to if called on to justify the observation that Dickens is not only a different kind of genius from James, but a genius of a greater kind. The creative life in him flows more freely and fully from deep sources – the depth, the freedom and fullness being the conditions of the Shakespearian suppleness.[28]

It is particularly this kind of reversal of judgment – James up, Dickens down, then Dickens up and James down – that leads certain critics to see similarities between evaluative criticism and the stock market, and, subsequently, to argue that the function of criticism is not evaluation. But, for all the problems raised here, I don't think they should lead us to the conclusion that evaluative criticism is fruitless and pointless. For one thing, Leavis's later judgment that Dickens is a greater novelist than James gets a good deal of collaborative support. Leavis's ability to change his mind here, and to recognize an error of judgment, can be considered a strength. What is surely called into question, though, is Leavis's habit of continually dismissing other writers while he advances the claims of those he admires. The problems raised here would be much less pressing if, in *The Great Tradition*, he had simply praised James and not found it necessary to disparage Dickens; as it is Leavis's reversal of judgment has invalidated much of the argument of that book, for Dickens is used as a whipping boy not only for James but also for Conrad. We must now consider most of the references to Dickens in *The Great Tradition* to be of historical value; they are not living criticism.

The presence, in Leavis's criticism, of the problems I have analysed does not *radically* undercut his achievement as a critic of fiction – I have after all emphasized the weaknesses rather than the strengths of his work. Nonetheless, the existence of these difficulties necessarily qualifies his final accomplishment as a novel critic. The deflection of Leavis's judgment in the instances where he slights questions of unity and responds mainly to the historical or moral import of the novel is troubling, for he grants the highest praise to works whose status as fully achieved art is quite problematical. But at least in the cases where we disagree with Leavis about the validity of the grounds of his evaluation – for example in his praise of *Adam Bede* for its historical value – critical discourse is still possible since the basis for his judgment is stated. Evaluative criticism can only be open to profitable discussion if a judgment is advanced with the reasons that support it, and at times – most glaringly in his rejection of Hardy – Leavis fails to back his judgment with a cogent argument. Where Leavis has, in the main, merely asserted his approval or disapproval, or tried to win our assent by a reliance on rhetoric, we are left with no grounds upon which to reply. At that point the possibility of 'the common pursuit of true judgment' is ended, and we are left only with the squabbling voices of conflicting opinions.

ii. Criteria

In the greater part of his criticism Leavis *does* offer 'reasons' to support his judgments; that is, normally he invokes certain criteria upon which his judgments are based. The exact nature and status of these criteria, however, is often difficult to determine. Many of the qualities Leavis values in a literary work are intimately connected to personal qualities he admires in the artist's character; consequently, many of his criteria involve judgments about the artist, as well as about the work. Moreover, Leavis's criteria seem to pass imperceptibly from being 'literary' to being more directly 'moral', and it is not always clear which term is more appropriate. Nor is it altogether obvious in what sense Leavis's criteria *are* 'moral'. By examining closely his use of two of his central criteria

– impersonality and maturity – we can get a better understanding of the general nature of Leavis's criteria and of the kinds of values implicit in his critical judgments.

(a) The Artist and Impersonality

Leavis's view of impersonality depends on a very definite conception of the artist and involves an equally definite conception of the relation between the artist's life and his work. Leavis thinks of the artist, whether poet or novelist, as an exceptional man – a man of exceptional capacity for experience. This view of the artist is first announced in *New Bearings in English Poetry*:

> Poetry matters because of the kind of poet who is more alive than other people, more alive in his own age. He is, as it were, at the most conscious point of the race in his time. ('He is the point at which the growth of the mind shows itself,' says Mr. I. A. Richards.) The potentialities of human experience in any age are realized only by a tiny minority, and the important poet is important because he belongs to this (and has also, of course, the power of communication). Indeed, his capacity for experiencing and his power of communicating are indistinguishable; not merely because we should not know of the one without the other, but because his power of making words express what he feels is indistinguishable from his awareness of what he feels. He is unusually sensitive, unusually aware, more sincere and more himself than the ordinary man can be. He knows what he feels and knows what he is interested in. He is a poet because his interest in his experience is not separable from his interest in words; because, that is, of his habit of seeking by the evocative use of words to sharpen his awareness of his ways of feeling, so making these communicable.[29]

The poet is an exceptional man, but he is an artist because he also has an exceptional power of communication; this is a position of great interest for it does not reduce the poetry to the poet's experience – rather his capacity for experiencing and for handling words are both essential. By emphasizing both the poet's experience and the dependence of his expression of it on his use of language, Leavis gives us a view of the artist that avoids the difficulty Murray Krieger finds in the views of T. S. Eliot and I. A. Richards:

> [Richards'] similarity to Eliot should be clear – Richards'
> poet does not need the poem in order to realize his
> experience – the organization of his impulses – any more
> than Eliot's poet, as defined in 'Hamlet and His
> Problems', needs it in order to realize his emotions. The
> experience of the one and the emotions of the other are
> completely formed and understood before they are
> embodied. The poets achieve their status primarily by
> their respective abilities to experience deeply or to feel
> deeply rather than to write well.[30]

In Leavis's description on the other hand the poet achieves his status by his ability to feel deeply *and* to write well, and the experience of the poem does not fully exist prior to the act of communication. This is a subtle view of the poet as a certain kind of man, and yet distinctly an artist.

It is not entirely clear that Leavis maintains this balance in his thinking about novelists. In describing the kind of novelist who is part of the great tradition Leavis emphasizes solely the nature of their response to life:

> It is in the same way true of the other great English
> novelists that their interest in their art gives them the
> opposite of an affinity with Pater and George Moore; it is,
> brought to an intense focus, an unusually developed
> interest in life. For, far from having anything of Flaubert's
> disgust or disdain or boredom, they are all distinguished
> by a vital capacity for experience, a kind of reverent
> openness before life, and a marked moral intensity.[31]

The difference of this from the description of the poet is obvious: the novelists are being praised for their capacity to respond to life and not also on their power of handling language to communicate that response. Nonetheless, whether writing about the poet or the novelist, Leavis offers us a view of the artist as an exceptional man.

The artist's achievement in his work is closely allied to his capacity for experience, but in the successful work of art the limitations of the purely personal are transcended by achieving impersonality. This impersonality, however, does not involve any clearly distinct separation between art and life, for the work derives from and remains deeply rooted in personal experience. Leavis's understanding of the artist and impersonality, then, obviously differs considerably from the more famous view of impersonality but forth by T. S. Eliot. Eliot, of course, in his doctrine of impersonality, does insist on a complete separation between the man and his work. And so deep was Eliot's influence on Leavis, that it took him some time before he gave his view of impersonality a distinct formulation.

At the very beginning of his career Leavis already held an exalted view of the artist, but he had not yet arrived at his own conception of impersonality. In *New Bearings in English Poetry*, in discussing Eliot's poem 'The Hollow Men', Leavis remarks that 'if we should be tempted to relate too crudely the 'mind that created'' with "the man who suffered" we have the various drafts to remind us that it is after all a poem we are dealing with'.[32] Surprisingly this lends support to Eliot's theory and at least acknowledges that a poem is a fictional embodiment and presents, or creates, a persona which cannot be identified with the man behind the poem; but Leavis generally minimizes this aspect of a poem. (I am not implying that Leavis believes that the speaker in a poem, or a character in a novel, is the author, but that there can be no artistic persona who does not reveal the author in some way. The difficulty, of course, lies in trying to determine to what extent Prufrock, for instance, reveals Eliot's attitudes, or Crazy Jane, Yeats's.) Even as late as *The Great Tradition* Leavis again, surprisingly, quotes Eliot's statement on impersonality with approval. Leavis writes of George Eliot's *Felix Holt*:

> The beneficent relation between artist and intellectual is to be seen in the new impersonality of the Transome theme. The theme is realized with an intensity certainly not inferior to that of the most poignant autobiographical places in George Eliot, but the directly personal vibration – the directly personal engagement of the novelist – that we feel in Maggie Tulliver's intensities even at their most valid is absent here. 'The more perfect the artist, the more completely separate in him will be the man who suffers and the mind which creates': it is in the part of *Felix Holt* dealing with Mrs Transome that George Eliot becomes one of the great creative artists.[33]

Given Leavis's view of the artist, and given the view of the relation between the artist's life and work *implicit* in many of his remarks, in *The Great Tradition*, on impersonality, it is extremely puzzling to find him, as late as 1948, referring favourably to Eliot's dictum. But either he had not yet realized his theoretical difference from Eliot, or he simply had not extricated himself from Eliot's influence. In any case, in writing *D. H. Lawrence: Novelist*, Leavis did come to have a sharper sense of his difference from Eliot, and after that book repeatedly attacked Eliot's conception of impersonality.

The essay 'T. S. Eliot As Critic' (1958) provides us with the clearest statement of Leavis's objections to Eliot's theory, and of his own view of the relation between the artist's life and work. In the essay Leavis attacks what he calls the 'falsity and gratuitousness' of Eliot's view, and dismisses as a 'wholly arbitrary dictum' the view that the mind of the poet ' "may partly or exclusively operate upon the experience of the man himself; but the more perfect the artist, the more completely separate in him will be the man who suffers and the mind which creates" '.[34] Eliot offers a view of the creative process, or imagination, working essentially in a vacuum and Leavis objects that

> nothing is done to supply the absent something answering to the verb 'create'...by the reference...to the 'intensity of the artistic process, the pressure, so to speak, under which the fusion takes place', for Eliot does nothing to explain or suggest what the process is, or where the pressure could come from...As if there were not something else, more important, to be said about the relation of the ode to the life, the living from which it derived the creative impulsion; derived something without full recognition of which there can be no intelligent appreciation of the 'artistic process' or the art.[35]

Leavis's position is now unequivocal; there can be no separation of the artist from the man, for the creativity of the art derives from and is dependent upon the pressure of personal experience. In rejecting Eliot's doctrine of the impersonality of art Leavis states:

> It is not then a coherent conception of art that is figured in Eliot's 'artist'. It *is*, however, a familiar ethos or case. 'The more perfect the artist, the more completely separate in him will be the man who suffers and the mind which creates': the perfection of this artist is something different from what we admire in *Anna Karenina*. No one with Tolstoy in mind as the type of the great creative writer

could have advanced that proposition: 'separate', for such
a use is not a possible word, whether one thinks of Tolstoy
or Lawrence...or Shakespeare – or George Eliot or Mark
Twain. But when we recognize that the artist implicitly
proposed is Flaubert, then the proposition becomes
intelligible, if not acceptable.[36]

In contrast to Eliot, Leavis insists that 'in contemplating the work
of one of the great creative powers we don't find ourselves impelled
to think of the pressure of the artistic process as something apart
from the pressure of the living – the living life and the lived
experience – out of which the work has issued; for that the work
has so issued,...we don't question'.

Leavis, of course, thinks of art as creativity, but he insists that
the greatest kind of creative writing is dependent on an intense
engagement with life. He explains Tolstoy's superiority over James
on just these grounds – that Tolstoy's work exemplifies a relation
between art and life that is characteristic of the highest kind of
creativity, a higher kind than James's. In contrast to James's
interest in a separable 'composition' and 'architecture' in art,
Leavis contends:

> The relation of art to life in Tolstoy is such as to preclude
> this kind of narrowly provident economy. It is an
> immensely fuller and profounder involvement *in* life on the
> part of the artist, whose concern for significance in his art
> is the intense and focused expression of the questing after
> significance that characterizes him in his daily living. This,
> of course, amounts to saying that Tolstoy is a different
> kind of man from James – he is the kind of man the
> greatest kind of artist necessarily is.[37]

Among modern critics, perhaps only Leavis would state this
position so baldly.

This view of art and the artist provides Leavis with an explanation
both of the source of the power of a work of art and of the reason
why it fails. There is, however, an obvious difficulty with Leavis's
position. If Eliot's theory of impersonality maximizes the distance
between the life of the artist and his work, Leavis's view minimizes
it; in fact, at times Leavis simply seems to eliminate the distance
and to suggest that the life in the work is a counterpart to the life
of the man. And this does not seem to allow for any imaginative

or creative process in the sense that the work represents something new or that something new is infused into the work. One of the clearest examples of the problem involved here can be seen in Leavis's remarks on James in *The Great Tradition*. He claims that *The Bostonians* has an 'overt richness of life' not commonly associated with James. This use of 'life' doesn't necessarily imply that it is derived from the author, though it suggests that, but in contemplating James's limitations Leavis comments on James's concern for 'the finer essence':

> So peculiar an intensity of concern for consciousness might perhaps be seen as in itself an index of some correlated deficiency – an index of something, from the beginning, not quite sound, whole and thriving within and below. True, *The Bostonians*, with the poised wisdom of its comedy, and its richness of substance, derived from the experience and observation of childhood and youth, doesn't encourage such reflections. But even of *The Portrait of a Lady* it might perhaps be suggested that its effect of rich vitality isn't quite simply an expression of rich and free first-hand living.[38]

This fairly well equates James's achievement in art with his personal achievement in life. Particularly in the works of the later James Leavis finds signs of a lack of first-hand living, and he offers a remarkable analysis of the style of the late novels as an index of the life in James himself:

> The trouble with the late style is that it exacts so intensely and inveterately analytic an attention that no sufficient bodied response builds up: nothing sufficiently approaching the deferred concrete immediacy that has been earned is attainable. Of Henry James himself we feel that the style involves for him, registers as prevailing *in* him, a kind of attention that doesn't favour his realizing his theme, in the whole or locally, as full-bodied life.[39]

'Concreteness', it appears, is a direct manifestation of the richness of life of the author. With his view of the direct relation between the work and the life, Leavis moves quite naturally, in his critical analysis, from the art to an explanation in terms of James's life. The failure of the late novels, he contends, is to be explained largely by the fact that James did not live enough.

Repeatedly when explaining a *failed* work, Leavis makes the

move from work to life, explaining the failure by relating it to some
deficiency – lack of vitality, for example – in the author's life. In
explaining a failed or limited achievement, that is, Leavis's criticism
often operates in a border-land between the realm of strictly
literary criticism – as most modern critics would define it, that is,
focused only on the work – and a controlled kind of biographical-
psychological speculation about the nature of the author's life. In
his later work he came to argue more directly that any achievement
in literature depends upon the accomplishment of a wholeness in
life. In his lecture on Yeats he explains why, in his eyes, Yeats
achieved so limited a success: 'Why this should be so isn't hard to
understand. "Sailing to Byzantium" doesn't come out of any
wholeness of being or mastery of experience; its poetic or quasi-
musical satisfyingness as a totality is not an index of any permanent
stability achieved by the poet in life.'[40] Obviously Leavis does not
deem it possible that the imagination can transcend – and in so
doing create a wholeness – any personal failure to achieve self-
realization. Most notably Leavis's attacks on Eliot have emphasized
Eliot's limitations as a man: 'I have been moving towards the overt
judgment: Eliot's poetry hasn't a rich human experience behind it.
It reveals, rather, a restriction; it comes, indeed, out of a decided
poverty.'[41] This is very similar to the analysis of James's 'case', but
Leavis further argues: 'That the creative Eliot could not draw any
wholeness of being, or free flow of life, has consequences for
criticism, and the "social" poverty of the spirit – the unheroism (it
led him to call Lawrence a snob) – was a manifestation of the
disunity, the disability, the inner disorder that characterized
him.'[42] This kind of diagnosis of the man behind the poem lies
outside the bounds most modern criticism has established for its
rightful territory, but it seems to follow logically from Leavis's view
of the inseparability of the man and the artist. Leavis's procedure
here is, in a way, that of a literary critic for he always *begins* with
the novel or poem and analyses what he considers to be the
weaknesses (or strengths) there, and strictly speaking that's where
his job as a critic ends; but Leavis has no reluctance in then
explaining that a personal failure in life lies behind the artistic
failure. Even if this is a legitimate supposition, certainly when the
procedure gets to the point where Leavis is spending more time
venting his dislike of Eliot the man, rather than explaining, by an
analysis of the poetry, his response to the work, there is a deflection
of critical interest.

In his best criticism Leavis does focus his attention on the work, for, while he insists that a great work of art must have a 'rich human experience behind it', he further contends that, to some degree, a successful work *is* differentiated from the writer's life – by being impersonalized. The personal experience out of which the work comes is objectified, and the resulting impersonality is evident as a quality of the work itself. And when evaluating a poem or a novel one of the first things Leavis tries to determine is whether or not the work has this necessary impersonality.

In *New Bearings in English Poetry* impersonality was not yet one of Leavis's major criteria; only Pound's *Mauberly* and Eliot's *Gerontion* and *The Waste Land* are praised, and only in passing, for their impersonality. It plays a greater role in *Revaluation*, in Leavis's discussion of the Romantics; quite likely he was deliberately attempting to counter the association of 'Romantic' with personality and self-expression. In comparing Shelley and Wordsworth he emphasizes that Wordsworth's superiority is evident in the impersonality of his poetry:

> The self-projecting and ardently altruistic Shelley is, in the comparison, the narrowly limited and the egoist (which term, it may be added, applies with less injustice to Milton than to Wordsworth). Wordsworth, it is true, has no dramatic gift, and compared with Shakespeare's, the range of interests he exhibits is narrow. But he exhibits also in his poetry, as an essential characteristic, an impersonality unknown to Shelley.[43]

The contrast of egoism ('egoist') and impersonality is significant; Leavis frequently makes this opposition and it suggests that impersonality carries a moral connotation. In fact Leavis himself makes the connection explicit, for he immediately goes on to comment about impersonality: 'This characteristic (consider the capacity and the habit it implies) is closely associated with the social-moral centrality insisted on above.'

Keats's poetry is also praised in *Revaluation* for its impersonality, and here Leavis elaborates on his use of the term. He writes of *Hyperion*:

> The immediately personal urgency of the preoccupation with suffering and death comes out plainly in the passage describing his nightmare race against the burning of 'gummed leaves' (11. 106–34). But this personal urgency is completely impersonalized; it has become the life, the

informing spirit of the profoundest kind of impersonality. There is no element of self-pity – nothing at all of the obliquely self-regarding – about the attitude...There is no afflatus, no generous emotionality. The facts, the objects of contemplation, absorb the poet's attention completely: he had none left for his feelings as such. As a result, his response, his attitude, seems to us to inhere in the facts, and to have itself the authenticity of fact...His own acute and inescapable distresses...he can, without feeling them the less, contemplate at the same time from (as it were) the outside, as objects, as facts.[44]

The first two sentences unfortunately are not very helpful, though they make it clear that impersonality derives from a personal urgency; it is the remainder of the quotation that is of primary interest. Keats's attitude is not 'self-regarding' and he is not simply immersed in his feelings, but understands them and so transcends the merely personal; it is this objectivity that Leavis calls 'impersonality'.

By the time of writing *The Great Tradition*, impersonality had become one of Leavis's central criteria for distinguishing fully achieved art. He now values this quality so highly that he bases almost his entire claim for George Eliot's *Felix Holt* on its impersonality. A remark Leavis makes about George Eliot further illuminates his concept of impersonality: 'No life would have been possible for her that was not filled with emotion: her sensibility is directed outward, and she responds from deep within. At this level, emotion is a disinterested response defined by its object, and hardly distinguishable from the play of intelligence and self-knowledge that give it impersonality.'[45] That is, an emotion that is not self-regarding, or egotistical, but is 'defined by its object' – focused on something outside of the self – is impersonal. Moreover, an emotion is 'impersonalized' when it is understood by intelligence; or rather an impersonal response is one that includes emotion, intelligence and self-knowledge.

Leavis considers certain parts of George Eliot's work too personal – that is, too emotional – and in *The Great Tradition* asserts that Conrad is more completely an artist than she is because his work is impersonal:

He transmutes more completely into the created work the interests he brings in...he achieved a wholeness in art... not characteristic of George Eliot. But it must not be

concluded that the point about her is that her novels
contain unabsorbed intellectual elements...The relevant
characteristic, rather, is apt to strike the reader as
something quite other than toughness or dryness; we note
it as an emotional quality, something that strikes us as the
direct (and sometimes embarrassing) presence of the
author's own personal need. Conrad, we know, had been
in his time hard pressed; the evidence is everywhere in his
work, but, in any one of the great novels, it comes to us
out of the complex impersonalized whole...At her best
she has the impersonality of genius.[46]

This emotional quality of art, the sign that art is being used to
answer to the artist's personal need, much like a day-dream, is
always condemned by Leavis. In fact what Leavis condemns is very
much what Freud – who thinks that there is a similarity between
art and a day-dream – considers art to be. Impersonal art is not
an escape from reality but involves a disinterested grasp of reality.

Fully achieved impersonal art is disengaged from the writer;
what the novelist has created cannot be treated as a psychological
document. Leavis, in his essay on *Little Dorrit*, totally rejects
Edmund Wilson's interpretation of the novel as 'evidence' of the
personal trauma Dickens suffered as a child, and he insists that the
personal experience has been transmuted – understood and
impersonalized. The essay provides one of Leavis's central
statements on impersonality in art:

We can no doubt see some direct drawing on personal
history; but Dickens himself, intimately presented as
Clennam is, wasn't at all like Clennam. Clennam's past
has left him discouraged in vital spontaneity. The creative
force of life in him has no confident authority; he, we can
say with point, is *not* an artist. But in that set inquest into
Victorian civilization which *Little Dorrit* enacts for us he is
a focal agent – focal in respect of the implicit judgments
and valuations and the criteria they represent. We have
here, representatively manifest, the impersonalizing process
of Dickens's art: the way in which he has transmuted his
personal experience into something that is not personal,
but felt by us as reality and truth presented, for what with
intrinsic authority they are, by impersonal intelligence. His
essential social criticism doesn't affect us as urged

personally by the writer. It has the disinterestedness of
spontaneous life, undetermined, and undirected and
uncontrolled by idea, will and self-insistent ego, the
disinterestedness here being that which brings a perceived
significance to full realization and completeness in art. The
writer's labour has been to present something that speaks
for itself.

That Dickens's finest work has the impersonality of
great art is something I have to insist on.[47]

The phrase 'impersonal intelligence' makes it appear that Leavis
thinks of emotion as personal, and intelligence as impersonal; he
also comes close to equating impersonal and disinterestedness here.
Certainly impersonality and disinterestedness (with its Arnoldian
echo) are clearly opposed to the 'will and self-insistent ego'.

Leavis's view of impersonality involves a definite conception of
the creative process that produces it. In his introduction to *Daniel
Deronda* he explains:

Constantius offers to credit her with an impersonal
wholeness of creative impulse and conception that is
certainly lacking here. She expanded herself on the 'Jewish
question' because (partly, at least) of a personal emotional
need working in ways of which she is not sufficiently
aware, and in this the whole Deronda function is
involved..., she is not...engaged in her wholeness – not
engaged as an artist must be in order to create.[48]

Impersonality, that is, results from the creativity of the whole being
or whole psyche; in recent years Leavis came to use 'wholeness'
much as a synonym for impersonality. The artist does not create
with any special faculty – the imagination or fancy – but from the
depths of the whole psyche. Leavis comments further on this aspect
of the novel: 'One might be inclined to call the prepotence, more
or less subtle, in the Deronda part, of the element of nobly feminine
self-indulgence, the price paid, the self-compensation, for the
sustained impersonality and maturity of the rest.'[49] Self-indulgence
and self-compensation are clearly opposed to impersonality, but
'maturity' is a quality Leavis values highly and it seems closely
associated with impersonality.

(b) Maturity

Leavis repeatedly uses 'maturity' as a criterion in *The Great Tradition* (and throughout his criticism, though not to any degree in the book on Lawrence); James's art is praised for its subtlety and maturity, Conrad's *The Secret Agent* is commended for being 'truly classical in its maturity of attitude', but it is particularly in his writings on George Eliot that Leavis uses it as the main criterion. His whole revaluation of George Eliot is conducted largely by attempting to differentiate the mature and immature parts of her work. It is in *The Mill On The Floss* that he finds the greatest evidence of George Eliot's 'immaturity' – in effect, a lack of or abeyance of intelligence:

> But of course the most striking quality of *The Mill on the Floss* is that which goes with the strong autobiographical element. It strikes us as an emotional tone. We feel an urgency, a resonance, a personal vibration, adverting us of the poignantly immediate presence of the author...But the case is so: the emotional quality represents something, a need or hunger in George Eliot, that shows itself to be insidious company for her intelligence – apt to supplant it and take command.[50]

It's not entirely clear whether Leavis thinks of this emotional quality as immaturity or as a lack of impersonality (or both); he criticizes George Eliot for offering the soulful side of Maggie with an absence of criticism:

> That part of Maggie's make-up is done convincingly enough; it is done from the inside. One's criticism is that it is done too purely from the inside. Maggie's emotional and spiritual stresses, her exaltations and renunciations, exhibit, naturally, all the marks of immaturity; they involve confusions and immature valuations; they belong to a stage of development at which the capacity to make some essential distinctions has not yet been arrived at – at which the poised impersonality that is one of the conditions of being able to make them can't be achieved.[51]

Again we have a suggestion that maturity and impersonality are associated in Leavis's mind, although here maturity, or at least the ability to make 'mature valuations', depends on a 'poised impersonality'. Leavis then argues:

There is nothing against George Eliot's presenting this immaturity with tender sympathy; but we ask, and ought to ask, of a great novelist something more. 'Sympathy and understanding' is the common formula of praise, but understanding, in any strict sense, is just what she doesn't show. To understand immaturity would be to 'place' it, with however suble an implication, by relating it to mature experience.

Maturity, that is, involves understanding. This idea that the novelist must 'place' or judge characters and experience is easily related to Leavis's view of the moral pattern in a novel. (It is also similar to Yvor Winters' view that in a good poem the poet not only expresses an emotion, but provides an evaluation of it.) Leavis continues his criticism of the presentation of Maggie: 'In George Eliot's presentment of Maggie there is an element of self-idealization. The criticism sharpens itself when we say that with the self-idealization there goes an element of self-pity. George Eliot's attitude to her own immaturity is the reverse of a mature one.' This last sentence is rather irritatingly unhelpful (another of Leavis's tautological sentences), but we begin to see some of the attributes of immaturity – self-idealization, self-pity. And Leavis's objection to the ending of the novel indicates that immaturity includes a lack of self-knowledge. Leavis apparently considers a purely emotional response an immature one; maturity includes the play of intelligence that involves self-understanding. And his remark that 'Maggie Tulliver, in fact, represents an immaturity that George Eliot never leaves safely behind her', makes it evident that he really is talking about personal qualities of George Eliot herself, and not about the actions or 'ethic' of the novel.

The discrimination of most of the remainder of George Eliot's work is made on the grounds of maturity. He writes of the Transome theme in *Felix Holt*:

> If we ask how this art is so astonishingly finer and maturer than anything George Eliot had done before, the answer is in terms of a perception that is so much more clear and profound because the perceiving focuses the profound experience of years – experience worked over by reflective thought, and so made capable of focusing. What we perceive depends on what we bring to the perceiving; and George Eliot brought a magnificent intelligence,

> functioning here as mature understanding. Intelligence in
> her was not always worsted by emotional needs; the relation
> between the artist and the intellectual in her...was not
> always a matter of her intellect being enlisted in the
> service of her immaturity.[52]

Maturity involves control of the emotions by the intelligence, or,
at least, a proper balance of emotion and intellect. To be mature
is, in effect, to be intelligent. Leavis immediately goes on to argue:
'The beneficent relation between artist and intellectual is to be seen
in the new impersonality of the Transome theme.' Here – and this
seems Leavis's more characteristic position – the impersonality of
the *art* is dependent on the maturity of the artist.

Leavis discusses *Middlemarch* as a kind of battleground of the
maturity and immaturity in George Eliot – although he also uses
the term 'poise', a key term of praise, as equivalent to maturity.
He argues that Dorothea is 'a product of George Eliot's own
"soul-hunger" – another day-dream ideal self', and contends that
there is self-indulgence in the presentation of Dorothea's relations
with Lydgate; this failure of touch betrays a radical disorder:
'Offered as it is in a context of George Eliot's maturest art, it not
only matters more; it forces us to recognize how intimately her
weakness attends upon her strength...It is certainly her strength
as a novelist to have a noble and ardent nature – it is a condition
of that maturity which makes her so much a greater artist than
Flaubert.'[53] Again there is the suggestion of a kind of psychological
analysis of George Eliot herself – 'a radical disorder'; the immaturity or self-indulgence in the novel is traced directly back to
her. Finally, the weak part of *Daniel Deronda* is condemned for
its immaturity; and here Leavis points out that the most fervid
wordiness goes with the emotionality. There are obviously some
clear associations: maturity equals intelligence and self-
knowledge, immaturity equals emotionality, self-idealization and
self-indulgence.

At least two questions need to be raised about Leavis's procedure
and his criterion. First, how useful are terms like maturity and
immaturity? Secondly, what is the exact nature of this term?
Bernard Bergonzi, in an essay entitled 'Literary Criticism and
Humanist Morality' objects to literary criticism which becomes

> a kind of McCarthyite witch-hunt for traces of emotional
> inadequacy in a poet or novelist. 'Maturity', a carefully

achieved and difficult emotional poise, is the one saving
virtue; it is the critic's job to seek out its concrete
embodiment in works of literature; this is likely to be rare
enough, and most of the time the critic will be discovering
and condemning such vices as 'immaturity', 'insincerity',
'lack of emotional control', 'self-indulgence' and so on.
The equation of emotional failure, literary flaw and moral
flaw is constantly made. Now this seems to me a limited
way of talking about literature...critics move without
hesitation from passing judgement on the poem to passing
judgement on the poet...nothing is more wearisome than
being in a perpetual state of vigil for the ogre of
Immaturity.[54]

Although Leavis is not named here it seems likely that Bergonzi
is referring to him, and I think there is some justice in the irritation
he shows. In his revaluation of George Eliot Leavis does seem
somewhat over-zealous in detecting signs of immaturity in her
work. Instead of, say, making any distinctions between George
Eliot's presentation of Maggie and Dorothea they are both treated
as equal examples of immaturity. Moreover, at times Leavis's
explanations of this term fail to clarify its meaning: 'Maggie's
emotional and spiritual stresses, her exaltations and renunciations,
exhibit, naturally all the marks of immaturity; they involve
confusions and immature valuations.' Rather than being helpful,
this is simply tautological.

Leavis's use of maturity as a positive criterion can also be of
limited value. In his discussion of Conrad's *The Secret Agent* he insists
on the maturity of the novel and quotes passages to illustrate it,
leaving us to 'see' the maturity. I can, perhaps, best state my
objection to this method by introducing a contrasting work of
fiction. David Lindsay's novel (it's actually a romance) *A Voyage
To Arcturus* seems to me an impressive, although flawed work. It
is not the kind of fiction that Leavis ever showed any interest in,
for it does not offer us a criticism of civilization, and the controlling
interests of the novel are not primarily social and moral, but
metaphysical. If I wanted to win recognition for the book I would
praise not its maturity or complexity, but rather its 'imaginative'
and 'visionary' power. Having done this I could select passages of
the book which illustrate, to me, this visionary power, and, much
as Leavis has done, copy them out, repeating that they are

'visionary'. My criterion of 'visionary' might simply be rejected, but even if it were accepted, in order to make anyone *see* this quality I would have to develop my argument in some detail. Simply quoting passages that are supposed to represent 'maturity' or 'visionary power', and pointing to them, is insufficient.*

Perhaps the main question that needs to be asked about 'maturity' as a criterion is about the kind of term it is: can it be labelled distinctly as a moral or as an aesthetic term? However, this is part of a broader question about the nature and implication of many of Leavis's critical terms, so before attempting to answer this question I want to examine briefly one of the other major criteria Leavis uses to praise George Eliot's work: specificity. Leavis prefers *Daniel Deronda* to *The Portrait of A Lady* on the grounds of the greater specificity of Eliot's novel:

> It isn't that George Eliot shows any animus towards Gwendolen; simply, as a very intelligent woman she is able. . . to achieve a much *completer* presentment of her subject than James of his. This strength which manifests itself in sum as completeness affects us as a greater specificity, an advantage which, when considered, turns out to be also an advantage over James in consistency. And, as a matter of fact, a notable specificity marks the strength of her mature art in general.[55]

This passage suggests that Leavis finds a relation between maturity and specificity; maturity is associated with specificity, or perhaps, complexity. In fact we find Murray Krieger using 'mature' in just this way in explaining the criteria of the modern poetry critics he is discussing (Brooks, Empson, Tate, Winters, among others):

---

* The critical attitudes involved in using visionary and maturity as criteria obviously differ considerably; in fact, visionary can almost be seen as the antithesis of maturity – it suggests pure desire and freedom of the imagination, whereas maturity emphasizes desire in *relation* to actuality. In *Revaluation*, in referring to Keats, Leavis makes this very point about maturity involving a grasp of the 'real': 'Keats. . . in his marvellous development, offers some fine illustrations for a discussion of maturity – maturity manifested in technique, of feeling in relation to thought, of imagination and desire in relation to actuality' (*Revaluation*, p. 14). Shelley, like George Eliot in her moments of immaturity, suffers from both an abeyance of thought and a lack of grasp on actuality. These two distinguishing features of maturity are clearly intimately related.

Hence arises the demand from these critics that poetry be 'mature', that it see all round any experience and not cheat our life of its complexity, our world of its body. So completely have these critics absorbed what they could use of Richards that we find Brooks putting forth this demand in the words of Richards by calling for a 'poetry of inclusion' rather than a 'poetry of exclusion.'[56]

It appears that Leavis also adopted these terms from Richards and transferred them to his criticism of the novel. In explaining the superiority of George Eliot's art to James's, Leavis offers a further description of specificity – it is essentially inclusiveness:

The kind of complexity and completeness, the fullness of vision and response, represented by her Mr Gascoigne characterizes her rendering in general of the world to which he belongs. Henry James's presentment of what is essentially the same world is seen, in the comparison, to have entailed much excluding and simplifying. His is a subtle art, and he has his irony; but the irony doesn't mean inclusiveness – an adequacy to the complexities of the real in its concrete fullness; it doesn't mark a complex valuing process that has for upshot a total attitude in which all the elements of a full response are brought together...he can...be so limited and selective, and what is an essential condition of his selectiveness, so lacking in specificity compared with George Eliot. His world of 'best society' and country-house is, for all its life and charm, immeasurably less real (the word has a plain enough force here, and will bear pondering) than George Eliot's. He idealizes and his idealizing is a matter of not seeing and not knowing (or not taking into account) a great deal of the reality.[57]

Specificity involves inclusiveness – 'an adequacy to the complexities of the real in its concrete fullness'. In fact Leavis will use any of these terms – specificity, complexity, concreteness – to praise literature he admires; since they indicate a grasp of the 'real' he occasionally simply uses 'real' as his criterion.

(c) *The Nature of Leavis's Criteria*
We now have impersonality, maturity, and specificity, and I want to consider briefly the relation and status they have along with

Leavis's other key terms such as concreteness, realization, and, of course, life. I have described these terms as Leavis's 'criteria', but this is perhaps misleading. In his dispute with Wellek Leavis had insisted that standards could not be defined abstractly, and that literature was not, in effect, judged by any abstract criteria. What then are we to make of these terms of Leavis's? Are they not, despite his reply to Wellek, the premises of his criticism? John Casey's response to the problem indicates the rather perplexing status of Leavis's terms or criteria:

> It is easy to see how the groupings are developing; intelligence, self-knowledge, maturity, reality stand together against immaturity, self-dramatization, sentimentality, day-dream, self-indulgence. It is obvious that there is a large set of terms in Leavis's criticism which are closely interrelated, and sometimes even equated. We quickly see what the paradigmatic terms are...Leavis's 'key' terms are so thickly interrelated that it is at any rate misleading to talk about his 'premises' – as though 'life', 'maturity', etc. existed in isolation and *a priori*, to be accepted or rejected entirely in their own right. On the other hand there *is* a sense...in which they can be described as premises.[58]

It is in deciding in just what limited sense that they can be described as premises that the difficulty arises. Frank Kermode's response to this problem is rather different from Casey's. Kermode argues that 'they derive their force from repeated use, not from any merit of their own as critical terms. That is why Wellek asked Leavis what he was doing'.[59] Despite a negative tone in his remark, Kermode is not dismissing the terms, but observing that they are defined – derive their force – in use, and this is the crucial point for understanding them.

We can get a general understanding of Leavis's use of terms by considering his explanation, in his essay on Literary Studies in *Education And The University*, of the status of the term 'realization'. He criticizes Arnold's sonnet *To Shakespeare* as being a poem offered by an unrealizing mind, handling words from the outside. He then provides an explanation of his use of this term:

> But it will not do to say simply that in good poetry the metaphors are realized. In fact, there are hardly any rules that can, with any profit, be laid down: the best critical

terms and concepts one can find or provide oneself with will
be inadequate to the varied complexities with which the
critic has to deal. Take, for instance, the idea of
'realization' that was introduced with 'realized' and
'unrealized' – terms that will be used again for they are
indispensable. Any suggestion that these terms introduce a
simple or easily applied criterion may be countered with
the following passage.[60]

And Leavis quotes a passage from *Macbeth* which reveals various
degrees of realization. What Leavis says here about 'realization'
applies to all of his critical terms – they cannot be given abstract
definition, and we come to understand them by examining Leavis's
varied and flexible use of them. To fully comprehend the term
'realization', for example, it is necessary to look at different
instances where it is used; and this is true of his other terms, such
as maturity and specificity as well.

Without expecting abstract definitions, we can still ask questions
about the nature of these terms. What kind of qualities are
specificity and maturity – that is, can they be described as moral
qualities? I have attempted to convince a colleague that Leavis is
not simply or openly a moral critic by pointing to his discussion of
Daniel Deronda and the praise for specificity there, as well as to his
discussion of Conrad's *Heart of Darkness* where he attempts to
discriminate the successful art, a matter of concreteness and specific
particularities, from the unsuccessful, the vague and unrealized.
The reply I received was that specificity and concreteness were in
fact moral terms, and this seems to be John Killham's view of the
matter: 'Generally speaking his remarks tend to emphasize the
dependence of concreteness on a quality of moral seriousness.'[61] Yet
if specificity and concreteness are to be thought of as 'moral'
qualities, we must at least realize that 'moral' is being used in an
unusual way.

A similar problem arises if we try to think of maturity as a 'moral'
quality. Northrop Frye, in the course of raising his objections to
evaluative criticism, remarks: 'It is not hard to see prejudice in
Arnold, because his views have dated: it is a little harder when
"high seriousness' becomes "maturity", or some other powerful
persuader of more recent critical rhetoric.'[62] It is difficult to see
what 'prejudices' or moral assumptions are involved with praising
maturity in literature and condemning immaturity. The back cover

of my copy of *The Great Tradition* states: 'The criticism of F. R. Leavis has always been notable for his uncompromising association of literature and morality'; however, the notion of morality or of the moral involved in Leavis's criticism is unusual in some ways. In examining *The Mill on the Floss* Leavis writes about the maturity and immaturity in the novel. It seems to me that a critic concerned about morality (a vitalist, say) might object to the ethos of the novel, to the advocacy of renunciation and duty at the cost of passion and 'life'. (I am not saying that this is the ethos of the book; but it is a possible interpretation.) What the moral critic would be objecting to are values enacted by the characters; but this is not what Leavis does anywhere in his discussion of George Eliot – an author noted for her moral preoccupation.

It is rather difficult to define, or even focus, the moral nature of Leavis's criticism – a problem which has been noted by some of the critics who have written about his work. Vincent Buckley observes: 'In fact, while one is inclined to remember his influence as of a directly ethical kind, one is seldom conscious, in actually reading him, of any separable ethical stress at all.'[63] That is, in his criticism Leavis does not generally discuss what we normally think of as the ethical issues in the novels, nor does he make obviously moral evaluations. John Casey has gone into this matter in some detail and his conclusions are of great interest. Casey quotes Leavis's remarks on Jane Austen in *The Great Tradition*, then he comments:

> It is important to notice what Leavis does *not* say. He does not say that Jane Austen arrives at the right moral *conclusions* about life...Nor does he suggest that the moral code which emerges in Jane Austen's novels is one which, if we admire her as a writer, we should in some sense be prepared to adopt, or at least to approve. Indeed the question arises whether the word 'moral' is being used with anything like the force it traditionally has...The moral significance of her work, then, lies in its dealing seriously, or intensely, or maturely with experience. The opposite of this would be triviality, or sentimentality, or self-deception.[64]

As a description of what Leavis generally does, this seems accurate enough. Casey's point is that Leavis assesses morality in terms of the emotional qualities it displays, and he raises a question about the limitations of this kind of judgment: 'But the assessment of the quality of emotional or mental states is not the whole of morality. We do, after all, also judge a man's actions, and we often judge them in terms of their consequences.'[65] In fact it is this latter kind of judgment which we characteristically think of as a moral judgment. The relation between literature and morality we usually make is that literature provides an enactment of moral behaviour, and by so doing provides us with the material for moral judgment – such as evaluating Maggie's actions. Leavis is not primarily concerned with this kind of judgment, and so, Casey concludes:

> We are left with a certain paradox. Both Arnold and Leavis insist that the criticism of literature is inescapably moral, but they both see moral judgment as essentially the diagnosis of emotions, motives, character – an area where it is most like aesthetic judgment. The conclusion is, surely, unavoidable that their notion of the moral, in its extreme formalism, is fundamentally aesthetic.[66]

This is a rather startling conclusion, and for all the useful contrast it offers to the view of Leavis as a moralist or didact, surely Casey has gone awry. Leavis, of course, rejects the notion of any aesthetic realm, separated from the moral and would hardly have agreed that his notion of the moral represents an 'extreme formalism'. It seems to me that by 'moral' Leavis often means 'fully human'. We can see how his use of 'maturity', for example, accords with this use of 'moral': maturity includes understanding, self-knowledge and a full use of intelligence – in other words, a full realization of one's nature. To be immature is to fail to be fully human. This may not necessarily be the way we use the word 'moral' in ordinary discourse, but it is hardly an 'aesthetic' usage; in fact, it strikes me – and Casey grants this – as a very central use of 'moral'.

The advantage Leavis gains by using a term like 'maturity' should be obvious. It is a criterion that raises moral issues – very widely defined – without committing Leavis to a specific, or narrow, set of values. Writers of quite different points of view could earn Leavis's praise by showing a mature – serious – concern with life. Moreover, while in a wide sense the term 'mature' undeniably is moral, it never becomes *simply* a moral term in Leavis's hands; since it is used to speak of the success of literary representations, in itself it has a literary dimension – or at least it is used inseparably as part of Leavis's 'literary' judgment.

In fact, one needs to avoid making a sharp either/or distinction with Leavis's terms – avoid seeing them as simply literary or simply moral. Perhaps the best way to think of his various criteria is in terms of a spectrum, with some having a predominantly literary connotation, and others having a more directly moral implication. 'Realization', with its emphasis on the quality of achieved art, seems to me closest to the literary end of the scale, while concreteness, impersonality, and maturity seem to move us progressively closer to the moral end.

(d) Literary and Moral Judgment

At the furthest end of this spectrum we do, in fact, find Leavis making judgments that reflect an interest in morality in the ordinary, narrower, sense. As Michael Tanner, in his review of John Casey's book, remarks: 'The narrower moral view, that to be judged favorably a work must not only manifest a serious concern with moral values, but issue, in however subtle a manner, in attitudes which we ourselves can endorse – [is] a view which sometimes seems to be held by Leavis, though Casey ignores the fact.'[67] What Tanner calls the 'narrower moral view' I want to refer to simply as moral judgment, and to contrast it with the kind of judgment Leavis normally makes, which I will describe as a literary judgment – keeping in mind that I do not mean by this a merely 'literary' judgment divorced from moral concerns, but that this kind of judgment is not *simply* moral. By examining this contrast we will be able both to define more sharply the kind of judgment Leavis normally makes, and, to bring out more explicitly the moral basis of his criticism.

Fortunately we can see Leavis making both kinds of judgments in the same place – in his assessment of the late novels of Henry James. Leavis is critical of all three novels of James's 'major phase', but on different grounds. He argues that *The Wings of the Dove* is not a successful work and that the great, the disabling failure is the presentation of the Dove, Milly Theale: 'A vivid, particularly realized Milly might for him stand in the midst of his indirections, but what for his reader these skirt around is too much like emptiness; she isn't there, and the fuss the other characters make about her as the "Dove" has the effect of an irritating sentimentality.'[68] This kind of judgment seems to me clearly that of a literary critic – it is not an overt moral judgment. Leavis's focus is on the quality of the art; that is, he claims Milly is not realized, not successfully imaginatively created. The judgment of sentimentality is more difficult to label; it is an assessment of the emotional quality of the novel and is comparable to finding immaturity in a novel. It is a judgment of emotional quality, and is not 'moral' in the narrow sense. Leavis's negative evaluation of *The Ambassadors* is similar in nature to that he makes about *The Wings of the Dove*:

> *The Ambassadors* too, which he seems to have thought his greatest success, produces an effect of disproportionate 'doing' – of a technique the subtleties and elaborations of which are not sufficiently controlled by a feeling for value and significance in living. What, we ask, is this symbolized by Paris, that Strether feels himself to have missed in his own life?...Is it anything adequately realized?[69]

Again it is the failure to realize the imputed values that Leavis objects to, and not the nature of the values in themselves.

Leavis's evaluation of *The Golden Bowl* is based on different grounds and his rejection of that novel is openly and avowedly moral; it is in fact one of the few examples in Leavis's criticism where he rejects a work for presenting moral values that he finds unacceptable. In discussing *The Wings of the Dove* he had remarked that James's art 'has a moral fineness so far beyond the perception of his critics that they can accuse him of the opposite. This fineness, this clairvoyant moral intelligence, is the informing spirit of that technique by the indirections and inexplicitness of which these critics are baffled.'[70] It is quite disconcerting after reading this praise of James's moral perception to find Leavis, in discussing *The Golden Bowl*, also accusing him of the opposite. Leavis argues that in this novel, 'James clearly counts on our taking towards his main persons attitudes that we cannot take without forgetting our finer moral sense – our finer discriminative feeling for life and personality.'[71] Leavis contends that James sympathizes with Maggie and Adam, but that our sympathies are with Charlotte and the Prince, who 'represent life'; in other words, the valuations Leavis makes about the characters are contrary to James. Leavis dismisses the supposed ambiguity of the novel and finds only moral confusion. What we have to keep in mind is that Leavis is not objecting to the quality of the novel – that it is unrealized or sentimental – in fact, he seems to consider it successful at that level. Leavis's criticism is that James's interest in technique has clouded his moral judgment, that in the technical elaboration he has lost his 'full sense of life' and let his 'moral taste' slip into abeyance.

Leavis gives a fuller statement of his objection to this novel in a slightly later essay written in response to Quentin Anderson's argument about James's intentions in the late novels. Leavis answered:

> What we are not reconciled to by any awareness of intentions is the outraging of our moral sense by the handling of the adultery theme – the triangle, or rather quadrilateral, of personal relations. We remain convinced that when an author, whatever symbolism he intends, presents a drama of men and women, he is committed to dealing in terms of men and women, and mustn't ask us to acquiesce in valuations that contradict our profoundest ethical sensibility. If, of course, he can work a revolutionary change in that sensibility, well and good, but who will contend that James's art in those late novels has that power? In *The Golden Bowl* we continue to find our moral sense outraged.
>
> Actually we can see that James doesn't realize what violent accommodations he is demanding of us, for his own sense of life is in abeyance.[72].

This is a straight-forward moral objection to the novel, and resembles the kind of objection critics often make to some of Lawrence's work – to *The Fox*, for example, or Eliseo Vivas to *Aaron's Rod*. Leavis is not judging this novel to be immature but immoral.

If this provides the most obvious example of Leavis condemning a novel on moral grounds, I think his evaluation of *Hard Times* provides an instance where he praises a novel more for its ethic or ethos than for its art. Utilitarianism, or Benthamism, is as abhorrent to Leavis as it is to Dickens, and this is a case where Leavis acclaims a novel which supports his own moral vision. Leavis practically makes this point when he later contrasts *Hard Times* with *Little Dorrit*: 'In *Hard Times*, with its comparative simplicity as a damning critique of the hard ethos and the life-oppressing civilization, the identity of the affirmatives, or evoked and related manifestations of life and health and human normality, by which he condemns, with those of Blake is clear.'[73] Leavis wholly approves of the ethos of the novel – the confutation of utilitarianism by life – and my impression is that his praise of the novel as a whole is a rationalization of that moral approval. It is, significantly, the only place where we find Leavis pointing to a passage and saying approvingly: 'Here is the formal moral.'

Leavis's discussion of George Eliot is almost entirely free of the kind of moralistic judgment we find in his appraisals of *The Golden Bowl* and *Hard Times* – he is concerned with the impersonality, maturity and specificity of her art – but his concluding remark does almost read like that of a Victorian moralist:

> She exhibits a traditional moral sensibility expressing itself, not within a frame of 'old articles of faith'...but nevertheless with perfect sureness, in judgments that involve confident positive standards and yet affect us as simply the report of luminous intelligence...For us in these days, it seems to me, she is a peculiarly fortifying and wholesome author, and a suggestive one: she might well be pondered by those who tend to prescribe simple recourses.[74]

Again, though, it is interesting to note what Leavis does not say: she, and her novels, are 'wholesome' not because of the ethical code, but due to the nature of her 'moral sensibility'; here, however, the addition of 'traditional' implies a particular kind of moral sensibility. Leavis makes what is a much more straightforward commitment to the moral values of George Eliot's novels in the opening chapter of *The Great Tradition*. He quotes Lord David Cecil's description of George Eliot: 'She believed in right and wrong, and man's paramount obligation to follow right, as strictly as if she were Bunyan himself. And her standards of right and wrong were the Puritan standards. She admired truthfulness and chastity and industry and self-restraint, she disapproved of loose living and recklessness and deceit and self-indulgence.'[75] Leavis then comments:

> I had better confess that I differ (apparently) from Lord David Cecil in sharing these beliefs, admirations, and disapprovals, so that the reader knows my bias at once. And they seem to me favourable to the production of great literature. I will add (exposing myself completely) that the enlightenment or aestheticism or sophistication that feels an amused superiority to them, leads, in my view, to triviality and boredom, and that out of triviality comes evil.

This statement is unusually explicit for Leavis, and the qualities he disapproves of here – 'loose living and recklessness', 'deceit and self-indulgence' – are more obviously what we usually think of as moral (or immoral) qualities than is immaturity. The fact remains that his criticism focuses on the latter kind of quality, and this makes the view of him as a moralist somewhat more problematical.

One final problem needs to be considered here: Leavis's continual use of the term 'moral sense' or 'ethical sensibility'. It might be interesting to relate Leavis to the line of English moral-sense philosophers, but the obvious difficulty with Leavis's position, or with any moral-sense view, is that raised by Bernard Bergonzi. Bergonzi remarks on Leavis's essay on James in *The Common Pursuit*:

> What is significant is that he claims James's treatment of adultery contradicts 'our profoundest ethical sensibility' (the first meaning that the *Concise Oxford Dictionary* gives for 'sensibility' is 'capacity to feel'), but nevertheless concedes that a great novelist *could* work 'a revolutionary change in that sensibility', so that after reading him we could presumably feel that adultery was not, after all, wrong; indeed, one of Dr. Leavis's objections to the late James is that he lacks the power to bring about such a change. This is to make a very large claim indeed for the ethical potentialities of literature, though it follows inevitably from the assumption that morality is a question of the feelings and the sensibility, not of the reason, and that literature has a unique power of modifying the sensibility. As a Catholic, I find this position unacceptable. One does, of course, admit the existence of a moral sensibility; the feelings can play quite an important part in our making of moral decisions, but it is necessarily a subordinate part, and they cannot determine for us the fundamental issues of right and wrong...
>
> It is in this context that Lawrence's claim 'the essential function of art is moral' must be understood. Art teaches us how to live by refining our sensibilities, improving our emotional poise, purifying the springs of morality within us.[76]

This last point is of particular interest. Leavis evaluates with his own moral sensibility the moral sensibility – the maturity, serious-ness, reverence – of the novelist; it is in a sense the 'springs of

morality' he is concerned with. When one thinks how characteristically Leavis evaluates the attitudes expressed in novels, we can
see his assumption that our attitudes determine our moral actions.
(I. A. Richards calls attitudes 'incipient actions'.)

The objections that Bergonzi makes to Leavis's position, however, seem mistaken in a number of ways. First, Leavis's use of
'sensibility' is not identical with that of the *Concise Oxford Dictionary*
and it is misleading of Bergonzi to offer the dictionary definition;
as I've explained in chapter four, Leavis makes no clear separation
between sensibility and intelligence. Secondly, it follows that the
'assumption' that morality is a question only of the feelings and
not reason is Bergonzi's, not Leavis's. Bergonzi implies that the final
arbiter of our moral choices is primarily reason, not ethical
sensibility, and Leavis, in his essay 'James As Critic', gives an
explanation of the actual nature of moral choice that provides a
fitting reply:

> A great work of art explores and evokes the grounds and
> sanctions of our most important choices, valuations and
> decisions – those decisions which are not acts of will, but
> are so important that they seem to make themselves rather
> than to be made by us. The tone (or timbre) of this kind
> of formulation is not, indeed, characteristic of James: for
> criticism and statements of the grounds of criticism, in
> which...the word moral has 'religious' in close
> attendance, the student will go to Lawrence.[77]

Leavis seems to me to give a very accurate description of the nature
of such choices and valuations, and it is not one of 'reason' (Leavis's
position is fully in accord with Lawrence's). This does not mean
that reason is excluded from such choices, but that it plays only a
part in a decision reached by the whole being. This quotation has
the added advantage of drawing our attention to the fact that we
do not get to the centre of Leavis's work by just asking what he
means by 'moral' or how he uses the term 'moral sense'; there is
a more important aspect of life to Leavis than the 'moral' and that
is the 'religious'. We can only fully understand what qualities
Leavis desires in life and literature, what he means by 'religious',
by examining his writings on D. H. Lawrence.

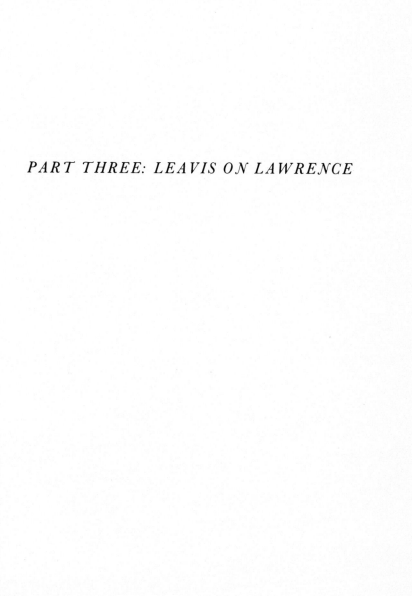

PART THREE: LEAVIS ON LAWRENCE

8

Leavis's Early Writings On Lawrence

F. R. Leavis's interest in D. H. Lawrence is at the centre of his literary criticism. Leavis wrote on Lawrence from the very beginning of his career as a critic: in 1930, the same year that he published his pamphlet on *Mass Civilization and Minority Culture*, he wrote another pamphlet, entitled simply *D. H. Lawrence*. It was clear even then that Leavis found in Lawrence the positive response to life, the concern for spiritual values that were necessary if cultural health was to be restored to modern civilization. After that first pamphlet Leavis dealt with Lawrence mainly in reviews until twenty years later when he began writing, in *Scrutiny*, the series of essays which he later published in 1955 as *D. H. Lawrence: Novelist*. Leavis's response to Lawrence develops from the early pamphlet of 1930 up to 1949, the year before his essay on *St. Mawr;* it shows a growing commitment to what Lawrence represents. But even in those early years Leavis recognized and especially praised the religious aspect of Lawrence's work; before discussing the development in Leavis's response to Lawrence, the nature of this early religious concern needs to be examined.

i. The Early Religious Concern

Leavis's literary criticism is generally considered to centre on a concern with moral values, or a moral sense, but the fact of the matter is that his *ultimate* concern is with the place of a religious sense in life and literature. Leavis 'defines' the nature of the religious sense that he regards as necessary to civilization primarily in his writings on Lawrence, whom Leavis sees as the pre-eminent

writer of our time largely *because* he expresses a religious response
to life. In supporting Lawrence, Leavis asserts his own view that
life has significance at a religious depth.

The term 'religious' first appears in Leavis's writings in 1932 in
a note on Lawrence, in *Scrutiny*, entitled 'Reminiscences of D. H.
Lawrence'. (Curiously Leavis's 1930 pamphlet on Lawrence makes
no use of the word 'religious'). From 1932 to 1934 there are
numerous references in Leavis's reviews and articles to Lawrence
and the religious sense he represents, and in these early essays the
main features of Leavis's religious position are set out. In that 1932
note Leavis praises Lawrence the man:

> Here was a man with the clairvoyance and honesty of
> genius whose whole living was an assertion of what the
> modern world has lost. It is plain from this books that he
> was not able to maintain steady confident possession of
> what he sought – wholeness in spontaneity; a human
> naturalness, inevitable, and more than humanly
> sanctioned; a sense, religious in potency, of life in
> continuity of communication with the deepest springs,
> giving fulfilment in living, 'meaning' and a responsive
> relation with the cosmos. But it is equally plain that he
> didn't merely seek.[1]

The qualities of life – wholeness, spontaneity, naturalness – that
Leavis claims Lawrence sought are very clearly the ones he himself
values most highly, but the key point is that these qualities are
'more than humanly sanctioned' and in touch with 'the deepest
springs'. These will be recurring terms in Leavis's attempt to
elaborate on, and define, his use of the word 'religious'.

With the appearance of Aldous Huxley's edition of *The Letters
of D. H. Lawrence* in 1932 Leavis now perceived a religious concern
embodied in Lawrence's work as well as in his life:

> But those who know his work will admit that his constant
> preoccupation is fairly to be called religious, even if they
> are dubious about his 'God'. What he sought was a
> more-than-human sanction for human life, a sense of the
> life of the universe flowing in from below the personal
> consciousness; he sought, one might say, a human
> naturalness; he aimed at 'planting' man again in the
> universe.[2]

I take it that any notion of the 'religious' involves a 'more-than-human sanction', but at this point it is not at all clear what, for Leavis, constitutes that sanction. However, this passage does expand Leavis's use of the word 'religious'. The idea of 'the life of the universe flowing in from below the personal consciousness' introduces a 'psychological' metaphor of depth that has a central place in Leavis's religious thinking. And Leavis's image of '"planting" man again in the universe' calls to mind his assertion that the plight of Western Civilization is that 'Humanity in its "triumph" over nature, has become uprooted.'[3] While the metaphor of 'uprooting' can be thought of primarily in social terms, referring to the destruction of the organic community, clearly, in Leavis's view, for a fulfilled life man must establish 'roots' in a religious sense.

In trying to understand what Leavis means by 'religious' we face the general problem of his mode of definition. As we have seen, Leavis never gives abstract, theoretical definitions of his criteria – 'moral', 'life' – or, of his critical terms – 'concreteness', 'realization' – but cites examples or passages of literary works that illustrate these qualities. With his use of the word 'religious' we get the same kind of concrete definition – he points to Lawrence and his works. Thus, Leavis argues:

> To talk of the 'religious sense' that he represents may
> sound weak, but it should not to those who read the
> Letters. For many today the essential thing is to meet such
> a sense in the concrete, dominating ('I am a passionately
> religious man'), and unmistakably an expression of health,
> courage and vitality. And we meet it, we find it, in
> Lawrence.[4]

In reviewing the Letters Leavis actually refers for the first time to Lawrence's religious 'sense', and he contrasts it with the attitude implicit in humanitarianism. He insists that Lawrence's religious response is not in any way 'Rousseauistic or romantic' and states: 'It is Lawrence's greatness that he convinces us of his actually believing in something "beyond his fellow men". He alone cannot give us the religion for lack of which the human spirit withers, but the fact that he lived and was so is a highly valuable fact.'[5] Leavis unquestionably emphasizes the limitations of a simply humanitarian or humanist attitude towards life – this is a point that he strongly reiterated throughout his career – and he is particularly

emphatic about it in *Nor Shall My Sword*. He does, it is true, in
Education And The University insist that literary criticism must be
'humanist' rather than religious, but his point there is that
'whatever else may be necessary, there must in any case be, to meet
the present crisis of civilization, a liberal education that doesn't
start with a doctrinal frame, and is not directed at inculcating
one'.[6] We can easily see how Leavis's reference to a religious sense,
rather than to an abstractly formulated religious position, fits in
here. He tends to think of Christianity as being doctrinal, and
obviously regards the fact that no dogma need be attached to a
religious sense as being an advantage.

The issues involved here are stated most clearly in Leavis's
review, in 1934, of T. S. Eliot's book, *After Strange Gods*. Certainly
the great difference in Leavis's and Eliot's concern with religion
is made apparent. Leavis observes:

> Mr Eliot's stress in this book, of course, falls explicitly
> upon the religious needs of the age. And, with conscious
> inadequacy, holding on to what one is sure of, one agrees
> that 'to re-establish a vital connexion between the
> individual and the race' means reviving, in a civilization
> that more and more, at higher and lower levels, fosters the
> chauffeur-mentality, what it may be crude to call the
> religious sense – the sense that spoke in Lawrence when he
> said 'Thank God I am not free, any more than a rooted
> tree is free.'[7]

While Leavis and Eliot are both concerned with the religious needs
of the age, Eliot, of course, attempts to meet them by invoking
Christianity:

> Mr Eliot has no need to talk hesitantly about the 'need for
> a religious sense'; he adheres to a religion, and can point
> to his church and recite its dogmas.
>   Nevertheless, those of us who find no such approach to
> tradition and orthodoxy possible can only cultivate the
> sense of health we have.[8]

Leavis here explicitly separates himself from orthodox Christianity,
and, despite his defence of the positive values of the nonconformist
tradition in English life, he never expressed any views that would
lead one to regard him as committed in any way to Christianity.
And he clearly thought it is better for the critic to remain

uncommitted to any specific doctrine. Eliot, on the other hand, came to argue that 'Literary criticism should be completed by criticism from a definite ethical and theological standpoint.'[9] It is generally agreed that Eliot's best criticism is his early work, and that his decline as a critic dates from the time of *For Lancelot Andrewes*, that is from the time of his conversion. To some degree, certainly in *After Strange Gods*, Eliot came to sacrifice literary criticism to theological or religious requirements. One of the great virtues of Leavis's reference to a religious sense is that it leaves his criticism much more open than the later Eliot can be. Leavis is able to respond fully both to Lawrence who is not a Christian, and to Eliot who is.

By 1934, then, the religious concern was already prominent in Leavis's work and was consistently associated with Lawrence; however, in 1934 Leavis extended his use of the term 'religious' to include Wordsworth's poetry. In *Revaluation*, except for a passing reference to Pope, it is only in connection with Wordsworth that Leavis makes use of the term 'religious', and it is of considerable importance that in considering the presentation of life at the depth or dimension that entails this word, he naturally thinks of Lawrence. In describing Wordsworth's poetry in Book II of *The Prelude* Leavis contends:

> The poetry, uninterrupted in the amended version, is
> complete and satisfactory; it defines convincingly –
> presents in such a way that no further explanation seems
> necessary – the sense of 'belonging' in the universe, of a
> kinship known inwardly through the rising springs of life
> and consciousness and outwardly in an interplay of
> recognition and response... 'Thank God I am not free,
> any more than a rooted tree is free.'[10]

Leavis frequently quotes this remark of Lawrence's as epitomizing the nature of the religious bond. Lawrence's comment is introduced to support what Leavis is saying about Wordsworth, but the description of the poetry also clarifies Leavis's interpretation of Lawrence's remark. What is taken as being 'religious' here is the sense of a bond or communion, of 'belonging' in the universe.

Leavis distinguishes between Wordsworth's supposed philosophy and his poetry, and maintains that Wordsworth had a wisdom to communicate which is embodied in his living work: 'What he had for presentment was a type and a standard of human normality, a way of life; his pre-occupation with sanity and spontaneity working at a level and in a spirit that it seems appropriate to call religious.'[11] In explaining that Wordsworth is more than a poet of Nature, Leavis says more about this religious sense:

> Wordsworth's preoccupation was with the distinctively
> human naturalness, with sanity and spiritual health, and
> his interest in mountains was subsidiary. His mode of
> preoccupation, it is true, was that of a mind intent always
> upon ultimate sanctions, and upon the living connexions
> between man and the extra-human universe; it was, that
> is, in the same sense as Lawrence's was, religious.[12]

This expands the concept of 'religious' to include the preoccupation with 'ultimate sanctions', though it still isn't made clear just what these are. In emphasizing that Wordsworth's primary concern is not with Nature but with man, Leavis compares it with Lawrence's concern with 'the deep levels, the springs, of life, the illimitable mystery that wells up into consciousness.' That is, the religious sense that Leavis finds in Wordsworth and Lawrence involves being in touch with the deepest sources in man, as well as the 'living connexion' with the 'extra-human universe'. There is then both an internal or 'psychological' metaphor and a definite external reference involved in Leavis's early statement of his religious position.

After he completed the Wordsworth essay in 1934, Leavis, with one exception, did not refer again to the religious sense, or use the word 'religious', until 1950 when he began the series of essays that formed *D. H. Lawrence: Novelist* (1955). Since Leavis became known in these years of the late 1930s and 1940s* it is perhaps not surprising that his critical position was generally thought to centre only on the moral values in literature; the religious element in his work was neglected. Yet even these books, and certainly *Revaluation*, if read carefully enough, reveal, or hint at, his religious interest. In *The Great Tradition*, in his essay on the later James, originally written in 1937, Leavis invokes both Lawrence and the term 'religious' as criteria for judging James. He explains what he considers to be the limiting characteristics of James's genius:

---

* In roughly this period *Revaluation* (1936), *Education And The University* (1943), *The Great Tradition* (1948), and *The Common Pursuit* (1952) were published.

It was not the explorer's or the pioneer's, and it had
nothing prophetic about it. It was not of a kind to
manifest itself in lonely plumbings of the psyche or
passionate questionings of the familiar modes of human
experience. It was not, in short, D. H. Lawrence's or
anything like it. James had no such immediate sense of
human solidarity, no such nourishing intuition of the unity
of life, as could make up to him for the deficiencies of
civilized intercourse: life for him must be humane or it
was nothing. There was nowhere in his work that preoccupation with ultimate sanctions which we may call
religious.[13]

In this passage Leavis extends his use of 'religious'. Here it involves
a 'sense of human solidarity' and an 'intuition of the unity of life'.
The first part of this does not seem to be specifically religious –
Conrad, for instance, insists on the importance of solidarity – but
certainly the sense of the 'unity of life' has a religious connotation.
Again, Leavis refers to 'ultimate sanctions' and in fact this seems
as central to his notion of 'religious' as is Lawrence's 'Thank God
I'm not free.' There are several places in Leavis's criticism, for
example his writings on *Aaron's Rod* and *Anna Karenina*, where he
speaks of 'laws of life' – which seems a synonym for sanctions – that
characters have broken at their peril. These laws or sanctions
underlying life are certainly part of what Leavis means by
'religious'.

The distinction Leavis makes between James, whose concerns are
moral, and Lawrence, whose concerns are religious, is similar to
the later distinction he makes between George Eliot and Lawrence.
In *The Great Tradition* the novelists are praised for their moral
intensity, and if one knows Leavis primarily through that book –
and it probably is his most widely-read work – the result is a limited
understanding of his concerns. Moreover, noting Leavis's praise of
George Eliot, James and Conrad in *The Great Tradition*, some critics
have been misled into thinking Leavis holds an essentially humanist,
and even agnostic, position. But his interest in Lawrence shows that
his criticism has a religious basis.

ii. Leavis's Developing Commitment to Lawrence, 1930–49

Despite Leavis's awareness and praise of the religious aspect of Lawrence's life and work, his attitude towards Lawrence in the 1930s was qualified in many ways. In the 1930 pamphlet he criticized Lawrence's treatment of sex, his invocation of the dark God, and his attitude towards mind and intelligence. But as Leavis quickly came to have a better understanding of the religious aspect of Lawrence's work, and as T. S. Eliot spoke out against Lawrence, Leavis consistently defended him and increasingly moved towards a fuller acceptance of his work. This growing commitment to Lawrence, then, provides an index of change; that is, the difference between the early pamphlet and the book is partly that the later Leavis is a vastly improved critic of the novel, but he also revises his understanding of intelligence, and this makes him even more sympathetic to Lawrence.

By the time of writing *D. H. Lawrence: Novelist* Leavis himself admitted that in 1930 he had not been qualified to write about Lawrence. In fact as early as 1933 with the publication of *For Continuity*, which contains the pamphlet, he had already rejected much of it, writing that 'I cannot read some parts of the early set appraisal without wincing'.[14] and he questions the purpose of reprinting rather than re-writing the essay. (For Leavis's fullest statement of his own awareness of the extreme limitations and inadequacies of the early pamphlet, see 'Lawrence After Thirty Years' in *D. H. Lawrence*, ed. H. Coombes.) The pamphlet is, however, of historical interest in being one of the first serious and significant attempts to assess Lawrence's achievement, and it is, of course, an essential document for tracing both the change and the continuity in Leavis's attitude to Lawrence. In some instances, notably in the judgment on the short stories and the tales, Leavis's early and later attitudes remain essentially the same, but his evaluation of individual novels changes almost completely. While the early pamphlet is written to gain recognition for Lawrence's genius, it is highly critical, pointing to limitations and the incompleteness of his wisdom; in contrast the later study is almost wholly laudatory.

Leavis makes very positive claims for Lawrence in the pamphlet, ascribing genius to him, a genius akin to Blake's. Further, in the face of the changes introduced by the machine Leavis maintains that Lawrence 'represents the splendid human vitality, the creative faith, and the passionate sense of responsibility'[15] that mankind desperately needs. These positive claims, however, are qualified in a serious way. Most importantly, Leavis judges Lawrence's wisdom to be inadequate is not giving a proper and full place to intelligence and the finer products of civilization. To accept Lawrence, he argues, we would have to surrender what Jane Austen stands for and the qualities of intelligence and civilization represented by E. M. Forster in *A Passage To India*: 'Against his preoccupation with primitive consciousness and "the old blood-warmth of oneness and togetherness" his concessions to "ideas" and "mind" show as little more than lip-service.'[16] That Lawrence was opposed to mind, ideas and intelligence is perhaps the fundamental criticism made against him. In his later book Leavis revised his judgment on this matter and insisted that Lawrence's genius was inseparable from his penetrating intelligence. Perhaps the main reason for this change is that Leavis comes to understand intelligence more as Lawrence conceives it, as an aspect of the whole psyche, inseparable from a vitality that Forster, say, is deficient in.

In changing his mind about the adequacy of Lawrence's wisdom, Leavis was also to change his evaluation of many of the individual works. In the pamphlet, for instance, he describes *The Rainbow* not only as difficult to get through, but as monotonous, limited in range and failing to communicate its intense concern. On *Women In Love* he is especially harsh, denying that it 'informs and leads into new places'. In 1930 Leavis gives an almost completely negative response to both *The Rainbow* and *Women In Love*, the two novels he later judges to be Lawrence's greatest achievement. Surprisingly Leavis thought *The Lost Girl* to be the 'best *novel*'. It is difficult to account for this preference, but the fact that he italicized the word 'novel' suggests the possibility that at the beginning of his critical career Leavis had a limited, almost formalistic sense of what a novel might be. It is partly, I think, this conception of the novel which led him to give high praise to *Lady Chatterley's Lover* for its concentrated, concrete presentation of pure passionate experience. The change in the later Leavis is apparent in his sharply lowered opinion of these two works. If singling out *The Lost Girl* and *Lady Chatterley's Lover* for praise now seems obtuse, it's only fair to observe that Middleton Murry preferred *Aaron's Rod* to the other novels, Catherine Carswell *The Plumed Serpent* and Anais Nin *Lady Chatterley's Lover*. The failure of Leavis and the others to recognize the achievement of *The Rainbow* and *Women in Love* is clearly an indication of the great originality of these two novels; the later novels lack this kind of profound originality, making it easier to respond to and comprehend them.

It took Leavis many years before he revised his evaluation of the novels, but it was very shortly after writing the pamphlet that his sense of Lawrence's greatness increased and he was cast in the role of Lawrence's strongest defender. The publication of Middleton Murry's *Son of Woman* in 1931 and T. S. Eliot's laudatory review of it caused Leavis to speak out more vigorously on Lawrence's behalf. In his essay 'The Literary Mind' (1932) Leavis explains what he considers to be the correct approach to Lawrence's writings. He insists that it is not as a prophet, but as an artist that Lawrence is important, that his 'thought' is secondary:

> His gift lay, not in thinking, but in experiencing, and in fixing and evoking in words the feelings and perceptions that seemed to him most significant. Lawrence's commentary on experience, his doctrine, must be approached by way of the concrete, the successful art; criticism of the doctrine cannot be separated from judgments concerning literary success or failure.[17]

That is, Lawrence mut be approached by the methods of literary criticism which involve a response of sensibility and intelligence. Leavis accuses Murry of ignoring the discipline of literary criticism; in attempting to extract a doctrine from Lawrence's work he uses his intelligence uninformed by sensibility. This is a central issue in criticism generally, and in Lawrence criticism in particular, and at this early stage Leavis was proposing the kind of approach he was later to apply so successfully. The quotation also reveals clearly a significant difference between the early and later Leavis. Here he makes a distinction between 'thinking' and 'experiencing' and consequently denies that Lawrence's gift was for 'thinking'. Later, however, he claims that Lawrence's genius entails his capacity for thought, for as Leavis comes to conceive of true intelligence it is in and of experience; no sharp separation is made between the capacity to 'think' and to 'experience'.

In the note on Lawrence 'Reminiscences of D. H. Lawrence', in the second issue of *Scrutiny*, Leavis speaks out on behalf of Lawrence the man, who is extolled above his writing:

> I have said elsewhere that he matters because he was a great artist. But the case is not so simple as that might

suggest. His art bears a peculiarly close relation to the man – 'the man who suffered' – and that is its importance. If we find him great, the supreme importance of his books is perhaps that they assure us that he existed. Those of them which are most successful as art are in some ways saddening and depressing. The fact of personal existence of which they assure us is perhaps the most cheering and enlivening fact the modern world provides. Here was a man with the clairvoyance and honesty of genius whose whole living was an assertion of what the modern world has lost. It is plain from his books that he was not able to maintain steady confident possession of what he sought...But it is equally plain that he didn't merely seek.[18]

Leavis's sense of what Lawrence the man achieved is partly qualified – 'he was not able to maintain steady confident possession of what he sought' – but he goes on to insist that Lawrence's 'best creative work was not fully representative of him. He himself – the personality behind the best stories – was a less equivocal incitement than these to the recovery of what has been lost. The man appears saner than the art.' Leavis, of course, while always thinking highly of Lawrence the man, comes to think of his works as representing a central and profound sanity.

Aldous Huxley's edition of *The Letters of D. H. Lawrence* (1932) had a decisive impact on Leavis's sense of Lawrence's greatness. Leavis wrote two separate reviews of the Letters, the first published in the *Listener*, October 1932. The higher evaluation of Lawrence is immediately apparent: 'Mr Huxley quotes me in his Introduction as comparing Lawrence to Blake; I should like to assert now my conviction that Lawrence was much the greater.'[19] The new knowledge gained about Lawrence from the Letters clearly helped Leavis to see the shortcomings of his 1930 essay: 'I confess that after reading the letters I am rather ashamed at having, in writing about him before, been so far from laying any stress on his centrality as against his eccentricities.'[20] The centrality now attributed to Lawrence is associated with the religious nature of his concerns.

Leavis also reviewed the Letters in the third issue of *Scrutiny*; the review was then reprinted in *For Continuity* under the heading 'D. H. Lawrence and Professor Irving Babbitt'. This rather incongruous title was chosen because the review concentrates as much on refuting Eliot's attitude to Lawrence (and the kind of attitude represented by Eliot's mentor, Babbitt) as it does in discussing the Letters. Leavis's point is that Lawrence represents a particular challenge to classicism, and the form of external authority Babbitt represents is inadequate to it. Against this kind of emphasis on orthodoxy and tradition Leavis quotes approvingly Lawrence's assertion that 'this classiosity is bunkum, but still more cowardice'. Eliot's negative response to Lawrence reveals the limitations of his classicism. Leavis begins his career as a critic in deep allegiance to Eliot, but he progressively moves away from Eliot as his commitment to Lawrence grows. At this early date, though, his sympathies are quite evenly divided, and he agrees that there is a reason for misunderstanding the novels which do suggest the fanatical and eccentric. Further he states that some of the negative observations Eliot makes about Blake could be applied to Lawrence.

Nonetheless, the Letters had a strong positive impact on Leavis and he gained at least three things from reading them: as I have pointed out, deeper insight into the religious sense Lawrence represents, new awareness of Lawrence's abilities as a literary critic, and greater understanding of Lawrence the man. In the review of the Letters Leavis advanced a new claim for Lawrence: that he was the finest literary critic of his time. It is Lawrence's acuteness in evaluation that causes Leavis to rank him so highly as a critic: 'His sense of value, like his spiritual insight and his intelligence, was quick and sure.'[21] The Letters confirmed Leavis's sense that Lawrence the man was greater than his writings; the novels, which are still described as reflecting an intense narrow concern, he contends do not fully represent him. In contrast to Eliot's view of Lawrence as a 'sick soul' Leavis finds him in the Letters to be 'normal, central and sane to the point of genius, exquisitely but surely poised, and with a rare capacity for personal relations.'[22] In further explaining the importance that Lawrence has for him, Leavis makes what may appear to be a surprising observation: 'Indeed, in our time, when the gap in continuity is almost complete, he may be said to represent, concretely in his living person, the essential human tradition; to represent, in an age that has lost the sense of it, human normality, as only great genius could.'[23] Here Leavis does not present Lawrence as representing any particular tradition, but rather he is praised as an embodiment of the 'essential human tradition' revealing what man can and should be. Leavis describes this exalted normality as belonging to a tradition because he does not think of it as purely individual achievement.

The following issue of *Scrutiny* contained an article by Leavis entitled 'Restatement For Critics' which carried on the argument about the proper approach to Lawrence. In the essay Leavis is answering a charge that *Scrutiny* refuses to be committed wholly, either to Eliot or Lawrence. Leavis's reply is an appeal for a critical stance: 'To suggest that one should "accept" Mr. Eliot or D. H. Lawrence is to insult both of them.'[24] Leavis's appeal is for a judgment entailing a real responsiveness and the necessary discriminations. He emphasizes that Lawrence is not a philosopher offering a system we accept or reject: 'What Lawrence offers is not a philosophy or an *oeuvre* – a body of literary art – but an experience, or, to fall back on the French again, an *expérience*, for the sense of 'experiment' is needed too. In him the human spirit explored, with unsurpassed courage, resource and endurance, the representative, the radical and central problems of our time.'[25] The emphasis on the exploratory nature of Lawrence's concern is consistent with Leavis's later position, but the denial that Lawrence offers us 'a body of literary art' is directly contrary to the insistence on his accomplishment as a novelist. Leavis then observes: 'More than one summing-up is possible, and it would be absurd to demand agreement with one's own; the stress will fall here for some and there for others.'[26] This is an important admission to keep in mind with regard to later critics who might disagree with Leavis about specific aspects of Lawrence's work while agreeing with the evaluation of him as a major writer. What Leavis was concerned about in 1932 was the total failure of Eliot and *The Criterion*, those concerned for 'order', even to recognize Lawrence's greatness.

The number of essays and reviews Leavis wrote on Lawrence between 1930 and 1933, shows how deeply he was involved with Lawrence at the very beginning of his critical career. Both the 1930 pamphlet and the important later review of the Letters were reprinted in *For Continuity* (1933), where Leavis placed them very much at the centre of the book, pointing to Lawrence as a source of health in the modern plight. Two other essays in the book, 'The Literary Mind' and 'Restatement For Critics', contain discussions of Lawrence, which means that a substantial portion of the book is concerned with him. H. Coombes argues that the book 'ought perhaps to be known as Leavis's first book on Lawrence'.[27] He then writes that '*For Continuity* sometimes seems to me the most important

single event in the history of Lawrence criticism',[28] even while he
concedes that 'the reprinted pamphlet contains a good deal of what
now seems inadequate, wrong and misleading commentary'.
Coombes's positive claims for the book must be considered to be
extravagant; *For Continuity* should be better known, it does have an
historical importance, it clearly sets Leavis's concern with Lawrence
in the context of his concern with the modern disintegraton, but
it failed for obvious reasons to win recognition for Lawrence. Before
this could be done Leavis had to focus on, and praise, the works
as well as the man.

Lawrence's influence and presence is very apparent in *Culture And
Environment* (also 1933) but the comments on him add little that is
new; the next major event in Leavis's response to Lawrence came
in 1934 with the publication of T. S. Eliot's *After Strange Gods*.
Eliot's attack on Lawrence in that book had the effect of turning
Leavis more decisively against Eliot. Leavis's review of the book,
republished in *The Common Pursuit* as 'Mr Eliot, Wyndham Lewis,
and Lawrence', established some of the main lines that his later
defense of Lawrence would take. Eliot made a series of charges
about Lawrence which Leavis attempts to deny and reject. He is
primarily concerned with the charge of an 'incapacity for what we
ordinarily call thinking'. Wyndham Lewis is brought into the
argument because Eliot praises his exposure of Lawrence's primitivism, but Lewis's analysis was based solely on *Mornings in Mexico*
which Leavis judges to be 'one of the very inferior books'. Against
Eliot's charge that there is lack of moral struggle in Lawrence's
books Leavis quotes the passage from *Lady Chatterley's Lover* on the
ability of the novel to inform and lead into new places. Leavis
concludes the review by asserting that 'the sense in which Lawrence
stands for health is an important one. He stands at any rate for
something without which the preoccupation (necessary as it is)
with order, forms and deliberate construction, cannot produce
health.'[29] And again the point is made that 'health' is not just a
moral or a psychological concern, but a religious one.

In this review, then, some of the main issues of the later book
are clearly outlined, but in 1934 Leavis's attitude to Lawrence is
still qualified: the concern with sex is regarded as excessive by any
standard of health, it is conceded that there is not all we need of
moral concern in Lawrence's work, nor can 'the sum of wisdom,
or anything like it' be attributed to him. Most surprisingly of all,
Leavis agrees that 'for attributing to him "spiritual sickness" Mr.
Eliot can make out a strong case.'[30] Despite Leavis's almost

complete disagreement with the approach and substance of *After Strange Gods*, and despite the strong impact of the Letters – with their evidence of Lawrence's 'religious sense' – his claims for Lawrence in 1934 were still considerably tempered.

Leavis's last major statement on Lawrence in the 1930s, and in effect his last essay on Lawrence until 1950, was the review of *Phoenix*, written in 1937 and republished in *The Common Pursuit* as 'The Wild, Untutored Phoenix'. The title indicates a new aspect of Eliot's criticisms that Leavis concerns himself with: the charge that Lawrence lacked a true education, an intellectual and social training. Leavis properly points to the contrary evidence found in E. T.'s memoir and insists that Lawrence enjoyed 'the advantage of a still persistent cultural tradition that had as its main drive the religious tradition of which Mr. Eliot speaks so contemptuously.'[31] That Lawrence was raised and educated in a living tradition becomes a major contention of Leavis's; it involves him in a defence not just of Lawrence's congregationalism but of the force of the whole Nonconformist tradition. In arguing against Eliot for a recognition of Lawrence's intelligence Leavis begins his fight with the literary world, especially Bloomsbury; like the disagreement with Eliot this will shape his final approach to Lawrence.

The review of *Phoenix* is as much centred on refuting Eliot as on discussing the contents of the book, but in that collection, as well as in *Studies In Classic American Literature* and the Letters, Leavis finds justification for his claim that Lawrence was the finest literary critic of our time. The qualities that Leavis regards as giving him this preminence are his intelligence and self-knowledge. And it is in terms of Lawrence's criticism that Leavis begins to redefine his notion of thought: 'If Lawrence's criticism is sound that seems to me because of the measure in which his criteria are sound, and because they and their application represent, if not what we "ordinarily call thinking", an extraordinarily penetrating, persistent and vital kind of thinking.'[32] Despite this high praise Leavis has still not advanced to his later view of Lawrence: here he acknowledges that 'the case that Mr. Eliot argues does, at its most respectable, demand serious attention'.[33] Nonetheless, the impact of *Phoenix* – the further recognition of Lawrence's achievement and insight as a literary critic – unquestionably was a decisive factor in eventually leading Leavis to re-assess the fiction, and by the time of *D. H. Lawrence: Novelist* all of his critical energy is devoted to showing how totally wrong Eliot is about Lawrence.

In the period 1937 to 1947 Leavis wrote most of the essays on the novel that he collected in *The Great Tradition*. During this time he wrote no essay on Lawrence and in fact hardly mentions him. But in a 1947 review of a collection of essays on T. S. Eliot, reprinted in *The Common Pursuit* as 'Approaches to T. S. Eliot', Leavis again refers to and praises Lawrence's criticism. In what was to become a standard procedure for Leavis, he stresses Eliot's limitations as a critic by contrasting him with Lawrence. Leavis remarks that Eliot is a great critic despite lacking the prime requirement of one: 'It is a qualification possessed pre-eminently by D. H. Lawrence, though he, clearly, is not to be accounted anything like as important in literary criticism as T. S. Eliot: a sure rightness in what, if one holds any serious view of the relation between literature and life, must appear to be the most radical and important kind of judgment.'[34] Actually Leavis later extended his claims for Lawrence's criticism, but his position here is salutary in many ways: Lawrence has had little recognition as a critic and has had a circumscribed influence, while Eliot has clearly been the major influence on modern criticism, and Leavis grants this. That this is so is partly due to the fact that the major revolution in modern criticism, the new criticism in the 1930s, like Leavis's own work then, concerned itself mainly with poetry and it was not until later years that critics followed Leavis in shifting their attention to the novel, where the impact of Lawrence's criticism could be felt.

The Letters and *Phoenix* contain a great number of literary judgments and it is in the force and rightness of these judgments that Leavis locates Lawrence's strength as a critic. And he argues that 'it is Lawrence himself who, as a subject, provides the capital instance of Mr Eliot's defect as a great critic'.[35] Against Eliot's competence as a technical critic concerned mainly with matters relating to his own poetic concerns, Leavis sets Lawrence's fully engaged judgment: 'Lawrence stood for life, and shows, in his criticism, tossed off as it was, for the most part, in the most marginal way, an extraordinarily quick and sure sense for the difference between that which makes for life and that which makes against it. He exhibits a profound, and for those who come to the criticism knowing only the fiction, perhaps surprising, centrality.' Even at this late date Leavis is apparently showing a preference for, or fuller acceptance of, Lawrence's criticism over the fiction, and he clearly is influenced by it. While the emphasis on 'centrality' as a key value term is part of Leavis's heritage from Arnold, the use of 'life' as his central value term he probably brought away from his reading of Lawrence's criticism. It should be noted that this marks a change in Leavis; in the 1930s he described Lawrence as standing for health, sanity or a religious sense, and while he continues to use these terms, from now on it will more frequently be 'life'. The concept of 'life' as a value term increasingly comes to dominate his criticism and the Lawrence study is very much an attempt to enforce the contention that Lawrence 'stood for life'.

One of the characteristics that Leavis and Lawrence have in common, and it is clearly what attracts Leavis to Lawrence's criticism, is a firm sense of 'that which makes for life and that which makes against it'; they both make very sharp separations. Leavis points to Lawrence's negative response to Joyce as evidence of the soundness of his critical judgment; on the other hand, Eliot backed Joyce against Lawrence and Leavis regards this as clear evidence of Eliot's failure as a critic. At least part of Leavis's negative response to Joyce is possibly due to this quarrel with Eliot; Lawrence and Joyce are so different that there is no question of Leavis wholly approving of Joyce or of including him in the great tradition, but I doubt if he would have set an either/or choice between them if Eliot hadn't already done so. In his fullest analysis of Joyce – in the 1933 review entitled 'Joyce and "The Revolution of the Word"' – he discusses what had then appeared of *Finnegans Wake* and very effectively argues a case against that work, explaining why he does not consider it a great novel; however, the same review indicates a real appreciation of and respect for *Ulysses*.

Leavis comments on Lawrence again in the introduction to *The Great Tradition*, where he sharply contrasts him with Joyce. (Leavis's remarks, in the essay 'Thought and Emotional Quality' (1945), about Lawrence's poem 'Piano' are only incidentally about Lawrence.) Leavis's criticism of Joyce is now extended to include *Ulysses* where he finds 'no organic principle determining, informing, and controlling into a vital whole...the extraordinary variety of technical devices'.[36] Lawrence on the other hand is described as 'a most daring and radical innovator in "form", method, technique. And his innovations and experiments are dictated by the most serious and urgent kind of interest in life.'[37] Leavis describes this interest in life as operating from the depths of Lawrence's religious experience, and argues that this deep controlling interest makes him more truly creative than Joyce. And for the first time Leavis contends that the spirit of Lawrence's concern with life relates him to George Eliot. By 1948, when this introduction was

written, Leavis had already defined several of the major claims that
he was to make for Lawrence: that he was the great genius of our
time, that his genius was especially that of a novelist, and one
belonging to the great tradition who represents significant development – and now, completely revising his 1930 assessment, Leavis
proposes that it is *The Rainbow* and *Women In Love*, as well as the
tales, that truly represent his genius.

Only two other relevant, though brief, pieces of writing come
between *The Great Tradition* and the essay on *St. Mawr* that initiated
the long series of essays that constitute the book on Lawrence. The
introduction to *The Great Tradition* indicates that Leavis was
already thinking of writing a book on Lawrence, but a letter from
H. Coombes in March, 1949 to the Editors of *Scrutiny* may have
given him the impetus to begin it in the following year. What
Coombes's letter shows is the absolutely deplorable state of the
response to Lawrence in the literary world: Lawrence was met with
total miscomprehension and was generally written about either to
be ridiculed or rejected. A glance at the excerpts in Coombes's letter
will give some idea of what a revolutionary achievement Leavis's
book on Lawrence represents. Leavis's introduction to the letter
announces what will be an important theme in his book, that,
contrary to the opinion given in the *Times Literary Supplement*,
Lawrence is not concerned primarily with sex: 'To this admirer of
Maupassant it may be replied that, while there is only one *Lady
Chatterley's Lover* in Lawrence's *oeuvre*, even in the special undertaking of that book he is preoccupied with the assertion of spiritual
values: it is Maupassant whose attitude to sex is crude.'[38]

Later in 1949 Leavis reviewed Keynes's *Two Memoirs*; the review
is reprinted in *The Common Pursuit* as 'Keynes, Lawrence And
Cambridge'. Leavis's hostility to Bloomsbury has a long history,
but it is in this review that we see him for the first time making
use of Lawrence's negative appraisal of Bloomsbury to support his
own critique. Keynes tries to explain away Lawrence's fierce
rejection of the 'civilization' represented by Bloomsbury, but
Leavis supports his judgment: 'That Lawrence, judging out of his
experience of something incomparably more worthy to be called
a "civilization", loathed and despised what was in front of him
merely because he saw just what it was, is inconceivable to
Keynes.'[39] Leavis claims that what Lawrence saw was a world of
self-enclosed petty egos without any reverence for life (that is, much
the same thing that Lawrence describes in the letter on Russell that

Leavis quotes in the essay 'Tragedy And The "Medium"'). After quoting Lawrence's description of Bloomsbury Leavis comments: 'The kind of triviality that Lawrence describes here is indeed a worse thing than Keynes was able to conceive it.'[40] This is a revealing comment; to both Leavis and Lawrence triviality signifies an abdication of responsibility and respect towards life, and their hostility to it is intense. Leavis tells us that 'out of triviality comes evil', a comment which is strikingly similar in significance to Lawrence's vision of evil in *St. Mawr*. I think this helps us to understand why Leavis values *St. Mawr* so highly, and why, of all Lawrence's works, he decided to write about it first of all; the essay on *St. Mawr* appears almost immediately after the review of Keynes and Bloomsbury. Twenty years after his initial pamphlet on Lawrence, Leavis committed himself to the task of attempting to establish Lawrence as the greatest writer of our time.

9

D. H. Lawrence: Novelist:
The Grounds Of Praise I

My aim, I repeat, is to win clear recognition for the
nature of Lawrence's greatness. Any great writer who has
not had his due is a power for life wasted. But the insight,
the wisdom, the revived and re-educated feeling for
health, that Lawrence brings are what, as our civilization
goes, we desperately need...When I think of the career
that started in the ugly mining village in the spoilt
Midlands, amidst all those apparent disadvantages, it
seems to me that, even in these days, it should give us faith
in the creative human spirit and its power to ensue fulness
of life.[1]

Thus Leavis states his purpose in writing *D. H. Lawrence: Novelist*.
Leavis is involved in an enterprise that is rather unusual in literary
criticism generally, but which is perhaps the summit of evaluative
criticism: he is attempting to 'make a case' for a writer, trying
almost single-handedly to win recognition for Lawrence's genius.

The success of Leavis's undertaking depends on the degree to
which he manages to convince us that his interpretation and high
evaluation of Lawrence, the grounds on which he praises him, are
in fact justifiable. On the whole, Leavis seems to me successful in
'making his case', but at times his concern with refuting T. S.
Eliot's view of Lawrence leads him into defending Lawrence on
inappropriate grounds. He overemphasizes the importance of
tradition to Lawrence, and both the value of Lawrence's work as
a record of tradition and more generally as social history. However,
in pointing to the criticism of civilization implicit in Lawrence's

fiction, and to the religious dimension of his art, Leavis establishes the central grounds on which Lawrence should be praised.

i. Lawrence and Tradition

Leavis's chapter on *The Rainbow*, entitled 'Lawrence And Tradition', centres on the attempt to refute once and for all T. S. Eliot's view of Lawrence and his background. An understanding of the context in which the chapter was written may help to clarify Leavis's purpose and method in it. The issue of *Scrutiny* which contained Leavis's essay on *Women In Love* also contained his review of Father Tiverton's book, *D. H. Lawrence and Human Existence*. In fact, Leavis's review ignores the book and concentrates on Eliot's foreword; his essays on *The Rainbow* seem almost a direct response to it. The foreword convinced Leavis that 'there is no way of getting Lawrence's genius recognized except by dealing with these fallacies and prejudices and misrepresentations' (319). Leavis has been criticized for the extent to which he quarrels with Eliot instead of concentrating directly on Lawrence's work, but many of those critics are resting on a recognition of Lawrence's merits that was won only by Leavis having discredited Eliot's view. Leavis's awareness of the great influence Eliot had led him to return again to this matter.

In the review Leavis refers back to *After Strange Gods* to explain the misconceptions Eliot had advanced, and in reply he tries to outline a proper conception of Lawrence's relation to tradition. To Eliot's charge that Lawrence was not brought up in a central and living tradition Leavis retorts: 'It is when I come to these things in Mr Eliot that I find myself saying: "I am a fellow-countryman of D. H. Lawrence". Mr Eliot is not' (320). This kind of response, and what it implies, has led some critics to state, quite rightly, that the Englishness of Lawrence is one of the central themes of *D. H. Lawrence: Novelist*. Certainly in Leavis's view, from this English background Lawrence brings a sense of the vital possibilities of life, a sense notably absent in Eliot.

A main point of the dispute between Leavis and Eliot centres on the nature of Lawrence's religious and intellectual background. Leavis has high praise for the cultural and religious tradition centred in the chapel of Lawrence's Congregationalism, claiming that 'to turn, as Lawrence did, the earnestness and moral seriousness of that tradition to the powering of a strenuous intellectual

inquiringness was all in the tradition' (321). Is Leavis right about
the strength of this tradition or are his claims just part of a sectarian
battle? The most convincing testimony to the breadth of D. H.
Lawrence's early education comes, of course, from Jessie Chambers;
her *Memoir* provides an inside report on the 'strenuous intellectual
inquiringness' of Lawrence's formative years. Her account of
Lawrence's voracious and wide-ranging reading is (or should be)
well-known.

Lawrence's own response to the Nonconformist tradition should
be carefully noted. The article 'Hymns in a Man's Life', which
Leavis refers to (see the footnote on p. 90) gives a totally positive
sense of the Congregationalist background. Lawrence explains that
'the hymns which I learned as a child, and never forgot...mean
to me almost more than the finest poetry, and they have for me
a permanent value'.[2] The permanent value they provided was to
fill him with a sense of wonder, which he describes as the natural
religious sense, a description of the 'religious sense' very similar to
Leavis's emphasis on reverence. Lawrence also explains that he
preferred the martial hymns to the sentimental ones and quotes a
favourite example: 'Sound the battle-cry / See, the foe is nigh. /
Raise the standard high / For the Lord'.[3] He concludes by
asserting: 'Here is the clue to the ordinary Englishman – in the
Nonconformist hymns.' When we think of the title and spirit of
Leavis's book *Nor Shall My Sword* the truth of Lawrence's assertion
about the formative importance of the Nonconformist hymns
(especially 'the foe is nigh') becomes strikingly apparent. This
article confirms Leavis's argument, but if we look at what Lawrence
says about the Nonconformist religion in *Apocalypse* we get a slightly
different perspective. Lawrence explains that in the chapels the
Bible was expounded dogmatically and morally, that is, in a way
that destroyed the sense of wonder. In fact, what Lawrence is
attacking here is not his own Congregationalism but Primitive
Methodism; the distinction must be kept in mind to understand
many of Lawrence's remarks about Nonconformism. Particularly
in his later years Lawrence repeatedly rejected the Nonconformist
idea of salvation; his comment in *A Propos of Lady Chatterley's Lover*
is typical:

> If we are to take the Nonconformist, protestant idea of
> ourselves: that we are all isolated individual souls, and our
> supreme business is to save our own souls; then marriage

> surely is a hindrance. If I am only out to save my own
> soul, I'd better leave marriage along...
> But supposing I am neither bent on saving my own soul
> nor other people's souls? Supposing Salvation seems
> incomprehensible to me, as I confess it does. 'Being saved'
> seems to me just jargon, the jargon of self-conceit.
> Supposing, then, that I cannot see this Saviour and
> Salvation stuff, supposing that I see the soul as something
> which must be developed and fulfilled throughout a
> lifetime, sustained and nourished, developed and further
> fulfilled, to the very end; what then?
> Then I realize that marriage, or something like it, is
> essential.[4]

This does not imply a rejection of what Lawrence learned from his
own religious background, but of Primitive Methodism. In 'Hymns
in a Man's Life', explaining why he thought it was good to be
brought up a Congregationalist, Lawrence points out that 'the
Primitive Methodists, when I was a boy, were always having
"revivals" and being "saved", and I always had a horror of being
saved.'[5] Perhaps the simplest, and most obvious, testimony of how
deep the influence of Nonconformism was on Lawrence is given in
the very fact that he would write such a book as *Apocalypse* (it is
his last book) and begin it by discussing the approach taken by the
Nonconformist clergymen to the Book of Revelation.

Leavis's review of Tiverton's book came in the June, 1951 issue
of *Scrutiny*; the following issue included a correspondence between
Leavis and Robert Wagner. In his reply Leavis explains how he
would go about establishing that Lawrence derived from his
upbringing the qualities which Eliot denies him. Leavis writes: 'I
should not quote general propositions or explicit statements of
attitude...I should point to the valuations and beliefs and radical
attitudes towards life that are conveyed in Lawrence's art. These
are such that the explicit traditional wisdom...of *A Propos of Lady
Chatterley's Lover* should strike no one as an incongruous or novel
presence in Lawrence's oeuvre.'[6] In the three essays, first published
in *Scrutiny*, which form the chapter 'Lawrence And Tradition',
Leavis applied this method to *The Rainbow*.

In Leavis's writings on *The Rainbow* T. S. Eliot's name is referred
to only infrequently, but his charge that Lawrence exemplifies 'the
crippling effect of a man not brought up in a living and central

tradition' lies behind Leavis's entire argument. Lawrence's own remarks on the Nonconformist tradition justify Leavis's view that this was a 'living' tradition, and Leavis attempts to prove it was a 'central' tradition by trying to establish a clear relationship between Lawrence and George Eliot. Leavis does succeed in showing some connection between the two novelists, but he exaggerates their similarity and their ties to a common tradition, and he is led, by his desire to refute T. S. Eliot, and by his own commitment to tradition as a source of value, to give a distorted reading of *The Rainbow*.

Leavis insists on the association with George Eliot partly to refute the notion of Lawrence as the prophet of the dark gods. In fact, he explains that there are 'tactical reasons for insisting on George Eliot's name as properly to be associated with his' (110). This 'tactical' manoeuvre is understandable in the light of the nature of Leavis's defence of Lawrence, but it results in a misrepresentation. Of the opening part of *The Rainbow*, dealing with Tom and Lydia, Leavis claims: 'It is not only that, in the life depicted, George Eliot would have recognized the known and poignantly familiar; she would have found nothing uncongenial in the ethical tone – the implicit moral and human valuations – of the present-ment' (110–11). Leavis devotes the next few pages of the chapter to an attempt to substantiate this observation. Referring to the scene between Tom and the child Anna he picks out references to 'mother' and 'church' as evidence that, great as are the differences, the relation to George Eliot is an essential one. He contends that the association of 'mother' and 'church' is felt 'as a presence that is being continued and re-emphasized; that of the pieties and the sanctions that have played so essential a part in life as these early chapters of *The Rainbow* have evoked it' (112). This is rather selective evidence and Leavis is demanding that the association of words carry an excessive significance. Further, this insistence on 'pieties and sanctions' seems more applicable to George Eliot, and to Leavis himself, than to Lawrence; while the 'dark gods' may not be essential to *The Rainbow*, Lawrence's insistence on the importance of the qualities associated with 'darkness' is, and Leavis's focus on 'pieties and sanctions' slights this aspect of the novel.

Leavis's argument about Lawrence's similarity to George Eliot, and about the influence of the common tradition, fails in another way to be convincing. It is apparently not in all of Lawrence's work that Leavis finds a clear indication of his affinity with this tradition, but primarily in *The Rainbow* (as well as *The Daughters of the Vicar* and *Fanny and Annie*). He comments: 'How different *The Rainbow* is from *Women In Love* we may fairly convey by observing that there is much about *The Rainbow* that makes us see it as being, clearly and substantially, in a line from George Eliot; as belonging to the same tradition of art – and of more than "art" immediately suggests" (101). Frank Kermode has argued persuasively about the influence of *Middlemarch* on *Women In Love*, but Leavis does not seem very interested, at this point, in arguing about this tradition of the novel: it's the effective presence of the wider cultural tradition that he wants to establish. But if Leavis cannot establish the presence of this tradition, or Lawrence's relationship or affinity to George Eliot, on the basis of *Women In Love*, then his claims for the force of this common tradition become more tenuous.

An even more serious problem is involved with Leavis's argument. If Lawrence 'belongs to the same ethical and religious tradition as George Eliot' (108), how does it come about that his work is ultimately 'religious' while hers is only 'ethical'? Leavis wants to argue that this tradition is absolutely central to Lawrence, and yet the continuity he demonstrates is merely at an ethical level. On the other hand he argues that the most important aspect of Lawrence's work is its religious quality – and he insists that this is exactly what *differentiates* Lawrence from George Eliot. This seems to radically undercut the importance Leavis attributes to the common tradition.

Not only does Leavis have trouble in establishing the common tradition, but his quarrel with Eliot on this points leads him into praising the novel on inappropriate grounds. On the basis of the presentation of Tom Brangwen and of his development, Leavis contends: 'That Lawrence was... brought up in the environment of a living tradition *The Rainbow* offers the most compelling kind of evidence. The book might have been written to show what, in the concrete, a living tradition is, and what it is to be brought up in the environment of one' (108). The novel does provide evidence of a truly living tradition, but when Leavis suggests that it 'might' have been written to show this, he is clearly overemphasizing his point. Lawrence is surely more concerned with presenting the predicament of living in the modern world.

Leavis's argument goes even further along these mistaken lines. As additional evidence of Lawrence's relation to George Eliot, Leavis cites the nature of Tom's quest for a fulfilling life; on the passage dealing with Tom's rejection of his drinking, Leavis comments: 'This might seem to be far enough from George Eliot. Yet the common tradition speaks emphatically in this comment on the drinking bout' (113). Leavis's argument at this point is curious at best; he is turning Lawrence almost into a mouthpiece of the tradition and obliterating his distinctiveness. When Leavis further claims that from this tradition Lawrence brings nothing merely residual, but his 'very formation', it almost seems as if he is concerned more to vindicate the tradition than Lawrence. He certainly places too great a value on the tradition; it may have formed Lawrence but it also formed many others who were not geniuses; there is only one Lawrence and the fact of his genius cannot be fully accounted for by his background.

Leavis not only overemphasizes the importance of the tradition to Lawrence, he also fails to indicate the most characteristic feature in Lawrence's handling of the tradition. Of Lawrence's presentation of the environment that Ursula was brought up in as a child and adolescent Leavis writes: 'Anyone who wishes to know what, in the concrete, in the matter of religion, a living tradition is – or has been in provincial England – would do well to consider these pages of *The Rainbow*' (138). To enforce this claim Leavis quotes a lengthy passage dealing with the coming of Christmas and the cycle of the Christian year. This certainly is convincing evidence and clearly shows Lawrence's religious tradition was one of real depth and wonder. But what Leavis does not bring out is the response to this tradition that is distinctively Lawrence's; that is, he was not simply formed by this tradition, continuing it; he criticized it, rebelled against it, made it his own. There is the matter of Ursula refusing to turn the other cheek and slapping her sister, in direct defiance of the Christian tradition; yet this act is very Laurentian. More importantly the last two pages of 'The Widening Circle' present a distinctively Laurentian insistence not on the Cross but on the Resurrection of the body to life – it is here where Lawrence is changing the import of his religious tradition that much of his strength lies, and Leavis, with his own greater emphasis on continuity, slights this fact.

Leavis's view of the relation between Lawrence and George Eliot and the English tradition has been challenged by other critics. Eugene Goodheart, for instance, in his study *The Utopian Vision of D. H. Lawrence* (1963), although he agrees that there are resemblances between aspects of life in *The Rainbow* and in George Eliot's work, comments: 'The unfortunate effect of underlining Lawrence's debts to tradition is that it tends to deprive him of the special claim that he makes upon us...Continuity with the past and the handing-down of inherited cultural attitudes – tradition in this sense does not figure in Lawrence. He is rather, in the phrase of Nietzsche, one of "the tablet-breakers".[7] Goodheart is partly misunderstanding Leavis's view of tradition here; for Leavis tradition is not so much as 'handing down' as a 'carrying on' which is a creative activity and involves finding new directions. However, there is a slight difference between Leavis's general view of tradition and his description in his chapter on *The Rainbow*; here he does come very close to describing tradition as simply a 'handing down'. Goodheart does not develop at length the comparison with Nietzsche but states: 'Like Blake and Nietzsche, Lawrence tried to unburden himself of the past.'[8] To the extent that we consider the past to be the outworn ideals that have caused man to become, in Lawrence's words, 'pot-bound', this is true enough, and certainly by the time Lawrence finished writing *The Rainbow* he had come to believe that man was being primarily constrained and stifled by what Ursula sees as 'the old, hard barren form of bygone living'. Lawrence himself remarked, in a letter of 9 July 1915: 'I am correcting the proofs of *The Rainbow*. Whatever else it is, it is the voyage of discovery towards the real and eternal and unknown land. We are like Columbus, we have our backs upon Europe, till we come to the new world.'[9] This kind of comment does not give Leavis's reading of the novel – the emphasis he places on tradition – much support.[10]

ii. *Lawrence as Social Historian and Social Critic*

Leavis's argument about tradition leads into a consideration of one of his main reasons for valuing the novel in general, and especially *The Rainbow*. He writes that 'if it should be necessary to show that there is more to be said about the place of the English Sunday in the history of English civilization, it would be enough to adduce this chapter [ten] of *The Rainbow*, so illustrating once again the incomparable wealth of the novel as social and cultural history' (139). In other words Leavis values the novel as a document and in this instance he uses it in a historical debate. Of the description of Ursula's experience of the English Sunday he states: 'That something valid and of great value has its record here is established as only the art of a great novelist *could* establish it' (140). It is one of Leavis's cardinal assumptions that the novel gives us our essential history more completely than the work of actual historians, and at times he seems to value *The Rainbow* primarily for its historical aspect. He praises the record Lawrence gives us not only of traditional religion and the English Sunday, but also of the cultural role of women at the Marsh and of the place of the vicar and class in that civilization. Leavis writes of this: 'It gives an inkling, too, of the supreme qualifications of a great novelist for the work of a social historian, for it illustrates the subtlety of Lawrence's study of an actual civilization' (109).

Leavis makes a more specific claim about Lawrence's role as social historian. Referring to Lawrence's description of the imaginative values brought to the women at the Marsh by the presence of the vicar and Lord of the Manor, Leavis argues:

> Lawrence knows, and renders with the insight and art of a great creative writer, what have been the conditions of his own individual development; to be brought up in the environment of a living tradition – he is recording, in his rendering of provincial England, what in the concrete this has meant to an actual civilization. As a recorder of essential English history he is a great successor to George Eliot. (110)

This quotation brings together all the matters I have been discussing – the relation to tradition and George Eliot, to the novel and history. It raises the question: is Lawrence as concerned to record English history as George Eliot? I think the answer must be no (actually more in the nature of 'no, but...'). Leavis contends that the developing story of *The Rainbow*, the changing conditions of life for Tom, Anna and Ursula gives us the changing history of civilization in England, since Lawrence's interest 'in the deeper life of the psyche cannot be an interest in the individual abstracted from the society to which he belongs' (128). This is true and has to be recognized as one of the conditions of Lawrence's greatness, yet his emphasis is more directly on exploring the deeper psyche than George Eliot's is. This is a matter of degree: George Eliot's psychological insight is profound, but she lays a greater stress on the historical, social conditions of the individual. The difference between *Middlemarch* and *Women In Love* on this matter is characteristic. Eliot recreates very specifically and in great detail the historical period, while Lawrence tends to move in the other direction – for example there are no direction references to the war. Lawrence himself has remarked that 'it was really George Eliot who started it all...It was she who started putting all the action inside.'[11] Lawrence has gone further inward and his focus is, to some degree, more on the individual than on the civilization. For example, the scene of Will and Anna on their honeymoon presents their experience in isolation from the outside world. This is a complex and difficult issue, but it touches on one of the fundamental aspects of Leavis's criticism, for he tends to praise only those novelists who show a keen awareness of the inter-dependence of the individual and society (or history). He is, for instance, very critical of, in fact rejects Virginia Woolf for her interest in the individual apart from the society to which she belongs; on the other hand he has praised John Dos Passos for the range of his interest in civilization and for directly relating the individual to society. It would not be accurate simply to say that Lawrence comes between or includes both of these writers. Woolf and Dos Passos provide an extreme contrast, but her work is more characteristic of the direction the modern novel took in its exploration of inner subjective experience and Lawrence is involved in this movement in the intensity with which he explores the deeper life of the psyche. In this sense he can not entirely be considered to be following George Eliot as a recorder of English history. Lawrence, then, deserves to be praised more for his exploration of the 'new world' and his exploration of the deeper life of the psyche than, as Leavis would have it, for any record he provides of a 'living tradition' or of 'essential English history'.

Leavis concludes his chapter on *The Rainbow* by again praising the novel's value as an historical record:

> And how much of England that can have no other record than the creative writer's there is in *The Rainbow*. The wealth of the book in this respect is such as must make it plain to any reader that, as social historian, Lawrence, among novelists, is unsurpassable. Actually he is, in the strict sense, incomparable. *The Rainbow* shows us the transmission of the spiritual heritage in an actual society, and shows it in relation to the general development of civilization... *The Rainbow* has...its historical depth. (151)

It's worth raising the general question involved here: do we in fact value literature, and in particular Lawrence's novel, for its historical record? Surely not. In the first place, since literature is a creation and not primarily a direct imitation, we should value it as a creative force and not as a document. To centre the value of literature in its historical aspect (which may be great) is to emphasize something of secondary value, and certainly Lawrence's central achievement in *The Rainbow* is not as a social historian (despite the fact that Leavis brings out how much the novel achieves in this area).[12]

The questionableness of the ground on which Leavis praises *The Rainbow* can perhaps best be brought out by contrasting the grounds on which he praises *Women In Love*. In his analysis of that novel he writes: 'I will consider the treatment of Gerald Crich's case. There we have peculiarly well exemplified the way in which, in Lawrence's art, the diagnosis of the malady of the individual psyche can become that of the malady of a civilization' (158). That is, Leavis praises *Women In Love* primarily for the penetrating diagnosis of civilization it enacts; and he generally locates the value of literature in this kind of creative criticism, not in literature's function as a historical document. In fact it seems that Leavis considers *Women In Love* a greater novel than *The Rainbow* on just these grounds: that in his implicit hierarchy of criteria the criticism of civilization is of greater importance than historical representation – and surely it must be agreed that this is so.

Leavis's discussion of *Women In Love* centres on the diagnosis of civilization in the novel. Later critics have taken exception to the extended emphasis Leavis's interpretation gives to Gerald (and the Crich family), in contrast to the much shorter examination of Ursula and Birkin. There is some justification to this complaint, since the lengthy treatment of Gerald and Gudrun arises partly from Leavis's desire to refute Murry's view that the novel is a personal document revealing Birkin–Lawrence, but Leavis also focuses much of his attention on Gerald because it is here, in the criticism of modern society, that he thinks the unquestionable strength of the novel resides. Leavis praises Lawrence's presentation of Gerald for being an analysis of both the disorder in the individual and in a civilization; that is, Leavis is arguing for a form of literary typology: 'In Gerald, in fact, we see the malady of the individual psyche as the essential process of industrial civilization' (164). And Leavis provides a useful clarification of the nature of the malady which Lawrence analyses: 'But mind, with its accomplice, will, does not, in Gerald, serve; it has established itself in the saddle, and its 'appliances' work the psyche from above. He suffers an attendant disadvantage, the lack of something that will and idea cannot supply: the sense of a meaning in life' (164). Gerald, that is, enacts the mechanization of man that is the result of industrial civilization.

In praising Lawrence's criticism of the 'technologico-Benthamite' civilization that Leavis himself has attacked directly in his own writings he explains that Lawrence's 'study of the individual psyche has led him to the diagnosis of a civilization in which the idealism he condemns (it amounts, he points out, to the same thing as materialism) has become a deadly enemy of life' (170). More specifically, he argues that the novel shows that:

> the 'plausible ethics of productivity' is not only an irrelevance in the face of this problem (What do you live for? is the way of putting it here): it represents, by the criterion that Lawrence's creative genius compels us to apply, a refusal of responsibility – of self-responsibility, or responsibility towards life. But so equally does Thomas Crich's idealism (167)

Here Leavis is concentrating on that aspect of literature that makes it of crucial importance to him: the enquiry into 'What do you live for?', the critique of false ends and values. His praise of *Women In Love* for its diagnosis of industrial civilization focuses on the strength of the novel, and here Leavis is pointing to an aspect of literature that is much more valid as a criterion of Lawrence's greatness than the insistence on his capability as a social historian in the discussion of *The Rainbow*.

iii. The Religious Sense and Reverence

In his analysis of *The Rainbow* Leavis explains what is at the centre of Lawrence's work, and why he values it so highly, when he describes it as being religious, and not, as George Eliot's is, simply ethical. Leavis, in comparing the two novelists, also wants to establish that there is this essential and profound unlikeness between them. He comments on the famous opening passage of the first chapter of *The Rainbow*, the proem of the novel, that not only does George Eliot not use words in this way but 'the kind of intense apprehension of the unity of life that they evidence is decidedly not in George Eliot's genius as it is of Lawrence's' (102). This sense of the 'unity of life' is part of what Leavis intends when he uses the word 'religious' to describe *The Rainbow*, but he also gives a further detailed account of the novel's religious quality.

Leavis distinguishes three main features in describing the religious nature of the novel: first, a reference to 'something' external to the individual, secondly, a quality of impersonal depth, and thirdly, the particular nature of Lawrence's concern with fulfilment. In a rather complex argument extending over ten pages (pp. 114–24) Leavis examines the nature of Tom's response to Lydia in order to illustrate the religious quality of Lawrence's work. He begins by quoting the passage from the novel portraying Tom's state of incompleteness:

> But during the long February nights with the ewes in
> labour, looking out from the shelter into the flashing stars,
> he knew he did not belong to himself. He must admit that
> he was only fragmentary, something incomplete and
> subject. There were the stars in the dark heaven travelling,
> the whole host passing by on some eternal voyage. So he
> sat small and submissive to the great ordering. (114)

This passage becomes Leavis's 'touchstone' in his later usages of the term 'religious' so it's worth calling particular attention to it here; the main point is that Tom 'knew he did not belong to himself'. After explaining Lawrence's view of otherness in personal relations Leavis asserts:

> Love for Lawrence is no more an absolute than sex is his
> religion. What, in fact, strikes us as religious is the
> intensity with which his men and women, hearkening to
> their deepest needs and promptings as they seek
> 'fulfilment' in marriage, know that they 'do not belong to
> themselves', but are responsible to something that, in
> transcending the individual, transcends love and sex too.
> (115)

It is not entirely clear what Leavis is referring to. What is it that transcends the individual? This remark is similar to the one he had made in the essay 'Tragedy And The "Medium"'. In explaining the nature of the tragic experience Leavis wrote:

> Actually the experience is constructive or creative, and
> involves a recognizing positive value as in some way
> defined and vindicated by death. It is as if we were
> challenged at the profoundest level with the question, 'In
> what does the significance of life reside?', and found
> ourselves contemplating, for answer, a view of life, and of

the things giving it value, that makes the valued appear unquestionably more important than the valuer, so that significance lies, clearly and unescapably, in the willing adhesion of the individual self to something other than itself.[13]

I think everyone would agree that this is a religious conception, but it's still not clear what it means – what is the 'something other'? While both remarks are of a religious nature they are also perplexingly vague in their invocation of 'something'. Leavis seems to be referring to 'something' *external* to the individual, but he perhaps is requiring us, to too great an extent, to provide our own interpretations of that which he points towards.

Leavis turns, in his discussion of *The Rainbow*, to examine the second aspect of the religious quality of Lawrence's art. He insists that the religious dimension which represents Lawrence's strength is inseparable from the poetic intensity of his art; the relation he is making between these two qualities 'poetic' and 'religious' is not immediately apparent. He quotes the passage dealing with Tom's decision to propose, then comments: 'It is the arduously achieved wholeness of resolution in him that acts. And this state is what expresses itself in the poetic intensity of the episode' (118). This helps us to see what Leavis is getting at: the quality of the prose, its 'poetic intensity', indicates a profound response and it is the sense of a response coming from 'the ground of being' that is religious. Tom's state outside the kitchen window, Leavis insists, 'is so much more than sensual passion (though that has its part), and it is something that entails the opposite of any assertion of will or of self. In the 'depths of his stillness' Brangwen contains, and lives, a resolution of the whole being' (120). Leavis then offers a summary of his argument in which he further describes the *source* of this religious quality:

> Lawrence's treatment of the relations between men and women – his central interest – illustrates something in his art to indicate the distinctive nature of which we have to use the word 'religious'. I have made the point that this characteristic is not something separable from the poetic intensity that distinguishes him from George Eliot. When we examine this intensity, as in the episode of Brangwen's courtship, what we find ourselves analysing is an effect to which a religious resonance inseparably belongs. In fact,

we are led by the analysis of such passages to the
recognition that the poetic intensity that characterizes
Lawrence's art in general, and leads to the mistaken view
that his genius is essentially 'lyrical', derives from a depth
and wholeness of response in him of the kind that he
illustrates, with a specific dramatic propriety, in
Brangwen. In Lawrence's wholeness, of course, there is the
marvellous intelligence of the great artist: his capacity for
an impersonal depth of response has an immediately wide
and varied application. But the vividness in his rendering
of all the varieties of life, human and non-human, *is* this
depth – depth that involves an impersonal wholeness.
(123–4)

The authentic religious response to life derives from this impersonal
depth, involving a transcendence of the ego, which is attained
pre-eminently by Lawrence.

Leavis then provides a third explanation of the nature of
Lawrence's religious concern in *The Rainbow*. He points out that
Lawrence's characters reach fulfilment, resolve the question 'What
for?', by achieving 'spontaneous-creative fulness of being'. Leavis
regards this state of being as essentially religious:

Life is 'fulfilled' in the individual or nowhere; but without
a true marital relation, which is creative in more than the
sense of producing children, there can be no 'fulfilment':
that is the burden of Lawrence's art. It is in the
establishment of a sure relation with the 'beyond' that the
creativeness of a valid marriage has its inclusive
manifestation. What the word 'beyond', with the
associated 'fulfilment' and the associated symbol, the
rainbow, points to is what all the varied resources of
Lawrence's dramatic poem are devoted to defining. (121)

What these words, as well as the term 'unknown', point to is the
religious sense conveyed in Lawrence's work. In analysing the
debate Will and Anna have on their visit to Lincoln Cathedral,
Leavis makes this point very clearly:

What we have to note is that the debate is a conflict in the
inner life of the married pair, and that the defeat or failure
on both sides has is significance in a failure of complete
'fulfilment' in marriage; a failure to 'create' (in a phrase

used later of Ursula), here in marriage, 'a new knowledge
of Eternity in the flux of time'. The positive religious
preoccupation of *The Rainbow* is *there*: a 'fulfilled' life has
achieved its religious validity. (131)

Leavis extends his use of 'religious' considerably here; this is not
really the same as Tom's knowing 'he did not belong to himself',
nor is it the same as the quality of depth he praises in Lawrence's
art. What Leavis proposes here is an even less orthodox, more
controversial use of the word 'religious'.

In discussing certain of Lawrence's other works Leavis adds the
term 'reverence' to help further define the religious quality of
Lawrence's art. In this chapter on *The Tales* Leavis contrasts
Lawrence's characteristic attitude of reverence with that of Maupassant and then adds in a footnote:

> I say Maupassant...But in reading these tales it is still
> more to the point to think, by way of contrast, of Mauriac,
> Eliot, and Evelyn Waugh, who have reputations as
> religious and specifically Christian writers. Unlike them,
> Lawrence (as I have noted) has a reverence for life,
> sensitive human feeling, and what seems to me a religious
> (as distinct from humanitarian – an adjective that so
> plainly doesn't apply to the other three) sense of human
> dignity. (258)

It is, of course, a point of extreme importance that Leavis can find
three avowedly Christian writers *not* fully religious. Eliot, Waugh
and Mauriac all represent a particular kind of Christianity – what
they all share to some extent is a distrust of the natural world and
a lack of faith in human creativity. They all lack the sense of the
inherent *sacredness* of the human world, the attitude towards life that
Leavis calls 'reverence'.

In his essay on *The Daughters of the Vicar* Leavis describes in
greater detail the reverence that gives the religious nature of
Lawrence's art its special importance:

> Lawrence is the greatest kind of creative writer; it can be
> said of him, as of Flaubert or T. S. Eliot it cannot, that his
> radical attitude towards life is positive; looking for a term
> with which to indicate its nature, we have to use
> 'reverence'. But 'reverence' must not be allowed to
> suggest any idealizing bent; and if we say that the

reverence expresses itself in a certain essential tenderness,
we don't mean that Lawrence is 'tenderminded' or in the
least sentimentally given. The attitude is one of strength,
and it is clairvoyant and incorruptible in its preoccupation
with realities. (77)

This essentially affirmative, yet realistic response to life Leavis finds,
and admires, in Lawrence, but not in the three 'religious' writers.
Leavis most fully explains the nature of the reverence of Lawrence's
art in his discussion of *St. Mawr*. Leavis praises Lawrence's supreme
intelligence in the tale but insists that 'formidably critical though
it may be, it is the expression of triumphant creativity, and the
associate of reverence and wonder...Lawrence can make
'wonder', as an answer to the potent actuality of Mrs. Witt, seem
so much more than a vaguely recoiling romanticism because for
him it is so much more' (245). Here 'wonder' is added to reverence
as defining the essential religious attitude. Lawrence, we might
recall, in 'Hymns In A Man's Life' defines wonder as 'the *natural*
religious sense'.[14] Further, 'reverence' and 'wonder' are central
Romantic words, and if Leavis accepts them as helping to define
an authentic religious response to life, it is one of a Romantic cast.
There seems little separation between Leavis's and Lawrence's
position here. It is for the power of this essentially religious
affirmation, made 'in the creative fact, his art; it is that which bears
irrefutable witness', that Leavis exalts Lawrence. His tale provides
an index of the kind of response to life that is desperately needed
for human fulfilment:

> What his art *does* is beyond argument or doubt. It is not a
> question of metaphysics or theology – though no doubt
> there are questions presented for the metaphysician and
> the theologian. Great art, something created and *there*, is
> what Lawrence gives us. And there we undeniably *have* a
> world of wonder and reverence, where life wells up from
> mysterious springs. It is no merely imagined world; what
> creative imagination of the artist makes us contemplate
> bears an unanswerable testimony. (246)

10

D. H. Lawrence: Novelist:
The Grounds Of Praise II

Much more explicitly than any of the novelists studied in *The Great Tradition*, Lawrence's art is praised for representing an affirmation of life. Moreover, in *D. H. Lawrence: Novelist* Leavis introduced for the first time his criterion of the normative, a more specific way of characterizing Lawrence's affirmation of life. In praising Lawrence on these grounds Leavis was invoking what became the central criteria of his criticism. There are, however, certain problems involved with Leavis's praise of Lawrence's affirmation of life. First, the 'life' that Leavis praises does not always accord with the 'life' that we actually find in Lawrence's fiction; at times, that is, Leavis imposes his own sense of life on Lawrence. Further, while Leavis convincingly argues that Lawrence's work, on the whole, is affirmative, he is forced to extend considerably his criterion of affirmation of life in order to take account of *all* of Lawrence's writings. And with much of Lawrence's work he repeatedly encounters difficulty in trying to establish that it does have normative bearings.

i. The Question of Critical Bias

Leavis argues that Lawrence represents the insight, wisdom and health – the 'life' – our civilization desperately needs. Although Leavis's over-all discussion does reveal to us Lawrence's work 'as it really is', as any critic with a distinct vision of his own will inevitably impose it, to some degree, on the writer he is discussing, Leavis does this in certain ways with Lawrence. At times Leavis offers us a slanted or distorted view of Lawrence; he reads his own

values and attitudes into Lawrence's work and then offers us these
as a source of health. In particular, Leavis reads into Lawrence's
work his own insistence on the importance of education, culture,
and the critical intelligence.

Leavis's interpretation of *The Rainbow* attempts to allay the
notion that Lawrence favours instinct against intelligence and
civilization. The proem of the novel presents two different orien-
tations towards life – the blood–intimacy of the men and the
intellectual aspirations of the women – and Leavis maintains that
Lawrence sides with the women: 'The life of "blood-intimacy"
. . .is, in the novel, a necessary and potent presence as something
to be transcended. The novel has for theme the urgency, and the
difficult struggle, of the higher human possibilities to realize
themselves – and no one who has read *The Rainbow* could call in
question the legitimacy of my "higher".'[1] He later asserts that the
Lawrence who wrote the opening of the novel 'was very close in
feeling to the aspiration of the Brangwen mother at the Marsh
Farm' (150). This gives an interpretation of the book that makes
it clearly compatible with Leavis's own emphasis on the importance
of education, culture, and intelligence, but is it correct? Is it true
to Lawrence or does it simply bring him much closer to Leavis
himself? How we regard this interpretation partly depends on what
Leavis means by 'transcended'; if he means that the 'blood-
intimacy' is something to be left behind (although it is not clear
that he does), then he would seem to be misreading the novel.
Unquestionably Lawrence values the 'higher-being', but the novel
shows the destructive consequences of the process by which 'blood-
intimacy' comes to be more and more left out of account as the
'higher-being' is sought in itself. The women decide that the higher
being is a matter of knowledge, of education, and when we come
to Ursula we see the consequences of stressing only one aspect of
life.

Leavis's interpretation presents Lawrence as an advocate of
intellectual culture and of the civilization of the age, 'the finer
contemporary human consciousness'. But his reading slights the
way in which Lawrence criticizes cultural aspirations for ignoring
deep areas of life. Leavis rightly argues that *The Rainbow* does not
exalt the life of the Marsh, that the initial theme is the transcending
of it, but Lawrence then turns his attention on the limitations of
the transcendence. Leavis's analysis of this theme in relation to Tom
is sound: the aspiration of the mother for the higher form of being

is there in his attraction to a foreigner and a lady. Ursula's problems and situation, however, are noticeably different; she does achieve the education that the mother desired for her children, but although she is educated, she is deracinated, cut off from the roots of her life. Late in the novel, Lawrence writes of Ursula:

> This world in which she lived was like a circle lighted up by a lamp. This lighted area, lit up by man's completest consciousness, she thought was all the world: that here all was disclosed for ever...But she could see the glimmer of dark movement just out of range, she saw the eyes of the wild beast gleaming from the darkness.[2]

All that the 'darkness' represents has been neglected in the quest for higher being.

Ursula's confrontation with the horses towards the end of the novel is a scene of indeterminate meaning; it is not enough to say that the horses represent only the instincts or the passions, but a remark Leavis makes about Tom is relevant here. He observes that the impulse and vigour in Tom's development towards higher being 'comes from the life that is to be transcended'; what Lawrence presents in the scene with the horses is the reassertion of those neglected forces of life. In his discussion of *The Rainbow* Leavis does not deal with Ursula's confrontation with the horses, and this is a striking, and revealing, omission. Leavis has overemphasized the values of the women in interpreting the novel, for what Lawrence seeks in *The Rainbow* is not the ascendancy of the women's aspirations, but rather a balance, a harmony, between the two aspects of life. Leavis has a greater belief in culture and education than Lawrence has and he reads this into the novel.

Leavis's interpretation of *Women In Love* does not raise similar objections; there is, I think, no question of his reading his own attitudes into the novel, and he convincingly shows that the novel does not 'represent a repudiation of mind in an extreme of abandonment to frenzied sexuality and the Dark Gods' (156). In *Women In Love* Lawrence is committed to the proper use of intelligence to achieve 'spontaneous-creative fullness of being' and Leavis fully endorses this kind of intelligence. However, in the chapter on *Women In Love* Leavis refers in terms of high praise to *Psychoanalysis and the Unconscious*: 'Here we have unmistakably the serenely triumphant reign of intelligence – intelligence that, in creative understanding, transcends the personal plight that feeds it. It is the intelligence of a great creative artist, whose imaginative achievements *are*, at the same time, achievements of intelligence' (153). In his later review of Father Tiverton's book, Leavis again praises *Psychoanalysis and the Unconscious* and argues that it reveals Lawrence's supreme intelligence; this insistence on Lawrence's intelligence is a recurrent theme of Leavis's study, but here I simply want to examine Leavis's claim that Lawrence is *committed* to intelligence.

Leavis argues that in *Psychoanalysis and the Unconscious* Lawrence not only displays intelligence but gives a full definition of it: 'What he undertakes to do in the book...is to set forth the conditions of health and wholeness in the psyche...The power of recognizing justly the relation of idea and will to spontaneous life, of using the conscious mind for the attainment of "spontaneous-creative fulness of being", is intelligence' (324). Again we are faced with a situation where Leavis is slightly re-making Lawrence, for it is not clear to me that the definition of intelligence Lawrence gives in the book is fully compatible with Leavis's. Lawrence concentrates in the treatise on criticizing the mechanizing effect of ideas and ideals (products of mind) and does not in fact advocate a view which gives the mind or mental consciousness a full place in the workings of the psyche. Leavis has always stressed the necessary and almost complementary role of the critical intelligence in the creative process, but for Lawrence 'the unconscious is the creative element'.[3] Lawrence's argument directs us towards recognizing the need of following the path of the unconscious, rather than of the whole psyche:

> For the whole point about the true unconscious is that it is all the time moving forward, beyond the range of its own fixed laws or habits. It is no good trying to superimpose an ideal nature upon the unconscious. We have to try to recognize the true nature and then leave the unconscious itself to prompt new movement and new being – the creative progress.[4]

This is not all that far from Leavis's position – he would agree we should not 'superimpose an ideal nature' – yet the total dependence on the unconscious Lawrence is advocating must surely be unacceptable to Leavis.

This aspect of Lawrence's thought, his faith in the creative unconscious, lends some justification to the comparison frequently made with Carl Jung; but Jung not only trusts in the unconscious, he distrusts the intellect so strongly that there are grounds for viewing him as an advocate of the irrational. Is Lawrence so clearly different? Leavis argues: 'Lawrence makes plain that without proper use of intelligence there can be no solution to the problems of mental, emotional, and spiritual health. We are committed, he insists, to consciousness and self-responsibility' (324). However the part Lawrence assigns to mental consciousness in this book is a very subsidiary one and the achievement of 'spontaneous-creative fulness of being' depends mainly on the unconscious. Lawrence assigns mental consciousness a more positive role than Jung would, but it is not equivalent to the stress Leavis usually places on the importance of the critical intelligence. There is also an element of occult thought in the book – Lawrence mentions the chakras – which Leavis must find alien. (I should add that the book reveals quite clearly Lawrence's belief that the individual can develop only through relationship with others. This commitment to the necessity of relationship makes Lawrence's interests essentially those of a novelist, not a poet, and also makes him, finally, quite unlike Carl Jung.) Lawrence's use of jargon in the book makes it difficult to endorse fully Leavis's high evaluation; the terms 'lumbar ganglion' and the 'thoracic plexus' are not particularly helpful in clarifying Lawrence's argument. Of the companion volume the *Fantasia*, which Leavis also praises, Frank Kermode writes: 'And there is no point, I think, in denying that there is a deal of rubbish in the *Fantasia*. Dr Leavis is surely exceeding reason and balance in asserting that it "has...the poise of lucid and sober intelligence" without explaining why, in this case, it smothers its basic theme in angry nonsense which the author will not even stand by.'[5] Here we very clearly have a situation where if Leavis's interpretation is as erroneous as it seems to me, then his valuation must be lowered.

Leavis again exaggerates the importance Lawrence attributes to intelligence in his interpretation of Count Dionys's role in *The Ladybird*. Leavis describes Dionys as a 'convincing dramatic presence as someone other than Lawrence himself' (63) and considers him part of the success of the tale. But Leavis's view of what the Count stands for is open to question: 'Representing, in his dark unknowness, the profound energies and potentialities of life that the conscious mind can only either serve or thwart, he represents, not the absence of "consciousness", but rather the necessary vital intelligence that, serving the whole life, can detect and expose the

unsurpations of will and "idea" (64). Vital intelligence, as Leavis
normally explains it, depends on a wholeness of being (his phrase
'serving the whole life' takes the stress here) and I don't think
Dionys can be considered to represent this kind of wholeness. There
is the matter of his anger which, however justified, almost dominates
him, and there are clear indications that he stands for darkness
rather than wholeness. As he tells Daphne: 'The true living world
of fire is dark, throbbing, darker than blood. Our luminous world
that we go by is only the reverse of this.'[6] Dionys is contrasted too
sharply with Basil to be taken as representing vital intelligence (that
is, including a full and proper use of mental, spiritual consciousness)
– and the extremity of the contrast weakens the story. Leavis and
Lawrence are both generally committed to the intelligence that is
a product of the 'whole man alive' and it is partly a similar
understanding of the nature of true, vital intelligence that makes
Leavis sympathetic towards Lawrence; but in certain instances –
such as in *Psychoanalysis and the Unconscious* and *The Ladybird* –
Lawrence sides less with intelligence or wholeness than with the
unconscious and darkness. In these cases Leavis can praise Lawrence only by misrepresenting him, by making it appear that
Lawrence considers the critical intelligence as important as he
himself does.

There are certain aspects of Lawrence's work which Leavis does
not share any deep sympathy with (that is, they are characteristically Laurentian but not at all Leavisite), and it is interesting to
observe how he deals with them. For example, *The Woman Who Rode
Away* is a work that he has very high praise for. In the tale the
woman loses her ordinary personal consciousness and gains a
passional cosmic consciousness, which, at least in a qualified way,
appears to be regarded as a positive in the story; but in this kind
of response and consciousness Leavis has no interest. He ignores it
and instead asserts: 'The poetic power of the tale is, in its creative
way, an earnestness and profundity of response to the problems of
modern civilization' (287). Leavis's response to the story *Sun*, which
he also judges to be one of Lawrence's most notable successes, is
even more instructive here. Again what is interesting are the
grounds on which he praises the story – for its diagnostic power,
for its criticism of life. He maintains that 'the point of *Sun* is not
to recommend to us some mystical, pseudo-mystical, or even merely
hygienic sun-worship' (296). This may not be the 'point' of the
tale, but the women's relation to the sun is being presented much

more seriously, and positively, than Leavis allows. Particularly in his later years, as he felt more and more cut off from society, Lawrence stressed the need for man to get in touch with the cosmos, to have a proper relationship with the circumambient universe – with the sun, the moon and the stars. This attitude of Lawrence's perhaps gets its fullest expression in *Apocalypse*, but it is a significant aspect of what *Sun* is about. This part of Lawrence Leavis is not interested in; for him the strength of the tale is that it 'presents a terrible criticism of an aspect of industrial megalopolitan civiliza-tion' (296) – the loss of the life of the body. By emphasizing the criticism of civilization in the story, and not the positive response to the sun, Leavis contains Lawrence within the range of his own interests, and within the range of his own sense of 'life'.

ii. Lawrence as Affirmative Writer

Leavis most insistently argues his case that Lawrence's work represents an affirmation of life in discussing *St. Mawr*: 'The intensity is not an intensity of repulsion and rejection; it is patently and essentially creative, a marvellous and triumphant expression of the creative force of life, in its very nature an affirmation' (255). It is not enough in Leavis's view for literature, however forcefully, to be simply critical, to present a thorough repudiation of a false, meretricious civilization. If, for instance, Lawrence had written this story omitting St. Mawr and offered only a satire on the shallow world of Rico, he would have given us a story similar to the work of Aldous Huxley. This kind of destructive analysis is not enough in Leavis's view to make a great writer, and in Lawrence 'the disgust, the exposure, and the rejection are utterly different from what one finds in Aldous Huxley: one can never be unaware of the affirmation, the positive, that gives them their "force"' (246).

Leavis's high praise of *St. Mawr*, then, rests with the positive, the 'life' that Lawrence symbolizes by the horse. Leavis quotes the passage about the body and emotions from *A Propos of Lady Chatterley's Lover* to illuminate the nature of the positive in the story, and asserts: 'St. Mawr, the stallion, *is* that life' (242). He argues that St. Mawr's break when he sees the dead snake is not viciousness, but 'a compelled protest of life', a re-assertion of vital instinct. There are a variety of values associated with 'life' that Leavis takes St. Mawr to stand for, but his main emphasis is on 'How far from merely sexual the significance of the stallion is –

how much more, indeed, has to be said than that he stands for forces
of life that the modern world frustrates. Standing, we see, for
the deep springs of life – for the life-impulsion' (250). Leavis's
explanation of the significance of St. Mawr is, it is true, exceedingly
vague here. While he makes the essential point that the significance
of the horse is 'far from merely sexual', when he attempts to
elaborate he falls back on an invocation of the word 'life'. He argues
that the horse "stands for forces of life' and then, to clarify that,
tells us that he stands for 'the deep springs of life – for the life –
impulsion'. This comes very close to being a tautological explanation, and is an instance where Leavis does fail to achieve precision
in the use of his cardinal term of value.

Leavis is more convincing when he describes the attempt to geld
St. Mawr as a hatred of the really living, as 'a determination to
eliminate every element of danger and wildness from life' (252).
This quality of wildness and openness – together with reverence
and wonder – is what Leavis means by 'life'. This is a sense of life
very close to Lawrence's own, and not at all easily accommodated
to the image of Leavis as a traditional moralist – a fact which it
would have been useful for some of the later critics of Leavis's work
on Lawrence to have noticed.

On the other hand, it does seem true that the 'life' which Leavis
values is not always identical with the 'life' Lawrence is presenting
and celebrating. In fact, two of the passages Leavis quotes bring
into fairly direct question whether the 'life' that Lawrence presents
in the horse is quite what Leavis makes of it. When Lou first sees
St. Mawr she is left in 'a great darkness', the horse 'looked at her
with demonish question' and looked at her 'out of the everlasting
dark' (239). And when Lou thinks of what the horse represents as
being only thing 'real', it is gushing 'from the darkness in menace
and question' (240). The repeated emphasis on darkness challenges
Leavis's view of a wholeness of life represented by St. Mawr. To
some extent, Leavis imposes his own sense of life on the story.

There is an additional difficulty with Leavis's argument about
the significance of St. Mawr. The problem that Leavis does not
adequately deal with is this: if St. Mawr is the focus of value in the
story, and an embodiment of the forces of life needed in the modern
world, how can he be inconsequentially dismissed when the story
shifts to America? If we argue that Lawrence uses the American
wilderness and the mountains as a final or preferable symbol of the
qualities lacking in the English civilization that Lou has left behind,

this would imply that what St. Mawr stands for is more limited than Leavis suggests. And there is a passage in the story that supports such a reading. As Phoenix drives Lou up to the ranch she thinks to herself: "When Phoenix presumed she was looking for some secretly sexual male such as himself, he was ridiculously mistaken. Even the illusion of the beautiful St. Mawr was gone."[7] Has St. Mawr been dismissed from the story because he was only an 'illusion'? To regard the American wilderness as representing something deeper and beyond what St. Mawr represents might save the unity of the story, but it would surely qualify Leavis's claim that St. Mawr stands for 'life'.

Leavis praises *St. Mawr* on the grounds that it is affirmative, but the ending of the story poses even further problems for accepting this view of the tale. He describes the concluding pages of *St. Mawr* as 'superficially so inconsequent and tailing off, essentially so *belonging* to the significance' (255). This is partly a claim that the story does have unity, but again Leavis has to try to convince us that our initial response – that the final pages *are* 'tailing off' – is false. When writing the later essay on the tales Leavis admitted to a doubt about the end of this story, a doubt whether Lou would have maintained her vigil in the mountains. The real question that must be asked about the ending is: just what is being affirmed – can we take Lou's retreat to the mountain to represent an affirmation of life? Leavis claims that 'the life she proposes on the ranch, with its history and its symbolic value, in the "wild America" is the antithesis of that represented by the Bloomsbury world she lived in with Rico. And we still feel that she truly apprehends, in this antithesis, something positive, a possibility of creative life, in spite of the closing sardonic comment' (256). 'Something positive' is not especially helpful in explaining what is being affirmed, but it can be agreed that Lou's retreat is not misanthropic; that it is a necessary retreat which adheres to life. Nonetheless, with Lou left in isolation, the tale is making a very paradoxical kind of affirmation.

The problems involved in Leavis's praise of Lawrence as an affirmative writer come up in a very direct way in his discussion of the shorter tales. Leavis gives a detailed analysis of *The Daughters of the Vicar* as an affirmation of life, and while the story is eminently suitable to his view of Lawrence there may be some question about whether it establishes that Lawrence is *characteristically* an affirmative writer. Leavis tells us that he selected the story for discussion because 'it is representative of Lawrence's genius in a central and profound way' (73). The question arises whether this story is truly representative, or whether Leavis selected it because it is affirmative. George Ford, referring particularly to the stories *The Prussian Officer* and *The Man Who Loved Islands*, claims that 'many admirers of Lawrence prefer to regard all of his writings as simply affirmatives and to overlook the kind of stories I have been discussing here'.[8] This certainly appears to be directed at Leavis and challenges his view of the very nature of Lawrence's work. Ford writes that 'Leavis finds "The Prussian Officer" unrepresentative of Lawrence...The present chapter will indicate, I hope, how representative the story is'.[9] Ford wants to argue that the sense of alienation, of separation and despair, which certainly is in this story, is representative of Lawrence's work. Part of the problem involved here is in deciding just what stories one takes to represent an author. To confine the discussion to the volume *The Prussian Officer*, I think there is more likely to be general agreement that *The Daughters of the Vicar* is of greater importance in Lawrence's work – that it is better – than the title story. If we are to base our selection on what is best in Lawrence then Leavis is not misrepresenting him. Moreover, it's worth noting that *The Thorn In The Flesh*, the other German military story in the book, is also affirmative. However, many of the other stories in the volume give a different impression of Lawrence. None of them is so clearly an affirmation or a 'triumph of life' as *The Daughters of the Vicar*, and several of the stories, including *The Shadow in the Rose Garden, A Sick Collier, The Christening* and *Odour of Chrysanthemums*, are about alienation, separation, death, the defeat of life. Lawrence's early tales obviously are not as completely affirmative as Leavis suggests.

With many of Lawrence's later stories Leavis himself acknowledges that they cannot be read as presenting an explicit affirmation of life. He praises instead their diagnosis or criticism of life and suggests that, at best, positive values are implied. In his chapter on the tales Leavis first discusses certain stories which he describes as being a 'triumph of life' or affirmative: *The White Stocking, Samson and Delilah, The Horse Dealer's Daughter, You Touched Me* and *The Fox*. But he then turns to examine a group of stories which present the 'defeat of life', and these stories he praises for their diagnostic power. One obvious difference between Leavis's approach to the more affirmative works, including the three tales he discussed at length in separate chapters, and his approach to the tales described as analysing a 'defeat of life', is that in discussing, say, *The Daughters of the Vicar, The Captain's Doll* and *St. Mawr*, his emphasis was on the presence and nature of Lawrence's positives; this seems to be one of the main reasons Leavis selected them for separate treatment. But as his survey of the tales makes clear, many of Lawrence's other stories are concerned less with presenting a clear affirmation of life than with diagnosing the failure of life. The significance of these tales has been a matter of some contention. Leavis insists that Lawrence's studies of failure derive from his positive concern with the conditions of fulfilment, and do not at all indicate any negative response to life.

England, My England, the first of the series of stories dealing with a 'defeat of life' that Leavis examines does support his view of Lawrence; even though it does not present a direct affirmation of value, its implications clearly are positive. Leavis focuses on the moral of the tale as it is enacted by Egbert: 'But of the complete failure of his life we are left in no doubt (and we are left in no doubt of the essential moral)' (279). The moral, the theme that Leavis singles out, is Egbert's refusal of responsibility and the impossibility of making a life without more engagement or commitment than he has. The point of the tale is that passion or love is not enough for a man's life; he also needs a creative purpose. There is an aspect of the story Leavis doesn't mention which supports the moral interpretation he gives to it and to all of Lawrence's work. Egbert's marriage fails because he does not represent anything beyond himself, and as a consequence of his personal and marital failure he relapses into a kind of primitivism: 'His heart went back to the savage old spirit of the place: the desire for old gods, old, lost passions, the passion of the cold-blooded, darting snakes that hissed and shot away from him.'[10] This is clearly presented as a moral failure; Lawrence is not advocating primitivism. Egbert's final attraction to dissolution and death is the result of his moral irresponsibility.

This story – whatever doubts are raised by *The Ladybird* and *Aaron's Rod* – is one of the best places to point to for proof that Lawrence's concern with power was a positive aspect of his genius, that it was a reflection of the intense responsibility he felt towards life. Lawrence tells us of Egbert: 'He was himself the living negative of power. Even of responsibility. For the negation of power at last means the negation of responsibility.'[11] We know that we are to take it as a fall, a moral failure, when Egbert's heart goes 'back to the savage old spirit of the place', for as Lawrence tells us of the power and belief of Godfrey Marshall: 'In the end, it is only this robust, sap-like faith which keeps man going.'[12] Egbert in contrast lacks this necessary faith; he 'could not bring himself to any more of this restoring or renewing business'.[13] In fact this story clearly establishes that Lawrence is not attracted to corruption and disintegration but insists on the need for positive creativity, that man realizes himself only by creating his world. This is the burden of Lawrence's later remark when he heard of the death of Percy Lucas, the prototype for Egbert: 'Yet, it seems to me, man must find a new expression, give a new value to life, or his women will reject him, and he must die.'[14]

The Man Who Loved Islands, which Leavis also examines as an example of 'the defeat of life', further supports his argument. Leavis does little more than write appreciative criticism of the tale, summarizing and praising it. He does, however, illicit a moral from the tale that is as central to Lawrence's (and Leavis's) view of life as the emphasis on responsibility: 'Lawrence's insistence on the "disquality" of the individual is inseparable from his clairvoyant preoccupation with the complementary truth: the truth that without his relations with other lives, the individual is nothing' (282). This story is inevitably involved in any discussion of whether Lawrence is essentially an affirmative writer, and there are those, like Kingsley Widmer and George Ford, who claim it reflects Lawrence's own nausea and alienation. Leavis interprets the tale as an exposure, a diagnosis of the illusion that the individual can sustain and develop himself in isolation or solitude. When we consider Lawrence's life-long insistence of the necessity of relationships, as well as his emphasis on the 'societal instinct' at the time of writing the story, I don't see how that interpretation can be seriously questioned.

In his chapter The Tales Leavis goes on, however, to discuss a group of stories which he claims exemplify Lawrence's irony: Mother and Daughter, Two Blue Birds and Things. These are stories generally about failure, and like the tales he describes as being about a 'defeat of life', Leavis praises them for their diagnostic power, not for any affirmations they embody. The important point here is that Leavis's treatment of both groups of these stories is quite uncharacteristic of his general criticism of the novel. In keeping with his interest in affirmative literature, Leavis normally focuses his attention on the positive qualities presented in a novel – those aspects of the work which reveal the possibilities of life. But none of the stories he is discussing, from *England, My England* to *Things*, represent this kind of directly affirmative literature; the positive is there only by implication, if at all. It is very striking that we find this extension of Leavis's normal procedure or normal criteria primarily in his work on Lawrence. (His praise of *The Secret Agent*, and perhaps *Victory*, are the only comparable examples I can think of.) It's not entirely clear that in what sense this series of tales supports the view of Lawrence as an essentially affirmative writer; diagnosis or criticism, after all, is not the same thing as affirmation and Leavis usually demands that the positive values be concretely realized, not just implied.

It is instructive to examine how Leavis attempts to deal with Lawrence's irony, and to note the positive quality that he does deduce from these later tales. He argues that one of the profits of comparing *Mother and Daughter* and *St. Mawr* is that

> it helps to explain the difference between Lawrence's
> ironic note everywhere and that of other writers who
> might seem to be practising the same kind of thing. What
> is so remarkable about Lawrence's irony is that, astringent
> as it may be, it never has a touch of animus; never a touch
> of that egoistic superiority which makes the ostensibly
> comparable work of other writers seem cheap – so often
> cheap and nasty. The difference one feels, is one of depth.
> What we notice is Lawrence's incomparable sensitiveness
> of touch and tone, and this, the juxtaposition of *St. Mawr*
> with *Mother and Daughter* suggests, is the index of the
> profound humanity that is implicitly present in the surface
> lightness. (288)

In effect, this quality of depth earns Leavis's praise in this group of later tales. While Lawrence may not be embodying clear affirmations in these stories, the depth of human experience rendered, Leavis implies, has the result of enhancing our sense of the possibilities of life.

iii. The Problem of the Normative

Leavis's praise of Lawrence's art on the grounds that it has normative bearings is clearly, as I have noted, a more specific way of praising Lawrence's affirmation of life. This more particular

claim for Lawrence's work, however, is open to serious question.
In fact, one of the most striking features of *D. H. Lawrence: Novelist*
is the repeated difficulty Leavis himself encounters in attempting
to argue that Lawrence's work *is* normative.

'Normative', as Leavis uses the term in his discussion of Lawrence, refers to a standard defined not by prophetic preaching, but
by art. As he explains in his analysis of *Women In Love*, the norm
a novel embodies is created or discovered in the process of writing:
'In fact, an experimental process of exploring, testing, and defining
does seem really enacted, dramatically, in the "tale"; so little are
we affected as by any doctrine formulated in advance, and coming
directly from Lawrence' (187). The novel, that is, is not didactic
but enacts its moral or norm. In discussing Birkin, and his relation
to Lawrence, Leavis gives a full explanation of the nature of
enactment and of the nature of the norms in the book: 'We realize
that in Birkin, who is far from being coextensive with the
"spontaneous-creative fullness of being" out of which *Women In
Love* comes, Lawrence, the whole creative artist, enacts a tentative
or kind of experimental process – a testing and exploring of the
conscious and formulated conclusions that Birkin thinks he has
settled in securely enough to act upon' (184). Leavis goes on to
explain how the norms or conclusions are those proper to a novel,
how they are derived, not from the views of a single character, but
from the novel as a whole: 'Self-dramatized in Birkin, the Lawrence
who formulates conclusions ("doctrines") and ponders them
suffers exposure to the searching tests and the impersonal criteria
that the artist's creative genius, which represents an impersonal
profundity and wholeness of being, implicitly and impartially
applies to them' (184).

In elucidating the normative bearings of Lawrence's work Leavis
provides some clarification of his own values. For example, he
seems to be in complete agreement with the moral or norm of *The
Rainbow*. He observes that Lawrence's insistence on fulfilment in
the individual carries with it a corollary: 'It is only by way of the
most delicate and complex responsive relations with others that the
individual can achieve fulfilment' (106). In the novel, he explains,
this theme is

> explored dramatically with the marvellous technical
> inventiveness of a great artist. There, in the novels, the
> treatment of the theme has for a major part of its implicit
> moral this further insistence: except between 'fulfilled'

individuals – individuals, that is, who are really
themselves, recognizing their separateness or otherness,
and accepting the responsibility of that – there can be no
personal relations that are lasting and satisfactory. (106–7)

The central relationship is that between a man and a woman, and
with reference to it, Leavis further explains the 'moral' of *The
Rainbow*: 'Life is "fulfilled" in the individual or nowhere; but
without a true marital relation, which is creative in more than the
sense of producing children, there can be no "fulfilment": that is
the burden of Lawrence's art (121). Leavis obviously endorses fully
this view of human relations.

Leavis's interpretation of *Women In Love* emphasizes the fundamentally moral import of the book, but here he raises some
questions about the normative implications of the novel. He insists
that the presentation of positive values gives the diagnosis in the
book its force:

The West African statuette...represents something that
we are to see as a default, a failure, antithetical – and so
significantly related – to the human disaster enacted by
Gerald Crich. A strong normative preoccupation, entailing
positives that are concretely present in many ways (we
have them above in the phrase "the goodness, the
holiness, the desire for creation and productive
happiness") informs the life of *Women In Love* – the life that
manifests itself in the definition and 'placing' of these
opposite human disasters. (175)

The normative aspect of the novel, Leavis argues, centres on the
relation of Birkin and Ursula: 'In Birkin's married relations with
Ursula the book invites us to localize the positive, the conceivable
and due – if only with difficulty attainable – solution of the problem; the norm, in relation to which Gerald's disaster gets its full
meaning' (182). This seems definite enough, yet there is a certain
ambiguity in Leavis's attitude on the question of whether *Women
In Love* is essentially a normative work. On the one hand he insists
that 'the perceptive reader will not assume any simple identity
between Birkin's own formulated view of his relations with Ursula
and what is conveyed by the "tale" (even though Ursula endorses
Birkin's normative conclusions in her parting talk with Gudrun)'
(188), and on the other hand argues that 'we sufficiently see their
union as successful to take, and take as significant, the contrast it

presents to the disaster of the other pair'. This seems to imply that
while Leavis accepts their relationship as normative (or nearly so),
he does not fully accept Birkin's formulation of it. Leavis's more
general position, however, is to argue that the position Birkin
advocates is confirmed by the book, that it is normative: 'Actually,
it seems to me, the position for which Birkin contends in his wooing
of Ursula does emerge from the "tale" vindicated, in the sense that
the norm he proposes for the relations of man and woman in
marriage has been made...sufficiently clear, and, in its intelligi-
bility, sufficiently cogent, to compel us to a serious pondering'
(184). Here Leavis is giving very qualified assent; he does not say
he accepts or believes in the norm, only that it deserves 'serious
pondering', which is surely not what we usually take 'normative'
to imply. And even in this limited sense Birkins's position does not
seem completely 'vindicated', for there are times when what he is
proposing is not entirely intelligible. An example occurs in the
chapter entitled 'Mino'.

> 'There is' he said, in a voice of pure abstraction, 'a final
> me which is stark and impersonal and beyond
> responsibility. So there is a final you. And it is there I
> would want to meet you – not in the emotional, loving
> plane – but there beyond, where there is no speech and no
> terms of agreement. There we are two stark, unknown
> beings, two utterly strange creatures.'[15]

It's difficult to regard this as normative in the sense of being
'sufficiently clear'. (The problem is partly that if the norm is to
include the 'unknown' and the 'beyond', it can't be made fully
cogent.)

Leavis later does give a completer assent to Birkin's position:
'Birkin posits a relation that shall be, in its vitality, stable and
permanent because the terms between which it subsists are real'
(187). But, if Leavis finally accepts the relation proposed by Birkin
as being normative, he is nonetheless critical of the degree of success
Lawrence has in realizing this norm, in embodying it in the relation
between Birkin and Ursula. In the chapter 'Lawrence And Art',
Leavis comments, as an afterthought to his earlier discussion of
Women In Love, that

> it might be said in criticism of that novel that the
> normative aspiration it clearly represents is not as fully

realized as Lawrence (one guesses) had, in the first
conception, hoped: the diagnosis represented by Gerald
and Gudrun is convincing – terribly so: but Birkin and
Ursula as a norm, contemplated in the situation they
are left in at the close of the book, leaves us wondering
(and, it must in fairness be added, leave Lawrence
wondering too). That is, if a certain symmetry of negative
and positive was aimed at in *Women In Love*, Lawrence has
been defeated by the difficulty of life: he hasn't solved the
problems of civilization that he analyzes. This criticism, if
it *is* a criticism, is different in kind from that called for by
the close of *The Rainbow*. (29)

Leavis seems to be thinking mainly of the isolation of Birkin and
Ursula at the end of the book, of the fact that they have no place
in society; the whole question of Birkin's relation to Gerald, and the
possible difficulties this introduces into the attempt to regard
Birkin's relation with Ursula as a norm, Leavis fails to discuss. The
latter part of Leavis's objection, that Lawrence hasn't offered a
solution, is, as Leavis himself suspects, surely invalid. His own
characteristic position is that the artist does not solve, or give
any final answers to the problems of life (his criticism of Blake's
Jerusalem for purporting to do this is a good example). Yet, while
art does not give final solutions, it does, in Leavis's view, present
positives or norms and much of the central value Leavis finds in
literature, above all in Lawrence, depends on the successful
creation or evocation of these values. If Lawrence's norm in this
novel is not fully realized, or not fully acceptable, then the basis
of Leavis's high praise is weakened.

The main difficulties with praising Lawrence's work for its
normative bearings are raised, however, not by *Women In Love*, but
by his later tales and novels. In certain of these stories we find
the most questionable aspects of Lawrence's work – such as the
view of the relation between men and women they often present.
On the whole Leavis attempts to defend this view, although where
obvious problems arise he himself raises questions about their
normative implications. In a story such as *The Fox*, however, we
encounter some decidedly unpleasant features of Lawrence's work,
and when faced with, say, the treatment of Banford, Leavis's
argument becomes evasive. And other unsavoury aspects of Lawrence's work, Leavis tends simply to ignore.

These difficulties can be seen in his discussion of *The Captain's Doll*. This tale, he insists, represents an affirmation of life, made by Hepburn, and Leavis contends there is nothing romantic about it; on the contrary,

> the effect of the holiday-excursion is to confirm the
> positiveness and the validity of Hepburn's ostensibly
> negative attitude – his repudiation of 'love' and his
> 'meaninglessness'. This attitude is truly one of insistence
> on reality, and the insistence, negative as it may have
> seemed to Hannele, the 'idea'-bound, expresses an
> ultimate – an unsentimental and unideal-vital faith, a
> profound assertion of life and wholeness. (228)

Yes, but...One can agree that the tale establishes Hepburn as a compelling concrete presence, and agree with the critique of romantic love, and still question whether Hepburn's positive, the nature of his affirmation, is acceptable, whether Hannele's final capitulation to him is 'credible and right'.

Leavis's main praise of the story is for the normative conclusion it presents; he praises the moral of the story. As they come down the mountain Hepburn states his position to Hannele, and Leavis describes this as 'perfectly dramatic, and it is at the same time an explicit statement of the burden ("moral"; one might say) of the tale or drama' (229). The negative aspect of the burden, the rejection of adoration as an ultimate, is easy to agree with, but Hepburn's positive, his insistence that a woman honour and obey him, or at least his formulation of his position, is difficult to accept unequivocally. Leavis argues that the tale does not represent any desire on Lawrence's part for a 'bullying male dominance', but rather: 'The traditional terms are no more paradoxically wrested than they are used naively to express a crude or simple attitude: they are revitalized in the service of a profound insight into the deeper human needs and desires' (231). The relationship of Hepburn and Hannele offers interesting parallels to the relationship of Birkin and Ursula (there is even the similar situation of coming down from the mountain or the world of ice and snow), but the norm that Birkin proposes for the relation of a man and a woman – 'star–equilibrium' – is surely preferable to Hepburn's 'honour and obedience'. It is difficult to concur with Leavis's assessment of *The Captain's Doll* that the 'common sense *is* profound' (234).

Leavis's interpretation of the story could be questioned; that is, it could be argued that Hepburn's position, his norm, is not fully endorsed by the tale. Just as Ursula continually criticizes, rejects or qualifies many of the things Birkin says, Hannele responds in a like manner to Hepburn:

> 'I want marriage. I want a woman to honour and obey me.'
> 'If you are quite reasonable and *very* sparing with your commands,' said Hannele. 'And very careful how you give your orders.'
> 'In fact, I want a sort of patient Griselda. I want to be honoured and obeyed. I don't want love.'
> 'How Griselda managed to honour that fool of a husband of hers, even if she obeyed him, is more than I can say.'[16]

This mocking tone towards Hepburn is maintained until the end and a full response to the tale has to consider the degree to which Hepburn is being effectively criticized. Yet while I would not reject an interpretation which suggested Hepburn's view is not fully endorsed, Leavis's reading is more likely.

Granting Leavis's interpretation, is the story essentially normative? Leavis actually qualifies or hedges on his sense of the normative implications of the tale. He first tells us that 'in defining the norm with which it is preoccupied (and the creative impulsion in *The Captain's Doll* cannot be separated from a normative concern – with which fact is bound up the dramatic impersonality of the art), it is with a significant propriety that he makes Alexander Hepburn invoke the traditional formulation' (231). This seems straight-forward enough, but Leavis then states that '*The Captain's Doll* does not propound or generalize; we do not find it laid down there, nor are we forced to deduce, that the mode of the manifestation of the difference between men and women must always and everywhere be this' (232). He then immediately adds that: 'We have to note of course that theme and creative impulsion are, as I have said, essentially normative.' If this is not a contradiction, it means that Leavis does not intend the normative implications of the tale, or of literature, to be rigidly held. Normative may describe how things 'ought' to be, but the implication is that this must be applied with some flexibility to the particularity of human experience.

The shorter tales provide even greater problems for Leavis in his

attempt to establish that Lawrence's work is essentially normative.
He insists that Lawrence is concerned not simply with sex but
'always with the relation between individual human beings – the
relations in all their delicate complexity' (263). To support this
statement Leavis examines two stories, *You Touched Me* and *The Fox*.
He argues that love is the theme of *You Touched Me*, but I doubt
that the tale really can be regarded as a love story dealing with
'relations in all their delicate complexity'. Matilda is a cultured
woman who reads, cares deeply for painting and music, while
Hadrian is completely indifferent to this – the relationship is based
on 'vital' needs. Leavis in fact admits that Matilda's marriage to
Hadrian is not an unqualified triumph of life. The tale presents us
with an apparently objectionable situation: the problem is to decide
whether Matilda is being manipulated by her father and Hadrian
or is acting according to her deepest desires. Leavis's position is that
'no simple judgement, no simple determination of the sympathies,
is in place. Nor do we feel ourselves incited by the close to work
out a sum of for or against by way of deciding whether Matilda
chose on the whole rightly and her father did well, or whether the
major truth is that she was cruelly compelled' (267). But surely we
do have to decide one way or the other – even if 'no simple
judgement is possible' – in order to evaluate the story. Even if
Leavis's response to the tale is a proper one, in being sufficiently
complex, it is a somewhat curious position in light of his insistence
on Lawrence's basic normative concern. Leavis hesitates about
drawing any conclusion or moral from this story, rather he claims:
'What we do feel is the challenge to realize the full complexity
presented, and the tale leaves us with a sharp sense of how much,
to what rare effect, this is an art calculated to promote one's
imaginative perception in the face of ordinary human life' (267).
Perhaps: but there is something evasive about this position.

Leavis has an even harder time trying to deal with the possible
normative implications of *The Fox*. He gives a more extensive
analysis of *The Fox* than of any other work discussed in the chapter
'The Tales', and he regards it as one of the supreme things among
the major tales. He describes the story as a study of youthful love
and of Henry's wooing writes: 'It is so humanly central, so strongly
delicate, so direct and untouched by convention in the imagining
and so inevitably right' (275). However, two aspects of this
'love-story' make it difficult to accept and praise the tale as
completely as Leavis does. The first is involved with Banford's

death. Banford is one of many Laurentian characters – Clifford Chatterley, Rico, Mr Massy, possibly even Skrebensky – who lack vitality, physical and spiritual, and who, in their very being, are dependent upon others. Lawrence tends to show a lack of compassion, if not an open animus, towards these characters. Lawrence's treatment of Banford and the others does make it seem that his 'reverence' for life is selective; it extends to the characters he approves of but not to the life-denying figures. His reverence for 'life' does not include sympathy for those not on the side of life. The relevant point with regard to *The Fox* is that Lawrence's animus towards Banford intrudes into the story and he appears to approve of her death; she must be killed so 'life' can assert itself. This is the most challenging, and perhaps finally the most dubious aspect of Lawrence's work (or at least of this tale) and I find the presentation of this 'life-morality' much more disturbing than Leavis does. It clearly creates problems in Leavis's attempt to establish that Lawrence is essentially a normative writer.

The other questionable aspect of the tale comes from the last five pages dealing with the relationship of Henry and March after they are married. Leavis notes that Henry insists all responsibility be relinquished to him but contends that within the context of the story this is acceptable. Again Leavis is slighting a certain problem. (I am not sure the ending is integrated with the rest of the story in the first place; it sems somewhat tacked on, disturbing the formal unity.) A serious question is raised by the kind of marriage relationship Henry desires. His desire to assume the responsibility means a submergence of March's personality; this is not the star-equilibrium proposed in *Women In Love* but a very one-sided relationship: 'She would not be a man any more, an independent woman with a man's responsibility. Nay, even the responsibility for her own soul she would have to commit to him. He knew it was so, and obstinately held out against her, waiting for the surrender.'[17] This is not a desire for the integrity of both partners, but for male domination. It might be possible to argue that March needs to be dominated in order to regain her feminity, so she 'would not be a man any more', but that also means she would not be an 'independent woman' any more, and that creates the problem. In any case it is difficult to regard their relationship as normative.

Of this kind of marriage relationship, and possibly referring to Banford's death, Leavis writes: 'We may think of normative conclusions that preoccupy Lawrence elsewhere, but the psycho-

logical truth of *The Fox* is so compelling, and the close belongs so
much to the concrete specificity of the situation presented, that the
tale can hardly seem involved in any questionable generality of
intention' (277). This is surely an admission on Leavis's part that
he too finds the implications of the story disturbing, but his
argument involves a sleight of hand. Why shouldn't we think of
normative conclusions here just as much as in any other Lawrence
story? All of Lawrence's work presents particular, concrete situ-
ations and Leavis's position generally is that they have a normative
bearing. Grant the position that Lawrence's basic impulse is
normative, then Leavis's argument here is an attempt to circumvent
the unpleasant aspects of the tale.

In his discussion of what he calls 'the lesser novels', Leavis's
argument that Lawrence is a normative writer runs further
aground. *Aaron's Rod*, for instance, presents even greater problems
than *The Fox* for regarding Lawrence's work as normative. Leavis's
evaluation of *Aaron's Rod* depends upon his insistence that the book
is profoundly moral. Aaron's 'case' centres on the impasse of his
marriage. Of Lawrence's presentation of Aaron's relationship with
Lottie, Leavis writes:

> It is a familiar situation, a familiar kind of life-frustrating
> deadlock. The presenting of it transcends ordinary moral
> judgments; to judge Aaron selfish and irresponsible for
> leaving his wife in the lurch with the children on her hands
> (though he provides for her financially) or to say that,
> whatever the total accounts of rights and wrongs may be,
> plainly the domineering, demanding, complaining woman
> was at fault and had made his life intolerable, wouldn't,
> we know, be to the point. The presenting sensibility and
> the inquiring intelligence engaged are, of course,
> profoundly and essentially moral; the moral concern goes
> far deeper than the level of those judgments. What is
> wrong here? What laws of life have been ignored that
> there should be *this* situation, this dreadful deadlock,
> between a man and a woman? These questions give the
> informing preoccupation. (36)

Leavis opposes 'ordinary moral judgments' to 'laws of life' and as
he usually comes close to equating 'moral' and 'life' I take it that
his emphasis here falls on 'ordinary'.

Leavis contends that the diagnosis the book presents of Aaron's case involves a rejection of the mistaken belief that love is a goal; the positive offered instead is the emphasis on singleness, the view that valid love depends on the ability to stand alone. This is partly true but the novel also offers other reasons for the failure of Aaron's marriage, and the positive the book leaves us with does not centre on singleness. In order to decide just what the values of the novel are we must determine to what extent they are equated with those held by Lilly, whom Leavis describes as a self-questioning or experimental self-testing on the part of Lawrence. Of the presentation of the leadership theme in the book, of Lilly's role as leader and saviour, Leavis argues that 'Lawrence's total attitude in the matter is complex and unsure of itself – unaware of what it amounts to' (37). There is some confusion here: Lawrence's attitude is described as 'complex', a term of praise, and yet as 'unsure' and 'unaware'. Which is it? Leavis seems to be arguing that Lilly and his ideas are not fully endorsed by Lawrence but are continually qualified (if not rejected) by the other characters; the passage which Leavis quotes (p. 43), from the discussion between Aaron and Lilly at the end of the novel, about the love mode and the power urge, is an interesting example. This last chapter is entitled 'Words', which suggests that Lawrence is undercutting the substance of their discussion, and not fully identifying with Lilly's ideas. Further, throughout the discussion Aaron either objects or disagrees as Lilly states his position, and since Lilly has the last word in the novel we don't get Aaron's retort – so we don't have to interpret the ending to mean Aaron will submit. Yet despite all these qualifying elements, Lilly's advocacy of the power mode, with its authority and obedience, is very seriously being considered by Lawrence. Lilly's leadership programme is a disturbing part of the novel and Leavis never does confront it, which seems a serious omission; it is not satisfactory to say simply that Lawrence is unsure of his attitude to these ideas. What Lilly proposes contradicts Lawrence's emphasis on standing alone as the necessary basis of a relationship. Lilly states at the end of the novel, in the passage Leavis quotes, that 'men must submit to the greater soul in a man for their guidance; a woman must submit to the positive power soul in a man, for their being' (43). As the solution to the marital and political problem Lilly proposes not singleness but submission; in both instances it is a disturbing solution, and can hardly be considered to have an acceptable normative bearing. This aspect of the novel Leavis has ignored. In fact, one must consider the possibility that Leavis *deliberately* ignored this controversial issue in order to make his defence of Lawrence more palatable.

Leavis does, however, present his own critique of the normative bearings of *Aaron's Rod*, and by implication, of Lawrence's work generally. He locates the primary weakness of the novel in Lawrence's presentation of Aaron, and argues that the book 'fails to give full imaginative realization to Aaron's case as one different from Lawrence's own. And "fails" seems the right word: that is, we are faced with an inadvertence, a default of imagination, which is very significant' (42). Leavis contends that the default of imagination is evident in Aaron's lack of feeling about his children; this lack is the most serious limitation he finds in Lawrence's normative 'wisdom or doctrine'. In the light of Lilly's unsavoury proposals, and the problems raised by such a tale as *The Fox*, I find this a curious position to take. Lawrence generally thought of human fulfilment in terms of the relationship between a man and a woman, and not in terms of the family, but that hardly seems the most questionable aspect of his normative 'wisdom'.

In trying to explain the nature of Lawrence's failure in *Aaron's Rod*, and to bring out the basis of his limitations, Leavis refers to *Kangaroo*, treating it essentially as a personal document, rather than a work of art. Identifying Somers with Lawrence, Leavis quotes the passage in *Kangaroo* describing Somers's dream, then comments:

> These pages bring us face to face with the abnormality of Lawrence's position – for it *is* as abnormality that we have to think of it in a writer whose preoccupation with the relations between men and women in marriage was so essentially normative in spirit. For all the emancipating triumph of intelligence represented by *Sons and Lovers*, the too-close relation established with him by his mother had its permanent consequences. The dream-confusion of the mother with Frieda is significant. (48)

He then goes on to add that,

> though he was supremely intelligent, with the intelligence that manifests itself in a rare degree of self-knowedge, clearly his peculiar experience of emotional forcing, strain, and painful readjustment had some lasting consequences that made it very difficult for him to be sure of his poise and centrality as a reporter on some of the most delicate problems his genius drove him to explore. (48)

While we can admire Leavis's honesty in reporting on what he finds, this description introduces a confusion into his view of Lawrence that he surely should have made some attempt to resolve. How is this description of the abnormality of Lawrence's position – an abnormality caused by the 'too-close relation' between Lawrence and his mother – to be reconciled with the repeated insistence of his health and sanity, on the wholeness essential to a normative writer? Early in his book Leavis argues that in contrast to T. S. Eliot 'there is no profound emotional disorder in Lawrence, no obdurate major disharmony; intelligence in him can be, as it is, the servant of the whole integrated psyche. It is the representative in consciousness of the complex need of the whole being, and is not thwarted or disabled by inner contradictions in him' (27–8). This represents Leavis's characteristic view of Lawrence and it supports his view of Lawrence as a normative writer; but it is called into question by his comments on *Kangaroo*. He simply leaves us with the issue and critics who are pro or anti-Lawrence could quite properly quote Leavis to support their argument. In fact, in these comments on *Kangaroo* Leavis is almost conceding enough to satisfy the critics most hostile to Lawrence. Certainly this description seriously qualifies the force of Leavis's argument.

Clearly then there are serious problems involved with Leavis's attempt to establish that Lawrence is a normative writer. There obviously are real difficulties with accepting the relationships in some of Lawrence's work as a description of the way life 'ought' to be. Leavis of course never puts it quite this way, that is, he doesn't equate 'norm' with 'ought'; in fact, he thinks of the normative bearings of a work as being flexible and variable – but only up to a point. 'Normative' does seem to imply a more specific and definite view of human relations than does 'moral', thus it is possible to recognize that Lawrence's works are not always, or necessarily, normative, yet still think of him as an essentially moral, affirmative writer. And it is really the view of Lawrence as a moral and affirmative writer that is the cornerstone of Leavis's interpretation and the essential ground of his high praise. For all the objections we may possibly raise to the specific parts of Lawrence's work, there can be little doubt, I think, that his work as a whole is, as Leavis insists, an assertion of life.

11

D. H. Lawrence: Novelist:
Leavis's Evaluation Of Lawrence

Leavis bases his claims for Lawrence on the two major novels, *The Rainbow* and *Women in Love*, and on the tales; he tells us that he wants 'the stress to fall unambiguously'[1] on these works. This means, of course, that Leavis's approach to Lawrence's work is radically selective, and the 'lesser novels' are given a very secondary place. Specifically Leavis asserts:

> His genius is distinctively that of a novelist, and as such he is as remarkable a technical innovator as there has ever been. It is *The Rainbow* and *Women in Love* that most demand attention. The need is to get recognition for the kind of major achievement they are. Together they constitute his greatest work, or perhaps it is better to say that, in their curious close relation and the separateness, they are his two greatest works. They represent the enormous labour, the defining of interests and methods, the exploration, the technical innovation, on which the ease of the later work is based. (18)

Even in this short passage we get a clear sense of the major problem Leavis faced: 'the need is to get recognition'. He had, that is, to 'make a case' for Lawrence, and certain aspects of his argument can best be understood as part of this general problem.

Leavis, however, has been triumphantly successful in winning recognition for the two major novels. Mark Spilka, Eliseo Vivas, George Ford, Colin Clarke and Stephen Miko, for example, have all, to a great extent, followed Leavis in regarding these as Lawrence's greatest works. And Leavis's essays on the two novels have received high praise. Mark Spilka in his study *The Love Ethic of D. H. Lawrence* acknowledges that he has 'relied heavily in chapters five and six on F. R. Leavis's excellent and definitive series on *The Rainbow* and *Women in Love* in *Scrutiny* Magazine'[2] Graham Hough, in his book *The Dark Sun*, also acknowledges a debt to Leavis's *Scrutiny* articles: 'I found little helpful criticism except that of Dr Leavis...I owe most to his chapters on *The Rainbow* and *Women in Love* which indeed leave little for a later hand to add.'[3] Leavis is almost single-handedly responsible for winning recognition for the originality and greatness of both of these novels, and this is one of his major achievements as a critic.

But Leavis's claims for the tales and his discussion of the 'lesser novels' are far more contentious. Primarily in these two areas we see the problems that arise in his attempt to 'make a case' for Lawrence: 'tactical' manoeuvres that override Leavis's normal critical practice, a strong reliance on rhetoric, deflection of judgment, and overstatement. Let me cite an example of the most obvious kind of difficulty Leavis gets involved in in his attempt to 'win recognition' for Lawrence and to 'deal with some of the grosser and absurder falsities' (13) about him. In the introduction Leavis renews his dispute with T. S. Eliot almost immediately, challenging his view that Lawrence lacks a sense of humour. Leavis points to the short stories *Things, Two Blue Birds, Jimmy and the Desperate Woman, Mother and Daughter* and *St. Mawr* as evidence of Lawrence's humour. But Leavis is not content to argue just that Lawrence has a sense of humour; he goes further: 'For the plain fact is that Lawrence is one of the great masters of comedy' (13). Leavis has become so concerned about refuting Eliot that he is led to making an extravagant claim for Lawrence. The tales that Leavis cites do not convince me, at any rate, that Lawrence is one of the 'great masters of comedy', but nor do I see it necessary to argue that this is part of his greatness. Leavis is not doing Lawrence a favour by making claims that are inessential, and perhaps false. As far as the lesser claim goes, Lawrence clearly does have a sense of humour, but I think of it first of all in connection with some of his prose writings, such as *Studies in Classic American Literature* and *Introduction To These Paintings*; of the novels I would point to *Kangaroo*, particularly in aspects of his treatment of Somers. In *Mother and Daughter* and situation is too disturbing and in *Jimmy and the Desperate Woman* the treatment is too sharply satirical to be truly humorous. As to the related view that Lawrence was characteristically angry Leavis writes: 'As for anger, no sensitive and highly vital man was ever less given to it, if we are to judge by his humour, irony and the tone of his writing in general' (13). Again the problem is that Leavis states this in an extreme form which makes it difficult to accept, for there are places in Lawrence's writings that display an open animus, and it is clear from what we know of Lawrence's life that he did suffer from moments or periods of intense rage. I am not implying that Leavis consistently overstates his case for Lawrence, but unquestionably, at times, his desire to win proper recognition for Lawrence does lead him to advance exaggerated claims.

i. The Lesser Novels

Leavis's discussion of the 'lesser novels' is a curious mixture of claiming too little as well as too much, and the 'tactical' manoeuvres – unusual in Leavis's criticism – involved in 'making a case' for Lawrence are most obvious in his discussion of these works. Quite simply, I think that, as part of his 'tactic', Leavis claims too little for Sons and Lovers and Lady Chatterley's Lover while, in effect, over-valuing Aaron's Rod and Kangaroo. His attitude towards Sons and Lovers is perplexing. He does grant it considerable distinction: 'This is not to dismiss Sons and Lovers, which is certainly a work of striking genius. But Sons and Lovers has not lacked attention; it has been widely appreciated, and the nature of its originality recognized' (18–19). This in itself is acceptable enough; it was for a similar kind of reason that Leavis had not included an essay on Donne in Revaluation. But then Leavis goes on to add: 'Remarkable as it is, its qualities and achievements, on the one hand, are obvious enough and on the other, they are not, I think, such as to suggest that the author was going to be a great novelist' (19). This is another matter; surely the novel is not only an indication of Lawrence's powers, but is proof of them. The Rainbow and Women in Love are superior novels, but Sons and Lovers seems quite clearly to be Lawrence's third best work, and itself must rank as one of the major modern novels. Leavis wants to select and emphasize only what is essential in Lawrence, to outline the canon, and his slighting treatment of Sons and Lovers is a serious misemphasis. It is surely a more significant manifestation of Lawrence's genius at that early stage than The Daughters of the Vicar. Quite probably, though, Leavis's attitude to Sons and Lovers is partly the result of his desire to win recognition for The Rainbow and Women in Love;

as part of his tactic he had to insist firmly that *Sons and Lovers* was not, as the conventional view would have it, Lawrence's best novel.

Leavis's final (1961) assessment of *Lady Chatterley's Lover* seems even more influenced by his desire to combat a mistaken and conventional view of Lawrence. In the Lawrence book, Leavis devotes only two pages to *Lady Chatterley's Lover* and over a page of this is the description of Tevershall that he had used in the 1930 pamphlet where he had praised the book highly. By 1955, however, Leavis had changed his evaluation considerably and no longer regarded the novel as one of Lawrence's best works; in fact he makes a point of approving more of the pamphlet *A Propos of Lady Chatterley's Lover*, for its poise and vital intelligence, than of the novel. The novel he criticizes as being '*too* deliberate – too deliberate, at any rate, to be a wholly satisfactory work of art, appealing to imaginatively sensitized feeling' (73).

In the chapter on the tales, Leavis contrasts the novel unfavourably with *The Virgin and the Gipsy*. Again, as far as the attempt to establish the essential canon of Lawrence's work goes, Leavis is open to criticism: even if we could feel 'more unreservedly happy' about *The Virgin and the Gipsy* than about *Lady Chatterley's Lover*, it is a slighter work. Our understanding and estimation of Lawrence depends more on the novel than on the novella, and Leavis's slighting treatment of the former while giving a comparatively extensive analysis of the latter is a questionable emphasis. While the issue is not exactly the same as that created by Leavis's apparent preference for *The Daughters of the Vicar* over *Sons and Lovers*, it is similar enough; and I believe that in both instances the novels are more important. (I do not mean to imply that as a general rule the novels are more important than the tales.) Even if Leavis is right that *The Virgin and the Gipsy* is 'better' than *Lady Chatterley's Lover* (that is, a more controlled and impersonal work) this does not necessarily make it more important or central. In this case the novella is more limited in scope, and its achievement is conditioned by those limitations. *Lady Chatterley's Lover* has an importance that perhaps transcends its level of achievement simply because it represents such a concerted effort on Lawrence's part to express something he felt was essential – just the fact it went through three versions indicates the importance it had for Lawrence.

In 1955 Leavis had not completely rejected *Lady Chatterley's Lover*, however; his criticism is tempered by some strong praise. He describes the book as courageous and claims: 'There is much that

is admirable about *Lady Chatterley's Lover*. The spirit that animates
the book is that strong vital instinct of health to which I have just
referred as the spirit of Lawrence's genius' (73). More specifically
Leavis claims that Lawrence relates his special theme with great
power to the malady of industrial civilization – especially in Connie's ride through Tevershall. Indeed, the note on which Leavis
concludes is *almost* a favourable one.

But in February 1961, just after the London trial of *Lady
Chatterley's Lover* (Penguin Books v. Regina), Leavis published an
article in *The Spectator* that presented a serious devaluation of the
novel. The article was later reprinted under the heading 'The
Orthodoxy of Enlightenment' as the last essay in *Anna Karenina And
Other Essays* (1967), Leavis's first book since the Lawrence study.
Leavis brings many new objections against the novel, yet on the
whole I think that we have here an example of Leavis's response
being affected by his battle against the ethos of the 'new enlightenment'. His judgment was influenced by what we might call
'literary politics'. Leavis reacted strongly to the danger that
Lawrence would become known mainly as the author of *Lady
Chatterley's Lover*. And, to give Leavis his due, this was a very real
danger. Anthony Beal, in his book on Lawrence, written just after
the trial, observes that '*Lady Chatterley's Lover* is undoubtedly the
most generally known of Lawrence's books, but it owes its fame to
its history of legal repression.'[4] In contrast to the position of the
new orthodoxy, Leavis states:

> A real advance, in the sense represented by Lawrence,
> depends upon the existence of a body of genuinely
> enlightened opinion, ensuring that the nature of
> Lawrence's genius and achievement shall be widely
> understood, so that these may have their proper force.
> *Lady Chatterley's Lover*, then – it is important that this
> obvious enough truth should be recognized – is a bad
> novel.[5]

Leavis criticizes the novel for being didactic and lacking impersonality, but he also offers two other objections that call into
serious question the intent of his negative evaluation. In almost
complete contrast to his earlier judgment that the novel presented
a penetrating diagnosis of industrial civilization he now argues:
'Of course, Mellors helps to give plausibility to the suggestion that
the treatment of the personal theme gives us at the same time a

diagnosis of industrial civilization. Actually, the evoked Midland *decor* remains merely *decor*. Industrial civilization doesn't really enter into a just appraisal of Connie's behaviour.'[6] Here there is no reference to the description of Tevershall that Leavis had praised, since 1930, as *locus classicus* for understanding the essential problems of modern life. Leavis does not actually mention the Tevershall passage – a fact of some significance itself – but I do not think that it can be implied simply that he now sees it as a set-piece, unintegrated into the rest of the novel; it is 'merely *decor*' and not penetrating diagnosis. This change clearly shows that Leavis overstates his case against the book; he is so determined to defeat the attitude of the new enlightenment that he implicitly contradicts a judgment he had maintained over twenty-five years.

Leavis's other final objection is a directly moral one: 'The suggestion that the book tends to promote respect for the idea of marriage is fantastically and perversely false. Lawrence, when he wrote it, had forgotten what marriage (as opposed to a *liaison*) was.'[7] This is one of the few overtly moral objections that Leavis makes in his criticism, and it's of striking interest here since he defends, for instance, Aaron's abandonment of Lottie in *Aaron's Rod*, and even, apparently, the presentation of marriage in *Samson and Delilah*. I do not see how he can dismiss the relationship of Mellors and Connie as a *liaison*, since, whatever may be wrong with it, it is as serious as the relation of Hannele and Hepburn in *The Captain's Doll* and much more involved and complex than that of Yvette and the Gipsy, both relationships Leavis apparently approves of. (Leavis discusses at length the normative implications of the relationship of Hannelle and Hepburn, which shows that he considers it as much a 'marital program' as the relation of Connie and Mellors.) His rejection of the relationship of Connie and Mellors here reflects, I think, his *determination* to make a case against the novel.

Some of Leavis's objections to the novel can be granted without dismissing it as completely as he does. The story centres on Connie, and in presenting her predicament and search Lawrence shows both sympathy and insight. In Connie's quest to escape the emptiness of her life, and life in industrial society, there is a clear indication of what Leavis had earlier (1955) described as the vital instinct of health. *Lady Chatterley's Lover* is without question a 'lesser novel', but it surely deserves a more favourable response than Leavis, in the face of 'the new enlightenment', gives it.

If Leavis is unduly severe in his evaluation of *Sons and Lovers* and *Lady Chatterley's Lover*, he is surprisingly appreciative in his account of *Aaron's Rod* and *Kangaroo*. Of all the lesser novels only *Aaron's Rod* gets any detailed attention in *D. H. Lawrence: Novelist*. Generally, Leavis argues that experience which remains private and personal is not art – art is impersonality. Of *Aaron's Rod* Leavis claims that some scenes are probably 'recent actual experiences of Lawrence's own, directly rendered' (33); in other words, in presenting experience directly without transforming or transcending it, the novel lacks impersonality. Despite this lack Leavis contends that 'what he is offering us is art or nothing' (32), an assertion which is never satisfactorily explained. In contrast to *Sons and Lovers* which offers an achieved insight into the 'case', a necessary attribute of impersonality, Leavis describes *Aaron's Rod* as 'far more tentative, much more like an actual immediate living of the problem; something experimental embarked on in the expectation that the essential insight will have sufficiently clarified and established itself by the close' (32). This is a fair description of the book, but it's tentative, self-exploratory quality is not the quality of art. Despite Leavis's placing of *Aaron's Rod* among the 'lesser novels' he grants it considerable distinction, but I think he accords the novel a higher value than it deserves, or at least a higher value than he has justified in his argument.

Leavis has high praise for *Kangaroo* although he devotes only brief space to an actual analysis of the novel.[8] He argues that both intelligence and complexity of attitude (the two being almost indistinguishable) are the prominent characteristics of *Kangaroo*. In Lawrence's treatment of politics and Australian life Leavis praises the intelligence that 'forbids him to deceive himself with any gross simplification of the reality' (56) and also points to the intelligence evident in the complexity and integrity with which the relation of Somers and Harriet is presented. He further asserts that 'the complexity of attitude that makes *Kangaroo* so unlike a day-dream in the discreditable sense is manifested in the subtlety and variety of the tone' (56). These are the terms of praise that Leavis usually applies only to works he admires greatly, but all he offers in support of this claim is the quotation of a passage (56–7) from the imaginary dialogue Somers has with Harriet, on which he comments: 'That tone, so characteristic of Lawrence, is a more remarkable thing than may at first appear; it should be examined in the whole chapter. It expresses an extraordinary poise and a completeness of attitude.

What might seem to be levity or humorous disengagement is an absence of bitterness and partiality, and not an absence of depth or seriousness' (57). This is surely one of the occasions in the book where Leavis is guilty of special pleading, where he must attempt to convince us that our normal response to the passage (certainly our first reaction) is mistaken. I am not convinced by his argument, the tone strikes me as being light and detached.

Leavis further contends that Lawrence's concern with power has 'its solemn utterance in *Kangaroo* as in *Women in Love* and *Aaron's Rod*, but all three novels exemplify Lawrence's astonishing flexibility of tone: the solemnity is offset by (say) Frieda's voice; by the characteristic Laurentian recognition of the complex and indocile reality' (57). It's difficult to agree that *Aaron's Rod* and *Kangaroo* have the rich flexibility Leavis claims for them – and the way he associates them with *Women in Love* here seems a curious failure of discrimination. Lilly's voice comes close to dominating *Aaron's Rod* by the end, and while Harriet introduces a qualifying voice into *Kangaroo* this is not enough to make the novel truly complex. Leavis obviously considers *Women in Love* to be a greater novel than *Kangaroo*, yet in the brief discussion he gives the latter novel he at no time indicates why it is inferior – he praises its intelligence, complexity and flexibility and leaves us wondering how, if it is all this, it is a 'lesser' novel. For a critic capable of great astringency, Leavis seems perplexingly lenient in this evaluation.

ii. The Tales

Much of Leavis's claim for Lawrence is based on his high assessment of the tales: *The Daughters of the Vicar*, *The Captain's Doll*, *St. Mawr*, and the various stories. Leavis devotes nearly half of the book to discussing these works and on many of the stories he is very convincing; but in certain places we find over-evaluation and a deflection of his judgment by his personal literary battles. I find Leavis particularly convincing in his assessment of such tales as *The Horse Dealer's Daughter*, *England, My England*, *The Captain's Doll*, and *Sun*, for example, but I think some questions need to be raised about his high praise of *The Daughters of the Vicar* and *The Virgin and the Gipsy*.

Agreement with Leavis's high evaluation of *The Daughters of the Vicar* depends very much on accepting the interpretation he gives of the nature of the relationship between Louisa and Alfred. If the

story simply rejected the false spirituality of Mr Massy and offered
a positive physical vitality, it would not warrant Leavis's strong
praise. Leavis convincingly shows that the attraction of Louisa and
Alfred is not of a simple physical kind, that Lawrence insists on a
necessary continuity of the physical and spiritual. In the presentation of this relationship the success of the tale, which is considerable, lies. But, as Leavis observes, Alfred is significantly opposed
to Mr Massy, and the 'body' represented by Alfred is in obvious
contrast to Mr Massy, whose body is 'unthinkable'. The trouble
is that, from the moment he is introduced, Mr Massy really is an
abortion and it doesn't take any great perspicacity on Louisa's part
to reject him completely. What Lawrence give us in this story is
a clear delineation of value; we know fully what he is for and what
he is against. There is some loss of complexity in this kind of story
and this lack – involving the clear, sharp separation of value – does
call into question the total success of the tale. It is in many ways
a typical Lawrence story – *The Blind Man, The Virgin and the Gipsy*,
and *Lady Chatterley's Lover*, for example, have a similar contrast
between what Lawrence affirms and what he criticizes – and the
success of these stories depends to a great extent on the depiction
of the characters and values he is rejecting. In this instance
Lawrence's presentation of and attitude towards Mr Massy involves
a similar animus to that which he displays towards Clifford
Chatterley, and this weakens the story. That Leavis chose to write
about *The Daughters of the Vicar* as an example of Lawrence's early
fiction rather than *Sons and Lovers* is of marked interest. The novel
is more complex in its evaluations and it is possible for critics to
argue that it sides with either the father or mother; the result of
this complexity is that the affirmation, the values of the novel, can't
be determined as easily as in the story. That is, *The Daughters of
the Vicar* is perhaps more amenable to the approach of the moralist
than of the literary critic, to the critic who himself reduces,
separates, life into distinct categories.

Leavis singles out *The Virgin and the Gipsy* for special praise since
he regards it as 'one of Lawrence's finest things...itself enough to
establish the author's genius as major and as distinctively that of
a novelist' (300). Leavis does not use the term dramatic poem (in
fact he does not apply this description to any of the stories examined
in this chapter), but it is the dramatic and poetic means through
which Lawrence establishes his values that makes him a novelist.
Of the use of the contrasting phrases 'life-unbeliever' and 'moral-
unbeliever', Leavis writes:

> The phrases get their force not only from the dramatic
> situation that seems to give us the state of mind they point
> to, but from what, more generally, has gone before in the
> tale. The phrase, 'life-unbeliever', for instance, resumes or
> focusses a complex work of definition that has been done
> by creative means. (301)

And of the presentation of the positive values of the tale, embodied
in the gipsy and Yvette's relation with him, Leavis states:

> The word one has to use is 'desire'. It is a necessary word,
> and Lawrence himself uses it, but it leaves, of course, a
> delicate work of definition to his art. The tale is
> concerned with defining and presenting desire as
> something pre-eminently real – 'real', here, having its
> force in relation to the nullity of life at the rectory. (305)

Leavis is convincing on this point; the values are enacted in the
story and do not depend on statement or assertion. There are
however problems involved in accepting this story not dissimilar
to those encountered with *The Daughters of the Vicar*. Leavis
maintains that 'there is nothing satiric about the exposure of the
rector and of the pieties and loyalties of the rectory; one can read
the tale without a thought of Samuel Butler... The intensity and
depth of Lawrence's positive preoccupation determine the tone'
(301). This is questionable; it seems to me that there *is* animus in
Lawrence's attitude towards the rector. Lawrence doesn't simply
'place' him but gives vent to his dislike of him: he is described as
being 'like a rat at bay' and 'like a cornered rat'. Leavis simply
ignores these obvious manifestations of Lawrence's animus. And
there is another problem related to the presentation of the rector
that Leavis doesn't consider. The rector turns against Yvette when
she befriends the Eastwoods, and Lawrence writes: 'The rector
looked at her insouciant face with hatred. Somewhere inside him,
he was cowed, he had been born cowed. And those who are born
cowed are natural slaves, and deep instinct makes them fear with
poisonous fear those who might suddenly snap the slave's collars
around their necks.'[9] This represents a kind of Calvinist election
with vengeance; one of the disturbing aspects of Lawrence's work
is that many of his life-unbelievers seem to be damned from birth
and are wholly without the possibility of redemption.

   As Leavis points out, for Yvette 'the gipsy represents the
antithesis of the rectory' (305) and the positive, the value he

represents, the 'real', is desire. This story is similar to *The Daughters of the Vicar*, but there is a striking difference: in the earlier tale Lawrence was concerned to vindicate love, and here it is desire, presented as an impersonal attraction – that is, the positives presented in the two stories are quite different. It may not be fair to take these two stories as an index of change in Lawrence, but it is difficult to accept Leavis's giving nearly as full approval to the presentation of desire as to the presentation of love.

My objections to *The Daughters of the Vicar* and *The Virgin and the Gipsy* are meant mainly to qualify Leavis's judgment; but there are places where his claims for Lawrence's stories can be directly challenged. For instance, he has high praise for the story *Two Blue Birds* as an example of Lawrence's ironic mode, but it strikes me as far too light to bear the substantial weight Leavis puts on it – there is mainly 'surface lightness' and the tone skirts being flippant. In Leavis's treatment of this story we have, I think, a case where his own hostility, animus, intrudes and deflects his critical judgment. He argues that the story does 'maintain perfectly the light tone of its irony. But to suppose that the lightness means any lack of seriousness or depth would be a mistake – it would be a mistake to suppose that *The Cocktail Party*, in which sin and sanctity figure with the gin, is more serious and goes deeper (the contrary seems to me true)' (292). But I doubt that the depth is in the story and suspect that Leavis's desire to exalt Lawrence over Eliot is one of the reasons he overpraises it. Moreover, Eliot is not the only literary figure Leavis uses the story against; it 'places' one of his other enemies. The husband in the story is a writer and after quoting a speech of his on the novel Leavis comments:

> We need to be told no more about the kind of author the
> husband is – or why the literary world has always
> instinctively hated Lawrence. He has more than once,
> with an irony the more final for being unmalicious,
> presented and placed the type: the successful modish
> writer who is wholly uncreative, and has essentially
> nothing to say, but who *has* his 'personality', his assurance
> of his place in the social-personal world that determines
> success in contemporary letters, and his uncreativeness,
> which enables him to be easily and acceptably in the
> mode. (294)

Leavis's high evaluation of this story makes sense only in light of his battle with the literary world. He is responding to the subject matter, to Lawrence's critique of the modish writer, and taking that for the full achievement which is not there.

Of much greater importance, Leavis's battle with the literary world, or more specificaliy with Bloomsbury, intrudes conspicuously into his discussion of what is perhaps the most problematical of all Lawrence's works: *St. Mawr*. It seems that it was largely due to Leavis's intense dislike of the 'civilization' respresented by Bloomsbury, the kind of civilization so severely criticized in the novella, that he began his discussion of Lawrence in *Scrutiny* with *St. Mawr*. Lou's vision of evil overwhelming the world is a direct response to the triviality of the civilization depicted in the tale – and Leavis, as I have pointed out at the beginning of this section, considers the Bloomsbury ethos inimical to life in a similar way; what is so totally lacking from such a world is everything represented by St. Mawr. There are other reasons why Leavis began with *St. Mawr*: he had just finished writing his first two essays under the new concept of 'The Novel As Dramatic Poem', the essays on *Hard Times* and *The Europeans*. They are both short, tightly organized novels; that is, they are the kind of work that would seem to be most amenable to the new approach to the novel he was developing, and *St. Mawr* is suitably short. Again, like the other two works, *St. Mawr* was largely unknown and neglected, and much of Leavis's novel criticism has taken the form of 'rescue work'. Finally, *St. Mawr* is one of the works Leavis had consistently admired – he praised it in the 1930 pamphlet. But most likely Leavis focused on *St. Mawr* because it exposes the emptiness of the 'Bloomsbury world'.

The essay published in *D. H. Lawrence: Novelist* actually differs in a significant way from the original essay in *Scrutiny*; Leavis has interpolated a long section that makes his association of the story with Bloomsbury explicit. (Bloomsbury was not actually mentioned in the original version of the essay.) Leavis's interpolation (the dialogue quoted on page 249, all of pages 250 and 251, and the long quotation on 252) partly extends the significance of St. Mawr, but primarily concentrates on identifying the trivial civilization in Lou's vision of evil with Bloomsbury. Earlier Leavis had argued that 'Rico is the antithesis of St. Mawr; he represents the irremediable defeat of all that St. Mawr stands for' (238), and in the interpolation he clarifies what Rico 'stands for': 'He is in the first place, we may say, Bloomsbury – the Bloomsbury Lawrence knew and had recoiled from' (250). Leavis then extends Rico's significance to include the literary world in general, the world Leavis has always regarded essentially as the enemy. This quarrel with Bloomsbury – and the literary world – is out of place here; this aspect of the book belongs more to literary politics than to literary criticism. It is certainly not fair to the Bloomsbury represented by either E. M. Forster or Virginia Woolf to equate it, or them, with Rico. Leavis's attraction to this story, the special place it has in his writings on Lawrence, is not clearly separable from his hostility to Bloomsbury.

Leavis offers an assessment of *St. Mawr* which appears startling (and must have been especially so on the first appearance of the essay in 1950): '*St. Mawr* seems to me to present a creative and technical originality more remarkable than that of *The Waste Land*, being, as that poem is not, completely achieved, a full and self-sufficient creation. It can hardly strike the admirer as anything but major' (235). This has proven to be the most controversial of all Leavis's judgments on Lawrence's works, and the tale has been the subject of widely differing evaluations. Leavis's high praise of the story, however, seems to me clearly exaggerated. I have previously mentioned the lack of formal unity in the novella, and there are other weaknesses in the tale, and in Leavis's defence of it.

Leavis brings to bear his concept of the novel as dramatic poem in explaining and evaluating the success of this story. In most of the essays Leavis wrote on Lawrence he argues that the work succeeds as a dramatic poem, – he particularly argues this point in his discussion of *Women in Love* – and one of the main areas of contention in his reading of Lawrence is whether there always is this kind of success. Leavis writes of the significance of *St. Mawr* that: 'It is developed and enforced by a wealth of poetic and dramatic means' (242). Leavis recognizes though that the significance of much of the story is not just implied but at times brought very close to open statement, and of an example of this method he writes:

> The discussion that follows between her and her daughter
> offers a good example of a method that, as part of the
> complex process of establishing his values and
> significances, Lawrence can use with great delicacy. They
> discuss what may be called his central theme, and while
> doing so in a wholly dramatic way, bring to the point of

explicitness the essential work of implicit definition that
has been done by image, action and symbolic presentation.
(243)

It is always open to question whether Lawrence's explicitness is not
being offered as a substitute for created art; in the conversation
under discussion the art does seem predominant. One of Leavis's
later examples, however, is open to criticism. Lou spots the dead
adder that St. Mawr has recoiled from, and 'on the discovery
ensues a "vision of evil"; it possesses her as she rides on to the farm.
It brings to explicitness significances that the action, the symbolism,
and the poetic means in general of the tale have intimated' (250).
If the story has successfully conveyed its meaning implicitly, then
why is the explicit statement of Lou's vision even necessary? This
may sound like a narrowly Jamesian objection, but Leavis does not
satisfactorily explain the purpose of Lawrence's explicit statements.
This problem arises in a more acute form in the story of the first
settlers in the mountains of New Mexico. Here Lawrence comes
close to interpolating an essay into the story, or at least makes
use of the Victorian convention of authorial intrusion where the
narrator can generalize at length about the implications of his
story. In this account of the settlers (and to a lesser degree in the
presentation of Lou's vision) there is a tension between Lawrence's
explicitness, his prophetic impulse, and his achieved art that is not
fully accounted for in Leavis's reading of the story as a dramatic
poem.

As I have explained, as an approach to the novel, the idea of
the dramatic poem implies an application of the methods of close
analysis of poetry to the novel, and in a sense this is what we find
in Leavis's essay on *St. Mawr*. The essay is twenty-two pages long
and includes about ten pages of quotations; Leavis makes great use
of 'words on the page'. This does not mean that he says much about
Lawrence's use of language: Leavis's criticism of the novel generally
focuses mainly on the values represented by characters not on the
novelist's use of language. This direct concentration on values
rather than on language is even more noticeable in the book on
Lawrence than in *The Great Tradition* which, in this matter, is in
some ways a transitional book. In the essay on *St. Mawr* there are
only two references to the quality of Lawrence's written language
an in each instance Leavis is trying to convince us of the force of

Lawrence's creative writing. He describes the opening pages of
St. Mawr as being 'something extraordinarily like careless ease'
(235), but argues that

> what looks like carelessness – the relaxed, idiomatic, and
> even slangy familiarity – is actually precision and vivid
> firsthandness. And we soon discover that there is no limit
> to the power of easy and inevitable transitions. For
> Lawrence writes out of the full living language with a
> flexibility and a creative freedom for which I can think of
> no parallel in modern times. (236)

Leavis advances this as a general claim for Lawrence's use of
language and as such it deserves assent, but in this particular
instance it is at best problematical whether 'everything is precisely
and easily *right*'. The flippancy of tone in the opening passage
prevents it from being a good example of Lawrence's best writing,
and I find Leavis's attempt to persuade us that the passage achieves
more than we would think on a first reading unconvincing. His only
other comment on Lawrence's use of language in the tale occurs
when he's examining the discussion between Lou and her mother.
Leavis praises their exchanges for their range and suppleness, then
writes: 'It is astonishing what Lawrence can do, in dialogue, with
complete convincingness; dialogue that starts from, and, when it
likes, lapses back into slangy colloquialism, yet, invoking the
essential resources of poetic expression, can hazard the most intense
emotional and imaginative heightening' (248). Again Leavis tries
to convince us that what we might take for careless writing is in
fact extremely precise, but it is striking that at just this point Leavis
himself relies on a heavily emotive use of language – 'astonishing',
'complete convincingness', and 'the most intense heightening'. It
is difficult not to consider the possibility that these are places where
Leavis is protesting a little too much – that in making his case for
Lawrence he overstates his argument in those very places where
Lawrence is vulnerable.

Finally, Leavis's general claim for the tales as a whole needs to
be scrutinized. Of the over eleven-hundred pages of tales he argues
that 'all but a very small fraction is transcendentally good' and
that of 'the nearly fifty tales there are only five or six that one
would mark as certainly to be excluded from a volume that should
represent Lawrence's strength' (308). I find it a highly arguable
point whether most, or many, of the stories not discussed by Leavis

are 'transcendentally good', but the main question here is that raised by Graham Hough in the condensed but excellent chapter on the tales in his book *The Dark Sun*. He follows Leavis in emphasizing the range and variety of the stories, but he also makes an observation that undercuts the kind of importance Leavis attaches to them:

> With all this diversity there is perhaps only one thing the tales have in common – and that is something negative; they are *not* the growing points of Lawrence's fiction...It is never, I think, in the short stories that a new phase of Lawrence's development opens. His new ideas are hammered out in the long novels (that is why a consistent development can be seen through them); and the short stories are related to these arduous voyages of exploration in a variety of ways...Precisely because it is not in these shorter tales that the original exploration is done, they are often superior in artistic organization to the long exploratory novels. In a restricted form, preaching and repetition are bound to be kept to a minimum; and those who say, as many do, that Lawrence's best work is in his shorter pieces have much reason on their side. In sustained realisation, in formal completeness there is certainly nothing to better the best of his shorter tales. But simply to prefer them probably implies some reduction in the importance of Lawrence as a whole.[10]

While Leavis does not prefer the stories to the novels, he certainly thinks of them as having a much more important place in Lawrence's work than Hough does. Hough follows Leavis in emphasizing the exploratory nature of the novels but denies this quality to the stories, and despite his claim for their 'artistic' superiority, is led into reading them as secondary and (as the emphasis of his book indicates) as less important. If we grant Hough his point, then we possibly have to allow that Leavis focused half his attention, and half his claim, on a secondary part of Lawrence's work, and that the more comprehensive treatment Hough gives to the novels brings us closer to the centre of Lawrence's achievement. Hough's point cannot be easily dismissed and it is very difficult to decide just what status Lawrence's tales have in relation to his novels. (Involved with this particular argument, to some extent at least, is the more general question of just how important any short

stories or novellas can be considered to be in relation to the form
of the novel; Hough refers to the stories as a 'restricted' form,
apparently meaning only 'shorter' but the connotation of being
'limited' seems close at hand.) No easy answer can be given here,
but I think it can be said that Hough mistakenly simplifies the
relation between the novels and the tales and fails to give the latter
the recognition they deserve. At times the stories and tales *are*
exploratory, the developing point of Lawrence's art. In *St. Mawr*,
whatever its faults, Lawrence clearly is breaking new ground: St.
Mawr symbolizes qualities that Lawrence wasn't able to present
fully in the world of his novels (and that includes Ursula's
encounter with the horses), and the use he makes of the landscape
(again different from that in *The Lost Girl*) is a new element. *The
Captain's Doll* is also exploratory. The relationship of Hannele and
Hepburn is not simply a repetition of that of Ursula and Birkin;
the association in Hepburn of the unknown and darkness indicates
a change from Birkin. Certainly from the time Lawrence finished
writing *Women In Love* it is plausible to argue, as Leavis implicitly
does, that his major effort, in terms of artistic organization and
exploration, goes into the stories and the tales. In fact after *Women
In Love* the long tale itself – *The Fox, The Ladybird, The Captain's Doll,
St. Mawr, The Virgin and the Gipsy*, (and *The Woman Who Rode Away*
and *The Man Who Died* could also be included here, and the latter
in its revitalization of myth could be considered the most profoundly
explorative work of Lawrence's later period) – comes into
prominence in Lawrence's work.

Many of these tales, then, are distinguished not only by their
'artistic organization' but also by their exploratory quality. Lawrence's best tales in fact are fully in accord with and clearly
exemplify Leavis's view of the nature of great art: they display no
separation between form and exploration; rather, the form is
inseparably bound to a searching exploration of human experience.
And Leavis has quite properly centred his praise of Lawrence on
those works which manifest both 'formal completeness' and a
profound enquiry into human life.

PART FOUR: THE LATER LEAVIS

12

Leavis's Revaluation Of T. S. Eliot

The publication of *D. H. Lawrence: Novelist* not only established Leavis as Lawrence's strongest defender, but it also marked the decisive turning point in his attitude towards T. S. Eliot.* After 1955 Leavis's original acclaim of Eliot increasingly gave way to a dissenting appraisal, and this change in his attitude towards Eliot is one of the major developments of his later work. The greater ambivalence in Leavis's response to Eliot reaches its culmination in the extensive critique of the *Four Quartets* which he presents in *The Living Principle* (1975). This revaluation of *Four Quartets* shows Leavis in a major confrontation with his one-time mentor and is particularly revealing of his basic assumptions, for in opposing Eliot's sense of reality he is forced to bring his own view of life to a new point of explicitness. In order to clarify the significance of Leavis's revaluation, however, it is necessary first to sketch briefly the history of his changing attitude towards Eliot's work.

In *New Bearings in English Poetry* Leavis had, of course, placed

---

* After 1955 Leavis, of course, continued to write on Lawrence, and in 1976 he produced *Thought, Words And Creativity: Art and Thought in* Lawrence. This later book, in its explicit concern with thought, does have a slightly different focus from the earlier one, but it does not seem to me that it alters nor even develops, in any serious sense, the view of Lawrence that Leavis put forth in 1955. Hence I see no necessity for giving the later book close examination. I do, however, take up the religious concern of the book in the next chapter. For a slightly different view from mine, one which does see the book as representing significant development in Leavis's position, see Michael Black's essay, 'Leavis and Lawrence: Extending Limits', in *English*, Spring 1977.

Eliot at the centre of his study and he praised especially Eliot's 'self-exploration' and the 'sincerity' of his poetry. Leavis has perhaps done more than any other critic to establish Eliot as the major modern poet, but almost from the outset his high praise of Eliot was counterpointed by a note of reproval that became increasingly stronger. His review of *After Strange Gods* indicated the lines along which his critique would develop. In that book Eliot enunciated a commitment to a type of orthodox religious position that Leavis found unsatisfactory, but more particularly Eliot's harsh assessment of D. H. Lawrence alerted Leavis to certain shortcomings in Eliot's own response to life, such as his negative attitude towards sex. As Lawrence came to take on a greater importance to Leavis he focused more and more on Eliot's limitations. At this point, however, he called into question only certain aspects of Eliot's criticism; his high regard for the poetry remained unqualified.

When the *Four Quartets* originally appeared Leavis accorded them the highest possible praise. In his review of the poems, entitled 'T. S. Eliot's Later Poetry' (1942), Leavis explicitly commended the exploration of the complexities of experience below the doctrinal or conceptual religious frame. He concluded by insisting that to Eliot 'might be adapted the tribute that he once paid to that very different genius, D. H. Lawrence; he pre-eminently has stood for the spirit in these brutal and discouraging years. And it should by now be impossible to doubt that he is among the greatest poets of the English language.'[1] Leavis is totally appreciative of Eliot's poetry here, but in the slightly later review, 'Approaches to T. S. Eliot' (1947), he returns again to the question of Eliot's limitations as a critic, especially those revealed in his predominantly negative response to Lawrence. Nonetheless, Leavis's assessment remains generally positive.

D. H. Lawrence: Novelist reveals a decided change in Leavis's attitude. In the appendix to that book Leavis contends: 'Mr Eliot's attitude towards Lawrence has a significance in respect to himself that, pondered, entails limiting and qualifying criticism of a kind for which the time is now very decidedly due.'[2] In answering Eliot's charges against Lawrence, he states his central objection to Eliot's own work: 'I am not, then, impressed by any superiority of religious and theological knowledge in a writer capable of expressing what is to me the shocking essential ignorance that characterizes *The Cocktail Party* – ignorance of the possibilities of life.'[3] By writing his book on Lawrence Leavis seems both to have committed himself more fully to the view of literature as an affirmation of life, and to have clarified his own sense of life. He subsequently opposed the attitudes of distaste and disgust, the implied rejection of life, found in Eliot's work.

In his writings of the last twenty years Leavis returned repeatedly – almost compulsively – to a consideration of Eliot. In fact, it is Leavis's concern with Eliot, rather than with Lawrence, that can be regarded as being almost an obsession. The change in his attitude towards Eliot is immediately apparent in his essay 'T. S. Eliot As Critic' (1958). Here for the first time Leavis treats Eliot as a 'case', one requiring a 'diagnostic approach'. He argues that the negative attitudes towards life in Eliot's criticism involve him in a self-contradiction and 'portend a radical failure of wholeness and coherence in him, and consequently a defeat of intelligence'.[4] He then goes on to attack Eliot's doctrine of impersonality – the separation of art and the artist which it involves – as a central manifestation of his case. Leavis counters with his own belief 'that without the distinguished individual, distinguished by reason of his potency as a conduit of urgent life and by the profound and sensitive responsibility he gives proof of towards his living experience, there is no art that matters'.[5] He here asserts a disagreement with the fundamental postulates of Eliot's criticism.

Leavis never repudiated Eliot's criticism entirely; he continued to acclaim the essays on the seventeenth century and values highly Eliot's insight into 'the dissociation of sensibility'. But, having challenged many of the basic attitudes and assumptions in the criticism, he began to re-assess Eliot's poetry. *Lectures In America* (1969) contains an essay supposedly on 'Eliot's Classical Standing', but even here Leavis cannot refrain from emphasizing Eliot's shortcomings, and the final note of his response is 'Yes, but...' Nearly half of *English Literature In Our Time And The University* (also 1969) is devoted to a concentrated examination of Eliot's criticism and poetry, culminating in the chapter 'Why "Four Quartets" matters in a Technologico-Benthamite Age'. This chapter represents Leavis's most sustained appreciation of Eliot's later poetry, but he then contrasts Eliot, in very unfavourable terms, with Lawrence. Lawrence, he claims, possesses the true intelligence that is the agent of the whole being, while Eliot, being a divided man, lacks fullness of life. Leavis's work clearly had been leading up to this basic contrast of Eliot and Lawrence and his discussion of Eliot in *The Living Principle* develops from this point.

Leavis's harsh assessment of *Four Quartets* in *The Living Principle* is, nonetheless, rather unsettling in the light of his original acclaim of the poem. To be fair to Leavis, in 1975 he was writing in a completely different situation. In his 1942 review he was trying to win recognition for a new poem; the recognition has since been achieved and he was now able to devote himself to his objections. And even here Leavis maintains a certain balance in his judgment; he praises even while he damns, but the emphasis is predominantly on the negative features of the poem:

> What I have been offering is both a recognition of Eliot's great importance and a severe adverse criticism. It is his using a major poet's command of the English language to bring home to us the spiritual philistinism of our civilization that makes him important to us. The criticism regards his fear of life and contempt (which includes self-contempt) for humanity. This combination of fear and contempt commits him to a frustrating and untenable concept of the spiritual.[6]

Leavis is trying to work out a complex judgment to the particular problem that he feels Eliot poses: 'What is offered, it seems to me, is decidedly not satisfying. No major artist, I am apt to say, is a "case". Yet one couldn't happily call Eliot minor. So he is in his special limiting way unique' (63). The upshot, however, of Leavis's judgment on the attitudes towards human life expressed in Eliot's poem is finally negative. Discussing the ending of 'Burnt Norton' he writes:

> My own tribute to Eliot's genius must be a profoundly convinced 'No'. The advantage offered by the present passage is that it invites me to point immediately to the grounds for this decision. They are contained in the last two lines of 'Burnt Norton'
>
> > Quick now, here now, always –
> > Ridiculous the waste sad time
> > Stretching before and after.
>
> What compels my 'No' is the assumed antithesis between the 'now' and time – for 'time' here, the waste, sad and ridiculous (what belongs to it 'can only die'), represents that which is only 'living'. (191)

Most of Leavis's critique is devoted to working out this judgment but there are certain questionable aspects to his argument. He

overstates his own 'case' against Eliot both by being rather
selective in the passages he chooses to analyse (he ignores some key
affirmative parts of the poem) and by exaggering the negative
implications of other passages. His treatment of the concluding
sections of the *Quartets* is particularly questionable. He places
considerable emphasis on the ending of 'Burnt Norton', but when
he comes to the last paragraph of 'East Coker', while he praises
Eliot as being 'unequivocally a great poet' here, he says almost
nothing about the final twenty lines. Some of these lines lend
support to Leavis's view of Eliot's negative attitude to human time:
'Love is most nearly itself / When here and now cease to matter'.
But much of the rest of the paragraph implies an active and positive
response to life: 'Not the intense moment / Isolated, with no before
and after, / But a lifetime burning in every moment', and, even
more forcefully, the closing lines:

> Old men ought to be explorers
> Here and there does not matter
> We must be still and still moving
> Into another intensity
> For a further union, a deeper communion
> Through the dark cold and the empty desolation
> The wave cry, the wind cry, the vast waters
> Of the petrel and the porpoise.
> In my end is my beginning.

A distaste for human time may be found even here – 'the dark cold
and the empty desolation' – but the *movement* of these lines is
positive. The ending of 'East Coker' is clearly quite different from
that of 'Burnt Norton' and certainly deserves more attention than
Leavis gives it.

Leavis does examine closely the conclusion of 'The Dry Salvages'
but his remarks here reinforce one's sense that he is *determined* to
make a case against Eliot. It is here, of course, that Eliot introduces
an explicit theological note: 'The hint half guessed, the gift half
understood is Incarnation.' In Leavis's earlier writings on this
poem he had been concerned to 'save' Eliot from his theological
expositors and insisted that the poem could not be reduced to any
doctrine. His praise of the *Quartets* for their exploration 'into the
concrete actualities of experience below the conceptual currency'
was invaluable. He argued that the poem generally was not an
affirmation or statement, but 'a tentatively defining exploration',
and of the specific reference to 'Incarnation' he wrote: 'This

poetry, in its "re-creation of concepts", is at the same time, and inseparably, preoccupied with the nature of acceptance and belief; one might, in fact, say, adapting Harding, that to take the place of the words "acceptance" and "belief" is its essential aim.'[7] Now, in *The Living Principle*, we find Leavis remarking about the same passage that not only is Eliot's affirmation not coercively entailed and lacking inevitability of issue out of what has gone before, but 'when we come to the theological affirmation we have to recognize that the emphatically firm explicitness is, for us, not acceptable, it is so clearly addressed by the divided man in an admonitory way to himself' (249). Perhaps most significant of all, Leavis even retracts to some extent his repeated praise for the sincerity of Eliot's poetry. While in the earlier article on *Four Quartets* he described them as 'a technique for sincerity', he now contends: 'The positive attribution of "sincerity" *could*, I think, propose itself only to be judged out of the question; it would imply something about the poet, in relation to this after all basic issue, that one's commentary is bound to negate' (248). A change of view as extreme as this can hardly be accounted for simply by a lapse of time; it reveals both an open distorting 'animus' on Leavis's part towards Eliot, and, a point to which I will return, a significant shift in Leavis's general position.

Leavis's animadversions on the *Four Quartets* need qualification, but, granting this, he can be relentless in pressing his argument home. After reading his critique it is difficult not to agree that something is seriously amiss in Eliot's attitude towards human life and time. Eliot's typical response is given in his description of the Underground in 'Burnt Norton', focusing on the 'strained time-ridden faces / Distracted from distraction by distraction / Filled with fancies and empty of meaning'; in his account, in 'East Coker', of the rural population of seventeenth-century England, 'Eating and drinking. Dung and death'; and in his sense of the fishermen in 'The Dry Salvages': 'There is no end of it, the voiceless wailing.' These characteristic responses justify Leavis's objection that 'Eliot's emphasis falls so heavily and insistently on illusion and human nullity that we must ask, in wonder, what reality – beyond the tormenting privation he so disturbingly evokes – he concedes to time' (218).

In considering Leavis's criticisms of Eliot there is a very important point to keep in mind. *Four Quartets* has generally had a mixed reception and there is a feeling, best expressed by Donald Davie, that the judgments on the poem divide simply on religious grounds:

the religious critics praise the *Quartets* and the secular humanists dislike them.[8] This seems simplistic and there has been criticism written from a definite, explicitly Christian point of view which has passed a judgment on the poem similar to Leavis's. The Catholic theologian William Lynch, for instance, argues that Eliot wants to leap off the line of time into eternity and he counters that we must 'go along with the time-ridden faces. For they are at least on the right track, and dealing with the right fact...Jumping out of our human facts will not help at all... The only answer, as in every case, would seem to be to deepen the fact and its possible levels, to enter more deeply into it.'[9] Further, we certainly should *not* regard Leavis as presenting his critique from any standpoint that can be labelled as just 'humanistic'. The nature of Leavis's position, in fact, needs to be further examined.

Leavis always insisted that 'negative' criticism was necessary largely in order to ensure that true genius gains its proper recognition. This, for example, was partly the reason for his repeated insistence on Auden's marked inferiority to Eliot in the 1930s. Now Eliot himself is being judged adversely, yet this is not being done primarily to gain recognition for any other writer – for the first time Lawrence is hardly mentioned. Blake, certainly, is referred to throughout *The Living Principle*, but it is not so much that Leavis offers us Blake as that he 'uses' Blake, along with Michael Polanyi and R. G. Collingwood, to help him define and express his own stance and attitude to life, which he sets against Eliot's. To describe this as 'moral' criticism seems inaccurate; it is almost a philosophical, and ultimately a religious position that Leavis puts forward. In the *kind* of judgment Leavis presents he obviously goes beyond the bounds most literary critics set for themselves. Most literary judgments are concerned with the question of whether a work reflects a serious purpose and whether that purpose is fully embodied or realized in the work. It is usually felt that there is no reason for taking a judgment any further than this; in fact, the general belief seems to be that all attitudes are a proper subject for art. But Leavis does not accept this and always insisted that the greatest literature represents an affirmation of life; his engagement with Eliot here provides a final test of his basic assumption. In order to meet this test he is forced to attempt a new clarity in stating his position. And it is this, finally, which makes Leavis a major critic: he has his own vision of life and of value to convey.

His entire career has centered, in fact, on the effort to assert a position which gets beyond subjectivity into a larger 'human world'. To say that the judgments we make are 'only personal' or 'merely subjective' would not only make criticism futile, but also limit us to very private, and isolated, worlds. But Leavis insists that this is a false account of the nature of human life, for he believes that the spiritual values which make us human belong to what he recently has come to call the 'third realm'. Reality and values transcend subjectivity; a poem provides a paradigm of the way in which the third realm exists: 'A poem is "there," a meaning is "there," but not in space, it is "concrete"...The antithesis "public" in the ordinary sense, and merely "private," isn't exhaustive. The poem we acceptingly discuss...is neither" (62).

Part of Leavis's objection to Eliot is that he fails to realize that the 'human world' exists in this manner. Leavis observes, for instance, that the English language 'represents an immemorial collaborative human creativity, and, in using the language [Eliot] enters into that collaboration – he implicitly recognizing that in an important sense he belongs to a community (the word takes on a new force) that has a very present depth in time: the life he lives in creating his poem is more than the personal life which, as a matter of fact, is itself never atomic or hermetically enclosed' (228). Not only language but the entire world of values and meaning arises through this process of collaborative creativity. Through this collaborative process, that is, – a model of which is provided by literary criticism, 'Yes, but' – a shared community of value is established, and, of greatest importance, we create our reality. It is this view of the nature of value and life, of the 'human world', that Leavis brings to bear in his revaluation of *Four Quartets*.

Leavis's commitment to human creativity as the source of our values and our sense of reality obviously sets him totally against Eliot's emphasis on the limitations, if not the futility, of human endeavour. As he states in examining 'Burnt Norton': 'The questions, how must reality be conceived, and what is the nature of the human situation, have been raised in a way that compels one to determine and verify one's own ultimate beliefs, and I am sure already that my answers to those questions are not Eliot's' (178). Leavis rejects, in fact, not just the attitudes in the *Quartets*, but any theological doctrines in the western tradition which make 'human nullity' a basic postulate. Explicitly and emphatically Leavis makes his own contrary, rebutting affirmation. 'There is no acceptable religious position that is not a reinforcement of human responsibility' (236). This emphasis on human responsibility is at the heart of Leavis's thinking and establishes the grounds for his critique of Eliot. For Leavis, whatever transcends man can work effectively only through human effort.

William Blake – along with Charles Dickens – became increasingly important to Leavis for typifying the kind of human creativity and responsibility which he values, and Leavis's renewed admiration of Blake intensified his criticism of Eliot. The title of *Nor Shall My Sword*, of course, is taken from the preface to Blake's *Milton*, and in the introductory essay to his book Leavis makes it explicit that he considers Blake, as well as Lawrence, Eliot's antithesis. And in *The Living Principle* he again 'uses' Blake to define Eliot's limitations. In rejecting Eliot's conception of the spiritual he asks: 'How could "spiritual reality"...*be* a reality for us...unless apprehended out of life, in which we are, and in terms of our human livingness? That is Blake's insistence when he says: "Jesus was an artist"' (181–2). These references to Blake help us to understand the significance of the change in Leavis's attitude towards Eliot: it reveals a shift in the values that underpin his work. The terms 'classic' and 'romantic' are perhaps too general to be more than mere pointers, but to the extent to which 'classic' represents a reliance on tradition and authority and 'romantic' a reliance on individual responsibility, Leavis's advocacy of Blake over Eliot indicates that he moved towards a more romantic position. In his later years he frequently quoted with approval Lawrence's comment: 'This classiosity is bunkum; still more, cowardice'. And, without question, Leavis came to take a more positive view of Romanticism itself: 'What Blake represents is the new sense of human responsibility that we may reasonably see as the momentous gain accruing to the heritage – to be taken up (that is) in the creative continuity – from among the diverse manifestations of profound change that are brought together under "Romanticism"'.[10]

The change in Leavis's response to Eliot indicates not only a shift in his values, but also a change in the *kind* of criticism he writes. Even in his 1942 review of the *Quartets* Leavis had remarked: 'In any case, to feel an immense indebtedness to Eliot, and to recognize the immense indebtedness of the age, one doesn't need to share his intellectually formulated conclusions, his doctrinal views, or even to be uncritical of the attitudes of his poetry.'[11] But Leavis began to write criticism in a somewhat more theoretical manner that seemed to demand this kind of confrontation. I hesitate to say that

Leavis became more 'philosophical' since he is so determined to
distinguish literary criticism from philosophy, yet his recent use of
R. G. Collingwood and Michael Polanyi indicates that if he himself
was not tending in that direction, he at least was showing a new
sympathy towards philosophers whom he could enlist in his own
cause. In fact, one of Leavis's criticisms of Eliot is that 'he should
be able to dismiss so easily the truly important thinkers of his own
times: I will specify here only Alexander, Whitehead and
Collingwood. In the work of these distinguished minds process,
development and the telic are *of* the vital principle informing the
thought' (235). Leavis obviously disagrees with Eliot about very
basic assumptions.

Of the philosophers it is mainly Polanyi to whom Leavis refers
in attempting to clarify his own attitudes and intellectually formulated conclusions:

> Yet I don't think that Polanyi – I confine myself now to
> him, because he...has still, it seems to me, to get due
> recognition as the great potential liberating force he is –
> would disapprove of the application of the word 'religious'
> to his own basic apprehension. And unless it has a
> religious quality the sense of human responsibility can't be
> adequate to the plight of the world that so desperately
> needs it. (236)

For Leavis, the kind of religious response Eliot offers, which negates
human responsibility, is inadequate, but so too is any acknowledg-
ment of human responsibility which denies the religious dimension
in life.

There are, however, certain limitations and difficulties involved
with this position, or vision of life, which Leavis sets against Eliot's.
If Eliot tends to slight the temporal for the eternal, Leavis moves
too much, perhaps, in the other direction. When he argues, 'the
reality that Eliot seeks to apprehend being spiritual, he assumes
that the spiritual must be thought of as the absolutely "other" –
the antithetically and excluding non-human' (203), it is easy to
sympathize with his forthright rejection of this view. The problem
arises with his remark that 'the ultimate really real that Eliot seeks
in *Four Quartets* is eternal reality, and that he can do little, directly,
to characterize' (175). It is true enough that poets have to
approach eternal reality indirectly, through the use of natural
images, but one gets the sense that Leavis's criteria practically

preclude the presentation of the eternal. All the passages in *Four Quartets* that he selects for praise are those dealing with the world of time and change. Particularly in his discussion of 'East Coker' Leavis only praises Eliot's presentation of the 'now' of the temporal present. And it is on identical grounds that he commends the opening of 'The Dry Salvages' and the All Clear passage in 'Little Gidding', of which he writes: 'The vivid precision of this is an involuntary recognition on Eliot's part of the reality of life, life in time' (250). Leavis typically conceives of reality – or at least the depiction of reality – in terms of precisions of concrete realization, specificities, and complexities. That there is, however, a possible narrowness and limitation involved with this conception of reality can be seen when he writes:

> It is made impossible for us to doubt that Eliot wants to
> discredit time, but to eliminate time from the real world
> would be to eliminate life. For life is process. 'Hence life'
> – I quote from Collingwood, 'like motion, is a thing that
> takes time and has no instantaneous existence'. Motion
> means change, and change is an idea that Eliot shies away
> from. (228)

This view of life – 'life is process' – does not allow the idea of the eternal a place. In fact, the passage I have just quoted concludes: 'On the other hand, to the living – and the poet of *Four Quartets* is living – the idea of perpetual unchangingness is insufferable.'

A further difficulty arises as Leavis tries to enforce his argument that Eliot is a 'case' in his denial of human creativity. Leavis regards this denial as a fundamental self-contradiction and also rejects Eliot's view that imprisonment in the enclosing self is the essential human condition. To refute Eliot Leavis refers to Blake's distinction between the selfhood and identity. Eliot can only believe in the selfhood, but Leavis is committed to a Blakean 'identity'.

> The identity is the individual being as the focal
> manifestation of creative life – the mode of manifestation
> in which alone, each instance being unique in its
> individuality, life can be pointed to as 'there'. When Blake
> said, 'Tho I call them mine, I know that they are not
> mine', he meant that when the artist is creatively
> successful the creativity to which the achievement belongs

is not his, though, while transcending the person he is, it
needed his devoted and supremely responsible service. The
creative power and purpose don't reside within his
personal self-enclosure; they are not his property or in his
possession. He serves them, not they him. The pride that
Blake defends as a virtue is conscious and resolute
responsibility. It goes with the belief in human creativity
that is not hubris; that belief is what I have been
endeavouring to define. (185)

While Leavis here certainly differentiates his position from the one
he attributes to Eliot, too many questions are left unanswered by
this passage. What, for instance, does the creativity of the artist
belong to? What, is 'transcending the person'? This problem occurs
again when, in discussing 'The Dry Salvages', Leavis asserts: 'The
importance of Eliot is that the challenge his genius represents
precipitates positive conviction and a robust expression of it' (231).
But Leavis does not totally meet the challenge. For his robust
expression he refers, once more, to Blake and Lawrence, then quotes
Collingwood and Polanyi. Quoting passages from the works of
these philosophers is not a proper substitute for a lucid argument
of his own. We are left with the impression that Leavis's position
is not as fully, or systematically, worked out as it needs to be if he
is going to make a decisive positive answer to Eliot.

While Leavis is not entirely satisfactory at the level of theoretical
generalization, he is still an excellent critic when he gets down to
the concrete details of poetry. His discussion of 'Little Gidding' is
too brief to be an adequate account of the whole poem but the first
few pages of his analysis, at least, are the best part of his revaluation
of the *Quartets*. One need not accept his judgment that 'Little
Gidding', coming after the explicit theological affirmation of 'The
Dry Salvages', represents a 'relaxed inferiority', to appreciate the
quality of his argument. Here Leavis undertakes what he does best:
he makes a comparative judgment between passages of poetry, and
his wider concerns are present only implicitly. In fact, Leavis's
evaluation of 'Little Gidding' is not, at least in any apparent way,
ideological, but is strictly literary. The opening 'mid-winter spring'
section he judges adversely and argues, fairly convincingly, that
the passage is weakened by its reliance on 'the simplest kind of
compressed simile'. Leavis insists that by depending on the phrase
'pentecostal fire' Eliot is offering us not a creative–exploratory use

of language, but doctrinal assertion. He quotes a sentence by D. W. Harding, 'The opening of 'Little Gidding'' *speaks of* renewed life of unimaginable splendour', and comments: 'The suggestion conveyed by "speaks of"... is felicitous because Eliot's mode of imparting his sense that the pentecostal theme is for him of central importance is in essence one of mere statement – statement so insistent as fairly to be called emphatic assertion' (253). This is the *kind* of judgment Leavis usually makes: Eliot does not realize or enact his significance in the poem. Against the poetic inferiority of the first movement he sets the strength of the All Clear passage: 'In the uncertain hour before the morning.../I met one walking.' Leavis is not adding anything new to Eliot criticism simply by commending this part of the poem. What is of interest is Leavis's reading of the passage; he argues that here at last Eliot achieves an impersonality that allows the judgment into his 'case' and that momentarily he sees himself as – well, as F. R. Leavis sees him. And on this point Leavis concludes his own 'case' against Eliot.

The kind of theoretical explicitness Leavis presents in his revaluation, in his attempt 'to determine and verify [his] own ultimate beliefs', and his recent interest in Polanyi show him turning in new directions. But on the whole Leavis's career is marked less by new starts than by a striking consistency of concern. It is perhaps not surprising that, having had his final say about Eliot, he should return in *Thought, Words and Creativity* (1976) to Lawrence. This revaluation of Eliot, then, while it reveals interesting new tendencies, is more important for bringing to completion a development in Leavis's work – his process of disengagement from Eliot – that is implicit almost from the beginning. The critique of *Four Quartets* in *The Living Principle* is a culmination of the long series of writings on Eliot in which that process is worked out; it will certainly stand as a major part of Leavis's critical achievement.

13

The Religious Spirit

In addition to his revaluation of T. S. Eliot, there is one other very striking development in Leavis's thought in the last twenty years: the extension he makes in applying the term 'religious'. This central aspect of Leavis's later criticism seems to have gone almost unnoticed. Even the very sympathetic, laudatory article in *The Human World*, entitled 'The Third Realm', which surveys Leavis's work of the 1960s makes no mention of the deeply sounded religious note in his more recent books. Leavis came to apply the term 'religious' to John Bunyan, and, more importantly, to William Blake and Charles Dickens; as well, he expanded his explanation of what he means by the word 'religious'.

This religious note in his later work develops from his study of Lawrence. In *D. H. Lawrence: Novelist* Leavis had 'defined' the religious nature of Lawrence's art and he thereafter relied greatly on this definition. For instance, in his response to C. P. Snow, 'Two Cultures', trying to enforce his conviction of the paucity of Snow's sense of life, Leavis argues that the dimension of depth conveyed by great literature is necessary to life:

> In coming to terms with great literature we discover what at bottom we really believe. What for – what ultimately for? What do men live by? – the questions work and tell at what I can only call a religious depth of thought and feeling. Perhaps, with my eye on the adjective, I may just recall for you Tom Brangwen, in *The Rainbow*, watching by the fold in lambing-time under the night-sky: 'He knew he did not belong to himself.'[1]

It has not been properly understood that Leavis answered Snow's 'scientism' not with 'literarism', but with an appeal to the importance of the religious sense in life. And Leavis repeatedly referred to this passage in *The Rainbow* as a *locus classicus* for conveying the nature of this religious sense. Leavis goes on to observe: 'It is characteristic of Snow that "believe" for him should be a very simple word.' For Leavis 'belief' is obviously a complex matter, but his recent writings add further clarification to the question of just what he does 'believe' in.

One of Leavis's most sustained efforts, since the Lawrence book, to explain the religious quality he values so highly occurs in his 1964 introduction to Bunyan's *The Pilgrim's Progress*. In describing Bunyan's work, Leavis writes:

> There is something irresistible and unanswerable about the
> steadfastness of inner life (Bunyan's own steadfastness,
> something so profoundly and essentially disinterested...)
> that carries the pilgrims through defeats, lapses, disasters
> and felicities. This, we recognize, thinking of Tom
> Brangwen in the first chapter of Lawrence's *The Rainbow*,
> is the effective 'knowing we do not belong to ourselves';
> and we recognize, though theologies may have become
> unacceptable or odious and we may feel that we have
> nothing left that Bunyan could have called 'faith' or
> 'belief', a change-defying validity.[2]

Leavis argues that the religious quality of the art derives from the whole man, and is clearly separable from Bunyan's theological intention: the doctrine implied in the allegory is of less importance than the religious sense which inheres in the art. We should recognize how problematical a 'religious' conception this is, though, when Leavis states 'we have nothing left that Bunyan could have called "faith" or "belief"'. Nonetheless, Leavis explains further:

> To attempt to say anything positive about the religious
> quality of *The Pilgrim's Progress* is a delicate matter. One's
> awareness of a religious significance as distinguished from
> a theological intention is challenged by that opening to the
> First Part...the dream convention...To consider its use is
> to recognize the way in which the personal intensity gets,
> in the creative presentment, while being for that none the
> less intense, a necessary impersonalization. This effect is

hardly separable from the sense we have of there being, in the order of reality in which this history is enacted, a dimension over and above those of the commonsense world.[3]

Bunyan's art expresses the impersonality characteristic of the religious sense, but, more importantly for Leavis, Bunyan's sense of the eternal, unlike that of T. S. Eliot, is expressed as part of a profoundly positive response to *this* life. Leavis contends that:

> the sense of the eternal conveyed by *The Pilgrim's Progress* and coming from the whole man ('trust the tale', as Lawrence said, not the writer) is no mere matter of a life going on and on for ever that starts after death. It is a sense of a dimension felt in the earthly life – in what for us *is* life, making this something that transcends the time succession, transience and evanescence and gives significance.[4]

This sense of significance, Leavis argues, is conveyed with 'great potency' by *The Pilgrim's Progress*, and it is essentially a celebratory sense:

> Music and dancing: this puritanism assumes that art is necessary to life. . . . 'Wonderful! Music in the house, music in the heart, and music also in heaven' – the exclamation suggests aptly that actual 'unpuritanical' sense of earthly life in relation to the eternal which informs *The Pilgrim's Progress*. This is the religious feeling, the unquestioned spirituality, that the creative work conveys.[5]

The most important use or extension, however, Leavis made of the adjective 'religious', after writing the Lawrence study, has not been with reference to Bunyan, but with reference to Charles Dickens and William Blake. In the last twenty years Leavis largely re-stated the themes of his early work and re-examined writers he had previously discussed; his reassessment of Dickens and the increased interest he showed in Blake are the only major new developments in his criticism. Essentially Lawrence alone had represented the religious sense Leavis feels is so necessary to civilization, but in the last few years he came to find it in Blake and Dickens as well. He apparently came to this conclusion by thinking of both of these writers as being similar to Lawrence. This was perhaps the principal reason behind his revaluation of Dickens:

'His power of evoking contemporary reality so that it lives for us today wasn't a mere matter of vividness in rendering the surface; it went with the insight and intelligence of genius. The vitality of his art was understanding. In fact, as I have gone on reading him I have come to realize that his genius is in certain essential ways akin to Lawrence's.'[6] Much as Leavis came to criticize T. S. Eliot for not being like Lawrence, so he came to praise Dickens for his essential affinity.

It is especially in *Little Dorrit* that Leavis finds a religious sense in Dicken's work similar to Lawrence's. Leavis insists that – even in 1970 – Dicken's genius has not been fully recognized because the religious quality of his work has been ignored. Replying to those who talk of Dicken's 'bourgeois and unspiritual conventionality' Leavis maintains that *Little Dorrit* reveals that 'what, at a religious depth, Dickens hated about the ethos figured by the Clennam house was the offence against life, the spontaneous, the real, the creative'.[7] Explaining the significance of the Marshalsea in the novel, Leavis argues:

> Actually, what Dicken's evocation registers is not attraction, but recoil – intense and 'placing'. It is an evocation of final human defeat as a subsidence into a callous living deadness of abject acquiescence. If we are to talk of 'religious sensibility', then what we have here is Dickens's vision of the Marshalsea as Hell: 'Abandon hope all ye who enter here'.[8]

In his essay on *Little Dorrit* Leavis associates Dickens and Blake on the grounds of their religious sense: 'Dickens is in the same sense as Blake a vindicator of the spirit – that is of life. The creativity he insists on as an aspect of disinterestedness is inseparable from the "identity's" implicitly recognized responsibility to something that (not "belonging to itself") it doesn't, and can't possess.'[9] Blake is much more readily thought of as a religious writer than Dickens, but Leavis argues: 'It is the prophetic books that give Blake his standing as a great addict of the specifically religious quest; but actually, for all the grist he affords the research-mills and the symbol-specialists, his concern for the spirit is of the same order as Dickens's – he is, whatever the difference is in emphasis and accent, religious in the same sense.'[10] And Leavis adds: 'With Blake and Dickens I associate Lawrence, so that we have a line running into the twentieth century.'[11]

The collocation of Blake, Dickens and Lawrence and the insistence on the importance of the religious spirit they represent is one of the pressing themes – perhaps *the* central theme – of Leavis's last books. In *English Literature In Our Time And The University* (1969) Leavis explains that Blake is a realist who finds himself wrestling with problems for which he can see no solution:

> Yet if he is not an optimist, neither is he a pessimist, and the religious spirit so strong in him doesn't tend towards fatalism or resignation. It expresses itself in the confidence, unquestioning but un-hubristic, that the creative life in man will be justified in its positive refusal to be resigned. The contrast of Blake to Bentham may serve to enforce the main point I have been trying to make. You could hardly attribute a religious spirit to the Benthamite inspiration...I mustn't now go off into a discussion of Dickens and his relation to Blake. But...the student should know that the line runs from Dickens to D. H. Lawrence, Eliot's (not George Eliot's) great opposite.[12]

Blake, Dickens and Lawrence confute the secular Benthamite vision of man, and it is these three, and not the 'formally' religious (Christian) poet, T. S. Eliot, who represent the authentic religious spirit. In Leavis's introduction to *Nor Shall My Sword* (1972) he returns to this theme again:

> Lawrence might have said of his own works what Blake said of his paintings and designs: 'though I call them mine, I know that they are not mine'.
>
> It is the Blake corroborated and reinforced by Lawrence that I have in mind when I contend that what desperately needs to be emphasized in the present plight of mankind is the essential human creativity that is human responsibility.[13]

And then Leavis adds: 'And, at the opening of the line that runs (one can point out) to Lawrence through Dickens, there is the potent authority with which Blake conveys his knowledge that in creative work he himself serves something authoritative – a living reality that is not his selfhood.'[14]

There are perhaps some problems involved with this collocation – it is difficult to find a parallel in Dicken's work to Blake's 'visionary' aim of presenting the restored Albion and Jerusalem

– but I want to concentrate here simply on examining the different explanations that Leavis himself gives, in his discussion of Dickens and Blake, of the 'something that transcends'. In his essay on *Little Dorrit* Leavis attempts to convey the positive manner in which the religious aspect of Dickens's novel manifests itself:

> It is impossible to discuss Amy Dorrit as disinterestedness (and the creative nisus that placed her at the centre of *Little Dorrit* is intrinsically normative) without being brought to an explicit recognition that the disinterested individual life, the creative identity, is of its nature a responsibility towards what can't be possessed. As Daniel Doyce knows,... the creative originality in him, though it entails resolution and sustained effort, isn't *his*: he is the focus and devoted agent. And I will permit myself to quote once again from that place in the opening of *The Rainbow* which I have found frequently an apt *locus classicus* – the place where we are told of Tom Brangwen that 'he knew he did not belong to himself'.[15]

Again Lawrence is the touchstone for defining the nature of the 'religious'. And again it is not entirely clear just what Leavis conceives of as transcending the individual. Unlike Lawrence he never refers directly to 'God', or uses the equivalent of Lawrence's other comparable terms, such as 'the creative mystery'. Generally Leavis speaks only of 'life' as transcending the individual, and he seems to be presenting a 'godless' religious conception. The discussion that follows the passage I have quoted above is of particular interest in this context. Leavis argues that everywhere in *Little Dorrit* there is the implicit insistence that the individual does not belong to himself, then he maintains:

> The reference to St Paul's is not just convention. It invokes institutional religion, of course, but not in the spirit of satiric irony. The institutional is invoked as representing something more than institution; as representing a reality of the spirit, a testimony, a reality of experience, that, although it is a reality of the individual experience or not one at all, is more than merely personal. That the appeal is to the living cultural heritage which has its life here and now, and is kept living as a language is, becomes manifest as we move through that last paragraph

of the chapter to the end. The inherited totality of the
values, the promptings, the intuitions of basic human
need, that both 'manner' and 'money', in their lethal
way, have no use for – that is what is being evoked. The
reader who really reads Dickens will hardly feel that there
is anything of rhetorical indelicacy in the overtly
associating reference to the New Testament theme. The
effect of it is to emphasize how essentially the spiritual, in
what no one could fail to recognize as a religious sense, is
involved in the whole evocation.[16]

This seems to suggest that what transcends the individual, and what
he 'belongs' to, is the 'living cultural heritage', which implies a
very humanistic 'religious' conception.

Leavis's discussion of Blake, however, suggests another view of
the 'something that transcends'. His response to Blake is best set
out in the introductory essay to *Nor Shall My Sword*, entitled '"Life"
Is A Necessary Word', and in a more recent essay, 'Justifying One's
Valuation of Blake'. In order to establish what makes Blake
important Leavis tries to distinguish Blake's position from that of
what he calls 'hubristic humanism'. Leavis quotes, approvingly,
the words of the theologian J. G. Davies in *The Theology of William
Blake*: 'We are bound to affirm that his doctrines fall within the
general tradition of Christianity...Blake was a genius and he knew
it; but he also knew that this was not a cause for pride; what he
was, what he did, was really the work of a higher power operating
all his artistic creation through him.'[17] Blake's awareness of, and
responsibility towards, this 'higher power' gives him his particular
importance. The terms in which Davies, an orthodox Christian,
refers to Blake's responsibility towards a 'higher power' are quite
similar to those used by Leavis. While Leavis is not really aligning
himself with Davies's position, it is not entirely clear how he differs
from it. In this case the fact that Leavis does not refer *directly* to
a 'higher power' seems to establish the difference.

A paragraph in Leavis's essay 'Justifying One's Valuation Of
Blake' is relevant here. Leavis refers to the distinction Blake makes
between the 'identity' and the 'selfhood':

The 'selfhood' is that which asserts itself and seeks to
possess from within its self-enclosure. The 'identity' is the
individual being as the disinterested focus of life: it was as
identity that Lawrence's Tom Brangwen 'knew he did not

belong to himself'. Blake was voicing the same recognition when he said of his paintings and designs: 'Though I call them mine, I know that they are not mine.' The reply made to Crabb Robinson's inquiry 'in what light he viewed the great question concerning the Divinity of Jesus Christ' is a parallel formulation: 'He said – *He is the only God* – But then he added – "And so am I and so are you."' Crabb Robinson goes on: 'Now he had just before (and that occasioned my question) been speaking of the errors of Jesus Christ. Blake, who knew he wasn't infallible, had no tendency to mistake himself for God.'[18]

This passage provides a further definition of Lawrence's phrase 'knew he did not belong to himself', but Blake's very paradoxical formulation of Christ and man both being God needs to be interpreted if it is to help us understand what Leavis signifies by Lawrence's phrase. The comment on these words of Blake made by Thomas Altizer, the noted 'Death-of-God' theologian, is worth noting:

> Crabb Robinson reports the late Blake as eagerly asserting: 'We are all coexistent with God; members of the Divine Body, and partakers of the Divine Nature.' But these words of Blake do not bear their usual Christian meaning; he is neither referring to a transcendent and numinous God nor for that matter to any meaning of God that is present in the Christian tradition.[19]

Altizer may be right, and he certainly shows that Blake's words are open to diverse interpretations, but Blake does refer to 'God', and Leavis's passage is one of the very few places in his writings where he even uses, albeit indirectly, the word 'God'. This is of particular interest because Leavis closes his essay with a statement that is without parallel in all of his writings. He returns to the theme of the conception of responsibility that makes Blake so important to us now, and then argues:

> Few educated persons will dispute the reasonableness of the assumption that there was once a time when there was, in the world of nature, no life. Life emerged, and no scientist or philosopher has begun to explain how, or by what causation – apart from the persistent offer to explain it away...Nevertheless Collingwood, a very intelligent

and conscientious and well-informed witness, reported only
(so to speak) the other day:

> This at any rate seems clear: that since modern science
> is now committed to a view of the physical universe as
> finite, certainly in space and probably in time, the activity
> which this same science identifies with matter cannot be a
> self-created or ultimately self-dependent activity. The
> world of nature or physical world as a whole, on any such
> view, must ultimately depend for its existence on
> something other than itself.

> That would seem to be closely related to the intuition,
> unmistakably and inevitably asking to be called 'religious'
> as the great writer conveys it, expressed in Blake's
> insistence that he does not belong to himself.[20]

This statement sounds rather like an argument for the existence of
God, and, to the extent to which the statement does point us in
that direction, it is a little surprising, because Leavis has never made
this kind of explicit (for him) declaration before. It almost seems
as if Leavis finally felt the need to offer a justification for his
'belief'.

In *The Living Principle* Leavis again quotes this passage from
Collingwood and argues that 'all writers of major creative works
are driven by the need to achieve a fuller and more penetrating
consciousness of that to which we belong, or of the "Something
other than itself" on which the "physical world ultimately
depend"'.[21] While this clearly expresses a religious viewpoint,
Leavis insists: 'My mind is not on possible theological or philosophical developments of the theme to which Collingwood's sentence points.'[22] Leavis wants to concentrate in this book on the
concerns of literary criticism, but he is acknowledging at least that
Collingwood's statement has theological implications.

Appropriately, Leavis's last book, *Thought, Words And Creativity*,
returns us again to Lawrence. And here, even more clearly than
in *D. H. Lawrence: Novelist*, Leavis's argument and praise centres on
the religious dimension of Lawrence's work. There are two slight
changes in Leavis's position that, perhaps, cause the increased
concentration on the religious concern. First, Leavis now calls
attention to the prophetic aspect of Lawrence's thought: 'To be a
great creative writer, born in England, at Eastwood, of a miner's
family, at that moment in history, was for a Lawrence to find

himself committed to a prophetic role. He was impelled inevitably, by his astonishing gifts, into a questioning examination of the deepest underlying conditions of civilized life.'[23] The questioning is at a religious depth. Secondly, Leavis's own change towards a more 'romantic' position brings him even closer to Lawrence. He writes, for instance: 'It is for the man to foster in himself openness, necessarily creative, to the unknown – to strive towards free, unbiased and uncommitted receptivity at the well-head; his living spiritual authority is a matter of that.'[24] For the early Leavis, 'spiritual authority' was derived largely from an 'external' tradition; now it is a matter of inner receptivity to the 'unknown' – the 'unknown' that Lawrence himself was so open to.

Leavis's discussion of the religious concern in *Women In Love* and *The Rainbow* is the best part of the new book, and in his analysis of both novels we see how literary criticism can become a form of penetrating social commentary. He values *Women In Love* so highly because of Lawrence's presentment, through the fate of Gerald Crich, of the malady that ensues when the religious base of life is ignored. Gerald, locked into his ego in his desire to be self-sufficient, and thus cut off from the 'hidden source', enacts the destructive tendency of our civilization. Leavis's study leads up to *The Rainbow* since it is here that the religious quality of Lawrence's work is most evident. In this novel Lawrence expresses a religious attitude which celebrates the reality of time, development and creative change. Moreover, in Lawrence's religious attitude the emphasis falls squarely on human responsibility: 'God gives me my manhood, then leaves me to it.'

Nonetheless, Lawrence brings home the dependency of creativity on the religious source: 'I know myself the ingress of the creative unknown. Like a seed, which unknowing receives the sun and is made whole, I open onto the great warmth of primal creativity and begin to be fulfilled.'[25] This is the crux of the matter for Leavis. Major human creativity is not arbitrary, nor does it derive simply from the self-enclosed individual. As Leavis explains: 'The creativity in me isn't mine – it doesn't belong to me.'[26] And without access to the creativity that comes from the source, the unknown, there is no significant creation. The major creative artist serves that which transcends man. Lawrence has his crucial importance because in his creativity he apprehends the new life promptings from the unknown, and in his fiction brings them into our midst.

What conclusions can we draw in the end about Leavis's

religious position? Andor Gomme, in *Attitudes to Criticism*, remarks that Leavis has never been fully precise about the 'something that transcends', and then argues:

> A more limiting statement of a specific religious viewpoint is irrelevant to literary criticism which asks for a free play of the intelligence on literature... It is in fact a mark of the tact and sense of relevance of Leavis's literary criticism that, in spite of his refusing to stop short of invoking sanctions, one cannot tell from his criticism what more specific position he holds.[27]

I sympathize to a great extent with Gomme's view, but, since Leavis himself admits there are questions for the theologian and metaphysician implicit in certain of his assertions, we can perhaps try to establish his position in more definite terms than Gomme thinks is necessary. One possible way of shedding some light on Leavis's views is by comparing them with the views of certain modern theologians. While I think one should be cautious about comparing the statements of a literary critic and a theologian, since their concerns are quite different, I also think that, where these interests touch, nothing is to be gained by keeping them rigidly compartmentalized.

As an initial framework for considering Leavis's position it will be useful to refer to Martin Buber's argument in *Eclipse of God*. In a chapter entitled 'Religion and Modern Thinking' Buber criticizes Carl Jung's reduction of God and religion to merely psychological processes:

> For if religion is a relation to psychic events, which cannot mean anything other than to events of one's own soul, then it is implied by this that it is not a relation to a Being or Reality which, no matter how fully it may from time to time descend to the human soul, always remains transcendent to it. More precisely, it is not the relation of an I to a Thou. This is, however, the way in which the unmistakably religious of all ages have understood their religion.[28]

Buber's stand is quite clear: one can only legitimately refer to 'God' if He is regarded as a transcendent Being and Buber totally rejects the 'religion' of pure 'psychic immanence', the attempt to completely include the divine in the sphere of the human self. For

Buber, but not for Jung, God is unmistakably an Other, external to man. If we regard Buber and Jung as defining the two possible ways of thinking about 'God', can we clearly say where Leavis stands? Leavis's repeated quoting of Lawrence's 'knew he did not belong to himself' might seem to align him with Buber, but there are difficulties in making this comparison. In the first place, while Leavis speaks of 'transcendence' he does not directly refer to a 'transcendent Being'. Nor, of course, does he refer to 'God'. 'Life', in many ways, is the word in Leavis's writings that takes the place of 'God' in Buber's. Leavis typically refers to 'the life of which the artist in his creativity is conscious of being a servant'. 'Servant' certainly carries religious suggestions, but there is no need to think of 'life' as involving the conception of a transcendent, or even merely immanent, God. It seems, in fact, just as plausible to align Leavis with the position represented by Jung as with Buber's. For instance Leavis writes of the poet that he is 'a focal conduit of the life that is one, though it manifests itself only in the myriad individual beings, and his unique identity is not the less a unique identity because the discovery of what it is and means entails a profoundly inward participation in a cultural continuity'.[29] Here the individual is being related to something 'outside' of himself to which he belongs, but the idea of a 'cultural continuity' is as human centred as is Jung's ideas of the collective unconscious. Neither concept needs the premise of 'God'. And yet, it does not seem satisfactory to equate Leavis's position with Jung's human orientated 'religion' either; Leavis too insistently points to something outside of, beyond, man. Perhaps we have to recognize that the opposed views of Jung and Buber do not exhaust the possible ways of thinking about what 'God' means.

It is true that Leavis's reluctance to be specific about the ultimate ground of the religious sense he refers to, as well as his reluctance to use the term 'God' at all, can lead one to doubt whether he holds to *any* kind of theistic conception. Yet, certainly before drawing that conclusion, we should consider the fact that some modern theologians have also shown hesitation in making explicit reference to God. W. Richard Comstock, in an article surveying recent trends in religious thought, explains that in contemporary attempts to refer in a secular fashion to 'God', 'one characteristic that almost all of them hold in common is a sense of reticence about direct reference to "God" either in language or in action. All direct characterization of "God" . . . [is] felt to be ambiguous, inadequate, inappropriate.'[30] Comstock then argues that 'this reticence is not considered to be a forthright denial of the actuality of "God", but a recognition of the inappropriateness of any direct and immediate form of orientation toward it'.[31] If we consider Leavis in this context there is no reason to take his reticence as implying a rejection of God. It may simply indicate a rejection of any traditional or conventional concept of God.

The views of John A. T. Robinson, another Englishman, who is also from Cambridge, may be of use here. In *Honest To God* Robinson argues for a radical recasting of the most fundamental categories of theology – including that of God. He states that he can even 'understand what those mean who urge that we should do well to give up using the word "God" for a generation.'[32] Robinson is deeply indebted to Dietrich Bonhoeffer and Paul Tillich in his attempt to find new ways of understanding, and formulating, the meaning of 'God' and of religious experience. Robinson cites approvingly Bonhoeffer's description of God as the 'Beyond in our midst' and, of great interest in this context, compares this with D. H. Lawrence's claim that 'Beyond me, at the middle, is the God.' 'Beyond', we should recall, is one of Leavis's key religious words. Robinson's comparison of Bonhoeffer and Lawrence suggests that at least one stream of modern Christian thought is dealing with religious questions in terms very like those of Leavis's.* And the statements from Tillich which Robinson cites offer an even closer analogy. He quotes from *The Shaking of the Foundations* where Tillich proposes a view of God as the 'Ground of our being':

> The name of this infinite and inexhaustible depth and ground of all being is *God*. That depth is what the word *God* means. And if that word has not much meaning for you translate it, and speak of the depths of your life, the

---

* Leavis and Bonhoeffer could be compared in many ways. Leavis finds the religious dimension in the fulfilment of human life, and Bonhoeffer finds God 'not on the borders of life but at its centre, not in weakness but in strength, not therefore in man's suffering and death but in his life and prosperity' *Letters and Papers From Prison* (London: Fontana Books, 1969), p. 69. And generally Leavis's celebration of *this* world finds support in Bonhoeffer's religious views. Unlike Eliot, Bonhoeffer does not countenance any leap out of time into the eternal. Also, Leavis's repeated insistence on the necessity of human responsibility is echoed in Bonhoeffer's call to man to accept the responsibility for his fate in 'a world that has come to age'.

source of your being, of your ultimate concern, of what
you take seriously without reservation. Perhaps, in order to
do so, you must forget everything traditional that you
have learned about God, perhaps even that word itself.
For if you know that God means depth, you know much
about him...He who knows about depth knows about
God.[33]

This is strikingly similar to Leavis's position. He repeatedly insists
– for instance in his reply to Snow – on the importance of acknowledging this depth in life, which he calls 'religious'. Leavis's
reference to 'the mysterious spring' of life is close to Tillich's 'the
source of your being', and they both emphasize the word 'ultimate'.
Tillich adds 'what you take seriously' as a description of God, and
while this may sound like a 'moral' formulation – the kind Leavis
presents in *The Great Tradition* – the emphasis on depth transforms
this into a religious conception. Tillich has no hesitation in calling
this depth 'God' and if this is not what has traditionally been meant
by the term, Tillich, and Robinson, insist that 'God' needs to be
re-understood.

I do not mean to suggest that Leavis is necessarily making an
explicit attempt to re-interpret the concept of God, but I take it
that he starts from a rejection of the traditional notion of God. One
certainly can, as Gomme suggests, properly discuss the religious
aspect of his criticism without asking very specific questions about
his terms and without invoking the term 'God'. It is, however,
striking that Leavis's religious thought can be compared to the
work of major modern theologians. And the fact that Leavis's
thinking on religious issues is both subtle and penetrating enough
to stand the comparison with a theologian of the stature of, say,
Tillich, adds a significant dimension to his total achievement.
Moreover, while the apparent vagueness of Leavis's position can
be considered a weakness, it also perhaps gives Leavis an advantage
over those theologians who attempt to conceptually define their
religious stance. For as Martin Buber observes, 'all definitions and
specific images of God tend to become idols; they always quickly
desire to be more than they are, more than signs and pointers'.[34]
Leavis's support of a religious sense and the undogmatic nature of
his references to the 'something that transcends' represent a
possible way of keeping a religious orientation towards life open for
modern man.

Leavis's thought about the religious dimension of life, then, represents a considerable achievement in itself. He does not, of course, present his religious views in an abstract way; rather he puts them forth – conveys his sense of a religious possibility – in a manner appropriate to a literary critic: by his references to Blake, Dickens and Lawrence he makes his support of a religious sense concrete. The work of these three writers provides a definite embodiment, a showing forth, of the religious spirit that is needed if health is to be regained in technologico-Benthamite society. And in pointing us towards Blake, Dickens and Lawrence as the source of wisdom, health and life that our civilization needs, Leavis shows a compelling centrality of judgment.

NOTES

Introduction

1 F. R. Leavis, 'Introduction', *Determinations* (1934; rpt. Folcroft, Pa.: The Folcroft Press, Inc., 1969), p. 2.

2 F. R. Leavis, 'The Responsible Critic', in *A Selection From Scrutiny*, ed. F. R. Leavis (Cambridge: Cambridge University Press, 1968), II, 297.

3 Ibid., p. 298.

4 F. R. Leavis, *English Literature In Our Time And The University* (London: Chatto and Windus, 1969), p. 170.

Chapter One *Leavis's View Of Society: The Past and The Present*

1 F. R. Leavis, 'Joyce And "The Revolution Of The Word"', in *For Continuity* (Cambridge: The Minority Press, 1933), p. 216.

2 F. R. Leavis, 'Bunyan Through Modern Eyes', in *The Common Pursuit* (1952; rpt. Harmondsworth: Penguin Books, 1966), p. 210.

3 F. R. Leavis, '*The Pilgrim's Progress*', in *Anna Karenina And Other Essays* (London: Chatto and Windus, 1967), p. 38.

4 'Literature And Society', in *The Common Pursuit*, p. 191.

5 F. R. Leavis, '"English", Unrest And Continuity', in *Nor Shall My Sword* (London: Chatto and Windus, 1972), p. 129.

6 'Literature And Society', in *The Common Pursuit*, pp. 188–9.

7 'Bunyan Through Modern Eyes', in *Common Pursuit*, p. 208.

8 Northrop Frye, *The Bush Garden* (Toronto: Anansi, 1963), p. 216.

9 '*The Pilgrim's Progress*', in *Anna Karenina And Other Essays*, p. 41.

10 'Literature and Society', in *The Common Pursuit*, p. 189.

11 'Bunyan Through Modern Eyes', in *The Common Pursuit*, p. 208.

12 Christopher Hill, *The Century of Revolution 1603–1714* (1961; rpt. London: Sphere Books Ltd., 1969), p. 33.

13 Raymond Williams, *The Country And The City* (New York: Oxford University Press, 1973), p. 37.

14 '"English", Unrest And Continuity', in *Nor Shall My Sword*, p. 126.

15 *English Literature In Our Time And The University*, p. 95.

16 Ibid., p. 91.

17 Frank Kermode, *Romantic Image* (London: Fontana Books, 1971), p. 155.

18 Ibid., p. 156.

19 Alfred North Whitehead, *Science And The Modern World* (1925; rpt. New York: The Free Press, 1967), p. 50.

20 *Anna Karenina And Other Essays*, p. 55.

21 Ibid., p. 56.

22 F. R. Leavis and Denys Thompson, *Culture And Environment* (1933; rpt. London: Chatto and Windus, 1964), pp. 1–2.

23 Ibid., p. 2.

24 Ibid., p. 75.

25 George Sturt [George Bourne], *Change In The Village* (London: The Country Book Club, 1956), p. 137. Quoted by Leavis on p. 67 of *Culture And Environment*.

26 *Culture And Environment*, p. 75.

27 George Sturt, *Change In The Village*, p. 65.

28 Raymond Williams, *Culture And Society 1780–1950* (1958: rpt. Harmondsworth: Penguin Books, 1968), pp. 252–3.

29 John Fraser, 'Reflections on the Organic Community', *The Human World*, no. 15–16 (1974), 74.

30 *Nor Shall My Sword*, p. 188.

31 Thomas Hardy, 'The Dorsetshire Labourer', in *Thomas Hardy's Personal Writings*, ed. Harold Orel (Lawrence: University of Kansas Press, 1966), p. 183.

32 Ibid., p. 181.

33 C. B. Cox and E. A. Dyson, eds., *Word In The Desert* (London: Oxford University Press, 1968) p. 3.

34 *Culture And Environment*, pp. 96–7.

35 'Mass Civilization And Minority Culture', in *For Continuity*, p. 16.

36 'D. H. Lawrence', in *For Continuity*, p. 139.

37 *For Continuity*, p. 17.

38 *Culture And Environment*, p. 3.

39 Ibid., p. 1.

40 Raymond Williams, *Culture And Society*, p. 250.

41 *Culture And Environment*, p. 48.

42 Ibid., p. 53.

43 Ibid., p. 100.

44 Ibid., p. 100.

45 *Nor Shall My Sword*, p. 60.

46 Ibid., p. 38.

47 Ibid., pp. 94–5.

48 F. R. Leavis, *Education And The University* (1943; rpt. London: Chatto and Windus, 1965), pp. 22–3. For Leavis's later use of this passage see *Nor Shall My Sword*, pp. 201–2.

49 F. R. Leavis, *Thought, Words And Creativity: Art Thought in Lawrence* (London: Chatto and Windus, 1976), p. 26.

50 Ibid., p. 86.

51 *English Literature In Our Time And The University*, p. 107.

52 *Thought, Words And Creativity*, p. 69.

Chapter Two *Language, Literature, And Continuity*

1 *Nor Shall My Sword*, p. 160.

2 *English Literature In Our Time And The University*, p. 43.

3 *For Continuity*, p. 13.

4 Matthew Arnold, *Culture And Anarchy* (1969; rpt. Cambridge: Cambridge University Press, 1966), p. 8.

5 *For Continuity*, p. 39.

6 'Prefatory: Marxism and Cultural Continuity', in *For Continuity*, p. 9.

7 'Under Which King, Bezonian?', in *For Continuity*, p. 164.

8 Matthew Arnold, *Culture And Anarchy*, p. 12.

9 *English Literature In Our Time And The University*, p. 180.

10 *For Continuity*, p. 15.

11 Ibid., p. 44.

12 *Nor Shall My Sword*, p. 89.

13 'Pound In His Letters', in *Anna Karenina And Other Essays*, p. 163.

14 Raymond Williams, *Culture And Society*, p. 249.

15 'The Literary Mind', in *For Continuity*, p. 64.

16 *Culture And Environment*, p. 81.

17 'Towards Standards of Criticism', in *Anna Karenina And Other Essays*, p. 223.

18 *Culture And Environment*, p. 82.

19 'How To Teach Reading', in *Education And The University*, pp. 118–19.

20 F. R. Leavis, '"Scrutiny": A Retrospect', *Scrutiny*, 20 (1963), p. 5.

21 *Education And The University*, p. 16.

22 Ibid., p. 18.

23 *English Literature In Our Time And The University*, pp. 54–5.

24 *Education And The University*, pp. 19–20.

25 F. R. Leavis, 'Introduction', *Mill On Bentham And Coleridge* (1950; rpt. New York: Harper and Row, 1962), pp. 16–17.

26 *Nor Shall My Sword*, p. 171.

27 Ibid., pp. 171–2.

28 Ibid., p. 102.

29 Ibid., p. 222.

30 F. R. Leavis, *The Living Principle: 'English' As A Discipline Of Thought* (London: Chatto and Windus, 1975), p. 37.

31 *Education And The University*, p. 16.

32 *English Literature In Our Time And The University*, p. 3.

33 *Nor Shall My Sword*, p. 27.

34 Solomon Fishman, *The Disinherited of Art* (Berkeley: University of California Press, 1953), p. 56.

35 *Nor Shall My Sword*, p. 93.

36 Ibid., pp. 60–1.

37 René Wellek, 'The Literary Criticism of Frank Raymond Leavis', in *Literary Views: Critical And Historical Essays*, ed. Carrol Camden (Chicago: The University of Chicago Press, 1964), p. 189.

38 *English Literature In Our Time And The University*, p. 53.

39 *Nor Shall My Sword*, p. 120.

40 Ibid., p. 114.

41 Ibid., p. 15.

42 Ibid., p. 12.

43 Ibid., p. 20.

Chapter Three　*The Educated Public*

1 *For Continuity*, p. 15.

2 *The Living Principle*, p. 12.

3 Raymond Williams, *Culture And Society*, p. 248.

4 'Introduction', *Determinations*, p. 4.

5 *Nor Shall My Sword*, p. 217.

6 Ibid., p. 218.

7 William Walsh, *The Use of Imagination* (1959; rpt. Harmondsworth: Penguin Books, 1966), p. 72.

8 Ibid., p. 76.

9 Raymond Williams, *Culture And Society*, pp. 255–6.

10 *Nor Shall My Sword*, p. 79.

11 F. R. Leavis, 'T. S. Eliot and the Life of English Literature', *Massachusetts Review*, 10, 1969, p. 16.

12 *Nor Shall My Sword*, p. 97.

13 F. R. Leavis, 'Mutually Necessary', *New Universities Quarterly*, Spring 1976, p. 135.

14 Northrop Frye, *The Critical Path* (Bloomington: Indiana University Press, 1971), p. 74.

15 *For Continuity*, p. 29.

16 F. R. Leavis, '*Scrutiny*: A Manifesto', *Scrutiny*, 1 (1932–3), p. 5.

17 *Nor Shall My Sword*, pp. 213–14.

18 *English Literature In Our Time And The University*, pp. 28–30.

19 Ibid., p. 182.

20 *Nor Shall My Sword*, pp. 150–1.

21 Ibid., p. 203.

22 *Education And The University*, p. 55.

23 *Nor Shall My Sword*, p. 203.

24 Ibid., p. 204.

25 Ibid., p. 98.

26 'Introduction,' *Determinations*, p. 4.

27 *The Living Principle*, p. 11.

28 *English Literature In Our Time And The University*, pp. 44–5.

29 'Towards Standards of Criticism', *Anna Karenina And Other Essays*, p. 221.

30 *English Literature In Our Time And The University*, p. 56.

31 *Nor Shall My Sword*, pp. 204–5.

32 *Anna Karenina And Other Essays*, p. 221.

33 *Nor Shall My Sword*, p. 217.

34 *English Literature In Our Time And The University*, p. 50.

35 Ibid., p. 57.

36 F. R. Leavis, *New Bearings In English Poetry* (1932; rpt. Harmondsworth: Penguin Books Ltd., 1967), p. 185.

37 Matthew Arnold, *Essays In Criticism*: First And Second Series (London: Everyman's Library, 1969), p. 13.

38 Donald Davie, 'British Criticism: The Necessity For Humility', *The Frontiers Of Literary Criticism*, ed. David H. Malone (Los Angeles: Hennessey and Ingollis Inc., 1974), p. 31.

39 'Literature And Society,' in *The Common Pursuit*, p. 188.

40 *For Continuity*, p. 194.

41 Anthony Cronin, 'Toward School With Heavy Looks', in *A Question Of Modernity* (London: Secher and Warburg, 1966), p. 121.

42 *Essays In Criticism*, p. 262.

43 F. R. Leavis, 'Correspondence', *London Magazine*, 2, no. 3 (1955), 77–8.

44 *Nor Shall My Sword*, p. 70.

45 Ibid., p. 68.

46 George Steiner, 'F. R. Leavis', *Language And Silence* (1967; rpt. New York: Atheneum, 1976), pp. 230–1.

47 Frank Kermode, 'Some Reservations', *New Statesman*, 66 (1963), 568.

48 *Thought, Words And Creativity*, p. 144.

49 George Steiner, *Language And Silence*, p. 231.

50 *Nor Shall My Sword*, p. 213.

Chapter Four *The Idea Of Criticism*

1 *For Continuity*, pp. 182–3.

2 'The Responsible Critic: Or The Function Of Criticism At Any Time', in *A Selection From Scrutinity*, II, 297.

3 Ibid., p. 301.

4 'Restatements For Critics', in *For Continuity*, p. 183.

5 *Nor Shall My Sword*, p. 112.

6 Bernard Heyl, 'The Absolutism of F. R. Leavis', *Journal of Aesthetics and Art Criticism* 13 (1954), 250.

7 *The Common Pursuit*, p. v.

8 F. R. Leavis, 'Catholicity Or Narrowness', rev. of *A Critical History of English Poetry*, by Herbert J. C. Grierson and J. C. Smith, *Scrutiny*, 12 (1944–5), 292.

9 F. R. Leavis, 'Mr. Pryce-Jones, The British Council And British Culture', *A Selection From Scrutiny*, I, 183.

10 *English Literature In Our Time And The University*, p. 47.

11 Ibid., p. 50.

12 'Literary Criticism And Philosophy', in *The Common Pursuit*, p. 213.

13 Ibid., pp. 213–14.

14 'Arnold As Critic', *A Selection From Scrutiny*, I, 262.

15 T. S. Eliot, *To Criticize The Critic* (New York: Farrar, Straus and Giroux, 1965), p. 13.

16 'Introduction', *Determinations*, p. 5.

17 'Arnold As Critic', *A Selection From Scrutiny*, I, 263.

18 Ibid., I, 264.

19 'Johnson And Augustanism', in *The Common Pursuit*, p. 114.

20 'Luddites? or There Is Only One Culture', in *Nor Shall My Sword*, p. 97.

21 Northrop Frye, *Anatomy Of Criticism* (New York: Atheneum, 1967), p. 9.

22 Northrop Frye, 'On Value Judgements', in *The Stubborn Structure* (Ithaca, New York: Cornell University Press, 1970), p. 70.

23 *Education And The University*, p. 74.

24 Ibid., p. 38.

25 D. H. Lawrence, *Twilight in Italy* (1916; rpt. London: Heinemann, 1970), p. 57.

26 'The Literary Mind', in *For Continuity*, p. 50.

27 Ibid., p. 51.

28 Ibid., p. 56.

29 *Education And The University*, p. 120.

30 Ibid., p. 116.

31 Ibid., p. 70.

32 D. H. Lawrence, 'John Galsworthy', in *Phoenix* (1936; rpt. London: Heinemann, 1970), p. 539.

33 *Education And The University*, p. 71.

34 'Imagery And Movement', *A Selection From Scrutiny*, I, 237.

35 *Education And The University*, p. 71.

36 'Sociology And Literature', in *The Common Pursuit*, p. 200.

37 F. R. Leavis, *Letters in Criticism*, ed. John Tasker (London: Chatto and Windus, 1974), p. 26.

38 'Introduction', *Determinations*, pp. 7–8.

39 Laurence Lerner, 'The Life and Death of Scrutiny,' *London Magazine*, vol. 2, no. 1 (1955), 68–77.

40 F. R. Leavis, 'Correspondence,' *London Magazine*, vol. 2, no. 3 (1955), 79–80.

41 Ibid., p. 80.

42 Ibid., p. 81.

43 F. R. Leavis, 'Criticism and Literary History', *Scrutiny*, 4 (1935–6), 96.

44 'The Function of Criticism At Any Time', *A Selection From Scrutiny*, II, 281.

45 'Mr Eliot And Milton', in *The Common Pursuit*, p. 9.

46 See Fredson Bowers, *Textual & Literary Criticism* (Cambridge: University Press, 1959), pp. 166–7. Leavis apparently mistook the revised version of *Roderick Hudson* for the original.

47 'The Function of Criticism At Any Time', *A Selection From Scrutiny*, II, 293–4.

48 'Rejoinder,' *A Selection From Scrutiny*, II, 312–13.

49 'The Function Of Criticism At Any Time', *A Selection From Scrutiny*, II, 284.

50 *Anna Karenina And Other Essays*, p. 224.

Chapter Five *From Poetry Criticism To Novel Criticism*

1 George Steiner, 'F. R. Leavis', in *Language And Silence* (New York: Atheneum, 1967), p. 229.

2 Ibid., p. 230.

3 Edmund Wilson, *Axel's Castle* (1931; rpt. New York: Charles Scribner's Sons, 1969), pp. 116–17.

4 René Wellek, 'The Liberary Criticism Of Frank Raymond Leavis,' in *Literary Views: Critical And Historical Essays*, pp. 177–8.

5 Bernard Bergonzi, *T. S. Eliot* (New York: The MacMillan Company, 1972), pp. 87–8.

6 *New Bearings In English Poetry*, p. 11.

7 'Mr Eliot And Milton,' *The Common Pursuit*, p. 31.

8 *The Common Pursuit*, pp. 183–4.

9 See for example *Nor Shall My Sword*, p. 63, where Leavis writes: 'Thirty years ago, I wrote a pioneering book on modern poetry that made Eliot a key figure and proposed a new chart.'

10 *The Common Pursuit*, p. 53.

11 F. R. Leavis, *Revaluation* (1936; rpt. Harmondsworth: Penguin Books, 1964), p. 17.

12 Ibid., p. 42.

13 Ibid., p. 65.

14 *The Common Pursuit*, p. 280.

15 'T. S. Eliot As Critic,' in *Anna Karenina And Other Essays*, p. 228.

16 Ibid., p. 177–8.

17 *New Bearings In English Poetry*, p. 139.

18 Ibid., p. 151.

19 *Revaluation*, p. 216.

20 *The Common Pursuit*, p. 17.

21 *New Bearings In English Poetry*, p. 71.

22 *Revaluation*, p. 49.

23 F. R. Leavis and Q. D. Leavis, *Lectures In America* (London: Chatto and Windus, 1969), p. 36.

24 *For Continuity*, p. 208.

25 Ibid., p. 210.

26 *Revaluation*, p. 48.

27 F. R. Leavis, '"*Antony And Cleopatra*" And "*All For Love*"; A Critical Exercise,' *Scrutiny*, 5 (1936–7), 160–1.

28 Ibid., p. 167.

29 *Revaluation*, p. 187.

30 Ibid., p. 188.

31 Ibid., p. 196.

32 D. W. Harding, quoted by F. R. Leavis, 'Johnson As Critic', in *Anna Karenina And Other Essays*, p. 206.

33 'Johnson And Augustanism', in *The Common Pursuit*, p. 109.

34 *The Common Pursuit*, p. 124.

35 Ibid., p. 130.

36 *English Literature In Our Time And The University*, p. 99.

37 *Education And The University*, pp. 125–6.

38 *Anna Karenina And Other Essays*, p. 228.

39 Ibid., p. 230.

40 Ibid., p. 231.

41 David Lodge, *Language Of Fiction* (London: Routledge and Kegan Paul, 1966), pp. 65–6.

42 F. R. Leavis, *The Great Tradition* (1948; rpt. Harmondsworth: Penguin Books, 1966), p. 143.

43 Ibid., p. 144.

44 Ibid., pp. 257–8.

45 Ibid., p. 272.

46 *Anna Karenina And Other Essays*, p. 94.

47 Michael Tanner, 'Philsophy And Criticism', *The Oxford Review*, no. 4 (1967), p. 66.

48 *New Bearings In English Poetry*, p. 115.

49 F. R. Leavis, *D. H. Lawrence: Novelist* (1955; rpt. Harmondsworth: Penguin Books, 1968), p. 57.

50 There is a very curious and uncharacteristic reference to 'sincerity' in Leavis's article, 'This Poetical Renascence,' *For Continuity*, p. 199. In the course of dismissing Stephen Spender's poetry, Leavis quotes a passage of it, then comments: 'Sincere? One does not doubt it; but "sincere" is not a very useful term in criticism.'

51 *New Bearings In English Poetry*, p. 98.

52 'How To Teach Reading', in *Education And The University*, p. 113.

53 *The Great Tradition*, p. 40.

54 Michael Tanner, 'Philosophy And Criticism', *The Oxford Review*, no. 4 (1967), p. 70.

Chapter Six *The Basic Concepts Of Leavis's Novel Criticism*

1 *The Great Tradition* (1948; rpt. Harmondsworth: Penguin Books, 1966), p. 15.

2 Ibid., p. 17.

3 David Lodge, *Language of Fiction*, p. 68.

4 Henry James, quoted in *The Great Tradition*, p. 40.

5 *The Great Tradition*, p. 40.

6 *Anna Karenina And Other Essays*, pp. 11–12.

7 *The Great Tradition*, pp. 41–2.

8 Ibid., pp. 249–50.

9 A. J. Waldock, 'The Status of *Hard Times*', *Southerly*, 9 (1948), 33.

10 *The Great Tradition*, p. 157.

11 *Anna Karenina And Other Essays*, p. 60.

12 *The Great Tradition*, p. 169.

13 Ibid., p. 231.

14 Graham Hough, *The Dream and the Task* (London: Gerald Duckworth and Co. Ltd, 1963), p. 50.

15 Ibid., p. 48.

16 *The Great Tradition*, p. 268.

17 Ibid., p. 69.

18 Ibid., p. 72.

19 *Anna Karenina And Other Essays*, p. 70.

20 Ibid., pp. 101–2.

21 Ibid., pp. 108–9.

22 'Johnson And Augustanism', in *The Common Pursuit*, pp. 110–11.

23 *D. H. Lawrence: Novelist*, p. 187.

24 *Nor Shall My Sword*, p. 56.

25 *Anna Karenina And Other Essays*, p. 12.

26 *The Great Tradition*, p. 10.

27 F. R. Leavis, 'James As Critic', Introduction to Henry James, *Selected Literary Criticism*, ed. Morris Shapira (London: Heinemann, 1963), p. xviii.

28 *Anna Karenina And Other Essays*, p. 14.

29 Ibid., p. 59.

30 Ibid., p. 84.

31 *The Letters of D. H. Lawrence*, ed. Aldous Huxley (London: William Heinemann, 1932), p. 68.

32 *The Great Tradition*, p. 219.

33 *Anna Karenina And Other Essays*, p. 114.

34 Ibid., p. 119.

35 Ibid., p. 120.

36 D. H. Lawrence, *Phoenix*, ed. Edward D. McDonald (1936; rpt. London: Heinemann, 1970), p. 238.

37 *Anna Karenina And Other Essays*, p. 130.

38 Ibid., p. 132.

39 Ibid., p. 133.

40 *The Great Tradition*, p. 257.

41 Ibid., pp. 253–4.

42 J. R. Harvey, 'The Leavis's Dickens', rev. of *Dickens the Novelist*, by F. R. Leavis and Q. D. Leavis, *Cambridge Quarterly*, 6 (1972), 89.

43 F. R. Leavis and Q. D. Leavis, *Dickens the Novelist* (Harmondsworth: Penguin Books, 1972), p. 285.

44 Ibid., pp. 285–6.

45 Ibid., p. 287.

46 Ibid., p. 296.

47 Ibid., pp. 296–7.

48 Ibid., p. 297.

49 Ibid., p. 301.

50 Ibid., p. 334.

51 Ibid., p. 342.

52 René Wellek, 'The Literary Criticism of Frank Raymond Leavis', in *Literary Views: Critical and Historical Essays*, ed. Carol Camden, p. 190.

53 George Steiner, *Language And Silence*, p. 230.

54 *The Great Tradition*, p. 11.

55 Ibid., p. 13.

56 Ibid., p. 16.

57 Ibid., p. 18.

58 Ibid., p. 19.

59 *Anna Karenina And Other Essays*, p. 49.

60 *The Great Tradition*, pp. 23–4.

61 Henry James, rev. of 'George Eliot's "Middlemarch"', in *The Future Of the Novel*, ed. Leon Edel (New York: Vintage Books, 1956), p. 89.

62 *The Great Tradition*, p. 24.

63 Ibid., p. 24–5.

64 'Introduction,' *Selected Literary Criticism*, ed. Morris Shapira, pp. xx–xxi.

65 *The Future Of The Novel*, p. 104.

66 *The Great Tradition*, p. 26.

67 Ibid., pp. 27–8.

68 John Gross, *The Rise And Fall Of The Man Of Letters* (London: Weidenfeld and Nicolson, 1969), p. 278.

69 *The Great Tradition*, p. 210.

70 Ibid., p. 28.

71 'The Americanness of American Literature', in *Anna Karenina And Other Essays*, p. 145.

72 *Dickens The Novelist*, p. 52.

73 Ibid., p. 356.

74 Ibid., p. 358.

75 *Anna Karenina And Other Essays*, pp. 145–6.

Chapter Seven *Judgments And Criteria*

1 F. R. Leavis, *The Great Tradition* (1948; rpt. Harmondsworth: Penguin Books, 1960), p. 17.

2 Ibid., p. 48.

3 Ibid., p. 49.

4 Graham Hough, *An Essay On Criticism* (New York: W. W. Norton and Company, Inc., 1966), p. 38.

5 *The Great Tradition*, p. 60.

6 *Anna Karenina And Other Essays*, p. 55.

7 *The Great Tradition*, p. 125.

8 Ibid., pp. 126–7.

9 Ibid., pp. 215–16.

10 Ibid., p. 221.

11 Ibid., p. 154.

12 Ibid., p. 235.

13 Ibid., p. 33.

14 F. R. Leavis, 'After "To The Lighthouse"', *A Selection from Scrutiny*, ed. F. R. Leavis (Cambridge: Cambridge University Press, 1968), II, 99.

15 J. M. Newton, rev. of *Anna Karenina And Other Essays*, by F. R. Leavis, *The Cambridge Quarterly*, 3 (1957–8), 362.

16 *D. H. Lawrence: Novelist*, p. 95.

17 Ibid., p. 288.

18 Ibid., pp. 206–7.

19 Ibid., p. 301.

20 Ibid., p. 304.

21 *The Great Tradition*, p. 29.

22 Ibid., p. 229.

23 Ibid., p. 31.

24 Ibid., p. 147.

25 Ibid., p. 149.

26 Ibid., p. 153.

27 *Dickens the Novelist*, p. 299.

28 Ibid., p. 326.

29 *New Bearings In English Poetry*, p. 19.

30 Murray Krieger, *The New Apologists for Poetry* (1956; rpt. Bloomington: Indiana University Press, 1963), p. 60.

31 *The Great Tradition*, p. 17.

32 New Bearings In English Poetry, p. 96.

33 *The Great Tradition*, p. 67–8.

34 *Anna Karenina And Other Essays*, p. 180.

35 Ibid., p. 180.

36 Ibid., pp. 180–1.

37 Ibid., pp. 11–12.

38 *The Great Tradition*, p. 190.

39 Ibid., p. 186.

40 'Yeats: The Problem And The Challenge', in *Lectures In America*, p. 75.

41 *English Literature In Our Time And The University*, p. 144.

42 Ibid., p. 139.

43 F. R. Leavis, *Revaluation* (1936; rpt. Harmondsworth: Penguin Books, 1964), p. 144.

44 Ibid., pp. 221–2.

45 *The Great Tradition*, p. 93.

46 Ibid., pp. 43–44.

47 *Dickens the Novelist*, pp. 291–2.

48 F. R. Leavis, 'Introduction' to *Daniel Deronda* by George Eliot (London: Panther, 1970), pp. 12–13.

49 Ibid., p. 13.

50　*The Great Tradition*, p. 51.

51　Ibid., p. 54.

52　Ibid., p. 67.

53　Ibid., p. 92.

54　Bernard Bergonzi, 'Literary Criticism and Humanist Morality', *Blackfriars*, 43 (1962), 14–15.

55　*The Great Tradition*, p. 101.

56　Krieger, *The New Apologists for Poetry*, p. 132.

57　*The Great Tradition*, pp. 105–6.

58　John Casey, *The Language Of Criticism* (London: Methuen & Co. Ltd., 1966), pp. 156–7.

59　Frank Kermode, 'A Tradition of *Scrutiny*', rev. of *Anna Karenina And Other Essays*, by F. R. Leavis, *Commentary*, 46, no. 1 (1968), 85.

60　*Education And The University*, pp. 76–7.

61　John Killham, 'The Use of "Concreteness" As An Evaluative Term In F. R. Leavis's "The Great Tradition"', *The British Journal of Aesthetics*, 5 (1965), 19.

62　Northrop Frye, *Anatomy of Criticism* (1957; rpt. New York: Atheneum, 1967), p. 22.

63　Vincent Buckley, *Poetry And Morality* (London: Chatto and Windus, 1959), p. 160.

64　Casey, *The Language Of Criticism*, p. 181.

65　Ibid., p. 184.

66　Ibid., p. 196.

67　Michael Tanner, 'Philosophy And Criticism', *The Oxford Review*, No. 24 (1967), p. 69.

68　*The Great Tradition*, p. 175.

69　*The Great Tradition*, p. 178.

70　Ibid., pp. 174–5.

71　Ibid., p. 177.

72　'Henry James And The Function Of Criticism', in *The Common Pursuit*, p. 228.

73　*Dickens The Novelist*, p. 301.

74　*The Great Tradition*, p. 139.

75　Ibid., p. 23.

76　Bergonzi, 'Literary Criticism and Humanist Morality', pp. 13–14.

77　F. R. Leavis, 'James As Critic', Introduction to Henry James, *Selected Literary Criticism*, ed. Morris Shapira (London: Heinemann, 1963), p. xix.

Chapter Eight *Leavis's Early Writings On Lawrence*

1　F. R. Leavis, *Scrutiny*, 1 (1932–33), p. 190.

2　F. R. Leavis, 'The Living Lawrence' in *D. H. Lawrence: A Critical Anthology*, ed. H. Coombes (Harmondsworth: Penguin Education, 1973), p. 269.

3　Ibid., p. 269.

4　*For Continuity*, p. 181.

5 'D. H. Lawrence and Professor Irving Babbit,' *For Continuity*, p. 156.

6 *Education And The University*, p. 20.

7 'Mr Eliot, Mr Wyndham Lewis And Lawrence,' in *The Common Pursuit*, p. 240.

8 Ibid., p. 241.

9 T. S. Eliot, 'Religion And Literature', in *Selected Essays* (London: Faber and Faber Ltd, 1969), p. 388.

10 *Revaluation*, pp. 135–6.

11 Ibid., pp. 137–8.

12 Ibid., p. 139.

13 *The Great Tradition*, p. 181.

14 *For Continuity*, p. 2.

15 Ibid., p. 140.

16 Ibid., p. 135.

17 Ibid., p. 57.

18 F. R. Leavis, 'Reminiscences of D. H. Lawrence', *Scrutiny* 1 (1932–3), 189–90.

19 F. R. Leavis, 'The Living Lawrence', in *D. H. Lawrence: A Critical Anthology*, ed. H. Coombes, pp. 268–9.

20 Ibid., p. 270.

21 'D. H. Lawrence and Professor Irving Babbit', in *For Continuity*, p. 153.

22 Ibid., p. 152.

23 Ibid., p. 158.

24 'Restatement for Critics', *For Continuity*, p. 179.

25 Ibid., p. 180.

26 Ibid., p. 180.

27 H. Coombes, 'Introduction', *D. H. Lawrence: A Critical Anthology*, ed. H. Coombes, p. 38.

28 Ibid., p. 39.

29 *The Common Pursuit*, p. 247.

30 Ibid., p. 246.

31 'The Wild, Untutored Phoenix', in *The Common Pursuit*, p. 236.

32 Ibid., p. 237.

33 Ibid., p. 238.

34 'Approaches To T. S. Eliot', in *The Common Pursuit*, p. 282.

35 Ibid., p. 284.

36 *The Great Tradition*, p. 36.

37 Ibid., p. 35.

38 F. R. Leavis, 'D. H. Lawrence Placed', *Scrutiny*, 16 (1949), 44.

39 *The Common Pursuit*, p. 256.

40 Ibid., p. 259.

Chapter Nine *'D. H. Lawrence: Novelist': The Grounds Of Praise I*

1 F. R. Leavis, *D. H. Lawrence: Novelist* (1955; rpt. Harmondsworth: Penguin Books, 1968), p. 15. All subsequent references in the text are to this edition.

2 D. H. Lawrence, *Phoenix II*, ed. Warren Roberts and Harry T. Moore (London: Heinemann, 1968), p. 597.

3 Ibid., p. 601.

4 Ibid., p. 503.

5 Ibid., p. 600.

6 F. R. Leavis, 'Correspondence: Lawrence and Eliot', *Scrutiny*, 18 (1951–2), 143.

7 Eugene Goodheart, *The Utopian Vision of D. H. Lawrence* (Chicago: The University of Chicago Press, 1963), p. 5.

8 Ibid., p. 6.

9 D. H. Lawrence, *The Letters Of D. H. Lawrence,* ed. Aldous Huxley (London: William Heinemann, 1932), p. 240.

10 We should however keep in mind a typical remark of Lawrence's, made in a letter 11 October 1916: 'I do really think we shall see this old order collapsing even in the outer world... I want to have some seed of a new spirit ready – I know the time is nearly come to sow it. We shall be like Noah, taking all the precious things into the ark, when the flood comes, and disembarking on a new world.' (*The Letters of D. H. Lawrence*, ed. Aldous Huxley, p. 240). In his new discussion of *The Rainbow* in *Thought, Words And Creativity*, Leavis himself quotes a similar reference – see p. 127 – to Noah and his ark in *Phoenix I*. In other places as well Lawrence indicates his desire that there should not be an absolute break with the past but a certain continuity. As he writes in the essay 'On Human Destiny': 'The fact of the matter is, the exquisite courage of brave men goes on in an unbroken continuity, even if sometimes the thread of flame becomes very thin' (*Phoenix II*, p. 627). In statements like these Lawrence is not all that far from Leavis's desire 'for continuity'.

11 D. H. Lawrence, as reported by Jessie Chambers [E. T.] in *D. H. Lawrence: A Personal Record* (1935; rpt. New York: Barnes and Noble, Inc., 1965), p. 105.

12 I should point out that Leavis gets some support in his position from Graham Hough in his chapter on 'The Novel And History', in *An Essay On Criticism* (New York: W. W. Norton and Company, Inc., 1966), p. 113. Hough writes: 'A large part of the superiority of *The Rainbow* to *Kangaroo* is that *The Rainbow* presents (among other things) a real stage in the social evolution of the English provinces, while *Kangaroo* is only a socio-political fantasy.'

13 F. R. Leavis, *The Common Pursuit* (1952; rpt. Harmondsworth: Penguin Books, 1966), p. 132.

14 D. H. Lawrence, *Phoenix II*, p. 599.

Chapter Ten '*D. H. Lawrence: Novelist*': *The Grounds Of Praise II*

1 F. R. Leavis, *D. H. Lawrence: Novelist* (1955; rpt. Harmondsworth: Penguin Books, 1968), p. 103. All subsequent references in the text are to this edition of the book.

2 D. H. Lawrence, *The Rainbow* (1915; rpt. London: Heinemann, 1968), p. 437.

3 D. H. Lawrence, *Psychoanalysis and the Unconscious and Fantasia of The Uncon-scious* (1921, 1922; rpt. New York: The Viking Press, 1921), p. 16.

4 Ibid., p. 16.

5 Frank Kermode, *Lawrence* (Bungay, Suffolk: Fontana/Collins, 1973), p. 90.

6 D. H. Lawrence, *The Ladybird*, in *The Short Novels* (London: William Heinemann, 1963), I, 27.

7 D. H. Lawrence, *St. Mawr* in *The Short Novels* (London: William Heinemann, 1963), II, 127.

8 George Ford, *Double Measure* (New York: W. W. Norton and Company, Inc., 1965), p. 89.

9 Ibid., p. 75.

10 D. H. Lawrence, 'England, My England', in *The Complete Short Stories* (London: William Heinemann, 1963), II, 323.

11 Ibid., 315.

12 Ibid., 313.

13 Ibid., 314.

14 D. H. Lawrence, *D. H. Lawrence: A Critical Anthology*, ed. H. Coombes (Harmondsworth: Penguin Education, 1973), p. 106.

15 D. H. Lawrence, *Women In Love* (1920; rpt. London: Heinemann, 1964), p. 137.

16 D. H. Lawrence, *The Captain's Doll*, in *The Short Novels*, I, 82.

17 D. H. Lawrence, *The Fox*, in *The Short Novels*, I, 69.

Chapter Eleven '*D. H. Lawrence: Novelist*': *Leavis's Evaluation Of Lawrence*

1 F. R. Leavis, *D. H. Lawrence: Novelist* (1955; rpt. Harmondsworth: Penguin Books, 1968), p. 15. All subsequent references in the text are to this edition of the book.

2 Mark Spilka, *The Love Ethic of D. H. Lawrence* (Bloomington: Indiana University Press, 1955), p. vii.

3 Graham Hough, *The Dark Sun* (London: Duckworth and Co. Ltd, 1956), p. viii.

4 Anthony Beal, *D. H. Lawrence* (London: Olive and Boyd, 1961), p. 92.

5 F. R. Leavis, *Anna Karenina And Other Essays* (London: Chatto and Windus, 1967), pp. 235–6.

6 Ibid., p. 240.

7 Ibid., p. 241.

8 Leavis's actual *analysis* of the novel comes essentially on pages 56 and 57; the earlier pages he had devoted to the novel, pp. 45–8, treat the novel as a document revealing Lawrence's relationship with Frieda and his mother; Leavis's later reference to the novel, pp. 67–9, is concerned primarily to show how it leads into *The Plumed Serpent*.

9 D. H. Lawrence, *The Virgin and the Gypsy*, in *The Short Novels* (London: William Heinemann, 1963), II, 61.

10 *The Dark Sun*, p. 168.

Chapter Twelve *F. R. Lewis's Revaluation Of T. S. Eliot*

1 *Education And The University*, p. 104.
2 *D. H. Lawrence: Novelist*, p. 318.
3 Ibid., p. 323.
4 *Anna Karenina And Other Essays*, p. 179.
5 Ibid., p. 179.
6 F. R. Leavis, *The Living Principle* (London: Chatto and Windus, 1975), p. 205. All subsequent references to this book will be indicated simply by the page number.
7 *Education And The University*, p. 102.
8 Donald Davie, 'T. S. Eliot: The End of an Era', in *T. S. Eliot, Four Quartets*, ed. Bernard Bergonzi (London: Macmillan, 1965), p. 153.
9 William Lynch, *Christ And Apollo* (Toronto: Mentor-Omega, 1960), pp. 173–4.
10 *Nor Shall My Sword*, p. 12.
11 *Education And The University*, pp. 103–4.

Chapter Thirteen *The Religious Spirit*

1 *Nor Shall My Sword*, p. 56.
2 *Anna Karenina And Other Essays*, p. 45.
3 Ibid., p. 44.
4 Ibid., p. 47.
5 Ibid., p. 48.
6 *Nor Shall My Sword*, p. 81.
7 F. R. Leavis and Q. D. Leavis, *Dickens The Novelist* (Harmondsworth: Penguin Books, 1972), p. 285.
8 Ibid., p. 314.
9 Ibid., p. 356.
10 Ibid., p. 357.
11 Ibid., p. 358.
12 *English Literature In Our Time And The University*, pp. 106–7.
13 *Nor Shall My Sword*, p. 19.
14 Ibid., p. 20.
15 *Dickens The Novelist*, p. 351.
16 Ibid., pp. 351–2.
17 J. G. Davies, quoted in *Nor Shall My Sword*, p. 13.
18 F. R. Leavis, 'Justifying One's Valuation of Blake', in *William Blake: Essays in honour of Sir Geoffrey Keynes*, ed. Morton D. Paley and Michael Phillips (Oxford: The Clarendon Press, 1973), p. 81.
19 Thomas J. Altizer, *The New Apocalypse: The Radical Christian Vision of William Blake* (Michigan State University Press, 1967), p. 65.
20 'Justifying One's Valuation Of Blake', in *William Blake: Essays in honour of Sir Geoffrey Keynes*, p. 84.
21 *The Living Principle*, p. 68.
22 Ibid., p. 67.

23 *Thought, Words And Creativity*, p. 134.

24 Ibid., p. 131.

25 Ibid., p. 135.

26 Ibid., p. 136.

27 Andor Gomme, *Attitudes to Criticism* (Carbondale and Edwardsville: Southern Illinois University Press, 1966), pp. 134–5.

28 Martin Buber, *Eclipse of God* (1952; rpt. New York: Harper and Row, 1957), p. 79.

29 *Nor Shall My Sword*, pp. 171–2.

30 W. Richard Comstock, 'Theology After the "Death of God"', in *The Meaning Of The Death Of God*, ed. Bernard Murchland (New York: Vintage Books, 1967), p. 242.

31 Ibid., pp. 242–3.

32 John A. T. Robinson, *Honest to God* (London: SCM Press Ltd, 1963), pp. 7–8.

33 Paul Tillich, quoted in *Honest to God*, p. 22.

34 *Eclipse Of God*, p. 46.

BIBLIOGRAPHY

1. D. H. LAWRENCE

(a) Works by Lawrence

Lawrence, D. H., *Aaron's Rod*, 1922; rpt. London: William Heinemann Ltd, 1961.

- *Apocalypse*, 1931; rpt. London: William Heinemann, 1968.
- *The Collected Letters Of D. H. Lawrence*, 2 vols, ed. Harry T. Moore, London: William Heinemann, 1962.
- *The Collected Short Stories of D. H. Lawrence*, 3 vols, London: William Heinemann, 1963.
- *The Complete Plays of D. H. Lawrence*, London: William Heinemann, 1965.
- *The Complete Poems of D. H. Lawrence*, ed. Vivian de Sola Pinto and Warren Roberts, 2 vols, 1964; rpt. London: Heinemann, 1972.
- *Kangaroo*, 1923; rpt. London: William Heinemann, 1960.
- *Lady Chatterley's Lover*, 1928; rpt. London: William Heinemann, 1961.
- *The Letters of D. H. Lawrence*, ed. Aldous Huxley, London: William Heinemann, 1932.
- *The Lost Girl*, 1920; rpt. London: William Heinemann, 1961.
- *Mornings in Mexico And Etruscan Places*, 1927, 1932; rpt. London: William Heinemann, 1968.
- *Phoenix*, ed. Edward D. McDonald, 1936; rpt. London: Heinemann, 1970.
- *Phoenix II*, eds. Harry T. Moore and Warren Roberts, London: William Heinemann, 1968.
- *The Plumed Serpent*, 1926; rpt. London: William Heinemann, 1955.
- *Psychoanalysis and the Unconscious and Fantasia of the Unconscious*, 1921, 1922; rpt. New York: The Viking Press, 1969. The Phoenix edition prints these books in reverse chronological order, so I consider the Viking edition preferable.
- *The Rainbow*, 1915; rpt. London: William Heinemann, 1968.
- *Sea and Sardinia*, 1923; rpt. London: William Heinemann, 1968.
- *The Short Novels of D. H. Lawrence*, 2 vols, London: William Heinemann, 1963.
- *Sons and Lovers*, 1913; rpt. London: William Heinemann, 1966.
- *Studies In Classic American Literature*, 1923; rpt. London: William Heinemann, 1964.

- *The Symbolic Meaning*, ed. Armin Arnold, New York: Centaur Press, 1962.
- *The Trespasser*, 1912; rpt. London: William Heinemann, 1961.
- *Twilight in Italy*, 1916; rpt. London: William Heinemann, 1970.
- *The White Peacock*, 1911; rpt. London: William Heinemann, 1960.
- *Women in Love*, 1920; rpt. London: William Heinemann, 1964.

(b) Selected Works on Lawrence

Beal, Anthony, *D. H. Lawrence*, London: Oliver and Boyd, 1961.

Bedient, Calvin, *Architects of the Self*, Los Angeles: University of California Press, 1972.

Carswell, Catherine, *The Savage Pilgrimage*, New York: Harcourt, Brace and Company, 1932.

Cavitch, David, *D. H. Lawrence and the New World*, London: Oxford University Press, 1969.

Chambers, Jessie [E. T.], *D. H. Lawrence: A Personal Record*, 1935; rpt. Barnes and Noble, Inc., 1965.

Clarke, Colin, *River of Dissolution*, London: Routledge and Kegan Paul, 1969.

Coombes, H. ed., *D. H. Lawrence: A Critical Anthology*, Harmondsworth: Penguin Education, 1973.

Daleski, H. M., *The Forked Flame*, London: Faber and Faber, 1965.

Eliot, T. S., Introduction to *D. H. Lawrence and Human Existence*, by Father Wm Tiverton, New York: Philosophical Library, 1951.

Ford, George, *Double Measure*, New York: W. W. Norton, 1965.

Goodheart, Eugene, *The Utopian Vision of D. H. Lawrence*, Chicago: The University of Chicago Press, 1963.

Hough, Graham, *The Dark Sun*, London: Gerald Duckworth, 1965.

Kermode, Frank, *Lawrence*, Bungay, Suffolk: Fontana/Collins, 1973.

Moore, Harry T., *The Life and Works of D. H. Lawrence*, London: Allen and Unwin, 1951.

Moore, Harry T., ed., *A D. H. Lawrence Miscellany*, London: William Heinemann, 1961.

Murry, John Middleton, *Son of Woman*, London: Jonathon Cape, 1931.

Nehls, Edward, *D. H. Lawrence: A Composite Biography*, 3 vols, Madison: University of Wisconsin Press, 1957.

Spilka, Mark, *The Love Ethic of D. H. Lawrence*, Bloomington: Indiana University Press, 1955.

Spilka, Mark, ed., *D. H. Lawrence: A Collection of Critical Essays*, Englewood Cliffs, N.J.: Prentice-Hall, Inc.

Tiverton, Father William, *D. H. Lawrence and Human Existence*, New York: Philosophical Library, 1951.

Vivas, Eliseo, *D. H. Lawrence: The Failure and the Triumph of Art*, Evanston: Northwestern University Press, 1960.

Yudhishtar, *Conflict In The Novels Of D. H. Lawrence*, Edinburgh: Oliver and Boyd, 1969.

2. F. R. LEAVIS

(a) Works by Leavis

(*i*) BOOKS

Leavis, F. R., *New Bearings In English Poetry*, 1932; rpt. Harmondsworth: Penguin Books, 1967.

– *For Continuity*, Cambridge: The Minority Press, 1933.

Leavis, F. R. and Thompson, Denys, *Culture And Environment*, 1933; rpt. London: Chatto and Windus, 1964.

Leavis, F. R., *Revaluation*, 1936; rpt. Harmondsworth: Penguin Books, 1964.

– *Education And The University*, 1943; rpt. London: Chatto and Windus, 1965.

– *The Great Tradition*, 1948; rpt. Harmondsworth: Penguin Books, 1966.

– *The Common Pursuit*, 1952; rpt. Harmondsworth: Penguin Books, 1966.

– *D. H. Lawrence: Novelist*, 1955; rpt. Harmondsworth: Penguin Books, 1968.

– *Anna Karenina And Other Essays*, London: Chatto and Windus, 1967.

– *English Literature In Our Time And The University*, London: Chatto and Windus, 1969.

Leavis, F. R. and Leavis, Q. D., *Lectures In America*, London: Chatto and Windus, 1969.

– *Dickens The Novelist*, Harmondsworth: Penguin Books, 1972 [1970].

Leavis, F. R., *Nor Shall My Sword*, London: Chatto and Windus, 1972.

– *Letters In Criticism*, ed. John Tasker, London: Chatto and Windus, 1972.

Leavis, F. R., *The Living Principle*, London: Chatto and Windus, 1975.

– *Thought, Words And Creativity*, London: Chatto and Windus, 1976.

Leavis, F. R. *et al.* eds., *Scrutiny: A Quarterly Review*, vols. I–XX, rpt. Cambridge: Cambridge University Press, 1963.

Leavis, F. R. ed., *A Selection From Scrutiny*, 2 vols, Cambridge: Cambridge University Press, 1968.

(*ii*) UNCOLLECTED ESSAYS

'T. S. Eliot – A Reply to the Condescending', *The Cambridge Review* (8 Feb. 1929), pp. 254–6.

'This Influence of Donne on Modern Poetry', *The Bookman*, lxxix (March 1931), pp. 346–7.

'The Age in Literary Criticism', *The Bookman*, lxxxiii (Oct. 1932), pp. 8–9.

Introduction to *English in Australia: Taste and Training in Modern Community*, by E. G. Biaggini. London: Oxford University Press, 1933.

Introduction to *Determinations: Critical Essays*, London: Chatto and Windus, 1934.

'English Letter', *Poetry: a Magazine of Verse*, xliii (Jan. 1934), pp. 215–21.

'English Letter', *Poetry: a Magazine of Verse*, xliv (May 1934), pp. 98–102.

'English Letter', *Poetry: a Magazine of Verse*, xlvi (Aug. 1935), pp. 274–8.

'Revaluations (XI): Arnold as Critic', *Scrutiny* VII (Dec. 1938), pp. 319–32. Reprinted in F. R. Leavis, ed. *A Selection From Scrutiny*, Cambridge: Cambridge University Press, vol. I, pp. 258–68.

'Revaluations (XIII): Coleridge in Criticism', *Scrutiny* IX (June 1940), pp.

57–69. Reprinted in F. R. Leavis, ed., *A Selection From Scrutiny*, vol. I, pp. 268–78.

'Retrospect of a Decade', *Scrutiny* IX (June 1940), pp. 70–72. Reprinted in *A Selection From Scrutiny*, vol. I, pp. 175–7.

'Hardy the Poet', *Southern Review* VI (1940–1), pp. 87–98.

'After Ten years', *Scrutiny* X (April 1942), pp. 326–8.

'Reflections on the Above [Criticisms of *Little Gidding*]', *Scrutiny* XI (Summer 1943), pp. 261–7.

'The Teaching of Literature: III. The Literary Discipline and Liberal Education', *Sewanee Review* LV (1947), pp. 587–609.

'Critic and Leviathan (3): Literary Criticism and Politics', *Politics and Letters* I (Winter–Spring 1948), pp. 58–61.

'Comment: D. H. Lawrence Placed', *Scrutiny* XVI (March 1949), p. 44. Reprinted in *A Selection From Scrutiny*, vol. I, pp. 156–9.

'Mill, Beatrice Webb and the "English School": preface to an unprinted volume', *Scrutiny* XVI (June 1949), pp. 104–26. Reprinted as Introduction to *On Bentham & Coleridge*, by John Stuart Mill, 1950; rpt. New York: Harper and Row, 1962.

'Lawrence and Eliot', Note in reply to Robert D. Wagner, *Scrutiny* XVIII (Autumn 1951), pp. 139–43.

'Comment: Mr Pryce-Jones, the British Council and British Culture', *Scrutiny* XVIII (Winter 1951–2), pp. 224–8. Reprinted in *A Selection From Scrutiny*, vol. I, pp. 280–302.

'The State of Criticism: Representations to Fr. Martin Jarrett-Kerr', *Essays in Criticism* III (1953), pp. 215–33.

'The "Great Books" and a Liberal Education', *Commentary* (Sept. 1953), pp. 224–32.

'Valedictory', *Scrutiny* XIX (Oct. 1953), pp. 254–7.

'The Responsible Critic', note in reply to Mr F. W. Bateson. *Scrutiny* XIX (Oct. 1953), pp. 321–8. Reprinted in *A Selection From Scrutiny*, vol. II, pp. 308–15.

'Literary Studies: a Reply [to W. W. Robson]', *Universities Quarterly* XI (Nov. 1956), pp. 14–25.

'George Eliot's Zionist Novel', *Commentary* (Oct. 1960), pp. 317–25. Reprinted as Introduction to *Daniel Deronda* by George Eliot, London: Panther, 1970.

'A Note on the Critical Function', *The Literary Criterion* V (Winter 1961), pp. 1–9.

'A Retrospect', in *Scrutiny* vol. XX: A Retrospect; Indexes; Errata. Cambridge: Cambridge University Press, pp. 1–24.

'James as Critic', Introduction to *Henry James: Selected Literary Criticism*, ed. by Morris Shapira, London: Heinemann, 1963.

Introduction to *Felix Holt* by George Eliot, London: Dent, Everyman's Library, 1966.

'Valuation In Criticism', *Orbis Litterarum*, 21 (1966), pp. 61–70.

Introduction to *The Image Of Childhood*, by Peter Coveney, rev. ed., Harmondsworth: Penguin Books, 1967.

'T. S. Eliot and the Life of English Literature', *The Massachusetts Review*, 10
    (1969), pp. 9–33.
'Eugenio Montale's "Xenia"', *The Listener*, 86 (1971), pp. 845–6.
'Wordsworth: The Creative Conditions', in *Twentieth-Century Literature in
    Retrospect*, ed. Reuben A. Brower, Cambridge: Harvard University Press, 1971,
    pp. 323–41.
'Lawrence After Thirty Years', in *D. H. Lawrence: A Critical Anthology*, ed. H.
    Coombes. Harmondsworth: Penguin Education, 1973, pp. 398–407.
'Justifying One's Valuation of Blake', in *William Blake: Essays in honour of Sir
    Geoffrey Keynes*, ed. Morton D. Paley and Michael Phillips, Oxford: The
    Clarendon Press, 1973, pp. 65–85.
'Memories of Wittgenstein', *The Human World*, 10 (1973).
'"Believing" In The University', *The Human World*, 15–16 (1974).
'Mutually Necessary', *The New Universities Quarterly*, Spring, 1976.

(iii) UNCOLLECTED REVIEWS
England Reclaimed, by Osbert Sitwell; and *The Dark Breed*, by F. R. Higgins, *The
    Cambridge Review*, 18 Nov. 1927, p. 114.
Critiques, by Augustus Rolli, *The Cambridge Review*, 24 Feb. 1928, p. 285.
'Words and Poetry', review of *Words and Poetry*, by George W. Rylands, *The
    Cambridge Review*, 6 June 1928, p. 510.
Retreat, by Edmund Blunden, *The Cambridge Review*, 12 Oct. 1928, p. 20.
The Skull of Swift, by Shane Leslie, *The Cambridge Review*, 18 Jan. 1929, p. 199.
Cambridge Poetry, 1929, *The Cambridge Review*, 1 March 1929, pp. 317–18.
Death of a Hero, by Richard Aldington, *The Cambridge Review*, 25 Oct. 1929, p. 61.
'More Gothick North', review of *These Sad Ruins*, by Sacheverell Sitwell, *The
    Cambridge Review*, 8 Nov. 1929, p. 100.
'Green Fields', review of *Near and Far*, by Edmund Blunden, *The Cambridge
    Review*, 15 Nov. 1929, p. 118.
'T. F. Powys', review of *Kindness in a Corner*, by T. F. Powys, *The Cambridge
    Review*, 9 May 1930, pp. 388–9.
Cambridge Poetry, 1930, *The Cambridge Review*, 16 May 1930, pp. 414–15.
'D. H. Lawrence', review of *Nettles*, by D. H. Lawrence, *The Cambridge Review*,
    13 June 1930, pp. 493–5.
Novels and Novelists, by Katherine Mansfield, *The Cambridge Review*, 28 Nov. 1930,
    p. 169.
'Intelligence and Sensibility', review of *Seven Types of Ambiguity*, by William
    Empson, *The Cambridge Review*, 16 Jan. 1931, pp. 186–7.
'Criticism of the Year', review of *Seven Types of Ambiguity*, by William Empson;
    Axel's Castle, by Edmund Wilson; *The Imperial Theme*, by G. Wilson Knight;
    Wordsworth, by Herbert Read; *Son of Woman*, by J. Middleton Murry; *Scrutinies*
    II, by Various Writers; *The Bookman*, lxxxi (Dec. 1931), p. 180.
'The Living Lawrence', review of *The Letters of D. H. Lawrence*, ed. by Aldous
    Huxley, *The Listener*, 5 Oct. 1932, pp. iv–vii.

'Lord, What Would They Say...?' review of *Visions of the Daughters of Albion*, by William Blake, *Scrutiny* I (Dec. 1932), pp. 290–1.

'An American Lead', review of *The Experimental College*, by Alexander Meiklejohn, *Scrutiny* I ((Dec. 1932), pp. 297–30.

'Resolute Optimism, Professional and Professorial', review of *Leisure in the Modern World*, by C. Delisle Burns; *Successful Living in this Machine Age*, by Edward A. Filene, *Scrutiny* I (Dec. 1932), pp. 300–1.

'Dostoevsky or Dickens?' review of *Light in August*, by William Faulkner, *Scrutiny* II (June 1933), pp. 105–8.

Aspects of Seventeenth Century Verse, ed. by Peter Quennell; *Henry Vaughn and the Hermetic Philosophy*, by Elizabeth Holmes, *Scrutiny* II (June 1933), pp. 108–9.

'Battles Long Ago', review of *Conquistador*, by Archibald Macleish, *Scrutiny* II (Sept. 1933), pp. 202–4.

The Christian Renaissance, by G. Wilson Knight, *Scrutiny* II (Sept. 1933), pp. 208–11.

'The Latest Yeats', review of *The Winding Stair and other Poems*, by W. B. Yeats, *Scrutiny* II (Dec. 1933), pp. 293–5. Reprinted in *A Selection From Scrutiny*, vol. I, pp. 89–91.

'The Case of Mr Pound', review of *Active Anthology*, ed. by Ezra Pound, *Scrutiny* II (Dec. 1933), pp. 299–301. Reprinted in *A Selection From Scrutiny*, vol. I, pp. 99–101.

'Auden, Bottrall and Others,' review of *Poems* and *The Dance of Death*, by W. H. Auden; *Festivals of Fire* and *The Loosening and other Poems*, by Ronald Bottrall, *Scrutiny* III (June 1934), pp. 70–83.

'Shelley's Imagery', review of *Verse and Prose from the Manuscripts of Percy Bysshe Shelley*, ed. Sir John Shelley-Rolls and Roger Ingpen, *The Bookman*, lxxxvi (Sept. 1934), p. 278.

Manifesto, ed. C. E. M. Joad, *Scrutiny* III (Sept. 1934), pp. 215–17.

'Dr Richards, Bentham and Coleridge', review of *Coleridge on Imagination*, by I. A. Richards, *Scrutiny* III (March 1935), pp. 382–402.

'Marianne Moore', review of *Selected Poems*, by Marianne Moore, *Scrutiny* IV (June 1935), pp. 87–90.

'Criticism and Literary History', review of *English Poetry and the English Language*, by F. W. Bateson, *Scrutiny* IV (June 1935), pp. 96–100.

'Hugh Macdiarmid', review of *Second Hymn to Lenin and other Poems*, by Hugh Macdiarmid, *Scrutiny* IV (Dec. 1935), p. 305.

'Doughty and Hopkins', review of *Charles M. Doughty: A Study of his Prose and Verse*, by Anne Treneer; Selected Passages from *The Dawn in Britain*, ed. by Barker Fairly, *Scrutiny* IV (Dec. 1935), pp. 316–17.

The Powys Brothers, by R. H. Ward, *Scrutiny* IV (Dec. 1935), p. 318.

'The Orage Legend', review of *Selected Essays and Critical Writings of A. R. Orage*, ed. by Herbert Read and Denis Saurat, *Scrutiny* IV (Dec. 1935), p. 319.

'Mr Eliot and Education' review of *Essays Ancient and Modern*, by T. S. Eliot, *Scrutiny* V (June 1936), pp. 84–9.

The Faber Book of Modern Verse, ed. by Michael Roberts; *The Progress of Poetry*, ed.
   by I. M. Parsons, *Scrutiny* v (June 1936), pp. 116–17.
'Mr Auden's Talent', review of *Look Stranger*, by W. H. Auden; *The Ascent of F.6*,
   by W. H. Auden and Christopher Isherwood, *Scrutiny* v (Dec. 1936), pp.
   323–7. Reprinted in *A Selection From Scrutiny*, vol. I, pp. 110–14.
Reading the Spirit, by Richard Eberhart, *Scrutiny* v (Dec. 1936), pp. 333–4.
'The Marxian Analysis', review of *The Mind in Chains*, ed. C. Day Lewis;
   Education, Capitalist and Socialist, by Beryl Pring, *Scrutiny* vi (Sept. 1937), pp.
   201–4.
'Advanced Verbal Education', review of *The Philosophy of Rhetoric*, by I. A.
   Richards; *Scepticism and Poetry*, by D. G. James, *Scrutiny* vi (Sept. 1937), pp.
   211–17.
'The Recognition of Isaac Rosenberg', review of *The Complete Works of Isaac
   Rosenberg*, ed. by D. W. Harding and Gordon Bottomley, *Scrutiny* vi (Sept.
   1937), pp. 229–34.
'The Fate of Edward Thomas', review of *The Childhood of Edward Thomas: a
   Fragment of Autobiography: As it Was...World Without End*, by Helen Thomas,
   Scrutiny vii (March 1939), pp. 441–3.
'Hart Crane from this Side', review of *The Collected Poems of Hart Crane*, *Scrutiny*
   vii (March 1939). pp. 443–6.
'Arnold's Thought', review of *Matthew Arnold*, by Lionel Trilling, *Scrutiny* viii
   (June 1939), pp. 92–9.
'Critical Guidance and Contemporary Literature', review of *The Present Age from
   1914*, by Edwin Muir, *Scrutiny* viii (Sept. 1939), pp. 227–32.
'The Great Yeats, and the Latest', review of *Last Poems and Plays*, by W. B.
   Yeats, *Scrutiny* viii (March 1940), pp. 437–40. Reprinted in *A Selection From
   Scrutiny*, vol. I, pp. 93–6.
A Short History of English Literature, by B. Ifor Evans, *Scrutiny* ix (Sept. 1940), pp.
   180–1.
Another Time, by W. H. Auden, *Scrutiny* ix (Sept. 1940), p. 200. Reprinted in *A
   Selection From Scrutiny*, vol. I, p. 114
East Coker, by T. S. Eliot, *The Cambridge Review*, 21 Feb. 1941, pp. 268–70.
'After *To The Lighthouse*', review of *Between the Acts*, by Virginia Woolf, *Scrutiny* x
   (Jan, 1942), pp. 295–8. Reprinted in *A Selection From Scrutiny*, vol. II, pp.
   97–100.
'An American Critic', review of *The Wound and the Bow*, by Edmund Wilson,
   Scrutiny xi (Summer 1942), pp. 72–3.
'Landor and the Seasoned Epicure', review of *Savage Landor*, by Malcolm Elwin,
   Scrutiny xi (Summer 1942), pp. 148–50.
'The Liberation of Poetry', review of *Auden and After*, by Francis Scarfe, *Scrutiny*
   xi (Spring 1943), pp. 212–15.
'Catholicity or Narrowness?', review of *A Critical History of English Poetry*, by
   H. J. C. Grierson and J. C. Smith, *Scrutiny* xii (Autumn 1944), pp. 292–5.
'Meet Mr Forster', review of *E. M. Forster*, by Lionel Trilling, *Scrutiny* xii
   (Autumn 1944), pp. 308–9.

'The Appreciation of Henry James', review of *Henry James: The Major Phase*, by
F. O. Mattheissen, *Scrutiny* XIV (Spring 1947), pp. 229–37. Reprinted in
A Selection From Scrutiny, vol. II, pp. 114–23.

'Henry James's First Novel', review of *Roderick Hudson*, by Henry James, *Scrutiny*
XIV (Sept. 1947), pp. 295–301.

'Poet as Executant', review of *Four Quartets, read by the Author*, *Scrutiny* XV (Dec.
1947), p. 80. Reprinted in *A Selection From Scrutiny*, vol. I, p. 88.

'*The Portrait of a Lady* Reprinted', review of The World's Classics edition of *The
Portrait of a Lady*, by Henry James, *Scrutiny* XV (Summer 1948), pp. 235–41.

'Beatrice Webb in Partnership', review of *Our Partnership*, by Beatrice Webb,
Scrutiny XVI (June 1949), pp. 173–6. Reprinted in *A Selection From Scrutiny*, pp.
216–19.

'Saints of Rationalism', review of *John Stuart Mill and Harriet Taylor: Their
Friendship and Subsequent Marriage*, by F. A. Hayek, *The Listener*, 26 April 1951,
p. 672.

'Shaw Against Lawrence', review of *Sex, Literature and Censorship: Essays by D. H.
Lawrence*, ed. Harry T. Moore, *The Spectator*, 1 April 1955, pp. 397–9.

'The Critic's Task', review of *The Energies of Art*, by Jacques Barzun, *Commentary*,
July 1957, pp. 83–6.

'Romantic and Heretic?', review of *D. H. Lawrence: A Composite Biography*, vol. II,
by Edward Nehls, *The Spectator*, 6 Feb. 1959, pp. 196–7.

'How Far Short of True Greatness?', review of *The Invisible Poet* [T. S. Eliot], by
Hugh Kenner, *The Guardian*, 8 April 1960, p. 13.

'Genius as Critic', review of *Phoenix: The Posthumous Papers of D. H. Lawrence*, *The
Spectator*, 24 March 1961, pp. 412–14.

'Done for Lawrence?', review of *A D. H. Lawrence Miscellany*, ed. by Harry T.
Moore, *The Guardian*, 24 March 1961, p. 15.

'The Oxford Tradition', review of *The Oxford History of English Literature*, vol. XII:
Eight Modern Writers, by J. I. M. Stewat, *The Spectator*, 2 Aug. 1963, pp.
150–1.

(b) Criticism on Leavis

(*i*) BOOKS, AND BOOKS WITH PARTS OR CHAPTERS ON LEAVIS

Buckley, Vincent, *Poetry And Morality*, London: Chatto and Windus, 1959.

Casey, John, *The Language Of Criticism*, London: Methuen and Co. Ltd, 1966.

Gomme, Andor, *Attitudes To Criticism*, Carbondale: Southern Illinois University
Press, 1966.

Green, Martin, *Science And The Shabby Curate of Poetry*, London: Longmans, 1964.

Gross, John, *The Rise And Fall Of The Man Of Letters*, London: Weidenfeld and
Nicolson, 1969.

Hayman, Ronald, *Leavis*, London: Heineman, 1976.

Lodge, David, *The Language Of Fiction*, London: Routledge and Kegan Paul,
1966.

Watson, Garry, *The Leavises, The 'Social', and The Left*, Brynmill, 1977.

Watson, George, *The Literary Critics*, 1962; rpt. Harmondsworth: Penguin Books, 1968.

Williams, Raymond, *Culture And Society 1780–1950*, 1958; rpt. Harmondsworth: Penguin Books, 1968.

(*ii*) ESSAYS IN BOOKS

Bergonzi, Bernard, 'Criticism and the Milton Controversy', in *The Living Milton*, ed. Frank Kermode. London: Routledge and Kegan Paul, 1960, pp. 162–80.

Bentley, Eric, Introduction to *The Importance of Scrutiny*, ed. Eric Bentley. 1948; rpt. New York University Press, 1964.

Cronin, Anthony, 'Toward School with Heavy Looks', in *A Question Of Modernity*, London: Secher and Warburg, 1966, pp. 111–22.

Lodge, David, 'Literary Criticism In England In The Twentieth Century', in *The Twentieth Century*, ed. Bernard Bergonzi, London: Sphere Books Limited, 1970, pp. 362–403.

Nath, Raj, 'F. R. Leavis: A Revaluation', in *Essays In Criticism*, Delhi: Doaba House, 1971, pp. 97–102.

Panichas, George A., 'The Leavisite Rubrics', in *The Reverent Discipline*, Knoxville: The University Of Tennessee Press, 1974, pp. 378–93.

Rahv, Phillip, 'On F. R. Leavis and D. H. Lawrence', in *Literature And The Sixth Sense*, Boston: Houghton Mifflin Company, 1969, pp. 289–306.

Stein, Walter, 'Christianity And The Common Pursuit', in *Criticism As Dialogue*, Cambridge: Cambridge University Press, 1969, pp. 59–85.

Steiner, George, 'F. R. Leavis', in *Language And Silence*, New York: Atheneum, 1967, pp. 221–38.

Trilling, Lionel, 'The Leavis-Snow Controversy', in *Beyond Culture*, New York: The Viking Press, 1965, pp. 145–77.

Walsh, William, 'A Sharp, Unaccomodating Voice: The Criticism of F. R. Leavis', in *A Human Idiom*, London: Chatto and Windus, 1964, pp. 106–27.

– 'The Literary Critic And The Education Of An *Elite*: Coleridge, Arnold And F. R. Leavis', in *The Use Of Imaginations*, 1959; rpt. Harmondsworth: Penguin Books, 1966, pp. 67–83.

Wellek, René, 'The Literary Criticism of Frank Raymond Leavis', in *Literary Views: Critical And Historical Essays*, ed. Carroll Camden. Chicago: The University of Chicago Press, 1964, pp. 175–93.

(*iii*) ARTICLES AND REVIEWS IN PERIODICALS

Anon. 'Dr. Leavis On Lawrence', review of *D. H. Lawrence: Novelist. Times Literary Supplement*, 28 Oct. 1955, p. 638

Anon. 'The Critic As Man', review of *Anna Kerenina And Other Essays. Times Literary Supplement*, 30 Nov. 1967, pp. 1121–2.

Bateson, F. W., 'The Alternative To *Scrutiny*', *Essays In Criticism*, 14 (1964), 10–20.

Betsky, Seymour, 'Mr Leavis On The Novel', review of *The Great Tradition*, *The Sewanee Review*, 57 (1949), 525–33.

Black, Michael, 'A Kind of Valediction: Leavis on Eliot, 1929–1975', *The New Universities Quarterly* (Winter 1975), 78–93.
- 'Leavis and Lawrence: Extending Limits', review of *Thought, Words And Creativity*, *English* XXVI, no. 124 (1977), 23–40.
- 'The Third Realm', *The Use of English* XV (1964), pp. 280–8.
- 'The Third Realm: Part Two', *The Use of English* XVI (1964), 21–31.
Bradbury, Malcolm, 'The Rise of the Provincials', *The Antioch Review*, 16 (1956), 469–77.
Brower, Reuben A., 'Scrutiny: Revolution From Within', *Partisan Review*, 31 (1964), 297–314.
Casey, John., 'Dickens and the great tradition', *Spectator* (Oct. 24, 1970), 477–8.
Coulson, Peter, 'The Attack on Leavis', *Essays In Criticism*, 13 (1963), 107–12.
Draper, R. D., 'A Short Guide to D. H. Lawrence Studies', *The Critical Survey*, 2 (1964–6), 222–6
Fraser, John, 'A Tribute to Dr F. R. Leavis', *The Western Review*, 23 (1958–9), 139–47.
- 'Leavis and Winters: Professional Manners', *The Cambridge Quarterly*, 5 (1970–1), 41–71.
- 'Leavis, Winters and "Tradition"', *The Southern Review*, 7 (1971), 963–85.
Ford, George, 'Leavises, Levi's And Some Dickensian Priorities', review of *Dickens The Novelist*, *Nineteenth Century Fiction*, 26 (1971–2), 95–113.
Gersh, Gabriel, 'The Moral Imperatives of F. R. Leavis', *The Antioch Review*, 28 (1968), 520–8.
Gifford, Henry, review of *D. H. Lawrence: Novelist*, *Essays In Criticism*, 6 (1956), 224–32.
Gomme, Andor, 'Why literary criticism matters in a technologico-Benthamite Age', review of *The Living Principle*, in *The New Universities Quarterly* (Winter 1975), 36–53.
Gregor, Ian, 'The Criticism of F. R. Leavis', *The Dublin Review* (Third Quarter 1952), pp. 55–63.
Gribble, James, 'Logical And Psychological Considerations In The Criticism of F. R. Leavis', *The British Journal of Aesthetics*, 10 (1970), 39–57.
Harvey, J. R., 'The Leavises' Dickens', review of *Dickens The Novelist*, *The Cambridge Quarterly*, 6, no. 1 (1972), 77–93.
Heyl, Bernard, 'The Absolutism Of F. R. Leavis', *The Journal Of Aesthetics & Art Criticism*, 13 (1954–5), 249–55.
Hirsch, David H., '"Hard Times" and F. R. Leavis', *Criticism*, 6 (1964), 1–16.
Holbrook, David, 'F. R. Leavis and "Creativity"', *The New Universities Quarterly* (Winter 1975), 66–77.
Inglis, Fred, 'Attention to education: Leavis and the Leavisites', *The New Universities Quarterly* (Winter 1975), 94–106.
Kermode, Frank, 'Some Reservations', *New Statesman*, 66 (1963), 568.
- 'A Tradition of *Scrutiny*', review of *Anna Karenina And Other Essays*, *Commentary*, 46, no. 1 (1968), 83–7.
Killham, John, 'The Use Of "Concreteness" As An Evaluative Term In F. R.

Leavis's "The Great Tradition"', *The British Journal of Aesthetics*, 5 (1965),
    14–24.

Knight, G. Wilson, '*Scrutiny* And Criticism'. *Essays In Criticism*, 14 (1964), 32–6.

Lerner, Laurence, 'The Life and Death of *Scrutiny*', *London Magazine* 2, no. 1
    (1955), 68–77.

McLuhan, Marshall, 'Poetic vs. Rhetorical Exegesis: The Case For Leavis
    Against Richards and Empson', *The Sewanee Review*, 52 (1944), 226–76.

Newton, J. M., 'For Poetry', review of *Anna Karenina And Other Essays*, *The
    Cambridge Quarterly*, 3 (1967–8), 354–69.

Poole, Roger C., 'Life *Versus* Death In The Later Criticism Of F. R. Leavis',
    Renaissance And Modern Studies, 16: 112–41.

Pradhan, S. K., 'Literary Criticism And Cultural Diagnosis: F. R. Leavis On
    W. H. Auden', *The British Journal of Aesthetics*, 12 (1972), 384–94.

Pritchard, William H., 'Discourses In America', review of *Lectures in America*,
    Essays in Criticism, 19 (1969), 336–47.

Robinson, Ian, 'The Third Realm: Ten Years Work by F. R. Leavis', *The
    Human World*, 3 (1971), 71–85.

Singh, G. S., 'Better History And Better Criticism: The Significance Of F. R.
    Leavis', *English Miscellany*, 16 (1965), 215–79.

Tanner, Michael, 'Philosophy and Criticism', review of *The Language Of
    Criticism*, by John Casey, *The Oxford Review*, no. 4 (1967), pp. 58–71.

– 'Literature and Philosophy', *The New Universities Quarterly* (Winter 1975),
    54–64.

Vivas, Eliseo, 'Mr Leavis On D. H. Lawrence', review of *D. H. Lawrence:
    Novelist*, *The Sewanee Review*, 65 (1957), 123–36.

Waldock, A. J. A., 'The Status of *Hard Times*', *Southerly*, 3 (1948), 33–9.

Wilding, Michael, 'The Literary Criticism of F. R. Leavis', review of *Anna
    Karenina And Other Essays*, *The Oxford Review*, no. 7 (1968), pp. 69–78.

Williams, Raymond, 'Out Debt To Dr Leavis', *Critical Quarterly*, 1 (1958),
    245–7.

3. OTHER WORKS CITED

Altizer, Thomas J. J., *The New Apocalypse: The Radical Christian Vision of William
    Blake*, Michigan State University Press, 1974.

Arnold, Matthew, *Culture And Anarchy*, ed. J. Dover Wilson, 1869; rpt.
    Cambridge: Cambridge University Press, 1966.

– *Essays in Criticism: First And Second Series*, London: Everyman's Library, 1969.

Bateson, F. W., *Essays In Critical Dissent*, London: Longman, 1972.

Bergonzi, Bernard, 'Literary Criticism and Humanist Morality', *Blackfriars*, 43
    (1962), 4–17.

– *T. S. Eliot*, New York: The Macmillan Company, 1972.

Bowers, Fredson, *Textual & Literary Criticism*, Cambridge: Cambridge University
    Press, 1969.

Buber, Martin, *Eclipse of God*, 1952; rpt. New York: Harper and Row, 1957.

Collingwood, R. G., *The Principles Of Art*, 1938; rpt. New York: Oxford University Press, 1974.

Comstock, W. Richard, 'Theology After the "Death of God"', in *The Meaning Of The Death of God*, ed. Bernard Murchland, New York: Vintage Books, 1967.

Cox, C. B. and Dyson, A. E., eds., *Word In The Desert*, London: Oxford University Press, 1968.

Davie, Donald, 'British Criticism: The Necessity For Humility', *The Frontiers Of Literary Criticism*, ed. David H. Malone, Los Angeles: Hennessey and Ingollis Ind., 1974.

– 'T. S. Eliot: The End of An Era', in *T. S. Eliot, Four Quartets*, ed. Bernard Bergonzi, London: Macmillan, 1965.

Eliot, T. S., *To Criticize The Critic*, New York: Farrar, Straus and Giroux, 1965.

Fishman, Solomon, *The Disinherited of Art*, Berkeley: University of California Press, 1953.

Fraser, John, 'Reflections on the Organic Community', *The Human World*, 15–16, 1974.

Frye, Northrop, *Anatomy of Criticism: Four Essays*, 1957; rpt. New York: Atheneum, 1967

– *The Bush Garden*, Toronto: Anansi, 1971.

– *The Critical Path*, Bloomington: Indiana University Press, 1971.

– *The Stubborn Structure*, Ithaca, New York: Cornell University Press, 1970.

Hardy, Thomas, 'The Dorsetshire Labourer', in *Thomas Hardy's Personal Writings*, ed. Harold Orel, Lawrence: University of Kansas Press, 1966.

Hill, Christopher, *The Century of Revolution, 1603–1714*, 1961; rpt. London: Sphere Books Ltd, 1969.

Hough, Graham, *An Essay On Criticism*, New York: W. W. Norton, 1966.

– *The Dream And The Task*, London: Gerald Duckworth and Co. Ltd, 1963.

James, Henry, *The Future Of The Novel*, ed. Leon Edel, New York: Vintage Books, 1956.

Kermode, Frank, *Romantic Image*, 1957; rpt. London: Fontana Books, 1971.

Krieger, Murray, *The New Apologists for Poetry*, 1956; rpt. Bloomington: Indiana University Press, 1963.

Lynch, William, *Christ And Apollo*, Toronto: Mentor-Omega, 1960.

Robinson, John A. T., *Honest to God*, London: SCM Press, 1963.

Sturt, George [George Bourne], *Change In The Village*, London: The Country Book Club, 1956.

– *The Wheelwright's Shop*, Cambridge: Cambridge University Press, 1963

Whitehead, Alfred North, *Science And The Modern World*, 1925; rpt. New York: The Free Press, 1967.

Williams, Raymond, *The Country And The City*, New York: Oxford University Press, 1973.

Wilson, Edmund, *Axel's Castle*, 1931; rpt. New York: Charles Scribner's Sons, 1959.

4. MISCELLANEOUS WORKS

Eliot, T. S., Introduction to *Selected Poems*, by Ezra Pound, 1928; rpt. London: Faber and Faber, 1968.

– 'Johnson's "London" and "The Vanity of Human Wishes"', in *English Critical Essays*, ed. Phyllis M. Jones, London: Oxford University Press, 1933, pp. 301–10.

– *Notes towards the Definition of Culture*, 1948; rpt. London: Faber and Faber, 1967.

– *On Poetry And Poets*, 1957; rpt. London: Faber and Faber, 1957.

– *The Sacred Wood*, 1920; rpt. London: Methuen and Co. Ltd, 1967.

– *After Strange Gods*, London: Faber and Faber, 1934.

– *Selected Essays*, 3rd enl. ed., 1951; rpt. London: Faber and Faber, 1969.

Ellul, Jacques, *The Technological Society*, 1954; rpt. New York: Vintage Books, 1964.

Empson, William, *Seven Types Of Ambiguity*, London: Chatto and Windus, 1930.

James, Henry, *Partial Portraits*, Ann Arbor: The University of Michigan Press, 1970.

– *Selected Literary Criticism*, Introduction by F. R. Leavis, ed. Morris Shapira, London: Heinemann, 1963.

Laslett, Peter, *The World We Have Lost*, London: Methuen and Company Ltd, 1965.

Leavis, Q. D., *Fiction And The Reading Public*, 1932; rpt. New York: Russell and Russell, Inc., 1963.

Murry, Middleton, *Aspects of Literature*, London: W. Collins, 1920.

– *The Problem of Style*, 1922; rpt. London: Oxford University Press, 1967.

Pound, Ezra, A B C of Reading, London: G. Routledge, 1934.

Richards, I. A., *Practical Criticism*, 1929; rpt. New York: Harcourt, Brace and World, Inc., 1967.

– *Principles of Literary Criticism*, 1925; rpt. New York: Harcourt, Brace and World, Inc., 1969.

– *Science And Poetry*, New York: Norton, 1926.

Rickword, Edgell and Garman, Douglas, *The Calendar Of Modern Letters. March 1925–July 1927*, 4 vols, New York: Barnes and Noble, 1966.

Snow, C. P., *The Two Cultures: And A Second Look*, New York: A Mentar Book, 1963.

Winters, Yvor, *In Defence of Reason*, Chicago: The Swallow Press, 1943.

INDEX